Heresy and Inquisition in the Middle Ages

Volume 1

Heresy and Heretics in the Thirteenth Century

YORK MEDIEVAL PRESS

York Medieval Press is published by the University of York's Centre for Medieval Studies in association with Boydell & Brewer Limited. Our objective is the promotion of innovative scholarship and fresh criticism on medieval culture. We have a special commitment to interdisciplinary study, in line with the Centre's belief that the future of Medieval Studies lies in those areas in which its major constituent disciplines at once inform and challenge each other.

Editorial Board (2014)

Professor Peter Biller (Dept of History): General Editor
Dr T. Ayers (Dept of History of Art)
Dr Henry Bainton (Dept of English and Related Literature)
Dr J. W. Binns (Dept of English and Related Literature)
Professor Helen Fulton (Dept of English and Related Literature)
Dr K. F. Giles (Dept of Archaeology)
Professor W. M. Ormrod (Dept of History)
Dr Lucy Sackville (Dept of History)
Dr Hanna Vorholt (Dept of History of Art)
Professor J. G. Wogan-Browne (English Faculty, Fordham University)

Consultant on Manuscript Publications:

Professor Linne Mooney (Dept of English and Related Literature)

All enquiries of an editorial kind, including suggestions for monographs and essay collections, should be addressed to: The Academic Editor, York Medieval Press, University of York, Centre for Medieval Studies, The King's Manor, York, YO1 7EP (E-mail: gmg501@york.ac.uk).

Publications of York Medieval Press are listed at the back of this volume.

Heresy and Inquisition in the Middle Ages
ISSN 2046–8938

Series editors
John H. Arnold, Department of History, Classics and Archaeology, Birkbeck, University of London
Peter Biller, Department of History, University of York

Heresy had social, cultural and political implications in the middle ages, and countering heresy was often a central component in the development of orthodoxy. This series publishes work on heresy, and the repression of heresy, from late antiquity to the Reformation, including monographs, collections of essays, and editions of texts.

Heresy and Heretics in the Thirteenth Century

The Textual Representations

L. J. Sackville

THE UNIVERSITY *of York*

YORK MEDIEVAL PRESS

© L. J. Sackville 2011

All rights reserved. Except as permitted under current legislation
no part of this work may be photocopied, stored in a retrieval system,
published, performed in public, adapted, broadcast,
transmitted, recorded or reproduced in any form or by any means,
without the prior permission of the copyright owner

The right of L. J. Sackville to be identified as
the author of this work has been asserted in accordance with
sections 77 and 78 of the Copyright, Designs and Patents Act 1998

First published 2011
York Medieval Press, York
Paperback edition 2014

ISBN 978 1 903153 36 9 hardback
ISBN 978 1 903153 56 7 paperback

A York Medieval Press publication
in association with The Boydell Press
an imprint of Boydell & Brewer Ltd
PO Box 9, Woodbridge, Suffolk IP12 3DF, UK
and of Boydell & Brewer Inc.
668 Mt Hope Avenue, Rochester, NY 14620–2731, USA
website: www.boydellandbrewer.com
and with the
Centre for Medieval Studies, University of York
www.york.ac.uk/medieval-studies

A CIP catalogue record for this book is available
from the British Library

The publisher has no responsibility for the continued existence or accuracy
of URLs for external or third-party internet websites referred to in this book,
and does not guarantee that any content on such websites is,
or will remain, accurate or appropriate.

This publication is printed on acid-free paper

Contents

to Pete

Acknowledgements

The first and most important acknowledgement that I can make here must be to Pete Biller, for all his guidance and friendship, and for the generosity he has shown with his time, knowledge, wine and more book loans than I care to remember.

I would like to thank the Department of History of the University of York, the Arts and Humanities Research Council, the British Academy and Bennett Boskey for their financial support in the various stages of this project. I am also grateful to the librarians of the Bodleian Library, the Bibliothèque nationale de France, the Biblioteca Apostolica Vaticana and the Biblioteca Casanatense. To Mark Ormrod and Mary Garrison, for their insight and suggestions, I offer my heartfelt thanks, and I am also immensely grateful to Pete Biller, Caterina Bruschi and Shelagh Sneddon for allowing me to use their edition of Doat 25 before its publication.

Other debts of gratitude are owed to my Mum and Dad, for their love; to Amy, for her intellectual and moral support; to Miggy, for salads and general loveliness; to John Arnold, for his advice and encouragement; to Helen Weinstein, for looking out for me; to my friends, with special mention in this category for Helen Lacey, Sethina Watson, Judy Frost and Mark Every, and my friends and colleagues at Exeter College, Oxford. And to Adam, for his patience.

Abbreviations

Acta sanctorum	*Acta sanctorum quotquot tot orbe coluntur, vel a catholicus scriptoribus celebrantur...* new edn, 65 vols. in 67 (Paris, 1863–1931)
AFP	*Archivum Fratrum Praedicatorum* (Rome, 1931–)
AHDLMA	*Archives d'Histoire Doctrinale et Littéraire du Moyen Âge* (Paris, 1926–)
Anselm of Alessandria, *Tractatus*	Dondaine, 'La hiérarchie II, III', pp. 308–24
Anonymous of Passau	Anonymous of Passau, <*Tractatus*>, ed. J. Gretser, *Lucae Tudensis episcopi, scriptores aliquot succedanei contra sectam Waldensium* (Ingolstadt, 1613), pp. 262–75
Aquinas, *SCG*	Thomas Aquinas, *Summa contra gentiles* in *Opera omnia*, 25 vols. in 23 (Parma, 1852–73), V
BAV	Biblioteca Apostolica Vaticana, Vatican City
BNCF	Biblioteca Nazionale Centrale di Firenze, Florence
BnF	Bibliothèque nationale de France, Paris
Brevis summula	*La Somme des autorités, à l'usage des prédicateurs méridionaux au XIIIᵉ siècle*, ed. C. Douais (Paris, 1896), pp. 114–43
Caesarius, *Dialogus*	Caesarius of Heisterbach, *Dialogus miraculorum*, ed. J. Strange, 2 vols. (Cologne, 1851, repr. Ridgewood, 1966)
Canetti, *L'invenzione*	L. Canetti, *L'invenzione della memoria: il culto e l'immagine di Domenico nella storia dei primi frati Predicatori*, Centro Italiano di Studi sull'Alto Medioevo, Biblioteca di 'Medioevo Latino' 19 (Spoleto, 1996)
Capelli, *Adversus haereticos*	*L'eresia catara. Appendice*: Disputationes nonnullae adversus haereticos. *Codice inedito Malatestiano del sec. XIII.*, ed. D. Bazzocchi (Bologna, 1920)
CF	*Cahiers de Fanjeaux* (Toulouse, 1966–)
D'Alatri, *Orvieto*	M. d'Alatri, *L'inquisizione francescana nell'Italia centrale del duecento*, Istituto Storico dei Cappuccini, Bibliotheca Seraphico-Capuccina 49 (Rome, 1996)
DEC	*Decrees of the Ecumenical Councils*, ed. J. Alberigo, et al., trans. N. P. Tanner, 2 vols. (London and Washington, 1990)

Disputatio	*Disputatio inter catholicum et paterinum hereticum: Die Auseinandersetzung der katholischen Kirche mit den italienischen Katharern im Spiegel einer kontroverstheologischen Streitschrift des 13. Jahrhunderts*, ed. C. Hoécker, Edizione Nazionale dei Testi Mediolatini 4, Series I, 3 (Florence, 2001)
Doat	Paris, BnF, MSS Collection Doat
Dondaine, 'La hiérarchie I'	A. Dondaine, 'La hiérarchie cathare en Italie. I Le "De heresi catharorum in Lombardia"', *AFP* 19 (1949), 280–312, repr. in Dondaine, *Les hérésies et l'Inquisition*
Dondaine, 'La hiérarchie II, III'	A. Dondaine, 'La hiérarchie cathare en Italie II and III', *AFP* 20 (1950), 234–324, repr. in Dondaine, *Les hérésies et l'Inquisition*
Dondaine, *Les hérésies et l'Inquisition*	A. Dondaine, *Les hérésies et l'Inquisition, XIIe–XIIIe siècles: Documents et études*, ed. Y. Dossat Variorum Collected Studes Series 314 (Aldershot, 1990)
Dondaine, 'Manuel'	A. Dondaine, 'Le Manuel de l'Inquisiteur (1230–1330)', *AFP* 17 (1947), 85–194, repr. in Dondaine, *Les hérésies et l'Inquisition*
Dossat, *Crises*	Y. Dossat, *Les crises de l'inquisition toulousaine au XIIIe siècle (1233–1273)* (Bordeaux, 1959)
Douais, *Documents: Textes*	M.-J.-C. Douais, *Documents pour servir à l'histoire de l'inquisition*, 2 vols. (Paris, 1900), II, *Textes*
Douais, *La Somme*/I, II, III, IV	*La Somme des autorités, à l'usage des prédicateurs méridionaux au XIIIe siècle*, ed. C. Douais (Paris, 1896)
Duvernoy, *Quercy*	Peter Cellan, *L'inquisition en Quercy: Le registre des pénitences de Pierre Cellan 1241–1242*, ed. J. Duvernoy (Castelnaud-La-Chapelle, 2001)
Foulques, *Consilium*	*L'eresia a Vicenza nel duecento. Dati, problemi e fonti*, ed. F. Lomastro Tognato (Vicenza, 1988), edn of Consilium domini Guidonis Fulcodii, pp. 193–203
Fredericq	*Corpus documentorum inquisitionis haereticae pravitatis Neerlandicae*, ed. P. Fredericq, 5 vols. (Ghent, 1889)
Friedberg	*Corpus iuris canonici*, ed. E. Friedberg, 2 vols. (Leipzig, 1879, repr. Graz, 1959), I, *Decretum magistri Gratiani*; II, *Decretalium collectiones*
García, *Lateran 4*	*Constitutiones Concilii quarti Lateranensis una cum Commentariis glossatorum*, ed. A. García y García (Vatican City, 1981)
Grundmann, 'Typus'	H. Grundmann, 'Der Typus des Ketzers in mittel-alterlicher Anschauung', in *Kultur- und Universalgeschichte: Festschrift für W. Goetz* (Leipzig and Berlin, 1927) pp. 91–107; repr. in *Ausgewählte Aufsätze*, Monumenta Germaniae Historica Schriften 25, 3 vols. (1976), I, 364–416

Humbert, *Opera*	Humbert of Romans, *Opera de vita regularis*, ed. J. J. Berthier, 2 vols. (Rome, 1888–9, repr. Turin, 1956)
JEH	*Journal of Ecclesiastical History* (London, etc., 1950–)
Kaeppeli, 'Une somme'	T. Kaeppeli, 'Une somme contre les hérétiques de S. Pierre Martyr (?)', *AFP* 17 (1947), 295–335
Lenherr, *Gratian*	T. Lenherr, *Die Exkommunikations- und Depositionsgewalt der Häretiker bei Gratian und den Dekretisten bis zur* Glossa Ordinaria *des Johannes Teutonicus*, Münchener Theologische Studien 3, Kanonistische Abteilung 42 (St Ottilien, 1987), edition of C.24 q.1 pp. 18–56
Maisonneuve, *Études*	H. Maisonneuve, *Études sur les origines de l'inquisition*, L'Église et l'État au Moyen Âge 7, 2nd edn (Paris, 1960)
Mansi	*Sacrum conciliorum nova et amplissima collectio*, ed. G. D. Mansi, 53 vols. (Florence, 1759–1927, repr. Graz 1961)
Moneta, *Adversus catharos*	Moneta of Cremona, *Adversus catharos et valdenses libri quinque*, ed. T. A. Ricchini (Rome, 1743, repr. 1964)
MOPH	Monumenta Ordinis Fratrum Praedicatorum Historica (Rome, 1933–)
MOPH 16	MOPH 16 (1935), *Libellus de principiis Ordinis Praedicatorum/Legendae sancti Dominici*
Paolini, 'Italian Catharism'	L. Paolini, 'Italian Catharism and written culture', in Biller and Hudson, pp. 83–103
Patschovsky and Selge, *Quellen*	*Quellen zur Geschichte der Waldenser*, ed. A. Patschovsky and K.-V. Selge, Texte zur Kirchen- und Theologegeschichte 18 (Gütersloh, 1973)
PL	*Patrologia Latina*, ed. J. P. Migne, 217 vols. (Paris, 1857–66)
Preger, Pseudo-David	W. Preger, 'Der Tractat des David von Augsburg über die Waldesier', *Abhandlungen der bayerischen Akademie der Wissenschaften* 14 (1879), 204–35
Pseudo-David, *De inquisitione*	*Thesaurus novus anecdotorum*, ed. E. Martène and U. Durand, 5 vols. (Paris, 1717), V, 1777–94
Raniero Sacconi, *Summa*	Raniero Sacconi, *Summa de catharis*, ed. F. Šanjek, *AFP* 44 (1974), 31–60
Rottenwöhrer	G. Rottenwöhrer, *Der Katharismus*, 4 vols. in 8 (Bad Honnef, 1982)
Salvo Burci, *Suprastella*	Salvo Burci, *Liber Suprastella*, ed. Caterina Bruschi, Instituto Storico Italiano per il Medio Evo, Fonti per la Storia dell'Italia Medievale, Antiquitates 15 (Rome, 2002)
Selge, Texte	*Texte zur Inquisition*, ed. K.-V. Selge, Texte zur Kirchen- und Theologegeschichte 4 (Gütersloh, 1967)

SOPMA	T. Kaeppeli and E. Panella, *Scriptores Ordinis Praedicatorum Medii Aevi*, 4 vols. (Rome, 1970–93)
Stephen of Bourbon, lib.1/lib.3	Stephen of Bourbon, *Tractatus de diversis materiis predicabilibus*, Corpus Christianorum, Continuatio mediaevalis 124/124B, 2 vols. (Turnhout, 2002–6), I, *Prologus, prima pars, de dono timoris*, ed. J. Berlioz and J.-L. Eichenlaub; III, *Liber tertius. De eis que pertinent ad donum scientie et penitentiam*, ed. J. Berlioz.
Stephen of Bourbon, *Tractatus*	Stephen of Bourbon, *De septem donis spiritus sancti: Stephani de Borbone tractatus de diversis materiis praedicabilibus*, ed A. Lecoy de la Marche, *Anecdotes historiques, légendes et apologues tirées du recueil inédit d'Étienne de Bourbon, Dominicain du XIIIe siècle*, Société de l'histoire de France, Publications 185 (Paris 1877)
Tocco	F. Tocco, *Quel che non c'è nella divina commedia. Dante e l'eresia, con documenti e con la ristampa delle questioni dantesche* (Bologna, 1899)
Vitae fratrum	Gerard of Frachet, *Vitae fratrum ordinis praedicatorum nec non cronica ordinis ab anno MCCII usque ad MCCLIV*, ed. B. M. Reichert, MOPH 1 (1896)
Vitry, Crane	The Exempla *or Illustrative Stories from the* Sermones Vulgares *of Jacques de Vitry*, ed. T. F. Crane (Ithaca, NY, 1894, repr. New York, 1971)
Vitry, Greven	Die Exempla *aus den* Sermones feriales et communes *des Jakob von Vitry*, ed. J. Greven (Heidelberg, 1914)
Wakefield, 'Notes'	W. L. Wakefield, 'Notes on some Anti-Heretical Writings of the Thirteenth Century', *Franciscan Studies* 27 (1967), 285–321

Introduction

I once heard, said Stephen of Bourbon, about a heretic who used the Scriptures to preach his error. In this way, he was successful in converting a certain young man to his belief. Once he was sure of the youth's conversion, the heretic told him that, in fact, he did not believe the Gospels, nor indeed in any of the Scriptures that he expounded. Confused, the young man asked the heretic, why then did you preach them to me? The heretic responded that, as a bird catcher mimics the whistle, or the voice, of his prey in order to capture them because the sound of his own voice would frighten them away, so the heretics use the Bible in order to lure people from the Catholic faith.[1]

The story appears in the vast collection of *exempla* written by Stephen in the middle years of the thirteenth century. It is a neat story, but with several overlapping layers, not all of which are immediately apparent. Most immediately, it presents a first-hand account: a heretic preaching his error to the people in an effort to win converts. His preaching, which is at the forefront of the story, would seem to depend at least initially on a use and exposition of the Catholic Scriptures for its support. That use of Scripture, though, is a more loaded image than it seems: first, it suggests literacy on the part of the heretic, and, secondly, it effectively constructs a pretended appearance for that heretic, and the idea that the public face of heresy is not the same as the one visible to the initiated.

Both the initial picture of heretics and their pastoral activity and the underlying constructs of literacy and false appearance are aspects of a Catholic picture that Stephen shares with most of his contemporaries, and ideas that recur throughout the corpus of anti-heretical literature. Their use here is distinctive, though – indeed, the peculiar form of this story is unique to Stephen – by virtue of their function within Stephen's collection. Vivid similes are Stephen's own stock in trade, so, even while this one seems plausible as the heretic's own words, some suspicion is provoked by the placing of such a sinister simile as the bird catcher's whistle in the mouth of the heretic. That suspicion is in fact confirmed by a quick glance at the immediate context of the story, where the same whistle – the same imagery and the same vocabulary – was used by Stephen to build a general theme of pastoral care and negligence throughout the rest of the chapter. Moreover, the heretic's rejection of Scripture stands in direct contrast to the accounts that Stephen gives earlier in his

---

1   Stephen of Bourbon, *Tractatus*, p. 430; Stephen uses this same motif in book four, though in a less colourful form, p. 309. My paraphrase.

1

text of heretical doctrine, accounts received from former heretics. It is that complex layering within and among genres, and the construction of heresy that emerges from it, that form the subject of this book.

The German historian Arno Borst, looking backwards from the 1950s, saw a clear and overarching pattern in the way that commentators and historians had written about Cathars. In a long introductory chapter, 'The Cathars in the Mirror of the Sources and Research', he traced a continuum of writing about the Cathar heresy from medieval and subsequent writers to 1950. For Borst, each successive era and ideology shaped the history of this phenomenon after its own image. Among Catholic and Protestant historians of the sixteenth to eighteenth centuries the heretics were regarded as the forerunners of the Protestant movement: from the Catholic viewpoint, they were representatives of the continuing presence of evil; for the Protestants, early manifestations of their own doctrine and a rival claim to the antiquity and continuity of the Catholic Church. To some later Marxist historians the heretics of the twelfth and thirteenth centuries were less the champions of religious dissent and more a symptom of class struggle as manifested in the context of a religious society.[2] Regardless of persuasion, in Borst's view, commentators ultimately fell into one of two broad groups: one dogmatic and systematic, with little love for the Cathars, usually on the side of the inquisitors; one directed towards practical morals, which took a more sympathetic view of the heretics – the 'friends of the Cathars'.

Borst's elegant rendering of this tradition, by now itself a canonical motif in reading the historiography of the subject, has been updated, expanded and adjusted in more recent surveys by Biller, which take into account Borst's own preoccupations, but the portrayal remains a useful way of understanding the *longue durée* of writing about heresy.[3] In this view the history of heresy can be seen, to some extent, as the history of mainstream ideas, or at least a reflection of them, its image constructed and reconstructed according to the role it has played.

If there can be said to be a common theme in recent scholarship then it has been a focus on the nature and production of the texts themselves and an increasing unwillingness to take the contents of those texts at face value. In contrast to the phases described by Borst, historians of heresy in the last forty or fifty years have been concerned to understand the mechanisms underlying

2 For the full version of this analysis, see A. Borst, *Die Katharer*, Monumenta Germaniae Historica Schriften 12 (Stuttgart, 1953), pp. 1–58; French translation by C. Roy, *Les Cathares* (Paris, 1984), pp. 9–53.

3 P. Biller, 'Cathars and Material Women', in *Medieval Theology and the Natural Body*, ed. P. Biller and A. J. Minnis, York Studies in Medieval Theology 1 (York, 1997), 61–81. Also, in *Texts and the Repression of Medieval Heresy*, ed. C. Bruschi and P. Biller, York Studies in Medieval Theology 4 (York, 2003): 'Texts and the Repression of Heresy: Introduction', with Bruschi. On post-war historiography see also J. Nelson, 'Religion in "Histoire totale": Some Recent Work in Medieval Heresy and Popular Religion', *Religion* 10 (1980), 60–85, especially on Marxist perspective.

the creation of the texts and the resulting potential for distortion of the information they contain: that is, to cease to see them as 'transparent or innocent conduits of information'.[4]

This trend has mostly been the result of the broader shift in historiographical practice brought about by the importation of literary and cultural theory into the discipline, without which vocabulary and environment such an approach could hardly have thrived. Certainly the difficulty of anti-heretical texts in particular makes them (perhaps) susceptible to such an approach, and has made a text-critical reading desirable and in fact necessary, as well as being part of the wider trend toward treating texts as a subject in their own right.[5] However, in the case of the study of heresy specifically, there are also deeper roots to consider.

Bruschi and Biller's introduction to their edited volume, which outlines the long tradition of heresy scholarship and its relationship with text, makes it clear that one of the principal places we must look for the drivers of the recent emphasis on text as subject has been the increasing availability of the texts themselves. Beginning in earnest with the work of Charles Schmidt in the middle of the nineteenth century, and Célestin Douais slightly later, the full range of anti-heretical texts was made available to scholarship on heresy, and in particular this meant the recovery and use of inquisition texts. The work was continued by the pupils of Schmidt and Douais, and by the end of the nineteenth century scholars were using the majority of what we would now think of as the core canon of material.[6] Underlying the focus on text, then, was the accumulation of what Nelson calls the 'formidable dossier of primary evidence', built up further by the work of scholars such as Antoine Dondaine, through whose editions the texts themselves were made available, where previously they had often been poorly known, or not known at all.[7] A wealth of information could now be brought to bear on studies of heresy, and of heretics, though it was not until later that the nature of that information was revisited.

If the increasing use and accessibility of source material provided the potential for a text-critical focus to work on heresy and its repression, the work of Herbert Grundmann provided the impetus and intellectual catalyst. Alhough its impact was not immediate, Grundmann's work on heresy was to prove influential in several ways. His book *Religiöse Bewegungen im Mittelalter*, first published in 1935, transformed the traditional treatment of heresy and mainstream religion as two separate entities into an approach which saw heresy as

4   J. H. Arnold, 'Inquisition, Texts and Discourse', in *Texts and Repression*, ed. Bruschi and Biller, pp. 63–80.
5   In large part as a result of Michael Clanchy's *From Memory to Written Record. England 1066–1307*, 2nd edn (Oxford, 1993).
6   For a detailed account of this development, see 'Introduction', in *Texts and Repression*, ed. Bruschi and Biller.
7   Nelson, 'Religion in "Histoire totale"', pp. 61–2.

3

one element in a broader continuum of religious groups and ideas, an approach which has been taken for granted by subsequent scholarship.[8] Earlier than this, though, in 1927, Grundmann had published a groundbreaking article that outlined the rhetorical topoi that were employed by medieval authors of anti-heretical texts to describe their subject.[9] The article, 'Der Typus des Ketzers in mittelalterlicher Anschauung', argued that the spotlight ought to be on the texts themselves, and on their representation of heresy, as constructed entities that ought to be understood in a more complex way than simply as records of what happened. This approach was further refined throughout Grundmann's career by his article on the use of the term 'literate' in the Middle Ages and by the appearance, almost forty years after that first breakthrough, of his study of the mechanisms of inquisition trial records and the difficulties of interpretation posed by these deceptively straightforward documents.[10] Despite the significance of Grundmann's early work scholarship, in English-speaking circles at least, was slow to absorb its implications, and its influence owes a lot to the initiative of Robert Lerner, who pushed for a translation of *Religiöse Bewegungen* and made effective use of Grundmann's theories in his own work.[11]

As in Borst's later survey, the reflection of mainstream concerns was also something Grundmann highlighted with regard to the texts themselves – the danger that, in simply reproducing the material that the texts contain with no attention to how that material was arranged or filtered, the preoccupations and perspective of the authors, the mainstream church, would be reproduced in modern scholarship. It was that concern which informed the new wave of work on heresy that began to emerge in the 1970s, when the focus began to shift away from what the texts had to say with regard to heresy and heretics per se, and towards a desire to deconstruct the language and content of those texts to get at how they said it, and why, and how that affected our understanding of the information they contained.

This new trend, which sought to place the examination and critical analysis of text at the forefront, had perhaps been signalled in 1970 by an expanded

---

8 H. Grundmann, *Religiöse Bewegungen im Mittelalter: Untersuchungen über die geschichtlichen Zusammenhänge zwischen der Ketzerei, den Bettelorden und der religiösen Frauenbewegung im 12. u 13. Jahrhundert und über die geschichtlichen Grundlagen der deutschen Mystik* (Berlin, 1935); translation by S. Rowan, with an introduction by Robert Lerner, *Religious Movements in the Middle Ages: The Historical Links between Heresy, the Mendicant Orders, and the Women's Religious Movement in the Twelfth and Thirteenth century, with the Historical Foundations of German Mysticism* (Notre Dame, 1995).

9 Grundmann, 'Typus', 91–107; reprinted in Grundmann, *Ausgewählte Aufsätze*, Monumenta Germaniae Historica Schriften 25, 3 vols. (1976), I, 313–27.

10 H. Grundmann, '*Litteratus-illiteratus*. Der Wandel einer Bildungsnorm vom Altertum zum Mittelalter', *Archiv für Kulturgeschichte* 40 (1958), 1–65. H. Grundmann, 'Ketzerverhöre des Spätmittelalters als quellenkritisches Problem', *Deutsches Archiv für Erforschung des Mittelalters* 21 (1965), 519–75, reprinted in Grundmann, *Ausgewählte Aufsätze*, I, 364–416.

11 R. E. Lerner, *The Heresy of the Free Spirit in the Later Middle Ages* (Berkeley, CA, 1972).

edition of Norman Cohn's *The Pursuit of the Millenium*.[12] Although at the same time Le Roy Ladurie's chronicle of French rural life, *Montaillou*, treated Fournier's extensive register as an unproblematic source of information, studies implementing the methodology advocated by Grundmann, by Robert Lerner on the heresy of the Free Spirit and by Grado Merlo on the Waldensians established a more deconstructive reading of sources for heresy as the norm.[13] By the 1980s, then, heresy had become something that could no longer be understood at face value, and a text-critical approach was increasingly entrenched as the accepted way to read and use the sources for heresy – in fact, it was to come to dominate the work of the succeeding decades, and this in both general studies and specific works, a fact evinced by essay collections such as *The Concept of Heresy in the Middle Ages*, which focuses on ideas of heresy through a series of largely text-orientated articles.[14] More directed still have been two collections dedicated to texts and text-critical problems with regard to heresy: *Heresy and Literacy*, edited by Peter Biller and Anne Hudson, gave new impetus to this area of inquiry, while the more recent *Texts and the Repression of Heresy*, edited by Caterina Bruschi and Peter Biller, follows up and develops further this approach to the subject.

Perhaps because of the nature of their content and structure, but also surely in part as a result of Grundmann's insight, a large part of recent work in this vein has been based on the sources emanating from the milieu of inquisition –

---

[12] Originally published in 1957, the new edition (London, 1970) was expanded and given a new subtitle, with a corresponding shift in focus, from urban collectives to specifically the atomised poor, not those entrenched in agricultural or artisanal networks – dissenters labelled as heretics by the established authorities. Cohn dealt again with heresy in his book *Europe's Inner Demons* (London, 1975), which was concerned with the ancient stereotype of the midnight orgy as applied to the heresy of the Free Spirit. Cohn showed the topos as a stock image wheeled out against any politically dissenting or challenging group, although, unlike Lerner, he still saw the Free Spirit as a coherent group.

[13] Ladurie's methodology was critiqued effectively by Leonard Boyle, who saw the book as paying insufficient attention to the context of the information or to the filters through which it had passed into Fournier's collection, L. E. Boyle, 'Montaillou Revisited: Mentalité and Methodology', in *Pathways to Medieval Peasants*, ed. J. A. Raftis, Papers in Medieval Studies 2 (Toronto, 1981), pp. 119–40. That critique was echoed five years later by Renato Rosaldo, 'From the Door of his Tent: The Fieldworker and the Inquisitor', in *Writing Culture: The Poetics and Politics of Ethnography*, ed. J. Clifford and G. E. Marcus (Berkeley, CA, 1986), pp. 77–97. The more deconstructive methodology was introduced by Lerner, in *The Heresy of the Free Spirit*, and by G. G. Merlo, *Eretici e inquisitori nella società piemontese del Trecento: con l'edizione dei processi tenuti a Giaveno dall'inquisitore Alberto de Castellario (1335) e nelle Valli di Lanzo dall'inquisitore Tommaso di Casasco (1373)* (Turin, 1977), pp. 9–15. Carol Lansing has also used Italian sources, in particular the inquisition records of Orvieto, to undertake a microcosmic study of Italian Catharism, and the ways in which it was defined by its Catholic opponents, C. Lansing, *Power and Purity: Cathar Heresy in Medieval Italy* (Oxford, 1998). See also on Merlo: C. Bruschi, *The Wandering Heretics of Languedoc* (Cambridge, 2009), p. 11, n. 2.

[14] W. Lourdaux and D. Verhelst (ed.), *The Concept of Heresy in the Middle Ages (11th–13th C.)*, Mediaevalia Lovanensia, Series 1, Studia 4 (Louvain, 1983).

John Arnold, James Given, Thomas Scharff, Caterina Bruschi and Mark Pegg in particular have all read through inquisition texts to discuss the mechanisms that produce and underlie them, though with different perspectives and conclusions.[15] But inquisition texts are not the only set of anti-heretical sources to have been read in this way. Dominique Iogna-Prat and, earlier, Marie-Humbert Vicaire have examined the polemicists' treatment of heresy, and Lorenzo Paolini – also an eloquent and informative commentator on inquisition materials – has used polemical material in order to answer questions about lay literacy and its relationship to heresy.[16] Other work, not on polemic, but, like Iogna-Prat's book, focused on traditions of anti-heretical writing within specific religious orders, has been carried out by Beverly Kienzle for the Cistercians and Bernard of Clairvaux, and by Luigi Canetti and Anne Reltgen-Tallon for the Dominicans.[17]

The move to a deconstructive reading has from the beginning had written through it a strong tendency to scepticism, though this has manifested itself along a spectrum ranging from the functional to the more radical. At the functional end, historians such as Peter Biller and Bernard Hamilton have directed the mistrust engendered by this trend towards generating more nuanced readings of the source material and dismantling assumptions. Several of Biller's articles have identified strands of construction in anti-heretical sources or refined the way in which we understand their use, as with, for example, the

---

[15] J. H. Arnold, *Inquisition and Power: Catharism and the Confessing Subject in Medieval Languedoc* (Philadelphia, PA, 2001); J. B. Given, *Inquisition and Medieval Society: Power, Discipline and Resistance in Languedoc* (Ithaca, NY, 1997); T. Scharff, 'Schrift zur Kontrolle – Kontrolle der Schrift', *Deutsches Archiv für Erforschung des Mittelalters* 52 (1996), 547–84; Bruschi, *The Wandering Heretics of Languedoc*; M. G. Pegg, *The Corruption of Angels: The Great Inquisition of 1245–46* (Princeton, NJ, 2001). Problems in the application of this approach to the thirteenth century have been highlighted by reviews of *The Corruption of Angels* by Biller and by Hamilton: B. Hamilton, review in *American Historical Review* 107 (2002), 925–26; P. Biller, review in *Speculum* 78 (2003), 1366–70. See also S. McSheffrey, 'Heresy, Orthodoxy and English Vernacular Religion 1480–1525', *Past and Present* 186 (2005), 47–80 (p. 47 and n. 2); P. Biller, 'Cathars and the Material World', in *God's Bounty? The Churches and the Natural World*, ed. P. Clarke and T. Claydon, Studies in Church History 46 (Woodbridge, 2010), pp. 89–110 (pp. 91–3, 109). See also J.-L. Biget, 'I catari di fronte agli inquisitori in Languedoc (1230–1310)', in *La parola all'accusato*, ed. J.-L. Biget, J.-C. M. Vigueur and A. Paravicini Bagliano (Palermo, 1991) pp. 235–51; J. Théry, 'L'hérésie des bons hommes. Comment nommer la dissidence religieuse non vaudois ni béguine en Languedoc (XIIe-début du XIVe siècle?)', *Heresis* 36 (2002), 75–117; G. G. Merlo, 'Il senso delle opere dei frati Predicatori in quanto "inquisitores hereticae pravitatis"', *Quaderni de Storia Religiosa* 9 (2002), 9–30.

[16] M.-H. Vicaire, 'Les Cathares albigeois vus par les polémistes', *CF* 3 (1968), 107–28; D. Iogna-Prat, *Order and Exclusion: Cluny and Christendom Face Heresy, Judaism, and Islam (1000–1150)*, translation by G. R. Edwards (Ithaca and London, 2002), originally published in French as *Ordonner et Exclure. Cluny et la société chrétienne face à l'hérésie, au Judaïsme, et à l'Islam 1000–1150* (Paris, 1998); L. Paolini, 'Italian Catharism and Written Culture', in *Heresy and Literacy*, ed. Biller and Hudson, pp. 83–103.

[17] B. M. Kienzle, *Cistercians, Heresy and Crusade in Occitania, 1145–1229: Preaching in the Lord's Vineyard* (York, 2001); Canetti, *L'invenzione*; A. Reltgen-Tallon, 'L'historiographie des Dominicains du Midi: une mémoire originale?', *CF* 36 (2001), 395–414 (p. 398).

use of the topos of heretical illiteracy and the variations in its application over space and time.[18] In other places he has looked at the mechanisms of this construction, those devices that define the picture of heresy that we receive from our sources; this work has been focused particularly on inquisition records and treatises, and more recently also on legal texts.[19] Likewise, Merlo's book of 1984, tellingly entitled *Valdesi e valdismi medievali*, which translates neatly as 'Waldensians and Waldensianisms', demonstrated different past realities of Waldensian groups that were given coherence by the regard of their persecutors. In this view there was no one authentic Waldensian tradition, but rather a rich and contrasted articulation, easily obscured by labels.[20] Claire Taylor, unusually bridging both early and inquisition-period heresy, engages with text-criticism and contextual material, weaving them together in a way that does not require us to discard the whole substance of the texts' content.[21]

Further along the spectrum, Robert Moore's work has been highly influential in promoting an idea of heresy as partly or wholly constructed. The *Origins of European Dissent* presents heterodoxy and orthodoxy as a struggle for power and posited, broadly, that what we think of as heresy was in fact resistance to centralizing authority expressed through religious means, either as dissent on the one hand, or in the established church hanging onto tradition on the other.[22] In this reading 'heresy' was a collection of dissenting elements rather than a heretical movement per se and, moreover, a dissent that arose spontaneously from developments in native spirituality (this argument standing in opposition to the thesis of eastern origin, since it is necessary for this reading to remove the possibility of that doctrinal connection.) The line of *Origins* was taken further still by *The Formation of the Persecuting Society*, which, as Carol Lansing observes, extends the idea that heresy must exist relatively to a view of heresy as deliberately created by a Catholic bureaucracy to justify the entrenchment of their power and authority.[23] A similar approach has been taken to eleventh- and twelfth-century heresy, always more problematic in its

---

18 P. Biller, 'The *topos* and Reality of the Heretic as *illiteratus*', in his *The Waldenses, 1170–1530: Between a Religious Order and a Church*, Variorum Collected Studies 676 (Aldershot, 2000), pp. 169–90.

19 P. Biller, 'Through a Glass Darkly: Seeing Medieval Heresy', in *The Medieval World*, ed. P. Linehan and J. Nelson (London, 2001) pp. 308–26; '"Deep Is the Heart of Man, and Inscrutable": Signs of Heresy in Medieval Languedoc', in *Text and Controversy from Wyclif to Bale: Essays in Honour of Anne Hudson*, ed. H. Barr and A. M. Hutchison, Medieval Church Studies 4 (Turnhout, 2005), pp. 267–80; 'Goodbye to Waldensianism?', *Past and Present* 192 (2006), 3–33.

20 G. G. Merlo, *Valdesi e valdismi medievali: itinerari e proposte di ricerca* (Turin, 1984).

21 C. Taylor, *Heresy in Medieval France: Dualism in Aquitaine and the Agenais, 1000–1249* (London, 2005).

22 R. I. Moore, *The Origins of European Dissent* (Toronto, 1977).

23 Lansing, *Power and Purity*, pp. 12–13; R. I. Moore, *The Formation of a Persecuting Society: Power and Deviance in Western Europe, 950–1250*, 2nd edn (Oxford, 2007, orig. 1987). See also U. Brunn, *Des contestataires aux 'Cathares': discours de réforme et propagande antihérétique dans les pays du Rhin et de la Meuse avant l'Inquisition* (Paris, 2006).

sources, by Guy Lobrichon.[24] The more sceptical approach and attitude that characterizes the work of Lobrichon and Moore has been current especially in French scholarship, particularly that of Monique Zerner and in the continuing work of Jean-Louis Biget, and is perhaps most easily accessible through a collection of articles with the deliberately ambiguous title *Inventer l'hérésie?*, which looks at evidence for heresy in the eleventh and twelfth centuries – that is, heresy pre-inquisition. As the title suggests, it explores the idea of heresy as a construct contained more or less entirely in the texts; a good example is Biget's article on the literary creation by the northern French and Cistercian writers of both the idea of the Albigeois as a centre for heresy, and the general application of the name to various heretical groups.[25] Out of this text-critical approach, then, a tendency to view these texts in a deconstructive way has emerged which has done much to improve our understanding of the texts and their significance and to undermine easy ventriloquism. It has led in several directions and with varying degrees of epistemological scepticism, in some instances to a view of heresy as entirely constructed from or by its sources.

Scepticism and a focus on text-criticism have brought with them a concomitant interest in laying out the subtext thus uncovered. The treatment of heresy presented by Brian Stock's work *The Implications of Literacy* is at once indicative of this trend as well as influential in its own right in its re-reading of the evidence for heresy in the eleventh and twelfth centuries in terms of textual relations.[26] Stock's ideas focus more on the presence and use of texts than on the nature of their content, but he is nevertheless concerned to unpick the representation of heresy to show what lies beneath once the veneer of rhetoric has been removed. In unravelling what the texts said to find what heresy actually was underneath, the answer has often been a political one: Biget's lengthy

---

24 Lobrichon argued that the letter of Héribert of Perigord, a text that seems to warn of early dualists, was in fact drawn from an eleventh-century document – not a letter, not written by Héribert – that was in reality a veiled, coded attack on the opponents of Cluniac reform, and not at all about heresy – effectively, as Claire Taylor has pointed out, removing the document from discussions of heresy. Subsequent to Lobrichon's article, however, the discovery of an earlier copy of the text and the demonstration of problems in Lobrichon's argument have enabled Taylor to bring the text back in from the cold. G. Lobrichon, 'Le clair-obscur de l'hérésie au début du XIe siècle en Aquitaine: une lettre d'Auxerre', in *Essays on the Peace of God: The Church and the People in Eleventh-Century France*, ed. T. Head and R. Landes, Historical Reflections/Reflexions Historiques 14.3 (1987), pp. 422–44, summarized in 'Arras, 1025, ou le vrai procès d'une fausse accusation', in *Inventer l'hérésie? Discours polémiques et pouvoirs avant l'inquisition*, ed. Zerner (Nice, 1998), pp. 67–85. Against Lobrichon's reading, see C. Taylor, 'The Letter of Heribert of Périgord as a Source for Dualist Heresy in the Society of Early Eleventh-Century Aquitaine', *Journal of Modern History* 26 (2001), 313–49.

25 J.-L. Biget, '"Les Albigeois": remarques sur une dénomination', in *Inventer l'hérésie? Discours polémiques et pouvoirs avant l'inquisition*, ed. M. Zerner (Nice, 1998), pp. 219–55. See on this Kienzle, *Cistercians*, p. 21.

26 B. Stock, *The Implications of Literacy: Written Language and Models of Interpretation in the Eleventh and Twelfth Centuries* (Princeton, NJ, 1983). Here, contact and interaction with 'text', broadly defined, is the common, shared characteristic, and not doctrine or the historical, typological coherence and significance seen or presented by the established church.

and thorough article on the Albi inquisition of 1299–1300 is a case in point.[27] But it is the process of identifying and removing the layers of construction put in place by the Catholic authors of the texts that has come to occupy centre stage.

Most studies of heresy now take for granted, therefore, that the 'insider' representation of heresy cannot be seen as unvarnished truth. The ways in which the church wrote about and represented those they placed on or beyond the margins of orthodoxy need to be processed and untangled in order to read them without, as Grundmann said, simply importing their perspective unchallenged. But that necessary deconstruction can, when taken to an extreme, lead to a complete unravelling of the construct or representation, to the dismissal of those elements identified as rhetorical or borrowed, and to an assumed disconnect between that construction and the thing described. The underlying idea of heresy, and the mechanisms that shaped and determined it, become secondary. Even where that is not the case, and the idea of heresy has been examined in many of the studies that we have looked at, the findings have been for the most part concentrated on particular fields of anti-heretical writing – often, but not always, inquisition materials.

The focus here is on the idea of heresy, rather than what is underneath it, and how it is put together across a wide range of texts written within a short time of each other and within a broader shared tradition than that provided by generic conventions and inheritance. The principal aim here will be to look for not what the sources can say about heresy so much as what they can tell us about Catholic ideas of heresy that lie behind them: how and from what parts the picture of heresy is put together, whether as part of a rhetorical programme or at a more structural level. The 'heresy' to which it is addressed will comprise, essentially, that which the contemporary church labelled as heresy. For the majority of the book heresy will remain undefined in order to explore the ideas and patterns from which it is constituted and which surround its use, and ultimately to try and understand what is meant or signified by the term. Two qualifications to this principle are, first, that, though several of our texts make reference to it, academic heresy will not be considered here in a serious way, and the focus will be on movements with a broad following; second, the terms 'Cathars' and 'Catharism' will be used as a deliberate shorthand for the sake of convenience for those who called themselves the Good Men and Good Women, and for their religion.

The best way to access the contemporary idea of what heresy was, and the patterns and rhythms in which authors wrote about it, is to look across the

---

[27] In it he argued that the investigation was defined largely by political motives, in particular those of Pope Boniface VIII and King Philip IV of France. For Biget, Catharism was connected more with political positions and interests of the officers of the king (who were Bernard de Castanet's enemies in the process) than with a popular heresy. Similarly, inquisition in Albi was also tied to politics, acting as an instrument of the church against the encroachment of royal power. J.-L. Biget, 'Un procès d'inquisition à Albi en 1300', *CF* 6 (1971), 273–341.

whole range of what was written through a comparison of different types of text. Given that the aim here is to encompass as wide a range of material as possible it is necessary to narrow the chronological scope from which it is drawn. The existence of anti-heretical material for the most part remains irregular until the middle of the twelfth century, through either accidents of survival or gaps in either the occurrence of heresy or the commentary upon it. The origins of western heresy in the murky depths of the eleventh century are hard to divine, largely as a result of the slight survival of evidence from that period. Twelfth- and thirteenth-century heresy was, in any case, very different from what had gone before and after the mid twelfth century there is a continuous production of material in a greater variety of genres. By the mid thirteenth century the major movements in high medieval heresy were well established and widely known. A contemporary tradition of anti- heretical writing had been established and writers in this tradition were now able to draw more on recent experience of, and had a greater familiarity with, the heretics of their time, where previously writers had tended to look to the Fathers for information and guidance.[28] Anti-heretical action had also expanded to its widest range and, with the establishment and growth of papal inquisition producing records and treatises alongside those more traditional areas of legislative action and polemical and homiletic writing, this was one of the highest and most diverse periods of Catholic activity toward and interaction with heresy; it is because of that richness of textual evidence that the middle of the thirteenth century will form the focus of our study.

This book is in two parts: in the first, four chapters will concentrate on one specific generic group of texts.[29] The aim in these chapters is to establish a broad pattern for each group, their basic meaning and point of view, and to analyse those groups in a way that gives common grounds for comparison. The second, smaller, part (chapter five) addresses the broader interpretative implications.

The principal textual treatments of heresy in this period can be divided, roughly, into four generic categories: polemical texts; texts designed for edification; canon-legal texts; and inquisition literature. For the sake of reference, the specific texts chosen in each group are described in detail at the beginning of their chapter. Broadly, however, canon-legal texts covers general textbooks, as well as specific anti-heretical legislation, while inquisition literature is made up of texts specific to inquisition, rather than heresy in general, and includes inquisitors' manuals and procedural documents such as depositions and sentences; the group that is called here 'texts for edification' is perhaps the most diverse of the four, containing, principally, preachers' tools, *exempla*

---

28 Biller, 'Cathars and Material Women', pp. 64–5.

29 The term 'text' is not being used here in the broad sense that Stock employs, of text as a set of ideas, but rather according to the more restricted sense in which it is used by John Arnold, as both a repository of fact and as a rhetorically constructed thing. Stock, *The Implications of Literacy*, p. 89; Arnold, 'Inquisition, Texts and Discourse', p. 63.

collections and hagiographical material. The contents of the chapter on polemic are largely self-explanatory. It is within these categories that the material is initially examined, though this is in large part for convenience, and, as will become increasingly clear, there is a great deal of overlap between these genres at their outer edges. Most of the texts that are considered here derive, not surprisingly, from a southern French or northern Italian context, though some of those could be seen to also have a sort of supra-national existence.

1

To Avoid Evil: Anti-heretical Polemic

Malum non vitatur nisi cognitum[1]

After the letters and sermons that greeted the first mutterings of dissent in the eleventh century, by the mid twelfth the anti-heretical treatise had re-emerged in the medieval west with the quickening of heresy and the growth of the schools.[2] Early attempts, with the possible exception of Peter the Venerable's *Contra petrobrusianos*, tended to remain within the sheltering framework of previously condemned heresy provided by the early church: Eckbert of Schönau's *Sermones tredecim contra haereticos* of 1163–7, the first major work on dualist heresy in the Middle Ages, nevertheless drew heavily on Augustine's *Contra manicheos* for authority and content.[3]

The new trend in polemic, which moved away from a patristic and towards a more identifiably 'high-medieval' mode, began in earnest around the turn of the century. The confession of the convert Bonacursus was reworked as a polemical tract against the Cathars; a text against Cathars and Passagians produced in Italy was an early scholastic response to heresy; and medieval anti-heretical polemic found its first known full-scale expression in Alan de Lille's *De fide catholica contra haereticos sui temporis* of 1199–1202, a four-book text that deals with heretics alongside other enemies of the church, here Jews and Muslims.[4] Several mostly French works on heresy survive from the early

---

1 *Brevis summula*, p. 114.
2 D. Iogna-Prat, trans. G. R. Edwards, *Order and Exclusion: Cluny and Christendom Face Heresy, Judaism, and Islam (1000–1150)* (Ithaca, NY, 2002), p. 120. For a useful overview of anti-heretical polemic, see Rottenwöhrer, I.i, 47–91, and the 'list of polemical sources' appended to W. L. Wakefield and A. P. Evans (trans.), *Heresies of the High Middle Ages* (New York, 1969, repr. 1991), pp. 633–8.
3 Iogna-Prat argues that, while anti-heretical polemics of the new medieval type continue to use the response of the early church as their frame of reference, from the 1150s two trends developed. Authors could either 'retreat within it', as St Bernard did, or, like Peter the Venerable, use it to develop a new way of writing a polemic against heretics: *Order and Exclusion*, pp. 120–47. Eckbert of Schönau's *Sermones* are in PL 195, 11–98.
4 Bonacursus, *Manifestatio haeresis catharorum quam fecit Bonacursus*, PL 204, 775–92; Pseudo-Praepositinus of Cremona, *The* Summa contra haereticos *Ascribed to Praepositinus of Cremona*, ed. J. N. Garvin and J. A. Corbett (Notre Dame, 1958); Alain de Lille, *De fide catholica contra haereticos sui temporis*, PL 210, 305–40.

years of the thirteenth century, perhaps most importantly the later work of Durand of Huesca, a former follower of Valdes, against the Cathars.[5] After these first decades, however, nearly all the polemical writing that appeared against heretics emerged from northern Italy, out of which context came the texts that are examined in this chapter, all of which were written in that region between about 1230 and 1250.[6]

Summa adversus catharos et valdenses[7]

Moneta of Cremona was a master of arts at the university of Bologna, and 'famous throughout Lombardy' at the time of his entry into the Dominican order in 1218 or 1219.[8] He was reputedly a close friend of St Dominic and also served as an inquisitor.[9] Moneta's *Summa adversus catharos et valdenses*, extant in sixteen manuscripts and known in six more now lost, is a long and scholarly work written in or around 1241 and edited only once, by Thomas Ricchini in 1743.[10] It is divided into five books: book one deals with the arguments of

---

5   The *Liber contra manicheos* of 1222–23, though he also wrote the *Liber antiheresis* in *c.*1191–3. On Durand, see M. A. and R. H. Rouse, 'The Schools and the Waldensians: A New Work by Durand of Huesca', in *Christendom and its Discontents: Exclusion, Persecution and Rebellion, 1000–1500*, ed. S. L. Waugh and P. D. Diehl (Cambridge, 1996), pp. 86–111, esp. pp. 87, 100–101.

6   There is one unpublished French work that is peripheral to the polemics, but which will not be looked at here: Benedict of Alignan's *Tractatus fidei contra diversos errores super titulum de summa trinitate et fide catholica in decretalibus*, of *c.*1261. See M. Grabmann, 'Der Franziskanerbischof Benedictus de Alignano († 1268) und seine Summa zum Caput Firmiter des vierten Laterankonzils', in *Kirchengeschichtliche Studien P. Michael Bihl, O.F.M., als Ehrengabe dargeboten* ed. P. I. M. Freudenreich (Strasburg, 1941), pp. 50–64, and Wakefield and Evans, *Heresies*, p. 636, no. xxvi; the text remains unedited, though some of the appendices to the *summa* were published by Douais, 'Les hérétiques du Midi au XIIIᵉ siècle: Cinq pièces inédits', in *Annales du Midi* 3 (1891), 367–80. There is also a recent edition of another, slightly later Italian polemical text by Andrew of Florence, *Summa contra hereticos*, ed. G. Rottenwöhrer, Monumenta Germaniae Historica, Quellen zur Gesistesgeschichte des Mittelalters 23 (Hannover, 2008). Andrew had been a heretic for fourteen years before his conversion, as he tells us in his prologue, and again later in the text, pp. 3, 39, 68. His *summa* is arranged, over nineteen chapters, as a series of careful arguments against heretical positions which are addressed to a hypothetical opponent. His text is very similar in style, tone and format to the other polemics treated here; in fact it contains echoes of most of them throughout, particularly of Moneta's.

7   Moneta, *Adversus catharos*. Biographical and bibliographical information from *SOPMA*, III, 137–38; *Dictionnaire de théologie catholique*, 15 vols. in 30 (Paris, 1923–50), X, 2211–15; and introduction in Wakefield and Evans, *Heresies*, pp. 307–8. See Rottenwöhrer, I.i, 59–63.

8   'In tota Lombardia famosus'; *Vitae fratrum*, p. 169.

9   The entry in the *Dictionnaire de théologie catholique*, X, 2211, mentions a dedication of 1243, 'master Moneta, OP, doctor of Theology, residing in Bologna'.

10   For a list of MSS see *SOPMA* III, 138–39, and IV, 201. On the date of the text: a passage in Ricchini's edition, based on BAV MS Reg. Lat. 428, p. 245, indicates the date *c.*1244, though in two MSS the same passage indicates 1241; see Wakefield and Evans, *Heresies*, p. 744, n. 1; *SOPMA*, which also dates the text to 1241.

absolute dualists and Catholic replies on God and the devil, creation, angels and men, prophecies and miracles. Book two addresses those of mitigated dualists on the same topics. Three and four argue against both groups on Christ, John the Baptist, the Virgin, the Holy Spirit, the Sacraments and Apocalyptic doctrine; and, finally, book five defends Catholic teaching and covers teaching on oaths, secular justice, usury and free will; this last part contains Moneta's limited material on the Waldenses, as well as brief treatment of philosophers.

Summa contra haereticos[11]

This is a reasonably long text that deals solely with the Cathar heresy, refuting points of Cathar doctrine and affirming the corresponding Catholic teaching in alternating sections. An ascription to James Capelli, lector at the Franciscan convent at Milan, was made by Molinier, who, working from the Milan manuscript that bears James' name, first described the treatise in 1888. Ilarino da Milano suggests that James may also have been an inquisitor, and certainly there are indications that the author of this work may have been connected to the process of inquisition. The ascription to James is not secure, however, and the treatise was published as an anonymous work in excerpts, and then in its entirety (by Döllinger and Bazzocchi respectively), from the Cesena manuscript, which has no ascription. The text survives in four manuscripts, while a fifth, now lost, is documented in the 1381 catalogue of the Franciscan convent at Assisi.[12] Molinier and Ilarino da Milano both place this text somewhere between 1240 and 1260, though Wakefield and Evans suggest, based on several passages comparable with the *c.*1241 Summa of Moneta of Cremona, that it was 'prepared' by about 1240: the possibility of a common source for the shared material would, however, reduce the significance of the comparison.[13] Wakefield also demonstrates the dependence of the author on earlier preachers' manuals for much of the material that comprises the chapters on orthodox belief.[14]

Disputatio inter catholicum et paterinum hereticum[15]

This text is an exposition and refutation of Cathar doctrine framed within the

---

11 Capelli, *Adversus haereticos*. Biographical and historiographical information taken from Wakefield and Evans, *Heresies*, pp. 301–2. See Rottenwöhrer, I.i, 57–59. There is a more recent critical edition, by P. Romagnoli in her 1991–2 Bologna doctoral thesis ('Pseudo-Giacomo de Capellis, "Summa Contra hereticos"'), which could not be consulted for this study.

12 A. Dondaine, 'Durand de Huesca et la polémique anti-cathare', *AFP* 24 (1959), 228–76, repr. in Dondaine, *Les hérésies et L'inquisition* (p. 266).

13 W. L. Wakefield, 'Notes on Some Anti-heretical Writings of the Thirteenth Century', *Franciscan Studies* 27 (1967), 285–321 (pp. 309–15). See also below, p. 16, n. 19.

14 Wakefield, 'Notes', pp. 299–304.

15 *Disputatio*. See Rottenwöhrer, I.i, 66–67.

form of a *disputatio, or debate, between a Catholic and a heretic*. It seems to have had a very wide circulation; Hoécker puts the number of extant manuscripts at fifty-three. These fall into two families: a shorter Italian version, the version that will be used here, and a longer, later French redaction, with added material on the Eucharist. The author refers to himself, in the eighth chapter, as a layman, but apart from this there is very little else known about him and there has been some debate over his identity.[16] Martène and Durand, in their edition of this text, marked the work as anonymous, but from a pun that he makes on the etymology of 'George', we can at least assume that this was the author's name.[17] Partly on this basis, Schmidt and Ilarino da Milano attributed it to the Dominican inquisitor Gregory of Florence, later Bishop of Fano, but Dondaine, and with him Hoécker, have rejected this attribution.[18] Several parts of the *Disputatio* can be related to other texts contemporary with it. One passage on the transmigration of souls is found in both the *Disputatio* and the *Summa* attributed to Peter Martyr, for which Kaeppeli suggests a common source. There are also places in which a close resemblance can be demonstrated between George's work and that of Moneta, and, though Borst rejects any relationship between the two, the similarities would seem to suggest at least some level of dependence or relationship.[19] Ilarino da Milano dates the *Disputatio* to shortly before 1250; Wessley suggests that an earlier date can perhaps be inferred from references to the death penalty within the text. Hoécker places this text in the first third of the thirteenth century, at some point between 1209 and 1234.[20]

Liber suprastella[21]

The author of the *Liber suprastella*, Salvo Burci, was a native of Piacenza, a member of the notarial family 'Burcius' and, according to Bruschi, probably

---

16 *Disputatio*, p. 46.

17 'Falso enim ero GEORGIUS, si terras domini mei non excolam'; *Disputatio*, p. 47.

18 C. Schmidt, *Histoire et doctrine de la secte des Cathares ou Albigeois*, 2 vols. (Paris, 1848–9), II, 230; Ilarino da Milano, 'Fr. Gregorio O.P., vevosco di Fano e la "*Disputatio inter catholicum et paterinum hereticum*"', *Aevum* 14 (1940), 85–140; Dondaine, 'Manuel', p. 174–80.

19 Kaeppeli, 'Une somme', 295–335 (p. 325, n. 38); S. Wessley, 'The Composition of Georgius' *Disputatio inter Catholicum et Paterinum hereticum*', *AFP* 48 (1978), 55–61; Wakefield, 'Notes', pp. 297–9; A. Borst, trans. C. Roy, *Les Cathares* (Paris, 1984), p. 21, n. 1; see *Disputatio*, pp. lxix–lxx.

20 Wessley, 'Composition', p. 55 and n. 3; *Disputatio*, p. xi, pp. xxxv–xlii; Wakefield and Evans, *Heresies*, p. 290. See also S. Hamilton, 'The Virgin Mary in Cathar Thought', *JEH* 56 (2005), 24–49.

21 Salvo Burci, *Suprastella*; biographical and bibliographical information taken from introduction, pp. vii–xxxvii. Excerpts have also been edited by Ilarino da Milano, *Il 'Liber supra Stella' del piacentino Salvo Burci contro I catari e altri correnti ereticali*, in *Eresie medievali: Scritti minori* (Rimini, 1983), 205–367, orig. publ. in *Aevum* 16 (1942), 272–319; 17 (1943), 90–146; 19 (1945), 218–341.

either connected to episcopal inquisitions or in some contact with the heretical fringe. Like the author of the *Disputatio*, Salvo was a layman and, though he was not a scholar, he was certainly schooled. The *Liber Suprastella*, dated very precisely to Sunday, 6 May 1235, was commissioned by Monachus de Cario. Bruschi points out that the de Cario family had close links with the Speroni family, whose name had been compromised by associations with heresy, and suggests that this commission was the de Carios' attempt to assert their orthodoxy. The book is apparently a response to a heretical work by the name of *The Star*, hence the title, and is a rather rambling and incoherent work nominally dealing with all heresies, but really with the Cathars and the Waldensians. Its prologue is written by a separate author who was apparently trying to impose some kind of generic identity on a text that the editor characterizes as a variable and above all hurried composition, written 'di getto'. The text is extant in one manuscript only, recovered by Döllinger in 1890.[22]

Summa contra hereticos[23]

Another *Summa contra hereticos*, this survives in two manuscripts, both Italian products of the thirteenth or early fourteenth century. It has been studied in depth by Kaeppeli, who places the date of the text in the region of 1235 and suggests the ascription to Peter Martyr. The author was certainly a Lombard and a Dominican, and clearly very familiar with heretics, and Kaeppeli's case for Peter's authorship, though conjectural, has been convincing to other specialists, including Dondaine and Caldwell, and will be assumed here for the sake of convenience.[24] It is clear from internal references that the *Summa* is intended to be in four parts, though in neither manuscript is the fourth part extant, and part of the third is also missing, or perhaps was never finished. Neither manuscript contains the text's prologue. The Perugia manuscript has a table of contents that shows the text divided into titles, and further subdivided within those, though these divisions are not apparent in either manuscript, both being devoid of any rubrication or navigational apparatus. Nevertheless, the text has a clear plan that is sustained throughout, and which Kaeppeli likens to that of Moneta. The first book is against the errors of Cathars, or rather Patarines, with regard to the credo and the sacraments, and ends with a short defence of the consumption of meat, eggs and cheese; this book takes up two-thirds of the text as it survives. Book two refutes the errors of five groups

---

22 In Florence, Biblioteca Medicea Laurenziana; see Salvo Burci, *Suprastella*, pp. xxix–xxxii.

23 Kaeppeli, 'Une somme', extracts on pp. 320–35. The Florence manuscript BNCF Conv. soppr. MS 1738 was consulted for this study. On Peter see A. Dondaine, 'Saint Pierre Martyr: Études', *AFP* 23 (1953), 69–107; C. Caldwell, 'Peter Martyr: The Inquisitor as Saint', *Comitatus* 31 (2000), 137–74; D. Prudlo, *The Martyred Inquisitor: The Life and Cult of Peter of Verona ([martyred] 1252)* (Aldershot, 2008).

24 Kaeppeli, 'Une somme', pp. 296–7; pp. 312–19.

of heretics – the Predestinarians, Circumcisors, Speronists, Waldensians and Rebaptizers – and the third book treats errors that are common to all groups. Kaeppeli suggests that the moral and religious practices of the Cathars would have been the subject of the fourth.[25]

These texts, though all emerging within the same twenty- or thirty-year period, and all from the Lombardy region, nonetheless present quite a wide spectrum of quality and style. Moneta's *Summa* is clearly the work of an accomplished and well-read academic: it is a complex theological and scholastic treatise. Peter's *Summa* is similarly learned and similar in approach, though it uses dialogue more freely and is more lively than Moneta's. The work of the Pseudo-James is also a learned work, especially in those parts that refute heretical doctrine. The two lay texts are not without learning, though Salvo's work is perhaps a little more lacking than George's, which is a relatively sophisticated theological work; however, both seem to reflect a less formal arena of discussion. For the most part these works address Cathar heresy; the Pseudo-James and George exclusively so. Although Moneta and Salvo both claim to treat Catharism and Waldensianism they both give far greater space to the former. Peter Martyr's text aims to encompass all heresies, and does so with more success than the others, but the errors of the Cathars are his main concern – even the heretical voice of the shared errors of the third part frequently sounds dualist in tone. Despite the differences in character, though, the similarities in the structure of these texts and in the ways that they represent their subject are such that several common features in their construction of heresy stand out, and none more so than that of heresy as an educated and intellectual phenomenon.

Each of Moneta's chapters is devoted to one point of heretical error and looks like a standard scholastic response to a problem of contradictory interpretations. He first systematically addresses all the authorities and arguments that are used to support that error and sets up the heretical argument as the thesis. He then presents the Catholic position in terms of counter-argument and solution, working through and refuting the points made. The exchange is therefore presented as an argument that alternates between two positions, indicated as *contra* and *solutio*. The Catholic position always, of course, offers the final resolution of the problem. The same dialectical, systematic structure is adopted by Peter Martyr, the Pseudo-James and George, though presented in the latter two within a framework of spoken, rather than written, debate, and in the first by a mixture of the two. This method is less apparent in the structure of Salvo's treatise than in those of the other writers, but his work still has a studied texture of academic method: he tries to respond to each point in turn and refute from authority, and he uses scholarly terminology.

---

25 Ibid., pp. 298–301 and n. 5.

The heresy presented in these exchanges is therefore one of complex theological ideas that proceed from a basis in authority. For the most part the principal source of those authorities is Scripture, and in almost every case that authority is drawn from the New Testament, although Moneta's heretical opponent makes substantial use of Old Testament material as well, and Peter Martyr seems to expect that the 'Patarine' will make use of both Old and New Testament authorities.[26] Occasionally, the texts show the heretics making reference to patristic writers such as Augustine and even Chrysostom, but such occasions are not common and usually appear because the heretical opponent is citing those writers not in support of his own point but as a proof used by his Catholic opponent.[27] Moneta does, though, include a Cathar argument based on a *dictum* of Aristotle, and the reliance on *auctoritates* is also bolstered in places by a use of logical arguments and arguments drawn from natural philosophy. Moneta, Peter, the Pseudo-James and Salvo all include heretical positions supported by *rationes*, and both Peter Martyr and his opponent also make use of Aristotle: he is the most cited of the secular authorities in Peter's text, and in fact language and arguments of this type are much more at the forefront of this text as a whole.[28] One of the few surviving Cathar texts, the *Liber de duobus principiis*, which uses both Aristotle (or rather a text that its author believed to be by Aristotle) and Roman Law as source material, would seem to support these representations.[29] Presented as a series of doctrinal

---

26 'Quia nusquam reperies in veteri vel novo testamento'; Peter Martyr, Conv. soppr. MS 1738, fol. 4r. Andrew of Florence states that he will use authorities drawn from both Old and New Testaments in defending Catholicism and confounding heretical depravity. In places he seems to expect his heretical opponent to reject these proofs, once reinforcing his point with a quotation from Peter 'si prophetam nolles recipere' and, in his final chapter, on bodily resurrection, switching from Old to New Testament proofs 'quia de veteri testamento quedam induximus, heretice, ad probandam resurrectionem contra insipientiam tuam, qui malitiose negas eandem', pp. 12, 130. Nevertheless, he uses the Old Testament freely in his work, the book of Isaiah and the Psalms especially, and the heretical positions that he sets up also seem in places to rely on Old Testament proofs. On Cathar use of Old Testament, see also P. Jiménez-Sánchez, 'Le "Traité cathare anonyme": un recueil d'autorités à l'usage des prédicateurs cathares', *Heresis* 31 (1999 for 1996), 73–100 (pp. 85–91).

27 Capelli, *Adversus haereticos*, pp. clxxxii, ccvii; *Disputatio*, pp. 18, 29, 45, 47, 63, 58.

28 Moneta, *Adversus catharos*, p. 23, also perhaps p. 83, and see below, p. 30, n. 70. Peter Martyr, Conv. soppr. MS 1738, e.g. discussions of the highest good, fol. 41r; of the manner in which the Holy Spirit is present in the sacraments, fol. 62v. Pseudo-James also seems to make use of Aristotelian terms: Capelli, *Adversus haereticos*, pp. xxi, xxxii, cl–cli, cxcix. See also Andrew of Florence, *Summa*, p. 124.

29 Though this reference is in fact misattributed, the author clearly believed it to be from Aristotle. A. Dondaine, *Un traité néo-manichéen de XIIIe siècle: Le* Liber de duobus principiis, *suivi d'un fragment de rituel cathare* (Rome, 1939), pp. 141, 143, 82. Paolini shows Italian Cathars using patristic authorities, as well as material from theologians and philosophers, and possibly the Ordinary Gloss. Paolini also cites George as referring to a heretical *glossa*, but Hoécker gives this as 'bursa': L. Paolini, 'Italian Catharism and Written Culture', in *Heresy and Literacy*, ed. Biller and Hudson, pp. 97–8 and 100, n. 76; *Disputatio*, p. 46 and n. 111.

errors based firmly in the enumeration and exposition of usually Scriptural *auctoritates*, and expounded according to scholastic principles, heresy as it appears in these polemics is an inescapably learned phenomenon, not only because that is what the authors describe but also because it is engaged with as such. If heresy in these sources is something expressed in academic terms, all the polemics share the conviction that heresy is also something that can also be answered in those terms.

The learning, or otherwise, of heretics was not at this stage an unprecedented aspect of anti-heretical writing. The heretic as *illiteratus* was indeed one of the more prevalent elements of the re-emergent anti-heretical polemic of the twelfth century, the general pattern of which was to emphasize, and perhaps overstate, the ignorance of the heretics in question, principally through the use of words such as *rusticus* and *illiteratus*. Although it is important to remember, as Grundmann made clear, that in this context *illiteratus* principally indicated that a person was not Latin literate, rather than unable to read altogether, in contrast to our texts the use of that term is still significant.[30] Examinations of this topos have revealed two levels to the accusation of illiteracy; the principal element was a general division between the educated church and ignorant heretics, while a further distinction was sometimes made among the ranks of the heretics (when the internal constitution of a sect was under discussion without direct reference to the Catholic Church) between the cunning, sophistical leaders and their simple and deluded followers.[31] That duality represented the main line of the earlier Catholic attacks on heresy, the effect, if not necessarily the aim, of which was to neatly sidestep the need to deal with the error closely: it invalidated the heresy because the ignorance or superficiality of the heretic precluded its having any real substance, dismissing the error by dismissing the capability of its proponents. The one partial exception to this early pattern was the *Contra Petrobrusianos* of Peter the Venerable, in which, according to Iogna-Prat, Peter employed a 'defensive argument' that allied a more argumentative approach to the solely imprecatory style of his contemporaries.[32] The earlier attacks were therefore *ad hominem*, focused on the heretic's behaviour and personal qualities, and included little engagement with, or extensive reporting of, error.

The application of this device was not uniform: it had a weak tradition in northern French polemic but continued to be strong in the south of France

---

Raniero Sacconi describes John of Lugio using not only the whole Bible, but also natural philosophy and Roman Law: Raniero Sacconi, *Summa*, 31–60 (pp. 53, 56, 54).

30 H. Grundmann, '*Litteratus-illiteratus*. Der Wandel einer Bildungsnorm vom Altertum zum Mittelalter', *Archiv für Kulturgeschichte* 40 (1958), 1–65.

31 P. Biller, 'Northern Cathars and Higher Learning', in *The Medieval Church*, ed. Biller and Dobson, pp. 25–53 (pp. 48–9), and introduction to *Heresy and Literacy*, ed. Biller and Hudson, p. 4.

32 See Iogna-Prat, *Order and Exclusion*, pp. 120–47, and see below, p. 195.

until the 1190s, after which time it was rarely employed against Cathar groups, though some writers in this region continued to employ the illiterate heretic device against the Waldensians beyond this date. Where it did maintain a strong tradition, well into the thirteenth century, was in German discussions of heresy, in the several handbooks written for inquisitors, though, perhaps significantly, the principal concern in this region was with Waldensianism.[33] The thirteenth-century polemical treatment of Cathar heresy, which emerges from an Italian context, abandoned this imagery and no longer centred on the simple duality of literate churchmen/illiterate heretics. In the first place, the manner in which these texts engage with their subject represents a departure in its own right. Unlike the earlier polemical approach, which rarely discussed error, the later texts engage precisely with that error and little else. Where the thirteenth-century construct also departs from most of the earlier material, and where Catharism seems distinguished from descriptions of Waldensianism in particular, is in its depiction of heretical use and application of Scriptural and occasionally philosophical knowledge. What is striking, therefore, is not only that the heresy, or rather the Cathar heresy that these texts present, is a learned phenomenon, but also that it consists primarily, and in fact almost entirely, of doctrinal and theological error, rather than the more externalized, behavioural error of belief presented by earlier texts, or indeed by some of the other genres to be considered later.

Vestiges of the language of that topos linger on in the thirteenth-century polemics; despite the impression of learning that is carefully and deliberately created through these polemics a certain amount of invective that paints both the heresy and heretics as stupid, or foolish, finds its way into the *Disputatio*, the Pseudo-James and the *Liber suprastella*. It is most common in the latter two – Salvo manages to call the heretics foolish six times in seven lines.[34] The type of language exhibited here is much more restricted in the sober prose of Moneta and Peter Martyr. Wherever it does occur in our polemics, though, it is belied by the manner in which each of these texts engages with its subject, which always presents a learned doctrine grounded in text and text-production, and even occasionally with learned individuals who either create or transmit that doctrine. Aside from those heretics named by Moneta and

---

33 P. Biller, 'The *topos* and Reality of the Heretic as *illiteratus*', in Biller, *The Waldenses*, pp. 169–90; also 'Northern Cathars', p. 48, and 'The Cathars of Languedoc and Written Materials', in *Heresy and Literacy*, ed. Biller and Hudson, pp. 61–82 (p. 80); A. Patschovsky, 'The Literacy of Waldensianism from Valdes to *c*.1400', in *Heresy and Literacy*, ed. Biller and Hudson, pp. 112–35 (p. 127).

34 'Stulti et insensati eretici, non est autem mirum si stulti estis eretici, quia stulta loquimini; stultorum enim in anima penitus et stulta proferre consuetudo est … [quotation from Matthew 21.12] … O stulti, ubi erat tunc corpus Christi? Stulti estis'; Salvo Burci, *Suprastella*, pp. 20–21.

Peter, the Pseudo-James uses the term *magistri* of at least some of the heretics he presents and Salvo mentions a certain *medicus* called Andrew as a source.[35]

The passage of time partly accounts for this change in the polemical approach to heresy, these texts being written after a lapse of time that had allowed the accumulation of knowledge about and confidence to describe contemporary heresy without over-reliance on models provided by the Fathers. Similarly, the developments in learning and teaching techniques and a change in authorship make for a different kind of text from the previous, largely monastic, productions. But it is also not coincidental that texts that are responding to heresy in a northern Italian context, as these polemics are, should present a different sort of texture and tone.

Peter of les Vaux-de-Cernay's history presents a picture of Languedoc before the crusade, where preaching and debate and the exchange of lists of *auctoritates* and *rationes* between the opposing parties were common. In Peter's account the participants vary from Catholic preachers to Cathars and Waldensians and also include lay observers of either Catholic or heretical sympathies.[36] By the middle years of the century that picture to some extent remains valid, and public debates between heretical and orthodox figures seem to have been common in northern Italian cities, as they had been in southern France in preceding years. Paolini points to two famous public debates that took place in 1260s Vicenza between the Cathar and Catholic bishops of that city. Salvo himself tells us that the Albanenses and Concorrezenses met often to resolve the schism between them, providing a further layer of contact and conflict in the debates that appear to have been frequent between the different Cathar churches.[37] But while heretics are often seen to debate with each other – whether Cathars with Waldensians, or different factions of either with each other – more pertinent to our discussion

---

35 *Doctores* and *magistri* began to appear among the Cathar ranks from the end of twelfth century. In a letter preserved in Matthew Paris's *Chronica majora* Yves of Narbonne, telling of his induction into Cathars secrets, relates that the Cathars told him that they sent their 'capable students' to Paris from most Lombard and some Tuscan cities, to study logic or theology, in order to bolster their own error and overthrow the Catholic faith. Paolini, 'Italian Catharism', p. 88; Yves of Narbonne to Gerald archbishop of Bordeaux, Wakefield and Evans, *Heresies*, p. 186; for analysis of this letter see Biller, 'Northern Cathars', pp. 50–51. Capelli, *Adversus haereticos*, 'magistri' (p. cviii), also a heresiarch (p. cxii). This would traditionally be the author of a heresy, but here, and elsewhere, it can mean both this and a high-ranking heretic such as Lugio or Raniero. 'Sic audivi quod Andreas medicus predicabat qui dicebatur esse de vestris': Salvo Burci, *Suprastella*, p. 314.

36 Peter of les Vaux-de-Cernay, *Hystoria albigensis*, ed. P. Guébin and E. Lyon, 3 vols. (Paris, 1926–39), I, 47–9. Peter the Chanter says that, if you want to talk to heretics, then to do so outside church and away from Christians, and that if they say something just in debate, then it ought to be recognized; N. Bériou, *L'avénement des maîtres de la Parole: la prédication à Paris au XIIIe siècle* (Paris, 1998), p. 39.

37 Stephen of Bourbon says that he has heard Waldensians quarrelling among themselves, according to the level of their indoctrination: Stephen of Bourbon, *Tractatus*, p. 299.

are those occasions on which the heretics are in dispute with Catholics, particularly the friars. Mendicant hagiography provides one obvious example: St Dominic can be seen with some frequency to enter into debate with heretics, and though in St Dominic's case the accounts refer to an earlier period, later anti-heretical saints such as Peter Martyr and Anthony of Padua can likewise be seen disputing publicly with the heretics.[38] But debates are visible throughout the wider mendicant tradition: one Franciscan inquisitor near Rome publicly questions a heretic on his beliefs about creation and salvation.[39]

The picture presented by these sources is reflected in the inquisition records; the penances of Peter Cellan, in particular, present many occasions where deponents report having witnessed a *disputatio*, or heard that someone *disputavit* about points of faith. One layman 'debated with the Friars Minor whether man ought to kill' on the basis of what he had learned from the Waldensians. Another describes accommodating three heretics for a day and a night, during which time 'there was a dispute between them and the priest of that place for almost the whole day'.[40] This 'disputatiousness' is identified by Paolini as a characteristic of the Cathar groups, and one that had troubled Catholic commentators, such as Joachim of Fiore, for some time.[41] Even as late as the 1320s Bernard Gui was warning less experienced scholars not to be too ready to take heretics on in public.

The *Disputatio* is consciously presented by its author as proceeding according to 'the manner of the heretics', 'more hereticorum', understood in this context to mean the scholastic method of dialogue in which the text is constructed.[42] The fact that a layman can use this phrase as a shorthand for

---

38 For examples of St Dominic and Peter Martyr in debate, see below, p. 83; L. de Kerval (ed.) *Sancti Antonii de Padua vitae duae quarum altera hucusque inedita* (Paris, 1904), pp. 220–21.

39 P. L. Oliger, 'Liber exemplorum fratrum minorum saeculi XIII (excerpta e cod. ottob. vat. 522)', *Antonianum* 2 (1927), 203–76 (pp. 272–3).

40 'Disputavit cum Fratribus Minoribus utrum homo deberet occidere'; 'fuit disputatio inter ipsos et sacerdotem loci quasi per totum diem'; Duvernoy, *Quercy*, pp. 96, 222. See further examples, pp. 64, 68, 78, 102, 112, 132, 160, 174, 182, 184. A nice example can be found in the penance of one Bernard Raimond, who, having heard the Waldensians preach, decides to visit the Cathars, 'volens temptare qui essent milieres [sic, r. meliores]', and see below, p. 134, n. 92. After spending time with the Cathars, 'disputavit cum quodam de fide hereticorum et Valdensium, et approbavit fidem hereticorum'; Duvernoy, *Quercy*, p. 146. One of the more extended examples of debate with the mendicants can be found in the depositions of the *credens* Peter Garcias; see below, pp. 131–2.

41 This can also be more general than debates; references to the heretics teaching and preaching are frequent throughout the anti-heretical corpus, including some of the polemics: see, for example, Salvo Burci, *Suprastella*, pp. 6, 342, Capelli, *Adversus haereticos*, pp. x, xi, xvii, lxxxiii. See also Andrew of Florence, who sometimes uses 'predicas' in place of or in addition to 'dicas' when addressing his opponent: Andrew of Florence, *Summa*, pp. 30, 59, 69, 73. On Cathar preaching see J. H. Arnold, 'The Preaching of the Cathars', in *Medieval Monastic Preaching*, ed. C. Muessig (Leiden, 1998), pp. 183–205. Paolini, 'Italian Catharism', pp. 90–91; Salvo Burci, *Suprastella*, pp. 5–6.

42 *Disputatio*, p. 4 and n. 6. The same usage occurs in the *Vitae fratrum*, where a young Peter

academic debate is suggestive. It points to a general familiarity with, and recognition of the condition of, heretical learning among his readership, which, to judge from the manuscript tradition, seems to have been wide, as well as an exterior existence to this learning, rather than simply a superimposed rhetorical framework. It also suggests a familiarity with heretics debating.

The two lay texts are both presented as tools for personal encounter with heresy, George's as a weapon, Salvo's as a defence against wiles, but both suggest contact and open debate. 'You have heard, Christians, a blasphemy of the cross!' exclaims George, before refuting the heretic's latest error.[43] The several connections between the texts both of Moneta and of the Pseudo-James with the *Summae auctoritatum* that are discussed in the next chapter might suggest that these, too, were closer to the real work of repression than is at first apparent; a text closely related to this set of polemics, the *Quaedam obiectiones*, of which more shortly, seems indeed to contain one of these *summae* as an integral part. This is not necessarily to argue that the polemicists intended their work for a scholarly heretical readership – Moneta is not talking to heretics but rather to an orthodox reader, despite the fact that he seems to address his heretical opponent throughout his long refutations – but it might suggest that, while their 'proximate' audience was orthodox, heretics nonetheless formed part of the 'ultimate' audience for these texts.[44]

A more physical suggestion of use might be found in a miniature copy of Moneta's *Summa*, to be found in a late thirteenth or early fourteenth century manuscript of the Bibliothèque nationale, Lat.3656. The latter is a tiny book, smaller than a modern sheet of A5, filled with notes and glosses and the occasional manicule pointing to relevant parts of the text. It is even slightly more miniature than the portable Bible of the Bibliothèque nationale manuscript Lat.174 that contains the first of Douais' *Summae auctoritatum*.[45] Another relatively small copy of (most of) Moneta can be found in Vatican manuscript Reg. Lat.428, which also contains Raniero Sacconi's handbook. The Florence manuscript of Peter Martyr's *Summa* is minute, only 154mm by 105mm.[46] The dimensions of these manuscripts evoke the ready portability of the vademecum books used by travelling preachers. The echo of an arena of verbal exchange and debate, much more immanent in the *Disputatio*, in Salvo and, to a lesser degree, in Peter's *summa*, suggests that the polemicists – certainly the authors of the lay texts, but also the others – involved as they were in the early

---

Martyr argues with his uncle: 'patruus nisus est ei probare per auctoritates, more hereticorum, quod dyabolus ista creaverat'; *Vitae fratrum*, p. 236.

43 'Audistis, Christiani, blasphemiam crucis!'; *Disputatio*, pp. 4, 72. Salvo Burci, *Suprastella*, p. 3.

44 The terms are D. L. d'Avray's, *The Preaching of the Friars: Sermons Diffused from Paris before 1300* (Oxford, 1985), p. 105.

45 See below, p. 45.

46 Kaeppeli, 'Une somme', p. 297.

days of inquisition, were in contact with heretical ideas in a direct, spoken form.

It is worth highlighting here Vicaire's suggestion that it was just such scholarly engagement that was partly responsible for the development of Cathar scholarship, of which the acceptance by the Italian Cathar leader John of Lugio of the whole Bible, for example, represents a significant step.[47] Beside this must be put Kaeppeli's suggestion that the heretic Peter Gallus may in fact have been one of the intended audience for Peter Martyr's *Summa*, since the text at one point addresses Gallus personally, exhorting him to return to the Catholic faith.[48] The 'Patarine' is even depicted cross-referencing his argument with the text in which he appears.[49] The same interaction can perhaps also be seen as one of the sources for the heretical content of the polemics. While the environment of northern Italy provides a plausible context for the occasionally more active texture of the polemics, however, with its disputatious heretics and high levels of lay literacy, it also supplies a more reliable source of content for the heretical material that the polemical authors argue against.[50] Though they rely on each other and borrow and import text from a variety of Catholic sources, the polemics can also be seen to use books produced by heretics in the construction of their texts.

Stephen of Bourbon, drawing on his experience as a Dominican and inquisitor in southern France in the middle of the century, relates a story in which a southern French noble, Robert of Montferrand, who died in 1234, had, over forty years, carefully collected books from all sects, including those of the local heretical groups.[51] That books containing the Gospels and the New Testament were owned and revered by heretical groups of this period is attested by the raggedy survival of a few such texts, and by their presence in reports of rituals performed by sect leaders, but, beyond the ritual function of sacred texts, heresy can also be seen to generate and exist within a written tradition all of its own.[52] Heretical books, not just of Scripture but also of doctrines and accompa-

---

47 M.-H. Vicaire, 'Les Cathares albigeois vus par les polémistes', *CF* 3 (1968), 107–28.

48 'Exi ergo, Petre Galle, de medio babillonis ... et veni ad ecclesiam dei, ubi est bonitas eius, que maior tibi apparebit quam fuerit iniquitas tua', Kaeppeli, 'Une somme', pp. 305–7. Possible hints of desire to convert also in *Disputatio*, pp. 26, 63, and in Salvo Burci, *Suprastella*, p. 315.

49 'Unum autem peto a Lectoribus istius operis, ut si qua argumenta, vel responsiones contra Haereticos sibi visa fuerint debilia, non me mordeant'; Moneta, *Adversus catharos*, p. 2; 'ut supra me credere inseruisti in prologo tuo', Kaeppeli, 'Une somme', p. 301, n. 5.

50 On lay literacy see Salvo Burci, *Suprastella*, pp. xxii–xxiii.

51 'Per quadraginta annos posuerat curam et diligenciam congregare libros omnium sectarum'. Not wishing his curiosity to be misconstrued, on his deathbed, he orders them destroyed: 'fecit autem dictos hereticos libros extrahi de loco dicto, et in oculis suis comburi'; Stephen of Bourbon, *Tractatus*, pp. 275–6.

52 A heretic using Gospel/Testament in ritual: Capelli, *Adversus haereticos*, p. cxxxviii: 'textum evangeliorum super caput eius imponit'. Pseudo-James also makes reference to apocrypha: ibid., p. xciii.

nying exegesis, are attested by a wide range of writers, particularly in Italy, from academic theologians, including Aquinas, who drew on them for detail in their discussions of doctrine, to inquisitors who collected and used them for evidence. Raniero Sacconi uses a book written by the heretic John of Lugio which he says is a 'a large volume of ten quires, a copy of which I have. I have read it through and from it have extracted the errors cited above'. Anselm of Alessandria likewise owns and uses heretical books.[53]

For one of the polemicists the idea of heresy as something found in a book is a deliberate part of the way heresy is presented: Moneta makes his access to and use of heretical texts explicit at the very beginning of his work when he tells us that his information comes either from their own mouths 'or from their writings'. He refers several times to different anonymous texts and also uses two texts by named individuals: Tetricus, an absolute dualist, and Desiderius, a mitigated dualist attested in other sources, whose work was also owned and used by Aquinas.[54] Moneta is alone in citing a heretical book explicitly, but the presence of such texts can be felt through and beneath most of these polemical works.

Like Moneta, Peter Martyr also acquires information from conversation with heretics and cites converts as a source; in several places he mentions a heretical bishop named Peter Gallus. Though he never mentions a text we know that Gallus was the author of at least one treatise; he is well attested as a Cathar scholar and writer in other sources, including the work of Albertus Magnus, and Kaeppeli thinks it likely that Peter had some of Gallus' writings in front of him as he composed his *Summa*.[55] The title of Salvo's book would appear to define the entire work in terms of a specific heretical text; the prologue to the *Liber suprastella*, written by a different author, explains the title of this work by reference to a heretical treatise named *The Star*, to which Salvo's book is a reply: the higher star. Salvo himself makes no mention of this text, but the book's modern editor nonetheless sees Salvo as being in some part reliant on a heterodox text, importing elements from it which stand out in tone

---

53 'Quoddam volumen magnum X quaternorum, cuius exemplarium habeo et perlegi et ex illos errores supradictos extraxi'; Raniero Sacconi, *Summa*, p. 57; trans. Wakefield and Evans, *Heresies*, p. 343. Anselm of Alessandria, *Tractatus*, p. 319. On heretical books see P. Biller and A. Hudson (ed.), *Heresy and Literacy, 1000–1530* (Cambridge, 1994), *passim*.

54 'Vel ex scripturis suis'; Moneta, *Adversus catharos*, p. 2. See also, for anonymous texts, pp. 42, 94, 398. Wakefield also points to other possible heretical sources used by Moneta: Wakefield, 'Notes', p. 305 and nn. 74–7. On Desiderius: Moneta, *Adversus catharos*, pp. 248, 347, 357; Thomas Aquinas, *Contra impugnantes Dei cultum*, cap. 6, cited by Dondaine, 'La hiérarchie II and III', p. 292, n. 36. He also appears in several other accounts, including the *Vitae fratrum*, 5.iii, p. 239, and Anselm of Alessandria's account of the Concorrezenses: Anselm of Alessandria, *Tractatus*, p. 310. On Tetricus: Moneta, *Adversus catharos*, pp. 61, 71, 79. See also Wakefield, 'Notes', p. 305, nn. 74–7.

55 Kaeppeli, 'Une somme', pp. 310–11. See also Dondaine, 'Hiérarchie II', pp. 297–8; Peter Martyr, Conv. soppr. MS 1738, 97r.

and language.[56] And in fact the presence of heretical texts is more than incidental: they can be seen to constitute a source of the heretical material contained in these Catholic works, underlying and defining the structure of the polemics. The process is clearest in the work of Moneta, who employs heretical works throughout as a template for his response, working systematically from the text being refuted. That use is explicit where Moneta makes direct reference to proofs found in the writings of Tetricus, for example, but many of the heretical doctrines and expositions that Moneta refutes are presented in such detail as to also suggest the presence of a text.

This working method in Moneta can be illuminated by comparison to an analogous text entitled *Quaedam obiectiones hereticorum et responsiones Christianorum*; it is a much smaller text than Moneta's *Summa*, but one which has close connections with it.[57] The first part of this text, which Wakefield believes may be an extract from a longer work, is principally concerned with an extended response to Cathar objections to the God of the Old Testament. The refutation begins with the statement that 'the objections of the heretics in this chapter proceed from four roots', and the author then follows that four-fold framework systematically, quoting and answering the heretical articles with the same method and the same level of detail as Moneta.[58] Wakefield demonstrates the close relationship of the *Quaedam obiectiones* with the sixth chapter of Moneta's second book. The prologue is almost identical with the beginning of Moneta's chapter, although the use of the terms 'Albigenses' or 'Bugari' where Moneta's version uses Cathars leads Wakefield to suggest that the Doat text is more likely to be of French origin. The relationship between the two lies neither in the group names used for the heretics nor in the refutations, but rather in the statements of heretical argument, and it is Wakefield's opinion that both authors had access to the same written source of heretical doctrine.[59] The use by both authors of the same material to create different responses again suggests that engagement with pre-existing heretical sources drives the argument and informs the structure of the orthodox polemic.

The pattern that we see in the *Summa adversus catharos et valdenses* and in the *Quaedam obiectiones* is repeated in the other texts, which all present their opponents' views in great detail. It would certainly substantiate the importation of a

---

56 Salvo Burci, *Suprastella*, p. 3. The title of the *Liber Suprastella* would seem to presuppose the existence of a heretical text, but Bruschi suggests that perhaps the prologue writer was trying to make some sense out of the rather strange title; Bruschi has alternative suggestions for its source: Salvo Burci, *Suprastella*, p. xxii. Those elements that seem to derive from a heretical tract are collected by Bruschi into an appendix (pp. 449–72); Ilarino da Milano also argues for Salvo's direct knowledge: reference in Paolini, 'Italian Catharism', p. 100, n. 77.

57 The *Quaedam obiectiones* and its relationship to other texts is discussed in more detail in the next chapter.

58 'Obiectiones hereticorum in hoc capitulo ex quatuor radicibus procedunt'; Doat 36, fol. 92ʳ.

59 Wakefield, 'Notes', p. 300, n. 65, and pp. 307–8. The text can be found in Doat 36, fols. 91ᵛ–203ʳ; see also below, chapter 2, p. 44, n. 15. See Rottenwöhrer, I.i, 63–4.

heretical text into Salvo's book, as demonstrated by Bruschi, and Peter Martyr's use of Gallus' work, as well as Paolini's view that the author of the *Summa contra hereticos* was also in some part dependent on heretical texts, though breaking them down to fit his own scheme and never citing them.[60] It is not clear whether the author of the *Disputatio* worked from a heretical source, though there are passages that see him moving through precisely referenced Cathar doctrine point by point, in much the same way that Moneta does. He is not concerned to present himself as using or owning a heretical book for the errors that he includes, although the fact that one of his heretical arguments appears to share a source with Peter Martyr's text might suggest that he did.[61] To take an opponent's text and construct a refutation around it was standard scholastic practice – to 'use what they say as the basis of proceeding to a refutation of their errors' – and this is in essence what these polemics do.[62]

In the opening to his *Summa contra gentiles* Aquinas says that it is possible to argue against heretics because they recognize a common text in the New Testament. Beside the shared textual inheritance, the statement also presents us with the notion that heretical groups read and understand those texts and in a way that can provide the basis for discussion or argument.[63] The fact that the heretical doctrines discussed by the polemics can be seen to derive from heretical texts, at least in part, must indicate to some extent that the academic framework that the Catholic texts use was not just a structure into which the ideas of their opponents were artificially inserted, but a format common to both. Heresy is presented in these texts, deliberately and without exception, as a set of doctrines expounded according to scholastic principles, generated by and sustained in the contemporary idiom of intellectual debate, and, though it reaches its fullest expression in Moneta's work, the same pattern runs through each of the polemics. The interaction and exchange visible in these texts is a significant factor in the representation of heresy as learned, but also seems to reflect an established tradition of debate and argument from authority rooted in an independent textual tradition among their heretical opponents. The heretical texts and ideas that can be seen to underlie the polemics seem to be of a kind that would fulfil the criteria for a reception and use of learning that Patschovsky outlines in his examination of Waldensian literacy in this period, namely: a productive application of knowledge by an intellectually active

---

60 Paolini, 'Italian Catharism', pp. 100–101.

61 Kaeppeli, 'Une somme', p. 325, n. 38; *Disputatio*, p. 27, n. 64.

62 Moneta, *Adversus catharos*, p. 71; Paolini, 'Italian Catharism', p. 101. Aquinas, *SCG*, 2 I.ii [2]; translated as *On the Truth of the Catholic Faith. Summa contra gentiles*, ed. A. C. Pegis et al., 4 vols. in 5 (New York, 1955–7), I, 62. References in square brackets are to the page number in the printed version.

63 Aquinas, *SCG*, I.ii [2]. Hamilton demonstrates that the Cathar version of New Testament was derived from the Vulgate; see B. Hamilton, 'Wisdom from the East: the Reception by the Cathars of Eastern Dualist Texts', in *Heresy and Literacy*, ed. Biller and Hudson, pp. 38–60.

readership, and the development of original writings based on this reception of knowledge.[64] What he finds to be lacking in a Waldensian context at this time seems very close to what our Italian polemicists are presenting as the condition of Cathar literacy.

In the context of the heresy that these texts present, the learned/unlearned duality of earlier polemics would not, then, present a valid line of attack and, indeed, attacks of this type are no longer the location of the real polemic, but rather a rhetorical relic. Clearly, if it is necessary to present an opponent as capable not only of learned exposition, but of exposition of a common text, then the struggle becomes about two opposed readings, and which is dominant. Though there is still invective, the real polemic is elsewhere in our authors' representation of the exchange between heretical and orthodox doctrine.

The principal reconciliation of the problem of a learned heresy with its inherent wrongness occurs through the continuing emphasis that all our authors place on interpretation. This takes place at the most basic level through the manner in which these texts are structured: in couplets of heretical and Catholic exposition. Each text consistently reinterprets the authorities used to support heretical arguments before going on to outline a statement of the orthodox position, offering refutation both by statement of Catholic doctrine and by Catholic reinterpretation of heretical exposition. The same exchange between interpretation and re-interpretation remains the general pattern even in the more loosely structured text of Salvo. The fundamental role of correct interpretation is further emphasized by the concessions that are made where an overlap occurs: Moneta and George will both acknowledge the correctness of the heretical interpretation where it coincides with the orthodox one; in the *Disputatio* the heretic is allowed to make similar concessions to his orthodox opponent.[65] Where previous polemics would, if they dealt with heretical error at all, tend to report it as necessary information, the Catharism presented by these texts consists almost entirely of doctrine. In the course of that construction exegesis is presented and recognized as the medium of the conflict; this heresy is learned, but it is also an error of learning.

So Moneta tells his opponent that 'it is clear that you understand badly' or that his 'understanding is perverse', usually at the introduction of his alternate, Catholic, reading. The interpretation of the shared Scriptural basis offered by the heretics is shown to be based on a skewed, perverse or simply wrong understanding. The exchanges between Peter Martyr's two opponents are nearly always conducted in terms of rival interpretations, and both accuse

---

64 Patschovsky, 'The Literacy of Waldensianism', pp. 116–17.

65 Moneta, *Adversus catharos*, p. 82. Concessions from both Catholic and Heretic in the *Disputatio*, pp. 7, 9, 39, 46, 58. Moneta also makes allowance for heretical disagreement over interpretation, where the heretic questions Catholic interpretation; Moneta, *Adversus catharos*, p. 12.

the other of getting it wrong. In one exchange, on wisdom, the 'heretic' remarks: 'it is natural that the church of God should have little wisdom, especially in letters', before wryly enumerating all the instances in the Scriptures in which simplicity is extolled over wisdom and worldly knowledge, allowing him in the process to call Peter and John 'unlettered, and ignorant men'. The 'Catholic' responds in kind, explaining that it should be understood to mean that only wisdom that is contrary to faith is to be avoided, and that it is therefore 'clear that you, heretics, are all ignorant men, especially in the Scriptures'.[66] Pseudo-James begins his responses to heretical statements in a similar style: 'we shall prove your exposition to be false', as does George: 'the worst understanding'. Salvo echoes George, 'in this case they have the worst understanding', though, like Moneta and George, he allows his heretical opponent to make the same claim of 'it is not to be understood that …' against the Catholic proposition, perhaps again imported from heretical text or speech.[67] They do not understand, and so they are unable to reach the patent truth of Catholic teaching, against which heretical exposition is always set: 'you expound badly … but it is to be understood thus'.[68] The emphasis on interpretation is in itself is a development from the previous polemical trope, identified by Biller, in which heretical stupidity is demonstrated by their inaccurate understanding or misunderstanding of the Latin itself; now their Latinity is accepted, only their interpretation of it questioned.

The idea is extended where the lack of understanding that results in so much misinterpretation is shown to be the result of overreaching, or connected in some way to a fault of human reason operating without the guidance of faith: 'they are separated from the learned *magistri* of the Roman Church'.[69] Moneta makes an oblique attack on this level: he condemns the use of the Aristotelian *dictum* 'the principles of contraries are contraries' and other terminology derived from that philosopher by his heretical opponent, but later, in book five, he also makes a substantial attack on Aristotle in his own right. That attack is more explicit and more extended in the Pseudo-James, who links

---

[66] 'Patet quod male intelligis'; 'perversam intelligentiam'; Moneta, *Adversus catharos*, p. 86, also pp. 79, 138, 22, etc. 'Sed naturaliter quod ecclesia dei debet habere parvam sapientiam maxime de litteratura'; 'sine litteris, et ydiote'; 'patet quod vos, heretici, estis omnes ydiote, maxime in scripturis'; Peter Martyr, Conv. soppr. MS 1738, fols. 95ᵛ–96ʳ, quoting from Acts 4. 13. Exchange over the correct interpretation of authority is the usual mode in this text – that which discusses the prohibition on swearing is a case in point, fols. 110ᵛ–111ᵛ.

[67] 'Falsam esse vestram expositionem probabimus'; Capelli, *Adversus haereticos*, p. lxii; also pp. iv, cxlv, clviii, clxv, cxcvi, cci etc. 'Pessimum intellectum'; *Disputatio*, p. 13, also pp. 15, 28, 41, 56 etc. 'In istis rebus habent pessimum intellectum'; 'non est intelligendum quod …'; Salvo Burci, *Suprastella*, pp. 8, 13, 70 etc., and from the heretic, p. 13.

[68] 'Male exponitis … sed ita intelligitur'; *Disputatio*, p. 13. The same emphasis on interpretation runs through Andrew of Florence's text, for example: 'erras ergo, heretice, sic exponendo et interpretando scripturas', or 'pravus est intellectus tuus'; Andrew of Florence, *Summa*, pp. 19, 85.

[69] 'A doctis magistris Ecclesie Romane separati'; Salvo Burci, *Suprastella*, p. 10.

many of the Cathars' errors, such as their position on the Trinity, to their misapplication of human reason to mystery: 'because it is not possible to perceive the trinity by human reason ... they do not wish to believe'.[70] They learn too quickly to be able to understand, 'they read the gospels wishing to be teachers, but they do not understand the things they say', 'always learning and never arriving at the knowledge of truth'.[71] The Pseudo-James' dismissal of heretical interpretations is supported by accusations of invention created through a colourful vocabulary of stories, fables and fictions: stories, nursery rhymes, trifles, fabricated stories, deceits, histories. 'Deceitfully they fabricate many nonsenses', says the Pseudo-James, reinforcing this impression through verbs concerned with construction and invention: to invent, drivel, chatter, fabricate, suppose, scheme, embroider.[72] These words constitute a common thesaurus for most of these texts – Peter Martyr's text expoits it regularly – but the Pseudo-James seems to have the most fun with it.[73]

So the battle over interpretation is a final layer in the polemical construct of a learned heresy, which is further developed through the manner of the orthodox engagement with it. The academic nature of the heretical arguments is answered in kind by the polemicists, and the refutation of heresy is treated as, and framed within, a dialectical exercise. These polemics do not criticize the fact of books and learning in their presentation of heresy, only the error of the interpretation contained within them – an approach broadly in line with the general conception of heresy within broader currents of thirteenth-century theological thought.

Peter Lombard's *Sentences*, the standard textbook of theological education from the 1220s onwards, asks the question 'What makes a heretic and what a heretic is', and answers it with two quotations.[74] The first, from Hilary, makes

---

70 'Contrarium contraria sunt principia' (*broadly*: the starting-points of things that are contrary to each other are themselves contraries); Moneta, *Adversus catharos*, p. 23. On Cathar use of this *dictum*, see Biller, 'Northern Cathars', pp. 36–7. 'Quia humana non potest ratione cognoscere trinitatem ... credere nolunt'; similarly 'verum quia hereticus non credit ideo non intelligit ... multas quidem blasphemandi habens occasiones si sumpta scripturarum intelligentia consuetae naturae cursum vult attendere';Capelli, *Adversus haereticos*, pp. cxci, cli.

71 'Legunt evangelium, doctores esse cupientes, [sed] non intelligunt quae loquuntur'; 'semper discentes et nuncam ad scientiam veritatis pervenientes'; Capelli, *Adversus haereticos*, pp. xcvi, cxii; also pp. xl, xlix, lxxxi, cl. This motif is also used by Andrew of Florence, *Summa*, p. 35.

72 'Fabulas', 'nenias', 'figmenta', 'nugas', 'fabulas fingentes', 'hystoria', 'multa mendaciter fingunt deliramenta'; 'fabulare', 'delirare', 'garrire', 'fingere', 'opinari', 'machinari', 'intexere', Capelli, *Adversus haereticos*, pp. cxv, xlv, xciii, xlvii, xciv, lii, cx, cxii, cxlvi, xcii.

73 See similar list in Paolini, 'Italian Catharism', p. 85.

74 'Quid faciat hereticum et quid sit hereticus'. The text's author had of course himself narrowly escaped a charge of heresy over his Trinitarian doctrine, but had been defended at the fourth Lateran council against Joachim of Fiore, who was in turn branded a heretic in the second canon of the council. After this endorsement, the *Sentences'* orthodoxy was

heresy a crime by virtue of incorrect understanding: 'for heresy is from understanding, not from the Scriptures; and thought, not speech makes the crime'. The other quotation, from Augustine, defines the heretic as one who invents or follows false and new opinions; the same quotation is used by Gratian in the twenty-fourth *causa* of the *Decretum*.[75] The definitions here and, more important, the majority of Peter's treatment are all about interpretation; increasingly prominent in the material to which scholars were now exposed, therefore, was a discussion of heresy that had an abstract presentation, of a doctrinal heresy developed through argument. By the time Aquinas had come to address heresy in the middle of the thirteenth century, as part of his long treatise against the enemies of the church, the *Summa contra gentiles*, the idea of heresy as an interpretative error had become firmly entrenched. Aquinas' approach in this text is similar to that of the fourth Lateran council in some respects, in that he first defines the 'truth' and then outlines all other opinions as wrong by definition, as it were, in contrast to the Catholic reading. This means that, where there is an overlap in understanding, the church is able to agree with some heretics while standing against others, although their continuing condition as heretics might suggest that there is more to their status than error.[76] Aquinas distinguishes between heretics and Catholics in terms of attempted understanding on the one hand and diligent reading on the other. The emphasis is placed firmly on interpretation, even more so where authorities used by Arius, Sabellius and Plotinus are reinterpreted in scholastic mode in order to demonstrate that the authorities are sound, and only the interpretation wrong.

The previous approach, which allowed the dismissal of heresy via the ignorance of its authors/followers, therefore now gives way to a presentation of a developed exegetical and textual tradition based on educated method and means, which accepts and engages with this tradition. The tension that this creates – between the presence of a learned doctrine based on the same foundation as Catholicism on the one hand, and on the other the fact that heresy must be condemned as false and foolish – is resolved in the shift of emphasis from a result of ignorance to an error of learning. The path to correct – that is, Catholic – understanding is careful attention to the text.[77] The diligent reader

---

assured, and once Alexander of Hales had begun lecturing on the text a decade later, the text, and the principles contained within it, began to be diffused throughout the academic community. For a useful summary of the context and production of this text, see P. Biller, *The Measure of Multitude: Population in Medieval Thought* (Oxford, 2000), pp. 29–31.

[75] 'De intelligentia enim haeresis, non de Scriptura est; et sensus, non sermo fit crimen'; and again, 'intelligentiae sensus in crimine est'; Peter Lombard, *Sententiae in IV libris distinctae*, ed. I. Brady, Spicilegium Bonaventurianum 4, 2 vols. in 3 (Grottaferrata, 1971–81), *Sententiae* IV.xiii.2, Brady, II, 314–15.

[76] Aquinas, *SCG* I.xx, IV.vii; [18, 55]; trans. Pegis et al., I, 106, IV.i, 55.

[77] Moneta, *Adversus catharos*, e.g. p. 141.

is invoked in both the *Liber suprastella* and the work of the Pseudo-James as the antidote to heretical doctrine, 'the falsehood of which exposition the careful reader is able to show'.[78]

As may already be apparent, built into the polemics' depiction of heresy as a set of errors is another, of heresy as inherently divided. This division extends beyond the distinctions made between different groups; the groups themselves are also internally divided. All the texts, with the exception of the *Disputatio*, divide the Cathar beliefs into a minimum of two camps, and sometimes more, but always on doctrinal grounds, to create a picture of a variegated set of ideas and doctrines.[79] That picture of division is in part achieved through the structure of the texts themselves: Moneta devotes book one to the arguments of absolute dualists, book two to those of mitigated dualists and three and four to the arguments of both. The Pseudo-James is initially organised in a similar way (the division of the later parts is less strict), and the author also draws comparisons between different groups – one group thinks (x), though others think (y), and they all agree on (z): 'opinions are diverse among them'.[80] Although the first part of Peter's treatise is aimed at Patarines as a group, he too is careful throughout to delineate the different strands of error within the group as a whole, and this is done consistently, even though he never gives them individual group names. The *Liber suprastella* is not really organized around this principle, but it nonetheless describes divisions between the groups and in fact does so in more detail than the other texts here, which are concerned with such distinctions mostly in terms of the organization of their own texts. Salvo describes a greater complexity of division, dealing with the different churches of the Albanenses, of Concorezzo and of Bagnolo. Like his fellow Piacenzan Raniero, Salvo describes the rivalry between the Albanenses and the Concorrezenses – not only a division between churches, but also an irreparable divide.

The brief treatments given to Waldensianism also take care to distinguish between different groups. Peter gives a brief history to explain the rift between the different Waldensian groups that he describes, before describing their different errors.[81] Moneta is likewise careful to provide different proofs against

---

78 'Cuius expositionem diligens lector falsitatis potest arguere'; Capelli, *Adversus haereticos*, p. cxlv.

79 The *Disputatio* seems to deal specifically with the doctrines of one of the Italian Cathar churches, perhaps the Bagnolenses; da Milano identifies George's opponent with this group, 'Fr. Gregorio, O.P.', 85–140 (p. 114); and so do *Disputatio*, p. xiv, and Wakefield and Evans, *Heresies*, p. 289. Raniero places this group at Mantua, Brescia, Bergamo, Romagna and (a small number) Milan. This is not one of the largest Cathar groups, only about 200 in total according to Sacconi's account: Raniero Sacconi, *Summa*, p. 50. Andrew of Florence describes doctrinal differences with some care, though without referring to the resulting groups by specific names: Andrew of Florence, *Summa*, pp. 98–112.

80 'Diverse inter eos sunt opiniones'. These examples are from Capelli, *Adversus haereticos*, pp. xxvi–xxviii, but they can be found throughout, e.g. pp. xxxviii, l–li, xciii, xciv, cxiv, cl.

81 Kaeppeli, 'Une somme', pp. 333–4; Peter Martyr, Conv. soppr. MS 1738, fols. 92ᵛ–93ᵛ.

the Poor of Lyons as against the Poor Lombards.[82] Salvo usually uses the names of both groups when talking to or about the Waldensians and will distinguish between them, or draw parallels with Cathar groups on the basis of their different errors.[83] Only the *Disputatio* makes no mention of these divisions, but, as it is addressed to one individual heretic, division and structure are neither available nor relevant to his construct.

Implicit beneath the idea of division is an idea of an underlying system that is nonetheless sufficiently coherent to contain differences built on a doctrinal basis. While the polemicists are little concerned to talk about anything other than doctrinal points, there is nonetheless an assumption that there is a wider, identifiable group that contains these distinctions within itself. At a most basic level all these texts present their subject material as a group, an identifiable body that can be given a name. All use the word 'sect' to describe the Cathars; the term 'Cathar' appears sparingly, but most of the authors rely on other group names, except for Moneta and the Pseudo-James, both of whom tend to rely more on the generic 'heretic'.[84] Salvo tends to use the names of the individual Cathar churches when naming his subject, while Peter Martyr and the author of the *Disputatio* use the northern Italian name 'Patarines', though George will more usually use the rather old-fashioned 'Manichee'. Discussion of the heretics is rarely any more concrete than the use of these group names, but the odd traces that do appear reinforce the impression of a coherent body internally divided, but which nonetheless has common features and attributes.

The Pseudo-James' *Summa* includes a brief and incongruous section that deals with the customs and lifestyle of the Cathars themselves, a section that the author acknowledges as a digression which departs from the otherwise doctrinal content of the work.[85] Here, the Pseudo-James presents his reader with a detailed account of hierarchical structures found in the Cathar churches, which include different orders, sacraments and rituals. The description is presented as a general structure that applies to all the different Cathar groups.[86] Moneta likewise speaks about heretical sacraments and gives a description of a common Cathar hierarchy as elements common to all; he also makes some reference to a common Cathar history.[87] The *Liber suprastella* assumes a common structure across all groups in the hierarchies of the Cathar churches.[88] Each of the polemicists is more concerned to talk about their subject in terms of a variegated but structured system of belief, and it is not

---

[82] Moneta, *Adversus catharos*, pp. 402–8.
[83] For example, Salvo Burci, *Suprastella*, pp. 69, 259–62, 288–9, 363, 424–6.
[84] Capelli, *Adversus haereticos*, p. xcv. *Disputatio*, p. 3. Salvo Burci, *Suprastella*, pp. 284, 290, 333.
[85] Capelli, *Adversus haereticos*, p. cxxxix: 'facimus digressionem, nunc ad propositum redeamus'.
[86] Ibid., pp. cxxxvii–cxxxix.
[87] Moneta, *Adversus catharos*, pp. 2, 296, 411, and see Wakefield, 'Notes', p. 313.
[88] Salvo Burci, *Suprastella*, pp. 349–50.

their principal concern to examine the behaviours and lifestyle of the groups whose errors they discuss; but, where those things are visible, their shared nature underlines the differences in belief that the texts are so careful to delineate as specifically division, rather than just diversity.

The intrinsic nature of such doctrinal division in the polemics' representation can perhaps be explained by their immediate context, since they agree with the later descriptions written by inquisitors in the region (and with the earlier *De heresi catharorum*). The hierarchical and way of life information given by the Pseudo-James, for example, reflects the account given in Raniero Sacconi's text, which also presents a picture of Catharism as a highly structured and hierarchical organization, and gives details of their sacraments and orders, as well as the doctrine that lies behind each of these. But the general impression of division and the descriptions of internecine conflict, such as the schism between the Albanenses and Concorrezenses, also match what we see for the region in other sources.[89] According to accounts in the handbook of Anselm of Alessandria, and in the anonymous *De heresi catharorum in Lombardia*, that division was long-standing and had come about after the visit of a Bogomil leader, papa Nicetas, in the 1160s. Subsequent to his visit to the west, say the authors of both texts, there were two schools of Cathar thought: the absolute dualists, who believed in two eternal creative principles, and the mitigated dualists, who held that there was only one eternal principle, but two creators. Most of the Cathars of southern France converted to the former variety after Nicetas' mission, but in Italy there remained deep divides between, and indeed within, the two groups.[90] Whether or not this story is accepted at face value, the divisions between northern Italian Cathar groups are fundamental to most descriptions of the region, and the polemics, all products of Lombardy, all represent to some degree a similar picture of an internally divided Catharism.

However, if the fundamentally divided nature of heresy that these texts present reflects what can be seen of their regional context, it is also occasionally made to serve another purpose. The third part of Peter Martyr's treatise begins with a list of reasons by which the Catholic Church can be shown to be the true one. His sixth reason, that the church should be universal, discounts heresies on the grounds that they are particular and regional.[91] For Salvo and the Pseudo-James the internal divisions of the Cathars also serve a polemical

---

89 Salvo Burci, *Suprastella*, pp. 5–7.

90 *De heresi catharorum in Lombardia* is edited by Dondaine, 'La hiérarchie I', 280–312 (pp. 306–12); Anselm of Alessandria, *Tractatus*, pp. 309–13. On Nicetas, see B. Hamilton's Introduction in Hugh Eteriano, *Contra Patarenos*, ed. B., J. and S. Hamilton, The Medieval Mediterranean: Peoples, Economies and Cultures, 400–1500 55 (Leiden, 2004), pp. 73–98.

91 'Sexta est, quia ecclesia debet esse catholica, id est universale, quia debet esse diffusa per universum orbem terrarum ... ac hereses omnes sunt particulares, aliquam certam mundi particulam tenentes, et ideo sunt omnes a tramite veritatis deviantes'; Peter Martyr, Conv. soppr. MS 1738, fol. 96ʳ.

purpose, and are taken as proof of their heretical status; because of their quarrels with each other 'they are clearly shown to be heretics', according to the Pseudo-James. Salvo draws the same conclusion after discussing the north Italian schism: 'in one body there are great divisions. Whence it is clear that they are not the Church of God, and this is read in the Gospel: Every kingdom divided against itself shall be made desolate. Therefore it is clear that they are the church of the devil.'[92] This latter is one of the criteria on which the Anonymous of Passau defines the true church, from which qualification the heretics are excluded on the basis of their divided nature.[93] Standing in contrast to this is a sense of the Catholic Church as a unity, from which the heretics are also divided. If Salvo feels that the heretics are the church of the devil this is 'because they were first, through Baptism, of the Roman Church; they cannot deny this'.[94] Peter likewise defines heretics as those who are separate from the faith, having once been part of the true church.[95] The Pseudo-James puts 'heretics, wandering from the unity of the catholic faith' together with other groups external to the Catholic faith, Saracens and other 'people who are damned'.[96] The *Disputatio*'s Patarine does most of the work in this regard, building a picture of a unified Catholic body through references to 'your' Augustine or Gregory, and 'your' Pope, though George himself also talks of Catholic unity and of the division of the heretics from it.[97]

Heresy is therefore defined by division, both within its own ranks and from the Catholic Church. If three of the texts occasionally exploit this division for polemical purposes, or tie it into a wider idea of the difference between church and outsiders, on the whole it passes without comment, since the polemicists are more interested in error than in the condition of those groups that subscribe to that error, though the division they describe implies and indeed necessitates a larger unity. Rather, the organization of the texts and their descriptions of their subject create an impression of heresy as inherently divided and composite, a structured system of belief that is defined by divisions based on doctrinal difference.

The concentration on heresy as a series of intellectual errors of understanding and the textual basis and milieux of the polemical material, together

---

[92] 'Ab invicem cum litigatione dissidentes ut per hoc manifeste heretici comprobentur'; Capelli, *Adversus haereticos*, p. cxii. 'In una quaque persona sunt divisiones magne. Unde manifestum est quod non sunt Ecclesia Dei, et hoc in Evangelio legitur: *Omne regnum in se ipsum divisum desolabitur*. Ergo manifestum est quod sunt ecclesie diaboli'; Salvo Burci, *Suprastella*, p. 6, quotation from Luke 11.17.

[93] Anonymous of Passau, p. 263, and see below, p. 147, n. 135.

[94] 'Quia primo de Romana Ecclesia per baptismum fuerunt, nec hoc negare possunt'; Salvo Burci, *Suprastella*, p. 6.

[95] Peter Martyr, Conv. soppr. MS 1738, fol. 98ᵛ.

[96] 'Ab unitate catholicae fidei heretici aberrantes'; 'Hominum qui dapnantur [*sic*, r. dampnantur]'; Capelli, *Adversus haereticos*, pp. cxii, vi.

[97] *Disputatio*, pp. 18, 29, 45, 47, 63, 58.

with the absence of any sustained discussion of lifestyle or practices, inevitably has the result that the heretical figure that appears as holder of these errors is an abstract entity. There are occasional appearances by some individual historical heretics, such as Tetricus, or Andrew the medic, or Peter Gallus, but they function more as authorities within the texts. The heretics to whom the polemicists address their responses and refutations are rhetorical creatures.

The 'rhetorical' heretic is most obvious in the *Disputatio*, the format of which demands the construction of a heretical opponent to argue against the similarly abstracted Catholic, but a similar principle is at work in the other texts. Each of the polemics constructs exposition and refutation as dialogue, often in the same mode as that used by George: a 'Catholic' and a 'heretic' speak their own position in the first person and address the other in the second. Only in the *Disputatio*, though, is the heretic consistently given a first-person voice. The other polemicists switch between that first- and second-person mode of dialogue and one which observes both positions from a third-person perspective: 'the heretic says', 'the Catholic says'. In both models the speaker is usually identified clearly in the rubric. So, the *Summa* of Moneta uses a label of *haereticus* to indicate heretical 'speech' and present the error under discussion, and the authors of both the *Liber Suprastella* and the *Summa contra haereticos* both present heretical doctrine as spoken by some unspecified third person or persons. The heretical positions in Peter Martyr's text are expounded by a 'heretic', or, in the first part, a 'Patarine', the response by a 'Catholic'. These heretics are hypothetical, abstract mouthpieces created to give voice to the doctrines and errors gleaned from books or debate, though there may be an echo of a genuine voice heard in discussion or in a text in the *forte dicent* formula used by Moneta, Salvo and George when positing a possible heretical statement. But the academic tradition of debate in which these texts are written necessitates the creation of these figures and the 'heretics' are primarily a rhetorical device that allows presentation of items for discussion.

Because it serves as a vehicle for ideas and not as the subject in itself, the heretical character is for the most part very thinly drawn. There are few of the rhetorical flourishes that we tend to expect in an anti-heretical text, which have been placed at the forefront of our memory of the texture of these materials by, on the one hand, Grundmann's brilliant article, and on the other the pushiness and colour of the images that are used by contemporary writers. The authors of polemics will occasionally liven up their debate with some of that imagery, including a small but reasonably consistent equation of heretics with serpents, but, while they were immersed in the anti-heretical tradition of their time, as a whole they employ the standard topoi of that tradition rather sparingly, largely because they are pertinent more to behaviour and actions and with the heretics themselves than to error.[98] Where this sort of imagery is brought to

---

98 See below, p. 177.

bear the polemicists tend to rely most on the theme of false appearance, characterizing the heretical figures as inwardly evil, in direct opposition to their outer piety.

The contrast between inner and outer conditions was by this time already an established trope of anti-heretical writing which centred on the association of heretics with the Biblical figures of the false prophets and the wolf in sheep's clothing.[99] For the most part in the polemics, though the wolf image is occasionally used, the depiction of heretics as cloaked, disguised figures is the more general form in which we find false appearance. The text that uses this topos the most is, unsurprisingly, the always more colourful *Summa contra hereticos* of the Pseudo-James, which is unusual enough in its quantity relative to the others to warrant a brief digression.

Traditionally, the Pseudo-James' work has been seen as remarkable for its moderation. The impression of moderation, however, relies on only a few passages in the text: a description of the ritual *consolamentum*, to which the Pseudo-James appends a dismissal of accusations that the Cathars actively kill those who submit to the rite; and a discussion of the Cathar position on matrimony, where he again defends them again against accusations of physical immorality. These two passages are among those shared with Moneta's text, but Moneta does not attach the same moderating pleas as the Pseudo-James. The tone of the work as a whole is hardly in keeping with this reading and, even taken in isolation, these passages seem less concerned with restoring the Cathars' injured reputation than a first glance might suggest. Though the author admits, and even insists on, the austerity of Cathar life, he then uses this to identify them as the false apostles that Paul describes in Corinthians. As such, they are also those that 'have the zeal of God, but not according to the knowledge of God', and so lead others astray both by their teachings and by 'exaggerating the malice and bad morals of clerics'. Using their asceticism to prove their error, rather than simply denying it, the author is able to more firmly and authoritatively reject their claims.[100] Similarly, though they are chaste, this is only a physical chastity: 'spiritually they fornicate and adulterate the word of God, however much their bodies may be chaste'. The author rejects the rumours of fornication because it is the persecution that they have endured on that account that allows the Cathars to claim apostolic status, while at the same time he rejects the basis on which the Cathars observe this chastity: 'they are all bound by their superstitious and false religion ... to the vow of continence'.[101] If he accepts the external truth of the Cathars' piety, he

---

[99] II Peter 2; Matthew 7. 15.

[100] 'Emulationem dei habent sed non secundum scientiam dei' (Romans 10. 2); 'maliciam malosque clericorum mores exaggerantes'; Capelli, *Adversus haereticos*, p. cxxxix.

[101] 'Spiritualiter fornicentur et verbum dei adulterent, tantum castissimi quidem sunt corpore'; 'supersticiosa siquidem, et falsa religione ... ad continentiae votum astringuntur'; Capelli, *Adversus haereticos*, pp. clvii–clviii; trans. Wakefield and Evans, *Heresies*, p. 306. See also Capelli, *Adversus haereticos*, pp. clxxi, xlv, l.

can dismiss it on doctrinal grounds, while demonstrating their lack of true understanding and reinforcing the superficiality of their piety. In other words, the Pseudo-James manipulates the topos of false appearance to bring a problematic element of Cathar appeal within the bounds of his theological and exegetical discussion and make it available to dismissal on the grounds of interpretation.

It is in this mode that false appearance operates where it appears in the other texts as well. It appears usually in connection to the learning of heretical figures and is to do with their leading astray of the simple-minded. Moneta warns that what seems like natural or logical reason is really sophistry; it is deceptive.[102] George, too, sees the Cathars as duplicitous (though his Patarine seems to hold the same opinion of the Catholic church).[103] The Pseudo-James, as we might expect, has the most to say on this subject, calling the Cathars pseudo-preachers and characterizing them as deceptive.[104] Only Salvo is able to offer something more optimistic: even the stupidest people can see how heretical the heretics are.[105] As with the issue of heretical learning, it is used to reconcile what the heretics appear to be with what they should be, though the theme of false appearance more broadly has roots in the competition between Cathars and the Catholic clergy for the appearance of holiness and zeal.

The main features of heresy in mid thirteenth century polemic are largely abstract. Above all, heresy is a learned thing, a series of doctrinal articles and a structured body of thought characterized by division but conceived in and expressed through an academic mode. The trend that was seeded by Eckbert, whose reliance on Augustine in answering heresy was nonetheless framed within an academic style of Scriptural exegesis, now occupies the mainstream, replacing the previously dominant Cistercian model. Both the manner in which the authors address the heretics in their texts and the way in which the texts are arranged attack heresy on the basis of interpretation: that is, they address the content of the heresy, not the condition of the heretic. More than this, if we can accept that it is more likely that these authors were all responding in their own way to a common opponent than that all of them, from trained theologian to over-zealous layman, were simultaneously seized by a common compulsion to be the next Augustine, then we must also see learning as a received element in the polemical construction of heresy. That is to say, that heresy is presented as learned because that was the guise in which it was encountered – that the polemicists were in contact with the wider 'textual community' of their local heretics and that this encounter, whether

---

102 Moneta, *Adversus catharos*, p. 23. *Disputatio*, pp. 13, 58, 70.
103 *Disputatio*, pp. 14, 56.
104 Capelli, *Adversus haereticos*: pp. xviii, xciii, civ; also pp. cxv, cxxi, cxxxix, clxxxvi.
105 Salvo Burci, *Suprastella*, p. 349: 'bene potest videri et etiam ab ydiotis quod estis pessimi erretici'.

written or oral, is as much a part of the source material as the anti-heretical tradition.[106] Given that the heresy the texts address appears to be at least in part drawn from encounters with heretical discourse either in spoken or, more probably, written form, it would seem that the increased influence of scholastic modes of argument on the response of the church was also operating in the work of their heretical opponents.

2

To Retreat from Sin: Texts for Edification

Per hoc a peccatis recederent et bonum appeterent[1]

It is a standard rhetorical trope, even in the polemical texts, and certainly in much of the legal material, to couple the coercive repression of heresy with a positive movement to reinforce Catholic teachings through word and example. Of the texts that talk about heresy in the mid thirteenth century a significant number are the product of that impulse: the impulse to correct and instruct, to edify and pre-empt that was part of the preaching revival of the thirteenth century. That drive by the papacy to improve the preaching offered by the Catholic church, and to control the right to preach more carefully, can be understood as in part motivated by heresy.

The landscape at the turn of the century featured heretical and other 'pseudo-preachers' as well as those sanctioned by the church, and preaching was a significant part of those group identities, central to the ideal of the apostolic life promoted by church and espoused by heretics and others.[2] Although towards the middle of the century the church had won the centre ground, it had not secured it, and preaching and the correct enactment of the *vita apostolica* remained a tool in 'the race between the institutional church and its rivals' to control lay piety.[3] Whether this was to be achieved through the repression of heresy by specifically anti-heretical preaching or through the promotion of an orthodoxy informed by heterodox challenges, it depended on the increased manpower and expertise offered by the mendicant orders and on the production and proliferation of new texts developed to support preaching, a 'rhetorical system of *ars praedicandi*'.[4]

---

1 Stephen of Bourbon, *Tractatus de diversis materiis predicabilibus*, Corpus Christianorum, Continuatio Mediaevalis 124/124B, 2 vols. (Turnhout, 2002–6), I, *Prologus, prima pars, de dono timoris*, ed. J. Berlioz and J.-L. Eichenlaub, 3.

2 D. L. d'Avray, *The Preaching of the Friars: Sermons Diffused from Paris before 1300* (Oxford, 1985), pp. 43–63.; J. H. Arnold, 'The Preaching of the Cathars', in *Medieval Monastic Preaching*, ed. C. Muessig (Leiden, 1998), p. 200; P. B. Roberts, 'The *Ars praedicandi* and the Medieval Sermon', in *Preacher, Sermon and Audience in the Middle Ages*, ed. C. Muessig (Leiden, 2002), pp. 41–62 (pp. 44–6).

3 D'Avray, *The Preaching of the Friars*, pp. 25–6. On competition, see also A. P. Roach, *The Devil's World: Heresy and Society, 1100–1300* (Harlow, 2005).

4 Roberts, 'The *Ars praedicandi*', p. 52, quoting Murphy; d'Avray, *The Preaching of the Friars*, pp. 51–62.

The various treatments of heresy with which this chapter is concerned are the product of that trend and development: either defences, both active and pre-emptive, against heresy itself, or texts conditioned by the presence and central role of heresy in the context of preaching. The texts fall into three main groups, the first of which comprises those texts known as *Summae auctoritatum*, lists of Scriptural references that could be used to support articles of faith, directed specifically against heretics. They are related to the polemics and aimed narrowly at heresy in particular, and so will be examined first. The second two groups are more general in scope: first, the collections of *exempla* that were coming into use in the mid thirteenth century, designed as a tool for preachers, to be used alongside the more traditional proofs of Scripture and reason in the construction of sermons;[5] and, lastly, a number of Dominican texts, written by members of the order for the benefit of their brethren, that deal with heresy and that provide further context for many if not most of the texts that are dealt with in this and the previous chapter. The three sets form a necessarily broad and more loosely defined category than the polemics; their aim is more often the edification or improvement of their ultimate audiences than attack, and heresy is not necessarily their principal focus.

Summae auctoritatum

The *Summae auctoritatum* belong to the species of texts that were developed to aid preachers, and are directed against heretics. They are, in essence, lists of Biblical materials and references that could be used to prove or disprove a series of different points of doctrine, under which headings the contents are organized. The main examples from our period that will form the basis of this section are all mendicant productions and come from northern Spain, southern France and northern Italy. Of these, five have been edited by Douais in his *La Somme des autorités*.

Summae I, II, III[6]

A '*summa*' in several pieces: Douais' first text is in the end folios of an Aragonese pocket Bible, probably Franciscan, while the second two are in the first folios of an even smaller French Bible. Because the last three chapters of I overlap with the first three of II, Douais regarded these two as representing two fragments of the same text; III he saw as a complementary text.[7]

---

5 J. Berlioz, '*Exemplum* et histoire: Césaire de Heisterbach (v.1180–v.1240) et la croisade albigeoise', *Bibliothèque de l'École des Chartes* 147 (1989), 49–86.

6 C. Douais (ed.), *La Somme des autorités, à l'usage des prédicateurs méridionaux au XIIIe siècle* (Paris, 1896). The edition of the texts to which I will hereafter refer as Douais I, II and III is found at pages 34–66; The *summa* to which I refer will be indicated in subsequent references within square brackets. See Rottenwöhrer, I.i, 72–3.

7 Douais, *La Somme*, pp. 7–10; F. Šanjek (ed.), 'Una "Summa auctoritatum" antiereticale (MS

Wakefield's discovery of a manuscript in Leipzig containing the entire text of I and II, followed by III, would seem to confirm this. We will therefore consider these three texts in conjunction with each other, as Wakefield does, as two complementary texts, the *Summa contra haereticos et manichaeos*, made up of Douais I and II, and the *Summa auctoritatum de sacramentis ecclesiae*, represented by Douais III.[8] Wakefield dates these texts to the early to mid thirteenth century, around 1225–50.

Summa IV[9]

An anti-heretical *summa* in a Dominican manuscript of the second half of the thirteenth century, to which period Douais also dates the text. He describes the manuscript as southern French and suggests that it was probably made at the Dominican convent at Toulouse. The manuscript also contains other Dominican theological works.[10]

Brevis summula contra herrores notatos hereticorum[11]

Another *summa* from the second half of the thirteenth century in an Italian hand, again contained in a pocket Bible, whose calendar indicates a Franciscan origin. Douais suggests that the other contents of this manuscript, together with the *summula*, show the whole to be aimed specifically at preaching against heresy.[12] The *summula*, originally thought to be of great significance to the study of Catharism, has since been shown to be less important owing to its composite nature. Dondaine showed that what Douais labelled as part three of the *summula* in fact reproduces an inferior version of an earlier Lombard text, the *De heresi catharorum*. Dondaine instead divided the text into six parts: a

---

47 della Bibliothèque municipale di Albi). Memoria di Raoul Manselli', in *Atti della Accademie Nazionale dei Lincei. 1: Classe di Scienze Morale Storiche e Filologiche* 6 (1985), 324–97 (pp. 335–97).

8 W. L.Wakefield, 'Notes on Some Anti-heretical Writings of the Thirteenth Century', *Franciscan Studies* 27 (1967), pp. 285–321 (pp. 299–300). See also W. L. Wakefield and Evans A. P. (trans.), *Heresies of the High Middle Ages* (New York, 1969, repr. 1991), p. 297.

9 Douais, *La Somme*, pp. 67–113; hereafter referred to as 'Douais IV'. See Rottenwöhrer, I.i, 70–71.

10 Douais, *La Somme*, pp. 28–30. Manselli contends that parts of this work refer to the Italian churches of Bagnolo and Concorezzo: R. Manselli, 'Una "Summa auctoritatum" antiereticale (MS 47 della Bibiothèque Municipale di Albi). Memoria di Raoul Manselli', *Atti della Accademie Nazionale dei Lincei. 1: Classe di Scienze Morale Storiche e Filologiche* 6 (1985), p. 335. See also below, p. 49, n. 37.

11 *Brevis summula*. See Rottenwöhrer, I.i, 67–8.

12 Douais, *La Somme*, p. 25. Dondaine did not believe that the compiler had put together these pieces with any intention of creating something coherent, but merely for his own use. He pointed to the lack of any title or prologue original to the compilation; the added prologue, written into the margins and containing a polemical tone entirely absent from the rest of the work, he saw as a later attempt to join the pieces into a whole: Dondaine, 'La hiérarchie I', pp. 295–6.

prologue, added by a later owner; general Cathar doctrines; doctrines specific to the three main Italian churches (taken from the *De heresi catharorum*); doctrines of the Albanenses, here misnamed Albigensians; a catalogue of the errors of the three Italian churches; a refutation of these errors.[13] Dondaine believed that the second, third and fourth parts of this text were so different in tone that they could not have been written by the same author. Wakefield and Evans agree with this assessment, but they add that the fourth part does share common characteristics with the catalogue and the refutation, and that the last three elements represent the work of one author. Wakefield also points to the similarity between the second part and part of Moneta's text, positing either a common source or even an adaptation of Moneta himself.[14] The date of the composition of this work is therefore problematic, but it was probably put together in the decade after 1250, although perhaps as late as 1270. The last part, then, the refutation, still provides a contemporary analogue to our other texts.

Quaedam obiectiones hereticorum et responsiones Christianorum[15]

Copied by the Doat scribes from a small manuscript in the Carcassonne archive, the *Quaedam obiectiones* is a French text that is connected both to Moneta of Cremona's *Summa* and to Douais IV. Wakefield considers the *Quaedam obiectiones* to be in fact two texts, though there is no indication from the Doat scribes that this text should be considered as something other than one whole: there is only one set of the usual introductory and concluding notes that give information about the source, and they bracket the whole of this text. Döllinger makes no distinction between the first and second halves in the extracts that he publishes, though Duvernoy also thinks that the text was originally two separate pieces. Whatever the relationship, the second part of the *Quaedam obiectiones* is a fuller version of Douais IV and therefore part of the same family of *Summae auctoritatum* to which that latter text belongs, probably dating from the second half of the thirteenth century.[16]

---

13 Dondaine, 'La hiérarchie I', pp. 294–302. Dondaine points out that both Douais and the text's other editor, Molinier, had never questioned the unity of the *summula*.

14 Wakefield and Evans, *Heresies*, pp. 351, 749, n. 9; Wakefield, 'Notes', pp. 306–7. Dondaine also highlights a relationship with Moneta, as well as a connection to the *Liber Suprastella*; Dondaine, 'La hiérarchie I', pp. 297–90.

15 Doat 36 on fols. 91ᵛ–203ʳ. See Wakefield, 'Notes', p. 300, n. 65 and pp. 307–8; Rottenwöhrer, I.i, 63–4. Wakefield identifies fol. 129ʳ, line 6 as the starting point of that text corresponding to Douais, *La Somme* [IV]. Parts of this have been edited by I. von Döllinger, *Beiträge zur Sektengeschichte des Mittelaltersm*, 2 vols. (Munich 1890), II, 375–6. See above, p. 27, n. 59. Duvernoy has also produced an edition, which is available on his website <http://jean.duvernoy.free.fr/> as *Summula contra hereticos. Un traite contre les Cathares du XIIIème siècle*, ed. J. Duvernoy (1987). Duvernoy puts the break between the two halves at the end of fol. 122ʳ.

16 Andrew of Florence, *Summa*, p. xxix.

BN MS Lat.14927 I, II[17]

Latin manuscript 14927 of the Bibliothèque nationale is a French manuscript of the late thirteenth to early fourteenth century which contains, among other mid thirteenth century texts, two *summae* of similar form to those edited by Douais. The differences in the section titles and in the references used show these to be of a different family, but they nonetheless display the same structures and concerns in their composition.

The first three of Douais' *Summae*, which we are treating together, and the two *summae* in MS Lat.14927 of the Bibliothèque nationale are lean, skeletal creatures. They contain little quotation and no exposition (except in one instance), and are really no more than lists of Scriptural references arranged under headings that describe their purpose: for example, 'in the first chapter it is proved that the father, and the son, and the holy spirit are one substance and one God'.[18] Their meagreness is quickly explained by their location, in the end leaves of small 'pocket' Bibles. The Bible into which Douais I is copied measures only 193mm by 133mm; that which contains Douais II and III is even smaller, only 170mm by 120mm.[19] The *summae* of 14927 occupy the first folios of a small collection of anti-heretical texts that measures 226mm by 165mm.[20] Their inclusion in these manuscripts places them squarely among the 'small, portable "vade-mecum" books ... produced in great numbers to meet the needs of the itinerant preaching friars'.[21] As Douais says, their inclusion here is suggestive of their use as portable tools of reference, but their necessary list form also means that it is not clear which part of the reference was supposed to carry the force of refutation, or indeed what interpretation the preacher would have placed upon it.[22]

Aside from ideas about their function that can be gained from their manuscript context, in fact, these list-like *summae* cannot by themselves tell us much about how they were used. However, the *Summa contra haereticos et manichaeos* and the *Summa auctoritatum de sacramentis ecclesiae* – that is, Douais I and II and Douais III – belong to a family of texts that has some plumper relatives, namely Douais IV and the second half of the *Quaedam obiectiones hereticorum et responsiones Christianorum*. Wakefield has demonstrated that three chapters of Douais IV bear a marked resemblance to chapters in Douais II, one of which is nearly identical, a resemblance that he feels must indicate a direct relationship

---

17 BnF MS Lat 14927, fols. 2ra–3rc; fols. 3rc–7rb. Wakefield, 'Notes', p. 301, n. 66. See also *Disputatio*, pp. cxxvii–cxxix.
18 'Primo capitulo probatur quod patris, et filii et spiritus sancti sit una substantia et unus deus'; Douais, *La Somme*, p. 34 [I].
19 Douais, *La Somme*, p. 7.
20 *Disputatio*, p. cxxvii.
21 D'Avray, *The Preaching of the Friars*, p. 57.
22 Douais, *La Somme*, pp. 7, 18.

of some kind. He further observes that the second part of the *Quaedam obiectiones* is in fact a fuller version of Douais IV, though the chapters, and in places the sequence of authorities, are not always the same.[23]

The fourth of Douais' *Summae* is similar in style and structure to the first three: it too is a collection of Scriptural authorities arranged under headings which describe the argument that they can be used to prove. The chapters also follow a similar sequence to Douais I, II and III, presenting expositions of Catholic doctrine as challenged by the implications of Cathar ideas, in a structure built around Catholic principles.[24] Though still in essence a list of authorities these are presented not as a series of citations but as part of an exposition; the references are usually quoted in full and here the interpretation or argument that derives from them, missing from the first three texts, is often given as well, for example: 'Mt.VI [26]: "Behold the birds of the air, for they neither sow, nor do they reap, nor gather into barns: and your heavenly Father feedeth them." Therefore creatures are his work.'[25]

Douais IV appears not in a portable book but in a manuscript containing general theological works, a version of its shorter cousins that was perhaps less intended for use in the field. Whether or not the *Quaedam obiectiones* ought to be seen as two separate texts as Wakefield suggests, its second part nonetheless provides another rendering of the expanded text, and as members of the same family as the more instrumental *Summae*, both it and Douais IV can be seen to represent a version of what these might have ultimately looked like once expanded and employed by a preacher.[26] We can look to the additional material provided by these two, and, by extension, by the *Brevis summula*, therefore, for a more precise idea of the function of the group as a whole.

The *summae* take the form of series of chapter titles, more or less elaborated, that describe points of Catholic doctrine. Heresy exists in these texts in negative, reflected in the doctrines defended and the choices made for inclusion. A summary of the titles of Douais I, II will quickly demonstrate the heretical ideas underlying them. While the first chapter of Douais I, II, the longest of the text, is concerned to prove the triune nature of God, the next three chapters address God's creative role in a manner that is unmistakeably a response to the contemporary dualist doctrines of creation that we know from other texts: God is creator of all that is visible and invisible; He is not only creator, but also the maker; God fashioned the [nature] of Adam, Eve and all bodies, an action

---

23 Wakefield observes that other texts of this sort, which cover the same areas, use different authorities, and he feels that this overlap in content and order must indicate dependence; Wakefield, 'Notes', pp. 300–301 and n. 65, 307–8.

24 One chapter of the sacramental section is suggestively concerned to prove 'quod homo non sit adorandus'; Douais, *La Somme*, p. 106 [IV].

25 '"Respicite volatilia celi quoniam non serunt, neque metunt, neque congregant in orrea, et Pater vester celestis pascit illa." Ergo creature sunt opera eius'; Douais, *La Somme*, p. 67 [IV].

26 Douais implies that these short, condensed works acted as complements to longer, more detailed informative works, though he does not say this explicitly; *La Somme*, p. 13; see also Wakefield, 'Notes', pp. 300–301.

described here with the very physical verb 'plasmare'.[27] The subsequent chapters similarly reflect dualist doctrines, asserting first the legitimacy of those Old Testament figures traditionally rejected by the Cathars (along with much of the Old Testament itself) as agents of the evil principle before moving on to mount a defence of the human soul, of several New Testament figures and of Christ's humanity.

Chapters nineteen and twenty, 'that God pours new souls into new bodies' and 'that the soul – not an angel – is in the body', together with twenty-three, 'that angelic spirits remained in heaven after the fall of Lucifer', make a fairly comprehensive treatment of the Cathar idea of the soul as a fallen angel trapped in a human body by Lucifer.[28] Chapters twenty-five and twenty-six address the contention made by some Cathars that Mary was not a physical being, stating not only 'that the most blessed Mary was a woman' but also 'that blessed Mary had a father and mother'.[29] The chapters on the nature of Christ insist very strongly on his physical existence, also denied by Cathar doctrine, a denial that prompts, in the course of the chapter on Christ's assumption of flesh from the Virgin, the only substantial piece of prose in this *summa*: a vitriolic attack against a 'insane and raving chief of heretics' which roundly dismisses the idea that Christ had only an 'imaginary body', and which is reproduced in the anti-heretical treatise by the Pseudo-James Capelli.[30]

Douais III and Douais IV and the *Quaedam obiectiones* are constructed along the same lines. Even though the focus of Douais III is exclusively on the sacraments of the Catholic Church, chapter titles such as 'that baptism is beneficial without the imposition of hands' and 'that men are [= can be] saved in carnal matrimony' clearly show the Cathar challenge underlying these statements of

---

27 '2: Probatur quod Deus qui est trinus personis et unus in essentia est creator omnium visibilum et invisibilum; 3: probatur quod Deus omnipotens non solum est creator set ethiam [*sic*] factor; 4: probatur quod omnipotens Deus Ade et Eve et aliorum corporum natura[m] plasmavit'; Douais, *La Somme*, pp. 36–7 [I].

28 'Quod Deus novas animas infundit novis corporibus'; 'quod anima est in corpore, non angelus'; 'quod spiritus angelici remanserunt in celo post lapsum Luciferi'; Douais, *La Somme*, pp. 45–7 [II]. It also shows a familiarity with the *Interrogatio Iohannis*, or secret supper. Wakefield and Evans, *Heresies*, place the *Interrogatio*'s first arrival in Europe in 1190. Raniero Sacconi says Nazarius learned the error of the Virgin Mary's angelic body from a Cathar bishop and elder son in Bulgaria; Anselm of Alessandria, writing in 1266–76, tells us Nazarius has a book called 'The Secret', and says something similar, that, contrary to Nazarius, Desiderius believes that Mary had a real body, Raniero Sacconi, *Summa*, p. 58; Anselm of Alessandria, *Tractatus*, p. 311; Wakefield and Evans, *Heresies*, pp. 344, 362; E. Bozóky (ed. and trans.), *Le livre secret des cathares*, Interrogatio Iohannis: *Apocryphe d'origine bogomile*, Textes, Dossiers, Documents (Série Annexe de la Collection Théologie Historique) 2 (Paris, 1980), p. 27.

29 'Quod beatissima Maria fuit mulier'; 'quod beata Maria habuit patrem et matrem'; Douais, *La Somme*, p. 48 [II].

30 'Insane et furiosum caput hereticorum'; 'fantasticum corpus'; Douais, *La Somme*, pp. 49–51 [II].

faith.[31] And neither is this a purely family resemblance: MS Lat.14927 I and II, is more skeletal even than Douais I, II, giving only the Biblical book and chapter reference under each heading, with no indication at all of the exact text to be used, but it is still noticeable that the headings present, in the same way as Douais' texts, positive statements of Catholic articles that are nonetheless dependent on the refutation of heretical articles.

Given the nature and structure of these *Summae*, it is perhaps to be expected that the picture of heresy that emerges from reading them is one consisting almost entirely of points of doctrine or belief. In their expression and structure these articles are presented as positive Catholic statements of faith, but the titles of these texts nonetheless direct them 'against heretics' and, even were that not the case, it is easy to retrieve the underlying construct of heresy on which the Catholic statements rest. Broadly, that construct is one which consists of a series of points, here given a Catholic unity by the framework in which they are set, which is based around the structure of Creation, Old Testament, New Testament, Resurrection and Catholic sacraments. This is not so much heresy itself, but heresy as it impacts on Catholic doctrine.

The refutation of the *Brevis summula* is unusual in its arguments in its free use of Old Testament authorities where the other texts restrict themselves mostly or entirely to the New Testament, a fact that is surely attributable to its Italian origin. Raniero's account of the Italian Cathar churches says that some of them accepted parts of the Old Testament as valid, and the texts that accompany the *Summula* similarly make it clear that the Italian Cathars' rejection of the Old Testament was not total. That John of Lugio, whose teaching accepted the Old Testament in its entirety, is mentioned here as a source, is suggestive.[32] The use of the Old Testament by the *Summula* at the same time serves to highlight further the almost complete absence of this material from the French sources. Despite the concern demonstrated by Douais I, II, Douais IV and the two *summae* of 14927 to prove the legitimacy of the Old Testament as a source of authority, their defence rests almost exclusively on New Testament authorities.[33] Where Old Testament authorities are used, and this is rare, they appear always at the end of the list of authorities.[34] The predominance of New Testa-

---

31 'Quod baptismus prodest sine manum impositione'; 'quod in matrimonio carnali homines salva[n]tur'; Douais, *La Somme*, pp. 59, 61 [III].

32 Raniero Sacconi, *Summa*, pp. 51–3; *Brevis summula*, pp. 116, 121. The identification of this heretic as the John of Lugio that Raniero describes is not entirely secure; see Wakefield and Evans, *Heresies*, p. 748, n. 3.

33 It may show, as Iogna-Prat demonstrates for Peter the Venerable in the Cluniac tradition (and Vicaire for Lugio in the Cathar), a desire to expand the base of reference for debate. D. Iogna-Prat, trans. G. R. Edwards, *Order and Exclusion: Cluny and Christendom Face Heresy, Judaism, and Islam (1000–1150)* (Ithaca, NY, 2002), p. 141; M.-H. Vicaire, 'Les Cathares albigeois vus par les polémistes', *CF* 3 (1968), 107–28. The first part of the *Quaedam obiectiones hereticorum et responsiones Christianorum*, beginning at fol. 91ᵛ, is concerned entirely with the defence of the Old Testament.

34 With the exception of chapter twenty-eight of Douais II, the chapter with the prose entry;

ment material perhaps reflects a concern that the arguments remain acceptable to Cathar opponents and suggests an intended arena for the use of these texts that makes their purpose more ambiguous than it would seem at first glance.

Douais saw these texts as intended in part for the instruction of the faithful; though informed by heretical opinions, they were essentially a reduced version of the Catholic faith for proper instruction, a catechism in order to avoid contamination. At the same time, he described the *Summae* as collections of witnesses used by preachers against heretics, alongside the Bible, which had the same virtue for attack as for defence.[35] These texts could be seen in either light. The refutation of heresy in the *Brevis summula* simultaneously provides a defence of Catholicism.[36] Certainly, the later author of the prologue saw the text as being aimed at the reinforcement of the faithful, the protection of the vineyard from the foxes; he emphasizes that those outside the faith are lost, and that people must be prevented from being led away by heretics – a concern with the defence of the flock, rather than an attack on those outside it. Douais IV presents the truth of Catholic doctrine as automatically excluding any different belief; 'it is clear by manifest reasons that faith is the foundation of virtues, and the highest good, and the first principle; and that there should be no division in it'.[37]

However much their statements of Catholic doctrine would appear to lend themselves to preaching to the faithful, the *Summae auctoritatum* in several places provide material more for debate than for sermonizing and raise questions about the nature of the context in which these texts addressed error. The *Brevis summula*'s prologue proposes the defeat of heresy by the example of good works, but also speech and authorities. More interesting, the refutation itself urges that Scriptural supports be demanded from heretics if they present their argument without: 'if the heretic says the contrary, say to him that he should show you through divine Scripture. If he says that he cannot, say that he strays foolishly from faith.'[38] If the polemics of the previous chapter can

---

Douais, *La Somme*: i p. 36, iiii p. 37, vi p. 38, xvi p. 44, xix p. 45 [I, II]; xvi (penultimate) p. 62, xxii pp. 64–5; chapter II, xxviii p. 49 [III].

35 Douais, *La Somme*, p. 113 [IV].

36 *Brevis summula*, pp. 133–42.

37 'Patet rationibus manifestis quod fides est fundamentum virtutum, et primum bonum, et principium; et quod in ea non debet esse divisio'; Douais, *La Somme* IV, p. 113. The same pattern appears in a much earlier example of this genre, which likewise responds to a heretical point by reinforcing the Catholic position; Manselli, 'Una "Summa auctoritatum" antiereticale', text of *Summa* in Appendix, ed. F. Šanjek, pp. 355–95. This '*summa*' is really a collection of fragments, inserted between the other texts in the manuscript – two Biblical texts, the Song of Songs and the Acts of the Apostles, and several patristic commentaries – which nonetheless seem to constitute something approaching a coherent body of work against heresy, specifically that of the Cathars. According to Manselli there are some connections between this work and that of the convert Bonacursus, pp. 335–6. The text is anonymous, but Šanjek believes the *summa* to be in a late twelfth, possibly early thirteenth century hand, either from Catalonia or Languedoc.

38 'Si herethicus [*sic*] dicit contrarium, dices ei quod ostendat tibi per Scripturam divinam. Si

seem in places to speak to more than one context, or to accommodate an active as well as an academic voice of attack, then this is even more true for their cousins the *summae*. And just as the *summae* are able to provide material for those polemics as well as for preaching, the debate of points of belief is a plausible context for the authors and users of the *Summae auctoritatum*, whether it is with undecided laity or with the heretics themselves. The one section of prose in the otherwise spare text of Douais I, II contains a suggestion, nothing more, of the text's use. The author, in a manner also typical of the anti-heretical polemics, sets out the heretical proposition before offering a rebuttal. After this string of proofs is finished comes the line: 'but now let them, subverters of the truth, respond again', to which end more proofs are supplied.[39] It is only a hint, but one that can be amplified by the longer texts.

The written text of Douais IV is intended for a Catholic audience: 'you should note, o Catholic, that heretics say this'. The author of this text nevertheless frequently employs direct address towards the heretics: 'if you wish to say, heretic'; 'o worthless heretic'; 'you cannot give …'.[40] The refutation section of the *Brevis summula* also occasionally uses a vocative/imperative to address his heretical 'opponent'.[41] However, while these heretics must of course be rhetorical, there are indications of a more active function. There is, for example, a great deal of the type of debate rhetoric similar to that found in the polemics, such as words and phrases that mean 'clearly' placed after expositions.[42] More suggestions of exchange can be seen at the very end of chapter sixteen of Douais IV, after the last Biblical citation: 'at this point the heretic should respond, because if he did not truly suffer, he did not truly rise again'; and again, after a quotation in chapter twenty-three: 'if however the heretic should say that …'.[43] Significantly, the explicit to Douais IV advocates debate with heretics as a means of defending the faith.[44]

If Douais IV's extended version of the lists of authorities suggests that we understand these texts as tools for attack, then a stronger suggestion is to be

---

dicat quod non potest, dicas quod stulte deviat a fide'; *Brevis summula*, pp. 115, 138. Douais, *La Somme*, pp. 71, 76, 77, 82, 92, 95, 96 [IV].

[39] 'Set respondeant iterum nunc subversores veritatis'; Douais, *La Somme*, pp. 49–51 [II].

[40] 'Nota tu, catholice, quod hoc dicunt heretici'; 'si velles dicere, heretice'; 'o heretice nequam'; 'nec potes dare'; Douais, *La Somme*, pp. 77, 75, 85 [IV].

[41] *Brevis summula*, e.g. pp. 359, 361, 371. The earlier *Summa auctoritatum*, edited by Šanjek, addresses heretics frequently in the second person, but just as often in the third, while the work as a whole is clearly addressed to an orthodox audience: e.g. pp. 360, 365, 380, 383.

[42] *Brevis summula*, pp. 142, 139, 141. There is a similar echo of debate rhetoric in the *Brevis summula* in phrases such as 'si forte dicat hereticus', 'si dicit spiritualiter' and 'si dicis, heretice'; also 'forte dicis' in the earlier *summa*, edited by Šanjek, p. 393.

[43] 'Hic respondeat hereticus, quia si vere non est passus nec vere resurrexit'; 'si autem dicat hereticus quod …'; Douais, *La Somme*, pp. 87, 99 [IV].

[44] 'Et quod de ipsa omnibus querentibus respondendum est, et quod de ipsa prius est disputandum. Que est prima et maxima cum hereticis altercatio'; Douais, *La Somme*, pp. 70, 73, 87, 99–100, 101 [IV]; *explicit* on p. 113 (though chapter 38 exhorts the faithful to avoid excommunicates: p. 110).

found in the Doat analogue. Here we not only find all the same echoes of dispute as contained in Douais IV, including the explicit urging confrontation, but the even fuller exposition of the authorities presented by this version also provides a further indication that this text was to function in a context not only of debate but of active debate. The chapter that argues the point 'that an oath can sometimes be taken without sin', after presenting and expounding its authorities, then bids the reader to 'note, in this article, there are four ways to proceed against a heretic'. There then follows an explanation of the four stages in which this particular argument can be constructed, including questions that can be used to prove the heretic wrong.[45] The purpose of the lists of authorities given by this text and its relatives was, at least in part, to be used in the dispute with heretics that the explicit in fact advocates. The last section of the *Brevis summula*, although it is a fuller text with greater amounts of exposition, is very like the other *summae* in its character. Where it departs from the others, though, is in the presentation of its arguments and refutations: these are offered as explicit contradictions of the Cathar doctrines that are outlined in the catalogue of errors, in a framework of chapter headings that begin *contra primum, contra secundum,* and so on. The first chapter is headed 'against the first: the heretics say that there are two gods and two principles', rather than the sort of reverse statement 'there is only one God' that we might expect from the other texts. The underlying presence of error is much more foregrounded here than in the other texts.[46]

At this point the significance of the several textual connections that Wakefield outlines between the *Summae auctoritatum* and the major polemical treatises of the period becomes apparent. The closeness of these two groups, so similar in their style, extends also to more direct relationships. The author of the Pseudo-James Capelli used *Summae auctoritatum* of the family to which the first four Douais texts belong in the construction of several of his chapters on Catholic doctrine. Less dependent relationships can also be seen with Moneta of Cremona's treatise, where Moneta seems to share some source material with both the *Quaedam obiectiones* and the *Brevis summula*.[47] If the two parts of the *Quaedam obiectiones* can be seen as a whole then the implications for the connection between the polemics and the *Summae* are significant, but even if this is not the case then the fact that they are presented by the Doat volume as a coherent whole contained in one manuscript would suggest that they were

---

45 'Quod iuramentum possit aliquando fieri sine peccato'; 'nota in hoc articulo quatuor modis procedit contra haereticum'; 'primo ut quaerens ab haeretico si iuramentum est peccatum ita quod nullo casu possit bene fieri qui respondebit quod sic, cui Catholicus respondebit fornicatio est tale peccatum sed Deus non potuit benefieri'; Doat 36, fols. 181ʳ–181ᵛ.

46 'Contra primum: dicunt heretici quod sint duo dii et duo principia'; *Brevis summula*, p. 133. In Šanjek's *Summa auctoritatum* heretical propositions are used in several places as the starting point against which the authorities argue, for example: 'auctoritates contra manicheos qui vetus testamentum restituunt [et] respuunt'; Šanjek, 'Una "Summa auctoritatum" antiereticale', p. 365.

47 Wakefield, 'Notes', pp. 301–4, 306–8.

closely associated in the original. A more concrete example of such an association is the manuscript that contains the two short *summae*, mentioned above as
analogues to the first three of Douais' texts, in MS Lat.14927 of the
Bibliothèque nationale. The two *Summae auctoritatum* are followed by an
extract from the *De heresi*, after which there appears a fragmentary Italian treatise against the Cathars, here called Patarines. This brief text takes the form of a
dialogue on Eucharistic doctrine between a Catholic and a heretic which
resembles very much the texture of the *Disputatio*, a copy of which it in fact
precedes. In such juxtaposition with texts framed as disputes, and a text of a
polemical purpose, suggestions of debate in the brief lists of our *Summae
auctoritatum* are reinforced.[48]

In general, and especially in what we can perhaps regard as the expanded
format of the fuller texts, the *Summae auctoritatum* in fact have more in
common with polemic than with homily, and the construction of heresy itself
resembles that presented by the polemics very closely. Although the discussion of each article is less developed, the language not as rich, nonetheless the
basic principle remains very similar: heresy here is a doctrinal thing and,
where it is more visible, it constitutes a developed theological system and
indeed little else. In the case of the Italian *Brevis summula* that system includes
a complex division of doctrine among different Cathar groups. Again, as in the
polemics, we can see the heresy of the *Summae auctoritatum* as learned, both in
terms of its expression through Scripturally based argument and in terms of
the Catholic reaction to it, which sees it as something to be engaged with
through exegesis and reinterpretation, addressing the error in an academic
mode. Indeed, if we can read the *Summae auctoritatum* at least in part as tools
for debate, then this engagement is a very direct one.

The use of the term 'heretic' in the *Summae* is also very similar to that found
in the polemics. While it is clear enough from the nature of errors refuted
within them that all of these texts are for the most part directed against the
Cathar heresy (though much of the sacramental argument would serve equally
against Waldensian error), *heretici* remains the most common term used
throughout all of these texts. The first three of Douais' *Summae* name their
subjects only in their incipits and explicits, and here they are called only 'heretics and Manichees'; the explicit of Douais III extends this to cover 'Manichees,
Patarines and heretics' as well as 'Passagians and Circumcisors, and against
many other heretics'. Douais IV addresses itself *contra hereticos*, but throughout
the text refers to them not only as heretics but also as *paterini*. Though the
Brevis summula includes detailed descriptions of the differences between the
Cathar groups in Italy which consistently use these specific group names to
refer to their subject, and though we know that the author of the refutation
knew the names of the different groups through his list of errors, which
describes and divides the heretics according to those names, within the refuta-

---

48 BnF MS Lat 14927, fols. 8vb–10ra.

tion itself only once is anything more specific than 'heretic' used.[49] Heretics remain, for the most part, rhetorical figures that provide a focus for the error, a mouthpiece, who here also have a more practical purpose as providing a framework for active debate. As with the polemical texts, though, the heretics are carriers of the errors that the texts address and not the subject under discussion.[50]

Exempla *collections*

The *exemplum* was one of the building blocks of the new wave of preaching. An illustrative story that could be exploited and adapted to carry home the central message of a sermon or exposition, it was one of the several tools developed for preachers in the course of the systematization of preaching techniques and the development of new *ars praedicandi*. Established as a separate genre between about 1170 and 1250, *exempla*, together with other tools such as *florilegia* and *distinctiones*, provided the raw materials from which sermons could be built. The Cistercian Caesarius of Heisterbach was one leading proponent of the *exempla* form, and his *Dialogus miraculorum*, designed for use within the monastery (though containing and preserving the imprint of the outside world), used these stories to educate and inform. In the century after 1250 dedicated collections of *exempla*, most of them Dominican productions, began to appear for the use of preachers in the field.[51] Stephen of Bourbon's *Tractatus de diversis materiis predicabilibus* is one of the earliest of these purpose-built collections, providing all the components that preachers might need not in the form of model sermons but as the individual *rationes, auctoritates* and *exempla*

---

49 Douais, *La Somme*, p. 66 [I, II, III]; Douais, *La Somme*, pp. 73, 86, 96, 98, 100, 104, 106, 107, 108 [IV]; *Brevis summula*, pp. 115, 130, 121–33; Stephen of Bourbon, *Tractatus*, pp. 286, 289, 299, 300, 303. Also note the juxtaposition of orthodox and heretical name, 'good man', in the *Summa auctoritatum* ed. by Šanjek, Manselli, 'Una "Summa auctoritatum" antiereticale', pp. 363–4.

50 Jiménez-Sanchez sees the anonymous Cathar treatise reproduced in part in the *Liber contra Manicheos* of Durand of Huesca, published by Thouzellier, as a preachers' manual for Cathar preachers, in a similar mould to the Catholic *Summae auctoritatum* that we have considered here, rather than as a coherent treatise; P. Jiménez-Sanchez, 'Le "Traité cathare anonyme" : un receuil d'autorités à l'usage des prédicateurs cathares', *Heresis* 31 (1999 for 1996), pp. 73–100 (esp. pp. 84–85); C. Thouzellier (ed.), *Un traité cathare inédit du début du XIIIe siècle d'après le* Liber contra Manicheos *de Durand de Huesca*, Bibliothèque de la Revue d'Histoire Ecclésiastique 37 (Louvain, 1961).

51 The study of *exempla* begins in earnest with J. T. Welter, *L'exemplum dans la littérature religieuse et didactique du Moyen âge: La* tabula exemplorum secundum ordinem alphabeti, recueil d'exempla *compilé en France à la fine du XIIIe siècle* (Paris, 1927, reprinted Geneva, 1973) and F. C. Tubach, *Index Exemplorum, A Handbook of Medieval Religious Tales* (Helsinki, 1981). For a useful summary, see Roberts, '*The Ars praecdicandi*', pp. 52–4. The online project *Thesaurus Exemplorum Medii Aevi*, under the direction of J. Berlioz, M. A. Polo de Beaulieu and P. Collomb, provides a searchable database of most of the collections used by Tubach: <http://gahom.ehess.fr/thema/>.

from which to build those models.[52] Between the two of them Caesarius and Stephen provide a great deal of material on heresy, including some now very familiar stories, such as Caesarius's account of the siege of Béziers. Further, for most of the *exempla* concerning heresy or heretics that are listed in the *Index exemplorum*, the collections of Stephen and Caesarius are the only sources cited. They are the principal mid thirteenth century authors writing or using *exempla* on heretics and certainly the only two that treat heresy as a topic in its own right.

Dialogus miraculorum[53]

Caesarius, the author of this text, was a monk in the Cistercian monastery at Heisterbach. It was out of his role there as master of novices that the *Dialogus miraculorum*, or *Dialogus magnus visionum atque miraculorum*, was born, between 1219 and 1223. Essentially a collection of spiritual anecdotes arranged as a dialogue between a monk and a novice over 746 chapters, and related in Caesarius's engaging style, it was intended to be used for the edification and instruction of novices in the order.[54] For Tubach, the *Dialogus* therefore represents the oldest surviving monastic *exemplum* tradition in Europe from this period, providing a link between the older monastic tale-tradition and the later mendicant sermon *exempla* collections, though in McGuire's view it is more proactive than this, combining the older story tradition with the contemporary developments in Cistercian written and oral culture.[55] The *Dialogus* was compiled slightly earlier than our period and it is difficult to know the precise role played by Caesarius's work in the development of the *exempla* tradition, but it was popular – it remains extant in over fifty manuscripts – and Caesarius remained interested in heretics and the question of heresy throughout his life.[56]

---

52 Stephen of Bourbon, lib.1, p. xxxviii.

53 Caesarius, *Dialogus*; translated as *The Dialogue on Miracles*, trans. H. von E. Scott and C. C. Swinton Bland, 2 vols. (London, 1929).

54 Berlioz, 'Exemplum et histoire', pp. 50–51; J. Berlioz, *'Tuez les tous, Dieu reconnaîtra les siens'. Le massacre de Béziers (22 juillet 1209) et la croisade contre les Albigeois vus par Césaire de Heisterbach* (Portet-sur-Garonne, 1994), p. 6; B. P. McGuire, 'Written Sources and Cistercian Inspirations in Caesarius of Heisterbach', *Analecta Cisterciensia* 35 (1979), 222–82 (p. 227). For the date of the text, see B. P. McGuire, 'Friends and Tales in the Cloister: Oral Sources in Caesarius of Heisterbach's *Dialogus miraculorum*', *Analecta Cisterciensia* 36 (1980), 167–247 (pp. 197–201).

55 Caesarius, according to Tubach, apparently draws mostly from Gregory's *Dialogues* and the *Vitae patrum* for his material, though he presents some of the older material within a contemporary setting; McGuire believes that Caesarius relied much more on contemporary Cistercian traditions. Of course, most of the heresy *exempla* deal with recent and current events, and are unlikely to be taken from earlier sources. Tubach, *Index Exemplorum*, pp. 521–2; McGuire, 'Written Sources', pp. 229, 236–7, 247; Berlioz, *'Exemplum* et histoire', p. 58.

56 One of his works, now lost, was, as McGuire observes, a dialogue 'contra hereticos huius temporis et errores eorum'. There is also a letter, 'satis longam', against the heresy of

Though Caesarius lived far from the *foveae hereticorum* that were the south of France and Lombardy, in the late twelfth and early thirteenth centuries there had been in his region several incidents of and inquisitions into heresy, notably in nearby Bonn and Cologne, and Caesarius's reports of the Cologne incident are recalling local and recent memory.[57] The stories of heresy spreading from the south were in any case accessible to Caesarius, as McGuire has shown, through the lively network of travellers and monks who passed through his abbey at Heisterbach and the 'great yearly exchange centre' of the General Chapter, and many stories from those regions are in fact included in the *Dialogus*.[58] There would therefore have been enough familiarity with heretics in and around Caesarius's community to allow their background presence to be accepted or their significance understood. So, heretics are included in an account of an earthquake in Brescia, for example, but bear no relevance to the moral or the narrative of the *exemplum*; they are simply present.[59]

McGuire describes the *Dialogus* as a 'finished work of monastic theology, spiritual experience, and moral instruction' in which the *exempla* are used to illuminate doctrine and 'straight historical narrative' is generally absent.[60] Nevertheless, Caesarius's stories are embedded in his own milieu, from which they take on colour and texture. Describing an exchange between an abbot and 'a certain knight' that he encounters, 'sitting on a horse and talking to his ploughman', Caesarius relates the knight's statement of his (heretical) views on the transmigration of souls:

> If [my soul] has led a good life, and won this reward from God, it will, when it leaves my body, enter into that of some future prince or king, or of some other illustrious personage, in which it will find happiness; or if it has lived ill, it will enter the body of someone both poor and wretched, in which it will find suffering.[61]

The scene and the doctrine are both envisaged within a contemporary framework of rural life and social hierarchy which Caesarius reproduces with characteristic economy and style. His ability to ground the abstract and even the

---

Lucifer, at the request of master John, 'tortoris hereticorum', described in a letter detailing his works to Peter, prior of Marienstatt; A. Hilka (ed.), *Die Wundergeschichten des Caesarius von Heisterbach*, 2 vols. (Bonn, 1933–7), I, *Einleitung, exempla und Auszüge aus den Predigten des Caesarius von Heisterbach*, p. 6.

57 See below, pp. 57–8 and n. 66. On heresy in north-western Europe, see J. Duvernoy, *Le Catharisme: L'histoire des Cathares* (Toulouse, 1979), Part 2, chapters 2–6.

58 McGuire, 'Friends and Tales in the Cloister', p. 224 and *passim*.

59 Caesarius, *Dialogus*, II, 251.

60 McGuire, 'Written Sources', pp. 258, 282.

61 'Quidam supradictorum Abbatum monachus, cernens quendam militem in equo sedentem loqui cum aratore suo'; 'Si bene vixit, et hoc apud Deum meruit, exiens de corpore meo, intrabit corpus alicuius futuri Principis, sive Regis, vel alterius cuiuslibet personae illustris, in quo delicietur; si autem male, corpus intrabit miseri pauperisque, in quo tribuletur'; Caesarius, *Dialogus*, I, 301; trans. Scott and Swinton Bland, I, 344.

supernatural in the physicality of the real world gives his stories an immediacy and vividness that can be, at times, alarming. He tells a story of two heretics who successfully convince the populace of their legitimacy through a series of 'miracles':

> They bade [the people] sprinkle flour over the pavement, and walked over it without leaving any trace of a footstep; in like manner they walked on water without sinking, and lastly, caused wooden huts to set on fire over their heads, and when these had been reduced to ashes, they came forth uninjured.[62]

At a loss to know how to combat so convincing an enemy, the bishop resorts to necromancy, ordering one of his clerks to summon the devil and ask him how they have obtained these powers. The devil obligingly answers that 'the indentures [*cyrographa*] under which they have become my vassals, are kept safe, sewn under their armpits, between the skin and the flesh, and it is by this charm that they perform their miracles, and are immune from all bodily harm'. Armed with this knowledge, the bishop has the men searched and 'the soldiers, as they had been instructed beforehand by the bishop, lifted up the men's arms, and discovering certain scars hidden beneath them, tore them open with their knives, and drew from thence the indentures [*chartulas*] which had been sewn up in them'.[63] Thus they are undone. Even a standard anti-heretical story is given colour and personalized, not only through familiarity with the eyewitness but through an injection of humour that is unusual in this context. Everard, canon of St Géréon, is staying in Verona and, through the hospitality of his host, finds himself in a typical underground heretical meeting, which includes all the familiar ingredients: people of both sexes listening to a heretical sermon, before the extinguishing of the lights signals the beginning of all manner of depravity. After six months Everard gets cold feet and stops going, but confesses all to Caesarius's source, Gotteschalk, reassuring him that 'you should know, brother, that I didn't attend heretical conventicles for the heresies, but for the girls'.[64] The inclusion of a joke here,

---

62 'Farinam in pavimento cribari iusserunt, et sine vestigii impressione super illam ambulaverunt. Similiter super aquas gradientes non poterant mergi; tuguria etiam super se facientes incendi, postquam in cinera sunt redacta, egressi sunt illaesi'; Caesarius, *Dialogus*, I, 296; trans. Scott and Swinton Bland, I, 344.

63 'Cyrographa mea, in quibus hominia mihi ab eis facta, sunt conscripta, sub ascellis suis inter pellem et carnem consuta conservant, quorum beneficio talia operantur, nec aliquo laedi poterunt'; 'milites vero, sicut ab Episcopo fuerant praemoniti, brachia eis levantes, et sub ascellis cicatrices obductas notantes, cultellis illas ruperunt, chartulas insutas inde extrahentes; Caesarius, *Dialogus*, I, 297, 298; trans. (adjusted) Scott and Swinton Bland, I, 338–41.

64 'Sciatis, frater, me non frequentare conventicula haereticorum propter haereses, sed propter puellas'. Caesarius's description of the underground scenes leaves little to the imagination: 'exstincta candela, unusquisque sibi proximam invasit, nullam habentes differentiam inter legitimam et absolutam, inter viduam et virginam, inter dominam et ancillam, et, quod horribilius erat, inter sororem et filiam'; Caesarius, *Dialogus*, I, 308. Scott

and the compelling reconstructions of physical settings, show Caesarius's depictions of heresy answering the wider demands of the pedagogic and didactic purpose of a text designed to provide 'spiritual experience, and moral instruction', as McGuire describes.

Within that model heretics and heresy can be seen typically to demonstrate a moral message or a Catholic article of belief within a wider discussion, though heresy itself can also be the subject of discussion in its own right. Like Stephen, Caesarius includes a section in which heresy is not merely contextual, but is the focus both of the *exempla* and of the moral that they convey. That discussion occurs within book five of Caesarius's collection *De daemonibus*, in chapters eighteen to twenty-five. These chapters describe, in the following order: two stories dating from the 1160s about heretics burned at Besançon and at Cologne; a chapter on the Waldensians at Metz; another on the Albigensians (a long chapter that includes the account of the siege of Béziers in 1209 and the meeting of the monk and the heretical knight); a story of academic heretics burned at Paris (the Amalricians); a story of heretics burned at Troyes; some more heretics at Verona (the obligatory chapter on sexual depravity, quoted above); and finally a heretical teacher who said that the devil was the ruler of this world.[65]

There is little distinction made in terms of the organization of the chapters along the lines of different sects; rather, they are all mixed in together: the Cathars, the Waldensians and the intellectual Amalrician heresy, with other, undifferentiated 'heretics'. Caesarius is not much interested in providing working descriptions of the heretics in question, but rather in seeking a moral message in their existence. The only occasions on which we are provided with more detail are within the accounts of the Albigensians and the Amalricians. For the most part the heretics included by Caesarius have few distinguishing features and tend to be described less in terms of belief than of actions and characteristics. Several common themes can be discerned in those characterizations, which apply in most cases, regardless of the depth of detail given about the heretics themselves.

As in the case of the Amalricians, heretics can be educated in Caesarius's world, but the level of that education varies by sect and according to the demands of the *exemplum*. Caesarius will sometimes emphasize the learning of the clergy in this context: the Bishop of Besçancon, for example, is learned, while the people are simple, and the heretics somehow neither, but are outside that construct, just as they are outsiders in the town, and their heresy is neither educated nor rustic, but diabolical. The heretics at Cologne are examined by learned men, but no mention is made of their errors, which in reality may have

and Swinton Bland rather neatly bowdlerize this as 'such scenes as were slanderously alleged by the heathen against the Christians in the early days of the church', I, 352.

65 Caesarius, *Dialogus*, I, 296–309. 'Amalricians' is not a name that Caesarius uses for this group, but it is used here for the sake of convenience. On depravity, devil worship and underground lairs see also Hilka, *Die Wundergeschichte*, I, 27, 149.

been quite complex, and with which Caesarius may have been familiar from his time there as a young scholar.[66] Meanwhile, the Waldensians are refuted by the clerks of Metz and for their part have to rely on a scholar that they have brought with them.[67] Heretical learning or a connection to it are never neutral for Caesarius, and are always glossed.

The heresiarch visited by the bishop of Cambrai and two other Catholic scholars, who we can presume to be a Cathar given the discussion of devil as creator that follows, is able to dispute a point with his visitors 'not only from the Scriptures, but also from reason'. The novice, remarking that he has heard that there are many heretics in Lombardy, receives the reply: 'no wonder, since they have their own masters in various cities, publicly reading [= lecturing upon] the scriptures and expounding them perversely'.[68] Though heretical learning is admitted by the latter example, at the same time it is made clear that it is turned to a perverse end. After the monk's description of the Albigensians the novice remarks that if they only had 'learned men' among them none of this would have happened. Caesarius, or the 'monk', to introduce his next chapter on the sect of the Amalricians, made up almost entirely of Paris theologians, replies that when learned men begin to fall into error the devil pushes them further than the illiterate – learning can be a tool of the devil if not applied within Catholic limits.[69]

Another noticeable feature of nearly all Caesarius's depictions of heretics is how frequently they are found in public, and how equally public and spoken is their mode of expression. One of the most common arenas in which we find heretics in this text is in the context of public debate or confrontation, usually with the local clergy or, in the case of an *exemplum* from Caesarius's sermon collections, with a papal legate.[70] Similarly, heretics are described in several places in Caesarius's stories as preaching, or impeding the preaching of the Catholics, and the Amalricians go on a three-month missionary journey from Paris to the dioceses of Paris, Lyons, Troyes and Sens.[71] Elsewhere, in another *exemplum* taken from his homilies, Caesarius tells us of 'the Albigensian heretics openly fighting against the Catholic faith'.[72] This public arena for heretics is something that is also common, in fact, to the *exempla* of Stephen and Jacques de Vitry.

---

[66] As McGuire points out, that fact is known from the *Dialogus* itself, book 6 chapter 4; McGuire, 'Written Sources', p. 275.

[67] Caesarius, *Dialogus*, I, 299–300.

[68] 'Non solum ex scripturis, sed etiam ex ratione'; 'Hoc mirum non est, habent enim suos magistros in diversis civitatibus, aperte legentes, et sacram paginam perverse exponentes'; Caesarius, *Dialogus* I, 309, 308; trans. Scott and Swinton Bland, I, 353.

[69] 'Viri literati [*sic*]'; Caesarius, *Dialogus*, I, 300–303; trans. Scott and Swinton Bland, I, 347.

[70] Caesarius, *Dialogus*, I, 297; I, 300; Hilka, *Die Wundergeschichte*, I, 210, 150–51: Albienses; interesting here, 'nullum ex scripturis admitteret testimonium hereticus'.

[71] Caesarius, *Dialogus*, I, 297, 300, 304, 306; Hilka, *Die Wundergeschichte*, I, 210, 150.

[72] 'Hereticorum Albiensium aperte fidem catholicam impugnancium'; Hilka, *Die Wundergeschichte*, I, 260, 171.

Despite their often public nature, Caesarius's heretics are also character-ized, as they are in other *exempla* collections and in the anti-heretical tradition as a whole, by deception and hiddenness. Hiddenness can apply to behaviour, as can be seen in the sensationalist account of secret, morally depraved conventicles held by Lombard heretics, but for the most part their hiddenness occurs rather in the context of their pretended appearance.[73] In his homilies Caesarius labels heretics as false prophets: 'in simple habits they approach simple men, they profer words of simplicity, and with lupine malice they fasten their teeth in them'.[74] In the same way, the two heretics that Caesarius describes at Besançon are marked, before anything else, by a false appearance, of piety and of nature: 'two men, simple in dress, but not in heart, ravening wolves rather than sheep ... pretending the deepest piety'.[75] It is by this decep-tion and their false miracles, which are powered by the devil, that they persuade people of their sincerity and of the truth of their teachings.

The equation between heretics and the devil, or diabolical forces, is almost omnipresent in Caesarius's description of heretics – they are the 'limbs of the devil' – and in his explanation for the hidden part of their nature.[76] Indeed, for Caesarius the devil represents, as McGuire puts it, a manifestation of all the evils of man, and is in fact a central part of Caesarius's whole text, but Berlioz also sees this diabolical connection as central specifically to Caesarius's conception of heresy and the heretic, and it is not hard to see why.[77] In nearly every case the heretics are either the agents of the devil or moved by the devil, or their doctrine is derived from him; in one story the devil himself is called up to say that the teaching of the heretics belongs to him: 'they preach what I have put in their mouths'.[78] Within book five, *De daemonibus*, though some of the chapters that contain heresy are concerned directly to discuss heresy in its own right, those discussions, like the other *exempla* included here, are all still subject to the overall demonic theme of the book. However, even outside the group of stories in that book, heretics are characterized above all by this connection. That diabolical involvement can in some ways be seen as a part of a wider construct that is visible also in the intervention of God in these stories; if the heretics are inspired or empowered by the devil then they are always punished by God, not by men, unless those men are acting clearly as the

---

73 Public defence: Caesarius, *Dialogus*, I, 308. 'Error non facit hereticum, sed defensio erroris'; in the letter to the prior of Marienstatt, Hilka, *Die Wundergeschichte*, I, 3. See also letter pref-acing *sermones dominicales*: 'non enim error hereticum facit, sed defensio erroris'; Hilka, *Die Wundergeschichte*, I, 21.

74 'In habitu simplici simplices adeunt, simplicitatis verba pretendunt et ... lupine malicie dentes in illos defigunt'; Hilka, *Die Wundergeschichte*, I, 208, 147–9

75 'Duo homines, non mente, sed in habitu simplices, non oves sed lupi rapaces ... summam simulantes religiositatem'; Caesarius, *Dialogus*, I, 296; trans. Scott and Swinton Bland, I, 338.

76 'Membra sunt diaboli'; Caesarius, *Dialogus* I, 309.

77 McGuire, 'Written Sources', pp. 260–61; Berlioz, *'Exemplum* et histoire', p. 52.

78 'Quae in ore illorum posui, illa praedicant'; Caesarius, *Dialogus*, I, 297; trans. Scott and Swinton Bland, I, 339.

agents of God. A tendency to remove the actual punishment from the responsibility of men is something that can also be seen within the Dominican tradition, but, given that the *Dialogus* as a whole is concerned with miracles, this dependence on supernatural forces is neither surprising nor exclusive to the sections involving heresy.

Tractatus de diversis materiis predicabilibus[79]

Stephen of Bourbon, a Dominican scholar and inquisitor, wrote his *Tractatus de diversis materiis predicabilibus* some time between 1250 and his death in 1261. What we know of Stephen himself can be gleaned mainly from this work and from a brief notice by the later Dominican, Bernard Gui, which describes the work and its author. The treatise is constructed around a scheme of the seven gifts of the Holy Spirit, though Stephen only reached the fifth gift, or book, before he died. This lengthy, though unfinished, work was intended as a manual for his brethren and aims to present authorities, arguments and *exempla* from which to construct sermons on any given subject.

Examination of Stephen's use and construction of heresy is at the moment made more difficult by the lack of a complete edition; Lecoy de la Marche extracted and edited many *exempla* from the work, selecting those that seem to derive from Stephen's more immediate experience. A new edition is underway, but so far only books one and three have been published, and the comparison between these and Lecoy's volume (each of the new volumes is the same size as Lecoy's) provides an instant demonstration of how much is missing from the latter. Nonetheless, Lecoy's edition is sound, if highly selective, and reading the two together can give a good impression of the overall nature of the text.

The stated aim of the *Tractatus* is to promote a Christian life among the simple by means of arguments reinforced by authority and illuminated by story, or, rather, to provide the means by which the 'proximate' Dominican audience of the text can construct sermons. Stephen's 'ultimate' audience is the congregation of the faithful and his concern is with their welfare and defence, not the attack of outsiders.[80] *Exempla* are at the heart of that purpose; they are given prominence beside, and perhaps over, the other elements of the work. Stephen introduces the work as a collection of 'authorities and reasons and various examples pertaining to the edification of souls', and opens by listing the good effects of *auctoritates* and *rationes*, which can prepare and teach men, instruct and stir them, cause them to move away from sin and towards good. It is in order to make these benefits effective, though, to carry them home, that Stephen provides *exempla*, which, he says, are especially effective in making

---

[79] Stephen of Bourbon, *Tractatus*; Stephen of Bourbon, lib.1/lib.3. See Rottenwöhrer, I.i, 153.

[80] Welter, but quoting Lecoy's introduction, points to the fact that the language of the *exempla* is often quite plain, and seems to be written for the purpose of bringing together simple stories for use of preachers; Welter, *L'exemplum*, p. 218.

impressions on the heart and in the memory, and are the most instructive to the simple. He goes on to cite Gregory, who proved, in his *Dialogues*, that deeds speak louder than words and *exempla* louder than preaching, and to point out that Christ taught first by example.[81] It is for these reasons that he collected various *exempla* from many sources, which he lists in great detail.

Stephen drew his material from a variety of sources. Apart from the Scriptures and the works of the Fathers, some of his stories are from early Christian texts, some from contemporary chronicles, from Lives of saints and rulers, and some from his own experience and that of others with whom he had spoken, reflecting a network of personal exchanges and interactions similar to that which McGuire outlines in Caesarius of Heisterbach's collection.[82] The material stemming from this latter source forms the basis of Lecoy's edition, and in this context we might expect Stephen to know something of heresy, given his background.

We know that Stephen acted as a papal inquisitor in France because he tells us so himself at various points throughout this text. Several times in the *Tractatus* his anti-heretical work provides the backdrop to an *exemplum*, or authenticity for its source – Stephen is always concerned to show from where he has acquired his material. He tells us that he has been present at and involved in the sentencing of a large group of heretics, and on two occasions he frames his story as part of his experience as an inquisitor, once in Forez and once when he was 'in a certain city, by apostolic mandate working against heretics and looking for [*or* questioning] them'.[83] We also know that he preached a crusade against the Albigensians at Vézelay, though the story he draws from this episode has nothing to do with heresy except that it was Stephen's reason for being in that place.[84] Heresy seems to be a sort of context for Stephen, at least at certain periods of his life, and it is perhaps surprising, therefore, that relatively few of his *exempla* are concerned with or mention contemporary heresy.

The number of occurrences of heresy in this text as a whole is, after all, relatively small. In those *exempla* that are drawn from his own experience, heresy is well-represented: in Lecoy's edition a relatively large proportion, 45 out of 519, or about 9 per cent, have some firm connection with heresy. However, most of these are clustered together; only 17 are outside the section dedicated

---

81 'Refertus auctoritatibus et rationibus et exemplis diversis ad edificationem pertinentibus animarum'; 'ad hec suggerenda et ingerenda et imprimenda in humanis cordibus, maxime valent exempla, que maxime erudiunt simplicium hominum ruditatem, et faciliorem et longiorem ingerunt et imprimunt in memoria tenacitatem'; Stephen of Bourbon, *Tractatus*, pp. 3–4; Stephen of Bourbon, lib.1, pp. 3–4.

82 Stephen of Bourbon, *Tractatus*, pp. 5–8; Stephen of Bourbon, lib.1, pp. 5–6. McGuire, 'Friends and Tales in the Cloister', *passim*.

83 Sentencing of heretics at Mont-Aimé, Stephen of Bourbon, *Tractatus*, pp. 150, 415. 'Cum ego in quadam civitate essem contra hereticos et inquirerem de mandato apostolico'; Stephen of Bourbon, *Tractatus*, p. 322, and in Forez, p. 196.

84 Stephen of Bourbon, *Tractatus*, p. 140.

to heresy and in the rest of the *Tractatus* heresy is comparatively uncommon. Though an examination of the Berlioz and Eichenlaub edition of book one doubles the number of *exempla* containing heresy we can find in Lecoy's selection from 3 to 6, the editors count 421 *exempla* in this book alone.[85] Likewise, the full edition of book three provides 12 *exempla* on heresy, in comparison to the 2 that appear in Lecoy, but the book as a whole contains 432 by Berlioz's count. In both books the stories not included by Lecoy all derive from early sources, but while this perhaps makes us feel more confident that in reading Lecoy's selection we have access to a fairly complete version of Stephen's depiction of the heretics of his own time and experience, it also underlines that, overall, Stephen draws as much on patristic sources as his own knowledge when a heretic is needed. The heretics of his own time he saves for his discussion of heresy itself.

Stephen dedicates a whole section of the *Tractatus* to the treatment of heresy. Each of the *Tractatus'* five books is divided systematically into titles, and then chapters, and each chapter has a theme, to the elucidation of which the arguments and their supporting authorities and *exempla* are all directed. The chapter *De heresi* appears in the seventh title, on Pride, of the fourth book, on the gift of Fortitude. Because heresy is here the subject, the organizing principle, rather than merely illustrative, the treatment that it receives here is different. In light of that difference, and the density of material, it seems helpful to treat the *De heresi* section separately from the incidence of heresy elsewhere throughout the text, using the full edition of books one and three as a control where possible.

Beyond the confines of the dedicated section of the *Tractatus* encounters with heresy are almost always in the form of the heretic: usually, though not always, an abstracted nameless figure. In book one, of the six *exempla* that include heresy in some form, in only one of these is the heretic, Pope Leo, named.[86] Of the three occurrences that Lecoy reproduces from book two only two actually feature heresy, again in the form of nameless heretics described no further than *heretici*. In the third book, heresy, or rather the preaching of the Albigensian crusade, is merely the context in which Stephen says he heard the (admittedly very good) story about a man with a 'great and horrible' toad immovably stuck to his face as a miraculous punishment.[87] Book three provides twice as many heresy stories as book one, including two versions of St Augustine's conversion from Manicheism, three stories about Arians (including Arius's unfortunate demise) and four about late antique saints

---

85 Stephen of Bourbon, lib.1, *tabula concordantiae exemplorum*, pp. 545–56; Welter gives the total number of *exempla* in the *Tractatus* at around 2,900; Welter, *L'exemplum*, p. 215.

86 Three antique: Hilary, Stephen of Bourbon, lib.1, p. 24; Theodosius pp. 207–8; Constantine p. 238. Three contemporary: St Dominic, Stephen of Bourbon, *Tractatus*, pp. 34–5/Stephen of Bourbon, lib.1, pp. 165–6; Alverniensis pp. 25–6/114–15; a mention of the Albigensian crusade pp. 36–7/176–7.

87 'Maximum et horribilem bufonem'; Stephen of Bourbon, *Tractatus*, pp. 79, 97, 140.

meeting 'heretics' or, in one case, 'Origenists'.[88] Book three also includes two *exempla* that concern contemporary heretics. In one, an anonymous heretic is seen to be confused by the arguments of a jester; the other presents us with the more developed character, 'a certain old woman', a contemporary of Stephen named Alberea, whom everyone thought a saint. Stephen tells us that, while she did indeed live an austere life, this was a result of her mistaken belief that everything was made by the devil, and Stephen identifies her as a Manichean heretic.[89]

Even if we discount the *De heresi* section of book four it still includes more contemporary incidents of heresy than the other books. Here we meet a distraught lady who, wishing to be burned as a heretic, is dissuaded and reassured by Stephen. We are also presented with the following: some heretics who attempt to argue with Catholic priests, but who must resort to attacking the priests' bad example when they are refuted via Scriptural argument and reason; a priest who becomes a heretic and leads others astray; a heretic who tries to confound St Francis and fails; and a notice of the burning of 180 Manichean heretics at Mont-Aimé, in whose trial and condemnation Stephen was personally involved.[90] Book five, by contrast, offers only one *exemplum*, containing 'a certain heretic'.[91]

Of all the examples mentioned above, in only two are the heretics named personally, though there is sometimes a designation by place of origin; this is the case with a heretic from the Auvergne, described in book one, who gave off a terrible smell when he was burned, though he is nonetheless distinguished no further than that he was 'quidam hereticus'.[92] More common is an identification with a group such as the Manicheans, though, with the exception of Alberea, this tends to be largely restricted to the heretics of antiquity; typically, the heretics in question are identified merely as such and distinguished only by opposition to the Catholic truth.

---

[88] St Martin of Tours, St Germanus of Auxerre and St Pachomius, whose tranquility is interrupted by the 'Origenist' heretics, whose noxious dogma renders them also physically odorous. Stephen of Bourbon, lib.3, pp. 68, 387, 185, 310, 354, 38, 300, 357, 387.

[89] 'Quedam vetula'; Stephen of Bourbon, *Tractatus*, pp. 148, 149–50; Stephen of Bourbon, lib.3, pp. 41–2. Here is a nice parallel with Pseudo-James Capelli, who argues several times that heretics' actions are right, but their motivations wrong. On Alberea, see P. Biller, 'The Earliest Heretical Englishwomen', in *Medieval Women: Texts and Contexts in Late Medieval Britain. Essays for Felicity Riddy*, ed. J. Wogan-Browne et al. (Turnhout, 2000), 363–76 (pp. 370–72). The twelfth *exemplum* in this book is not so much an *exemplum* as a series of similes that illustrate one of the qualities of confession – that it should be 'simplex'; Stephen of Bourbon, lib.3, p. 133.

[90] Stephen of Bourbon, *Tractatus*, pp. 196, 213–14, 215, 265, 415. Stephen also mentions the Mont-Aimé trial earlier, giving the number at 80; p. 150. There are *exempla* concerning a large dog, and an extinguishing of lights story, but these are describing superstition, rather than heresy, pp. 322–3. The story about St Francis is duplicated in the *De heresi* section, p. 304.

[91] Stephen of Bourbon, *Tractatus*, p. 430.

[92] Stephen of Bourbon, *Tractatus*, pp. 25–6; Stephen of Bourbon, lib.1, p. 114. Tubach cites only Stephen as a source for this *exemplum*.

In a few places some points of heretical belief penetrate the stories. Two of the heretics that appear in book three, namely the heretic who is confounded by the arguments of a jester and Alberea, refuse meat on account of their belief. Indeed, within Stephen's account is a brief report of Alberea's exposition of this belief before the inquisition. The heretic who confronts St Francis appears to hold a Donatist view of ministers, and the story of Theodosius in book one presents heretics denying the resurrection of the body. In this last case the heretical belief is an integral part of the narrative, in which Theodosius has tombs opened to prove them wrong, thus also proving the moral of the story, which is to demonstrate future corporal resurrection. Similarly, the heretic who attempts to denigrate St Francis claims that the priest from whom he is receiving Mass has a concubine; the heretic's failure exemplifies Stephen's argument, which has to do with irreverence. Where heretical doctrine appears it is as a necessary element in the progress of the narrative, and not the subject of it. Indeed, heretics are made to speak only when attacking the church, and never give voice to their own beliefs, which, if they appear at all, are described by Stephen. Although he mentions that there is a lot of heretical doctrine to be found in Milan he gives no indication of its content.[93]

Heresy, then, in the principal form in which it appears in this text outside the *De heresi* section, is a concrete, figural thing consisting of the actions and often even just the presence of an otherwise undifferentiated 'heretic', with little or nothing of heresy, or doctrinal error, presented. Error appears in this type of abstracted construct only when it serves the purpose of the story. In this context, heresy is only one part of the illustrative mechanism of the *exemplum* and subordinate to the purpose of that *exemplum* – that is, the illustration of some part of orthodox behaviour or belief – and also to the wider plan of the text. So, for example, the Auvergnat heretic must smell bad when he is burnt because Stephen wishes to show, by this example, in what condition heretics and other evildoers will suffer in Hell. That story functions as an illustration 'of their foulness and bad smell', which is one of a series of chapters that describes the torments of the damned in this title, which is on hell, and which in turn is part of the book on the gift of Fear.[94] In the same way as the appearance of heretical doctrine, mentioned above in the case of Alberea, heresy here is illustrative of something else. While here it is at least necessary that the figure be a heretic, and in some of the *exempla* these heretical figures have a historical ring to them, especially in the stories concerning the Order's founders, Diego and Dominic, there are occasions when the heretic is reduced to a mere device. When Stephen tells us that a heretic cut out a priest's tongue, here in order to give Mary, whose miracles are the subject of this chapter, the chance to restore it, he could have replaced 'heretic' with 'evil person', and the effect would have been the same. The rhetorical nature of the exemplary

---

[93] Stephen of Bourbon, *Tractatus*, pp. 213–14, 215.

[94] 'De feditate et fetore eorum'; Stephen of Bourbon, *Tractatus*, p. 25; Stephen of Bourbon, lib.1, p. 114.

heretic in these stories is perhaps best demonstrated by the fact that the story of St Francis' encounter with the Donatist heretic occurs twice in the *Tractatus*, but each time to convey different messages.[95]

Given that Lecoy's edition concentrates almost exclusively on the exemplary material from the *Tractatus*, it is difficult to look at the appearance of heresy in this text outside of its *exempla*. We can, though, look at the full text of books one and three for an idea of how heresy functions and is represented in the other two elements around which Stephen built his work: that is, authority and reason. In both books one and three, and it is only a very general control, it appears very rarely. There is very little discussion or mention of heresy in these parts of the text, even in places where it might be expected, such as the exposition on bodily resurrection, something that the Cathars denied, to much condemnation. In fact, there appears to be only one mention of heresy in the discursive parts of each book. Book three includes an almost throwaway reference to heretics as part of a series of similes that includes a fox and Julian the Apostate and that illustrates one of the qualities of confession – that it should be 'simplex', not made for nefarious purposes.[96] Book one has something more substantial: during a discussion on the proofs for the existence of punishment in Purgatory, in the course of the second chapter of the fifth title, there is a repudiation of heretics, especially Waldensians, who deny purgatory. Here we are given some detail of error – they say there is no place for souls except heaven and hell – which Stephen goes some way to refute, but it remains, as with the *exempla*, a subordinate part of the wider discussion of orthodox faith. One of the main things to be noticed here about Stephen's discussion is that his first response is to attack not the error but the holders of it, by comparing them to Biblical models that held the same tenets; they are hyenas, and devils, and the children of devils, and so 'they betray their stupidity'.[97] While he does refute a later point with authorities, this seems to be in order to show that they are sinners, and the attack, for it is quite polemical, remains focused around the heretics themselves.

A useful analogue to Stephen's non-*exempla* treatment here is to be found in a roughly contemporary and related work. Humbert of Romans' *Tractatus de habundantia exemplorum* is very similar to the *Tractatus de diversiis materiis* in both structure and intention, and it draws heavily on Stephen's work for its *exempla*, though its date is hard to pin down with precision. Kaeppeli and Panella give 1240–77 as the widest range for its composition; Boyer narrows

---

95 Stephen of Bourbon, *Tractatus*, p. 97; this story is also told by Caesarius, *Dialogus*, II, 31–3. Stephen of Bourbon, *Tractatus*, pp. 265; 304–5. It is perhaps unusual that Stephen does not use one of the many Dominican stories here, in which St Dominic argues with heretics and wins. Certainly he makes use of the *vitae* of St Dominic elsewhere.

96 Stephen of Bourbon, lib.3, p. 133.

97 'Manifestant eorum stultitiam'; 'non esse loca animarum descendentium nisi infernum et paradisum'; Stephen of Bourbon, lib.1, pp. 144–5.

the first date to 1263.[98] The surviving manuscripts of this work suggest that it had a reasonably wide distribution.[99] A collection of *exempla* that are woven, like Stephen's, into a didactic, moral narrative, and are subordinate to this framework, the work was compiled by Humbert for the use of preachers working 'for the edification and salvation of all'. For, as he tells us in a prologue highly reminiscent of Stephen's opening gambit, *'exempla* are more stirring than words, according to Gregory, and are more easily grasped by the intellect'.[100] The organization of Humbert's text is presented, like Stephen's, as being structured around the seven gifts of the Holy Spirit, though apparently only the first part of this was written, or survives. The book that we have, on the gift of Fear, is rather smaller than the first part of Stephen's text, but its division and chapter titles are almost identical to Stephen's.

Humbert's book seems to contain little material on heresy; though he lifts an enormous amount from Stephen, Humbert does not borrow any of his heretical *exempla*. There is, however, at the very beginning of the section dealing with Purgatory, a discussion of the 'heretics and particularly the Waldensians, who deny purgatory'. The discussion stands out as a contemporary element in a book otherwise dominated by material drawn from the Fathers and the early church, but, while the position of Humbert's treatment of the Waldensian error in the framework of the text resembles that of the *Tractatus*, the nature of this treatment is quite different. Unlike Stephen's rather polemical line, Humbert approaches the problem as a theological question, presenting first the Waldensian position, which is based on the words of Christ to the thief at the crucifixion, and then proceeding to a systematic refutation, devoid of invective and focused entirely on the error: 'next, against them is the Gospel, which they accept, where it is said ...', and then a little later, 'not only authority but reason is against them'.[101] Humbert's engagement with the subject on a purely doctrinal level throws into relief Stephen's continued treatment, even in this situation, of heresy through the figure of the heretic, not heresy as error.[102]

Heresy, then, in the majority of Stephen's text, appears always in the guise of the more or less defined heretic, and always in the service of the grand plan,

---

98 Humbert of Romans, *Humberti de Romanis De dono timoris*, ed. C. Boyer, Corpus Christianorum, Continuatio Mediaevalis 218 (Turnhout, 2008), p. xxi.

99 Eighty-four manuscripts of the whole or part of this work survive; Humbert, *Humberti de Romanis*, ed. Boyer, p. xxv; see also *SOPMA* II, 283–7.

100 'Ad edificationem omnium et salutem'; 'plus exempla quam verba movent secundum Gregorium et facilius intellectu capiuntur'; Humbert, *Humberti de Romanis*, ed. Boyer, p. 3.

101 'Heretici et praecipue valdenses qui negant purgatorium'; 'porro contra illos est evangelium quod recipiunt ubi dicitur ...'; 'item non solum auctoritas sed ratio est contra eos'; Humbert, *Humberti de Romanis*, Boyer, pp. 85–6.

102 The difference between the two might also reflect the division in Dominican traditions, between the southern and Paris Dominicans, that A. Reltgen-Tallon suggests: 'L'historiographie des Dominicains du Midi: une mémoire originale?', *CF* 36 (2001), pp. 395–414.

of the chapter, of the book, not an end in itself. It is, however, a common enough fact of life to be either really involved in different events, or to provide a plausible character. Heresy, or the figure of the heretic, is an integral part of the contemporary fabric of Stephen's experience.

Stephen's treatment of heresy as a subject in itself, *De heresi*, is contained within his discussion of Pride, the seventh of the titles within the fourth book of the *Tractatus*, on the gift of Fortitude. There is a further division within this section which provides five different kinds of information. As he always does, Stephen explains in a brief prologue the plan of what he is about to do, which it seems easiest to quote in full:

1. By which arguments against heresy the Catholic faith is shown to be true, and heresy confuted, and faith strengthened in believing hearts.
2. In what manner error, in its evil effects, is opposed to the good effects of faith.
3. In which evil conditions the heretic, deviating from faith, is entangled.
4. By which errors the heretics of our times – that is to say, the Waldensians and the Albigenses, called Patarines or Bulgars – are infected.
5. With which sophistries they attempt to conceal themselves, and how they may be detected.[103]

The first three parts – that is, the lists of things by which the Catholic faith is shown to be the true one, of the good effects of the Catholic faith, and of the evil conditions and qualities of heretics – form the bulk of the *De heresi* section, though Lecoy's edition abridges these sections quite significantly. However, his numbers 342 to 352 inclusive represent the unbroken text of the fourth and fifth parts in the original.[104] In the fourth section Stephen discusses error, with a description and refutation of heretical doctrine. In the fifth, he gives us four different ways in which a heretic may be recognized. As in the rest of the *Tractatus*, most of the *exempla* in these five parts that feature heresy, which is by no means all of them, treat it as a generic thing and are centred on the heretic. The difference in this section is that, though heresy appears in the *exempla*, it also determines or constitutes the subject of much of the surrounding material – that is, the discussion made up by *auctoritates* and *rationes*.

---

103 'Prima, per quas persuasiones contra heresim fides catholica vera esse monstratur, et heresis confutatur, et fides in cordibus credencium roboratur; secundo, quomodo error in suis malis effectibus bonis fidei effectibus adversatur; tercio, quibus malis condicionibus hereticus a fide devians circumvolvatur; quarto, quibus erroribus heretici nostri temporis, Valdenses scilicet et Albigenses, dicti Patareni vel Bulgari, inficiantur; quinto, quibus sophismatibus operire se conantur, et quomodo detegantur'; Stephen of Bourbon, *Tractatus*, p. 275.

104 Oxford, Oriel College, MS 68; Paris, BnF MS Lat. 14599. *De heresi* occurs at fols. 208[rb]–221[vb] and fols. 212[r]–240[r] respectively.

The first two sections concentrate on why the Catholic faith is superior to heresy. Stephen's defence of Catholicism in these parts is clearly built around a response to error, which, in a way similar to the structure and substance of the *Summae auctoritatum*, produces a discussion of orthodoxy that nonetheless reflects heresy. Section one is essentially a statement of faith. It involves, in the first place, a comparison of Catholicism not only with heresy but also with paganism and with Islam, an association that Stephen will make again in his list of heretical attributes. Stephen then goes on to demonstrate that, where heresy is divided, Catholicism is united under one God and one church, proven by the prophets. The second part sets out the good effects of the true faith, as defined by their difference from the effects of heretical belief and as a complement to the third section. In both discussions the *exempla* employed, whether they feature heresy or not, are, as with the other *exempla* considered so far, concerned with the elucidation of those main points, the demonstration of the truth of Catholic faith.

In the third section there is a shift, in as much as the *exempla* are now aimed at illustrating a discussion of which heresy is now explicitly the subject, although there remains an emphasis on the abstract and the generic and, rather than echo the previous two sections on the Catholic faith and treat heresy as a matter of belief, Stephen gives us instead a description of the characteristics of the heretic. 'Proud and conceited', 'poisonous', 'confused', 'avaricious and greedy': these characteristics revolve for the most part around defects in moral condition, and all our favourite anti-heretical staples are to be found here. Heretics are:

> Falsely adorned with pretended virtues, wolves dressed in the clothes of sheep; inwardly they are ravening wolves, having an appearance of piety, but denying the power thereof. The angel of Satan transformed himself into an angel of light, therefore it is no wonder if his ministers transform themselves into the ministers of justice.[105]

Next to the ravening wolves is invoked the image of Samson's foxes: the heretics are 'tied together in their posterior parts by their tails, because they are all intent on one thing, fighting the church, like Samson's foxes'. There is an emphasis on the harm that heretics do to others: 'they are defiled and they defile others'.[106] The fifth item on the list, that heretics are liars, includes an *exemplum* taken from the preaching of a bishop in the 'the land of the

---

[105] 'Falsati ornati, fictis virtutibus, lupi vestiti vellibus ovium mt.vi.c.[7.15] intrinsecus sunt lupi rapaces, tym.iii.b[5] habentes speciem pietatis virtutem negantes, cor.xi.d.[2 Corinthians 11. 14–15] angelus sathane transfigurat se in angelum lucis non ergo mirum si transfigurant se ministri sathane ut ministri iusticie'; Oriel MS 68, fol. 218va–vb, BnF MS Lat. 14599 fol. 233va–34ra.

[106] 'Elati et inflati', 'venenati', 'confusi', 'avari et cupidi'; 'sunt coadunati sive colligati ex parte posteriori in caudis quia omnis tendunt ad unum quia intendunt impugnare ecclesiam ut vulpes sampsonis qui habebant facies diversas colligatas caudas'; Oriel MS 68, fol. 218va–vb, BnF MS Lat. 14599 fols. 233va–34ra.

Albigensians' in which a simple man is persuaded by the words of some here-tics into believing his lamb to be a dog.[107] These are all personal attacks in which concern with error is peripheral.

The shift in the emphasis of the *exempla* is continued into the fourth section, but there is also a change in the general presentation of heresy, because here Stephen gives a description of the 'heretics of our times'.[108] What we find here is very similar to the treatment of heresy that might be found in the anti-heretical treatises, or a handbook for inquisitors, with descriptions of the background to the heresies and a detailed list of errors. In fact, the whole atti-tude of this section is incongruous; it stands out in tone and substance from the other parts of the book and sounds as though it is talking to a different audi-ence. At the end of the Waldensian section Stephen justifies the inclusion of this information: 'I have inserted these things here, thinking it good for the brethren, defenders of the faith, not to be ignorant of them.'[109] He acknowl-edges the difference in register of a piece surely not designed for sermons to the faithful, but in which instead we hear the voice of Stephen the inquisitor, and which was indeed used almost without alteration in Gui's later inquisition manual, the *Practica inquisitionis*.[110] The more detached, informative tone of the inquisitor breeds a different kind of representation to that found elsewhere in the *Tractatus*.

Stephen's main concern with regard to the 'heretics of our times' is to describe, rather than attack. For both groups, and he deals only with 'Waldensians and Albigensians', he describes their origin, their names and their errors. He includes details of their lands, their schools and their different regional names, as well as a description of internal differentiations between levels of initiation, but is mostly concerned with belief and their defence of it.[111] They are reminiscent of the heretics that appear in the polemical treatises and the *Summae auctoritatum*: learned and argumentative. They are shown, especially the Cathars, to argue from Scriptural authority and to include several *magister* figures among their ranks. There are even a few small exchanges in the dialogue format, like that used in the *Dialogus* and in some of the *Summae auctoritatum*, between a 'hereticus' and a 'Catholicus'.[112] The repre-sentation of heresy is not completely divorced from this figure at any point, which perhaps even becomes more tangible than elsewhere, as these are often drawn from people with whom Stephen has spoken personally, but the heretic does not *act*; rather, he believes, argues, misunderstands. The heretic now

---

107 'Terra albigensium'; Oriel MS 68, fols. 217vb–18rb, BnF MS Lat. 14599 fol. 232rb–va.

108 Stephen of Bourbon, *Tractatus*, p. 290.

109 'Hec autem inserui estimans fratres fidei defensores bonum non ignorare'; Stephen of Bourbon, *Tractatus*, p. 299; trans. (adjusted) Wakefield and Evans, *Heresies*, p. 351.

110 Also by another anthology containing material for inquisitors, Dondaine, 'Manuel', pp. 132–4.

111 Stephen of Bourbon, *Tractatus*, pp. 289, 300, 302.

112 Stephen of Bourbon, *Tractatus*, pp. 303–7.

carries a different content – not the rhetorical purpose of the story, but information, specifically, doctrinal information. Notably, in this section alone the heretics are differentiated carefully and in detail on the grounds of belief.

Stephen draws exclusively on his own experience for the illustration of this section and for the heretical arguments, obtained through discussions with 'a certain learned man who for a long time was of their sect'.[113] He also frames his account of the Waldensians within his own experience: 'as I myself came to know and found out, in the course of many interrogations and confessions – both of the *perfecti* and their believers – done according to law and taken down in writing from what they themselves said; and also from many witnesses received against them'. This is reinforced throughout the description of their error by frequent statements from the author that he has gained this information directly through confession or in conversation with members of this group: 'one of their leading teachers and emissaries drew for me the following distinction'.[114] However, he defers immediately to the authority of Augustine and Isidore for the initial doctrinal framework of the Cathar error: 'the Manichees, whose pestilence still infects many places, according to what blessed Augustine and Isidore say ...'[115] He continues to refer to the Cathars using the patristic name of Manicheans, not just here but elsewhere in the text, though we know that he is aware of more contemporary names such as *Cathari*, *Patereni* and *Bugari*. Stephen perhaps sees, or wishes to present, a continuous progression from Manichean history to his own time, 'un aperçu schématique des croyances cathares, à travers le prisme augustinien'.[116] This is a progression that he attributes to the Cathars themselves: as they appear here, they regard Mani as their founder, owing to Stephen's use of Augustine's description of the fourth-century group.[117] It may be that, for Stephen, the Cathars represent a more archetypal kind of heretic; he introduces this section with the quotation from the first letter to Timothy concerning the errors of the last days, verses often associated with heretics, and there may be a resonance

---

[113] 'Quodam litterato qui et diu fuerat de secta eorum'; Stephen of Bourbon, *Tractatus*, p. 303.

[114] 'Sicut ego cognovi et inveni per multas inquisiciones et confessiones eorum in jure, perfectorum quam credencium, ab ore eorum conscriptas, et per multos testes contra eos receptos'; 'quidam magnus magister et legatus eorum hanc distinctionem mihi faciebat'; Stephen of Bourbon, *Tractatus*, pp. 293–4, 296; trans. (adjusted) Wakefield and Evans, *Heresies*, pp. 346, 348.

[115] 'Manichei, quorum pestis adhuc multa loca inficit, secundum quod dicunt beatus Augustinus et Ysidorus ...'; also 'errores illius perversi dogmatis sunt hi qui colliguntur ex verbis beati Augustini, de tribus ejus libris'; Stephen of Bourbon, *Tractatus*, pp. 299, 300.

[116] Stephen of Bourbon, *Tractatus*, pp. 281, 303; J. Berlioz, '"Les erreurs de cette doctrine pervertie ...". Les croyances des Cathares selon le Dominicain et inquisiteur Étienne de Bourbon (mort. v.1261)', *Heresis* 32 (2000), 53–67 (p. 67).

[117] 'Item promissionem factam de Spiritu Paraclito mittendo dicunt in suo heresiarcha fuisse completam, quem dicunt fuisse Spiritum Paraclitum'; 'sicut magister eorum Manes Paraclitum se dicebat, ita dicunt ipse eos Paraclitos'; Stephen of Bourbon, *Tractatus*, pp. 302, 306.

here with the Biblical heretics' denial of marriage and food.[118] But it may also be a combination of a preference for established authority and an Isidorean need to derive a sect from a founder figure – easily done for the Waldensians in a way that is not as simple for the Cathars.

The fifth part returns to the format of the third part: a discussion that is primarily concerned with heresy, in the form of the heretic, who is now undifferentiated by belief and once again mostly generic. Stephen lays down four indications of a heretic: usurpation of office, diffusion of venom, hiding of affairs and sophistry. The term 'heretic' has moved back to a general usage after being used by Stephen with little distinction to describe the 'Manicheans' in the previous section. Some points here may be more applicable to one group than the other; the usurpation of the office of preaching and the owning of vernacular gospels must apply more to the Waldensians than the Cathars, and it is indeed to 'heretici Valdenses' that Stephen refers here.[119] The section on sophistry again draws on Stephen's inquisitorial experience of the difficulties of interrogation and echoes the similar account given by the Pseudo-David. Stephen closes the section by saying that 'those who propose the duality of things, as the Manichees do, can be refuted only with difficulty', but the scheme of elusive answers is not presented as specific to one group.[120] What is clear is that, even though the fourth section demonstrates that Stephen is fully aware of differences between contemporary heretics, this does not prevent him from creating, or perceiving, markers that can identify all heretics from their behaviour, regardless of their differences. Their doctrinal errors do not restrict a generic identity as 'heretics'.

The *Tractatus* presents us with a figural and, to varying degrees, abstract heretic allied to edifying vignettes. That pattern seems to dominate most of the appearances that heresy makes in this text; certainly, most instances outside the dedicated section, *De heresi*, show this type of construction, and this is in turn largely because these instances are within the context of *exempla* and so need to serve a higher moralizing purpose. Heresy does not feature much in the framework of the text, those parts made up of the *auctoritates* and *rationes* that Stephen describes in his prologue, and this is because heresy has its own dedicated section, in its right place according to the careful structure of the book, where it does form the framework. It remains contained within the figure of the heretic, but it is only here, where it forms the basis of discussion, that it is ever really described in terms of doctrine. It is also because the book is addressed to the edification of an orthodox audience, where tales of heretics' defeat, when safely cleansed of doctrinal content, provide plausible and useful illustration of the correctness of orthodoxy and the perils of dissent.

---

118 I Timothy 4. 1–3; Stephen of Bourbon, *Tractatus*, pp. 303, 304.

119 Stephen of Bourbon, *Tractatus*, p. 308.

120 'Illi autem qui ponunt rerum duplicitatem, ut Manichei, difficulter possunt convinci'; Stephen of Bourbon, *Tractatus*, pp. 313–14.

A landscape populated by heretics was clearly the source of much of Stephen's material, but it was also, ultimately, the context in which these stories were deployed. Anti-heretical preaching had gathered momentum in the first decades of the thirteenth century as the church began to respond more proactively to the challenge that heretics posed to their authority. Of the several preachers who led this campaign, Jacques de Vitry in particular made notably effective use of *exempla* in his preaching career and brought all this to bear on the problem of heresy.[121]

Jacques had a personal connection with the heresy of his time, having acted as a preacher for the Albigensian Crusade in the south of France in 1213 and 1214, and in Belgium and Rheims in 1228, but he was also generally concerned with the combating of heresy through preaching.[122] The preface to his life of the northern saint Marie d'Oignies directs the work to this end, as an answer to a request from the bishop of Toulouse for accounts of contemporary saints that could be used to preach against the heretics of his region. Though the life itself contains no heresy as such, Jessalyn Bird demonstrates clearly that the emphases that it places on the power of the Eucharist and sacraments were nonetheless shaped by an anti-heretical design.[123] Similarly, though relatively few of the *exempla* that Jacques included in his sermons contain or concern heresy, those that do reveal this common, underlying concern.[124]

Jacques tells of the daughter of the count of Toulouse, born into a heretical family but remaining firm in her Catholic faith until her mother calls an evil spirit to torment her. The girl's faith is reinforced by the Holy Spirit and the story ends when the evil spirit 'fell into the pit that he made' (a quotation from the seventh Psalm that Jacques also uses to describe the defeat of the Patarines at the hands of the *Humiliati*). Heresy is venomous and perfidious, and heretics 'wish to harm Catholics', and Jacques uses his sermons to demonstrate this.[125] His approach is not generally to address heretical ideas directly, though he

---

[121] J. Longère, *Œuvres oratoires de maîtres Parisiens au XIIe siècle: étude historique et doctrinale* (Paris, 1975), pp. 420–32.

[122] Vitry, Crane, pp. xxii–xxxiv. On Jacques's attitude toward and preaching against the Cathars see C. Muessig, 'Les sermons de Jacques de Vitry sur les cathares', *CF* 32 (1997), 69–83.

[123] J. Bird, 'The Construction of Orthodoxy and the (De)construction of Heretical Attacks on the Eucharist in *Pastoralia* from Peter the Chanter's Circle in Paris', in *Texts and Repression*, ed. Bruschi and Biller, pp. 45–61 (p. 54).

[124] According to Crane, there were four sermon collections from which Jacques's *exempla* were drawn: the *Sermones dominicales*, the *Sermones de sanctis*, the *Sermones vulgares*, which provide the content of Crane's collection, and the *Sermones communes vel quotidiani*, which provide the content of both Greven's and Frenken's collections; Vitry, Crane, pp. xxxviii–xlvii; Vitry, Greven; *Die* Exempla *des Jacob von Vitry: ein Beitrag zur Geschichte der Erzählungsliteratur des Mittelalters*, ed. G. Frenken (Munchen, 1914).

[125] 'Incidit in foveam quam fecit'; 'catholicis nocere cupiunt'; Vitry, Greven, 98, pp. 58, 99, 59. Jacques de Vitry, *The* Historia occidentalis *of Jacques de Vitry. A Critical Edition*, ed. J. F. Hinnebusch (Fribourg, 1972), p. 146. The same phrase is also in *Vergentis in senium* – 'se ipsum laqueis suae fraudis innectit, et incidit in foveam, quam paravit'; X 5.7.10, Friedberg, II, 782.

does occasionally do so: in the *Sermones vulgares*, in a sermon addressed to 'citizens and burghers', Jacques makes a defence of the administration of sacraments. The story relates how a certain man, 'from an excess of simplicity', would not receive the sacraments from an unworthy priest. God, to recall him from error, sends him a dream in which he sees a well from which a leper draws clear water in a beautiful vessel. When the man approaches to drink with the many others gathered there the leper refuses him, saying 'in what way will you accept water from the hand of a leper, you who scorn to accept the sacraments from an unworthy priest?' 'Most evil, therefore, is the doctrine of heretics', Jacques glosses, 'who say the virtue of the sacraments depends on the [moral worthiness] of the minister'.[126] More broadly, another *exemplum*, about a sea-going monkey, is used by Jacques to demonstrate that heretics, though preaching against the church out of envy, in fact are inwardly tormented as they know that 'their doctrine is perverse'.[127]

On the whole, Jacques's main tactic is to equate heretics with evil and to cast doubt on their intentions. So, some sheep, here representing those who lend their support to heretics, foolishly allow wolves to enter among them because they are protected by the dog; they are tricked by the wolves – that is, the heretics – into giving up their canine protector – that is, the prelates of the church; by these methods, Jacques tells us, heretics wish to make the clergy hateful to Christians, in order that they more freely invade the flock.[128] Thus Jacques associates heretics and their preaching with evil, while simultaneously bolstering the role of the church as protector. He also takes care to underline the necessity, and even inevitability, of their punishment by the Church. Two further *exempla* serve to illustrate heresy, or rather heretics, in this way: a certain rustic, remembering that his foot ailment was cured with hot onions, tries, unsuccessfully, to heal his neighbour's eye condition with the same remedy. So the same medicine does not cure all illnesses, and so the church does not treat all heretics in the same way; those wishing to return are reconciled, others put in prison, others handed over to the secular arm, depending on their obstinacy.[129] Similarly, two penitents receive unequal penance

---

126 'Ex nimia simplicitate'; 'quomodo de manu leprosa vis aquam recipere qui a malis sacerdotibus dedignaris accipere sacramenta?'; 'Pessima igitur hereticorum doctrina qui ex una ministri dicunt pendere virtutem sacramentorum'; Vitry, Crane, clv, p. 68; 'una' is not clear here – possibly a mistake for 'manu'.

127 'Perversa est eorum doctrina'. While travelling by sea to Santiago, a man, though already wealthy, has acquired even more wealth by selling the pilgrims badly measured and frothy wine. Seeing the purse in which he keeps this money, a monkey steals away with it and climbs the mast of the ship, putting the coins to its nose, and casting some into the sea as though they were filthy. The monkey and the purse are eventually retrieved by a sailor, and the man finds all his ill-gotten gains cast into the deep by the monkey; only his lawfully inherited money remains; Vitry, Greven, 102, pp. 60–61.

128 He also takes the opportunity to condemn the rejection of sacraments based on the merits of the minister; ibid., 96, p. 57.

129 Ibid., 100, p. 59. Likewise, an intended harm can unwittingly produce a good. In a matching eye-related story, a Saracen, seeking help from a woman for his eye complaint, is

depending on the level of their contrition; the one that has a hard heart receives a heavy penance. Jacques uses this to exemplify the hardness of heart, the obstinacy, that distinguishes heretics according to the Biblical model given by Titus, which he makes contemporary by the gloss 'who are called *consolati* or *perfecti'*.[130]

Jacques's stories are aimed not at coercion or debate, but at protection of the flock via preaching. His opposition to heresy is indirect; his message is about the relative value of heretics and the church's representatives and, while heresy may be a problem of belief, heretics also present a problem of allegiance. In a sermon on the theme 'that we should refresh ourselves in the treasury of the Scriptures before refreshing others', one *exemplum* shows Jacques in direct contact with heretics. It concerns an occasion on which he is involved in a debate in the Albi region with some heretics, here called 'little foxes' and unspecified by name, but identifiable as Cathars from the brief description of their error: 'they assert that the devil created all things visible and corporal'. The Catholic party are not succeeding, and the heretics are shouting that the Catholics are unable to convince them clearly by authorities. Jacques's party challenges one of the heretics to make the sign of a cross, and his inability to do so means that they are finally recognized as heretics.[131]

Here, where heresy appears within the story its presence is simply illustrative; a convenient demonstration of the sermon's theme, the uses of Scriptural knowledge. As with others of Jacques's and in fact Stephen's *exempla*, particularly those drawn from older sources, heresy is simply a part of the story's context – Jacques tells two stories about the Arians, who serve to illustrate the character of St Athanasius, while giving very little attention to the heresy that they contain.[132] In those examples that are drawn from Jacques's own time and experience, though, their presence in the background takes on a more immediate character of competition. The type of conflict with heretics that Jacques describes in southern France is also a part of his life. In his *Historia occidentalis*, first composed around 1221, Jacques gives a description of the *Humiliati* of northern Italy, who, he tells us, were particularly effective in combating the 'heretics whom they call 'Patarines'. As well as revealing their lies and confounding them in public, they caused many to return to the faith and turn against their own kind; the heretics are described here again as 'vulpeculae'.[133]

given quicklime by her servant, instead of ointment. He returns, cured, after eight days to thank the woman. The interpretation which Jacques gives to this story, which he says he remembers from his time in the east, is that while heretics try to harm Catholics, 'eos magis exercitatos et acutos in scripturis et fidei defensione reddunt'; ibid., 99, pp. 58–9.

130 Ibid., 101, pp. 59–60. Titus 3.10–11: 'hereticum hominem post unam et secundam correptionem devita, sciens quia subversus est qui huiusmodi est'.

131 'Vulpeculae'; 'asserunt quod omnia visibilia et corporalia creavit diabolus'; Vitry, Crane, xxvi, p. 9.

132 Vitry, Greven, 92, 93, p. 55.

133 'Hereticis quos patarinos appellant'; Jacques de Vitry, *Historia occidentalis*, ed. Hinnebusch, pp. 144–6.

Jacques's contact with, and respect for, the *Humiliati* perhaps grew out of his own attempts to preach against the 'Patarines' in this region while on his way to Rome to be consecrated as bishop of Acre, which he described in one of his letters. After nearly losing all his belongings and his books, his 'arma', in a swollen river, he arrives at Milan, which he calls a pit of heretics, 'fovea hereticorum'. He tries to preach there, but finds 'in the whole city hardly anyone who resisted the heretics', except for the *Humiliati*.[134] Anti-heretical preaching is not just about ensuring right belief, it is also about countering a powerful set of rivals.

Dominican sources

A significant tradition in mid-century writing about heresy is to be found within texts written by Dominicans for use and circulation within the Order. The lives of their saints and brothers, written for the edification of the brethren and the reinforcement of the Order, describe the early days of its development: a southern French landscape of trials, and miracles, and a reasonable number of heretics. The principal sources are hagiographical: early lives of the Order's founder Saint, Dominic, and its first martyr, Peter of Verona. Next to these there is also a collection of stories about the lives of the earliest Dominicans known as the *Vitae fratrum*. These stories do more than preserve and record the Order's origins. Luigi Canetti's *L'invenzione della memoria* looks specifically at the development of an internal tradition of the Order in these early works and shows the way in which they build a Dominican idea of themselves.[135] For Canetti, the development of Dominican identity is closely tied to, and indeed can be traced through, the development of the image of their founder-Saint, St Dominic, as he is redefined into a series of prototypes, or models, for the Order's contemporary needs.[136] And this is a specifically Dominican, rather than mendicant, tradition. A search for descriptions or discussions of heresy in the equivalent, contemporary Franciscan tradition, the lives of St Francis and of St Anthony and the Order's chronicles, yields a very scanty return in comparison to the Dominican texts. While the character of heresy is similar, there is no parallel with either the relative prominence that heretics have in the Dominican texts or in the role that they play in the formation of a regular identity.[137] Within Canetti's framework of a consciously created Dominican

---

134 'Vix autem invenitur in tota civitate qui resistat hereticis'; Jacques de Vitry, *Lettres de Jacques de Vitry (1160/70–1240), évêque de St.-Jean-d'Acre*, ed. R. B. C. Huygens (Leiden, 1960), Letter 1.34–54, pp. 72–3.

135 Canetti, *L'invenzione*.

136 This seems to be a perspective on the Dominican written tradition not dissimilar to the re-imagining of the lives of St Francis and the early Franciscan brethren by successive biographers in light of debates over poverty and the interpretation of the Rule. See, for example, J. Moorman, *A History of the Franciscan Order from its Origins to the Year 1517* (Oxford, 1968), pp. 278–91.

137 The main examples are: The holiness of St Francis confounds heretics and extols the

identity we can look at how heresy and the repression of heresy fits into the Dominicans' idea of themselves in terms of their origin, their vocation and their ongoing mission and activity.

Vitae of St Dominic

There are four main *vitae* of St Dominic from this period, beginning with that contained in the *Libellus* of Jordan of Saxony in 1232-3, an account of the origins of the Order, upon which the subsequent lives are ultimately based. There then follow the *legendae* by Peter Ferrandi (in 1235-39) and Constantine of Orvieto (in the mid 1240s; perhaps 1246?), as well as Humbert of Romans' version, which became the official Life of St Dominic for the Order in 1260, to the exclusion of those written previously, though it is essentially a cunning amalgam of the earlier accounts.[138]

Vitae of St Peter Martyr

There are three accounts of Peter Martyr's life and death from this period, the principal one being that by Thomas Agni of Lentino, written before 1267. It is from this text that the *Legenda aurea* version is lifted.[139] The other account, though much shorter, is apparently by a close friend of the Saint, Henry of Scacabarazzi, and is to be found in the *Vitae fratrum*.[140]

---

faithful; Thomas de Celano *vita prima*, pt.1, cap. xxii, p. 47; Thomas de Celano, *legenda chori*, para. 9, p. 122; Julianus de Spira, cap. x, p. 357. St Francis performs a miracle with a capon and confounds a heretic; Thomas de Celano, *vita secunda*, pt.2, cap. xlviii, pp. 177–8; see also Jacobus de Voragine (Iacopo da Varazze), *Legenda Aurea*, ed. G. P. Maggioni, 2nd edn, 2 vols. (Florence, 1998), II, 1028. St Francis converts Patarines; Henrici Abrincensis, *legenda versificata*. lib.vi. 1.140, p. 447. Page references are to *Legendae S. Francisci Assisiensis I*, Analecta Franciscana, sive Chronica aliaque varia Documenta ad Historiam Fratrum Minorum 10 (Quaracchi, 1941). Also, Anthony of Padua converts some heretics through preaching and debate: L. de Kerval (ed.), *Sancti Antonii de Padua vitae duae quarum altera hucusque inedita* (Paris, 1904), pp. 41–2.

138 All these 'lives' are to be found edited in MOPH 16 (1935): Jordan of Saxony, *Libellus de principiis Ordinis Praedicatorum*, ed. H. C. Scheeben, pp. 1–88 (translation of *Libellus* by Simon Tugwell: Jordan of Saxony, *On the Beginnings of the Order of Preachers* (Dublin, 1982). Tugwell advises reading the Scheeben edition alongside the older but more reliable *Acta Sanctorum* edition: Jordan of Saxony, *On the Beginnings*, Tugwell, p. xiii). Peter Ferrandi, *Legenda sancti Dominici*, ed. M. H. Laurent, pp. 197–260. Constantine of Orvieto, *Legenda sancti Dominici*, ed. H. C. Scheeben, pp. 263–352. Humbert of Romans, *Legenda sancti Dominici*, ed. A. Walz, pp. 355–433. There is also a brief abridged Life by Bartholomew of Trent, 1245–50, edited by B. Altaner, *Der hl. Dominikus. Untersuchungen und Texte*, Breslauer Studien zur Historischen Theologie 2 (Breslau, 1922), edition of text on pp. 229–39.

139 Thomas Agni de Lentino, *Legenda beati Petri Martyris*, in *Acta Sanctorum*, April 3, 29, cols. 686–719. Golden Legend version: Jacobus de Voragine, *Legenda Aurea*, ed. Maggioni, I, 421–42; translated as *Jacobus de Voragine, The Golden Legend, Readings on the Saints*, trans. W. Granger Ryan, 2 vols. (Princeton, NJ, 1993), I, 254–66.

140 *Vitae fratrum*, translated as *Lives of the Brethren of the Order of Preachers*, trans. P. Conway, ed.

Vitae fratrum

According to Simon Tugwell's examination of its development, the *Vitae fratrum*, sometimes *Vitas fratrum*, was originally begun by Gerard of Frachet in the 1250s as an instructional book for novices of the same type as Caesarius's *Dialogus miraculorum*, before it was gradually incorporated into the collection of stories about the Order's members that was started in the General chapter of 1255, of which Gerard, and subsequently Humbert of Romans, was editor. There is no one definitive manuscript version of this text.[141] It was a text aimed solely at the brethren and their edification, as well as the preservation of Dominican history; some of the stories that it contains have the character of *exempla*.

Heresy appears consistently in the Dominican tradition in connection with the Order's origins in Diego's mission in Toulouse in the opening decade of the thirteenth century. During this time Dominic was preaching as part of the anti-heretical movement which swept the south in these early decades, initially as a companion to his bishop, Diego of Osma, and then at the head of his own small group, and several significant encounters between Dominic and heretics are recorded in the various Lives. All of these texts cover similar ground with regard to Dominic's early encounters with heresy, of which a sketch follows, based on Jordan's account.

While on a mission to Toulouse Bishop Diego is moved to pity by the level to which heresy is ingrained in the region; meanwhile, his sub-prior, Dominic, converts their host, who is a heretic, by arguing with him all night: 'the heretic was not able to resist'.[142] Diego and his party then join a Cistercian legation sent to combat heresy, which is meeting with little success. Diego advises the monks to dispense with their excessive clothing and provisions and lead by apostolic example, as he himself then does, sending most of his followers home and retaining only a few who will stay with him and spread the faith. Among this number is, of course, the future St Dominic. Dominic is soon able to demonstrate his latent sanctity in a famous miracle, which Jordan places at Fanjeaux: at a public debate between heretical and Catholic groups, the written arguments of both sides are subjected to trial by fire.[143] Dominic's text, which has been chosen by the Catholic side to represent their views, leaps unharmed from the fire. The heretics understand this, according to Jordan, as a sign that

---

with notes and intro. B. Jarrett (London, 1955). *Vitae fratrum* account of Peter of Verona on pp. 236–48 and pp. 205–14 respectively.

141 S. Tugwell, 'L'évolution des *vitae fratrum*. Résumé des conclusions provisoires'; in *CF* 36 (2001), 415–18.

142 'Non posset hereticus resistere'; Jordan, MOPH 16, pp. 33–4.

143 The earliest account of this miracle, by Peter of les Vaux-de-Cernay, to which Humbert returns in his version, places it not at Fanjeaux, but at Montréal; *Hystoria albigensis*, ed. P. Guébin and E. Lyon, 3 vols. (Paris, 1926–39), I, 47–9.

Diego (not Dominic) is holy and has been sent to learn their faith. Diego founds the convent of Prouille to provide for the daughters of poor nobles who, because of their poverty, must be educated by heretics. He remains in Toulouse for two years, and dies on his return to Spain.

Dominic is now left on his own in an unofficial capacity, with only a few companions, and at this time the Albigensian crusade is launched in the region. No explicit connection between Dominic and the crusade is made by Jordan; he simply tells us that Dominic remains in the region until the death of Simon de Montfort, 'constantly preaching the word of God'. Though this is not specified as anti-heretical preaching, Dominic endures threats and mockery from the heretics with characteristic patience and an apparent desire for martyrdom. He tries to sell himself to save a man who follows the heretics only because they support him financially. Dominic apparently continues in this vein until the time of the Fourth Lateran Council, but no further details of this time are provided and heresy does not make another appearance in Jordan's account of the 'Origins of the Order of Preachers'.

What is interesting with regard to the role of heresy is the way in which the significance of these same basic events develops in the course of the later *legendae* and their representation of the Order's foundation, something that Canetti's evaluation of these sources makes clear. Perhaps the most obvious change is the gradual replacement over time of Diego with Dominic as the principal actor in this phase of the Saint's life, something which the promotion of Dominic's cult and the re-attribution to him of the role of founder made necessary.[144] The next of the lives to appear, Ferrandi's *legenda*, is certainly based on Jordan's original version, but adds a lot of its own material. Diego is still present in the same capacity, but now it is Dominic who is presented as the one who is initially moved by the heresy he sees in the Midi, and the miracle of the fire at Fanjeaux is accentuated when the text is made to leap a further two times from the fire.[145] Ferrandi follows the same pattern as Jordan until Dominic's attempt to sell himself, at which point he adds a story in which Dominic converts some Toulousain nobles from heresy by outdoing the heretics who are staying with them in his levels of abstinence and abnegation during Lent. That new section is striking in the invective that it introduces into the hitherto rather dry descriptions of the heretics inherited from Jordan, calling on many anti-heretical images, including ravening wolves and a false appearance of piety, to illustrate its attack. From this point, this story forms an integral part of the following lives. Ferrandi also adds that the heretics are

---

[144] Reltgen-Tallon, 'L'historiographie des Dominicains du Midi', pp. 395–414, 398.

[145] Peter Ferrandi, MOPH 16, pp. 216, 220. Ferrandi is perhaps influenced by Peter of les Vaux-de-Cernay's version, in which the paper leaps unharmed from the fire three times. He also doubles the number of times Dominic tries to sell himself, adding a reflection of the original (itself of rather dubious veracity) in which Dominic tries again to sell himself to help a woman whose brother is held by Saracens.

twisted with envy at Dominic's perfection.[146] With Constantine's account, the suggestion that the heretics wanted to recruit Diego is omitted from the Fanjeaux miracle account, and there is no mention of Prouille or its foundation. By the time we reach Humbert's *legenda*, again, it is Dominic who is initially disturbed by the heresy, as Humbert lifts this almost entirely from Ferrandi, but now it is also Dominic who is the founder of Prouille.[147]

The view of the Order's origins and the centrality of heresy that these texts present is refracted in a variety of ways through other Dominican texts. Stephen of Bourbon, for example, in an incidental remark, places the founding of the Order at Diego's abandonment of his retinue in order to preach in the Midi, but does not connect it with heresy.[148] At the same time, for Gerard of Frachet, heresy is the sole reason for the foundation of the Order. The first paragraph of his section on Brothers who have died for the faith, which begins with an account of the Martyrs of Avignonet and Peter of Verona, opens: 'the Order of Preachers having been founded by St Dominic in Toulouse, specially to combat heresy and errors' and goes on to make an explicit connection between this and the assignment of the office of inquisition to the brothers.[149] The Dominican chronicler William Pelhisson is equally confident that the repression of heresy represents the vocation and principal reason for the founding of his order: 'the blessed Dominic instituted the said order against heretics and their believers'.[150]

Perhaps more significant for the place of heresy in the Dominican tradition is the reinterpretation of Dominic's life and image in light of the Order's subsequent involvement in the office of inquisition. There has been some dispute, most notably between Thouzellier and Vicaire, over whether or not Dominic himself could ever be called an 'inquisitor'. Thouzellier believed that he was, if not an inquisitor, a 'precocious example of inquisitorial zeal', to use the phrase that so annoyed Vicaire, operating within a well-established papal tradition of repression. Vicaire thought the whole thing anachronistic, and that Dominic

---

146 Ibid., pp. 225–6, 228.
147 Humbert, MOPH 16, pp. 377, 382. Humbert leaves Ferrandi's account to revert to Peter of les Vaux-de-Cernay's for the fire miracle, making it not only a private event, but also placing it at Montréal, as Peter does.
148 Stephen of Bourbon, *Tractatus*, p. 79; this version does not appear to correspond to those found in any of the Lives.
149 'Cum ordo predicatorum a beato Dominico contra hereses et errores specialiter fuerit institutus Tolose'; *Vitae fratrum*, p. 231; *Lives of the Brethren*, trans. Conway, p. 201, though, curiously, Gerard doesn't mention any heretical involvement in his description of the murder of William Arnold and Stephen of St Thibéry and their party. The account of Dominic in the *Vitae fratrum* includes only one occurrence of heresy, and it is not one recorded in the *legendae*, perhaps because, being concurrent with Humbert's official account, this could not be a 'life' of Dominic; Canetti, *L'invenzione*, p. 479.
150 'Beati Dominici ... dictum Ordinem instituit contra hereticos et eorum credentes'; William Pelhisson, *Chronique (1229–1244) suivie du récit des troubles d'Albi (1229–1244)*, ed. J. Duvernoy, Sources d'Histoire Médiévales publiées par l'Institut de Recherches et d'Histoire des Textes (Paris, 1994), p. 34; see also pp. 64, 96.

did none of the things that mark inquisitorial behaviour, such as legal inquiry or interrogation of witnesses.[151]

Whichever is closer to the truth in real terms, in the written tradition of St Dominic at least, as Canetti shows, the Saint came to be represented more and more as a prototype of Dominican inquisitors. For Canetti, the 'providential anti-heretical significance' of Dominic's sanctity was tied to the Order's involvement in inquisition.[152] He concurs with Merlo's theory that the canonization of St Dominic to some degree sanctioned the office of inquisition, and extends this further by placing the canonization in the context of Innocent III's policy of 'confusio heretice', via persuasion and coercion. The canonization itself then arose partly out of a need, both of the Order and the pope, to legitimize this unpopular office.[153] The change in the lives appears first in the mid-century *Legenda* of Constantine. Up until this point in the hagiographical tradition all contact between Dominic and heresy had taken place very firmly in the years before Dominic founded his Order. Now Constantine adds two more examples post-foundation in the process of accumulating miracles around the figure of St Dominic that marks this version of the Life.[154] The first is a story in which a huge and unpleasant cat assails Dominic and nine ladies

---

[151] This debate can be found in *Annales du Midi* 80 (1968), 121–38.

[152] Canetti, *L'invenzione*, p. 103. Caldwell similarly makes a case for the *vitae* of Peter Martyr as part of a move to articulate Dominican identity through its saints, at a time when the order was undergoing some difficulties; (as Caldwell) 'Peter Martyr: The Inquisitor as Saint', *Comitatus* 31 (2000), 137–74, and (as Caldwell Ames) *Righteous Persecution: Inquisition, Dominicans, and Christianity in the Middle Ages* (Philadelphia, PA, 2009).

[153] Constantine, according to Tugwell, 'had all the instincts of the worst kind of hagiographer'; S. Tugwell, 'Notes on the Life of St. Dominic', *AFP* 65 (1995), 5–169 (p. 31). Canetti, *L'invenzione*, pp. 244, 96. All of the Lives of St Dominic are post-canonization, so the change in his image must be part of an ongoing process. At the time Jordan was writing his *Libellus* the office of inquisition was still young and had perhaps not yet built up the level of hostility that it later acquired. Papal policy certainly seems to have been to regard the Order as closely connected to anti-heretical activity, though Cistercians and Franciscans continued to make up an equally important part of the Papal inquisition. Gregory's original mandate for the commission for Dominic's canonization does indeed mention heresy. A letter sent by the Cardinals to the Order after the killing of Peter of Verona, which Gerard of Frachet reproduces, seems to regard the Order as being instituted to deal with heresy, at least in some capacity. A letter of Innocent IV to Raymond of Peñafort entitled *De haeresi extirpanda* similarly regards the Order in this light: 'in his autem, nobis fratres vestri ordinis Dominus specialiter voluit esse adjutores'; Mansi, XXIII, 568. However, not many of the witnesses of Dominic's canonization process seem to have felt heresy to be a significant part of Dominic's life; only two of the nine in the Bologna process and five of the twenty-three in the Toulousain process mention it. These are previous to the rewriting and reinterpretation of St Dominic's life, but even despite the developments in the tradition of Dominic the majority of his contact with heresy in these sources is presented as occurring in the period of his life before he founded the Order. There was surely more anti-heretical material to be found in Dominic's later involvement in preaching missions in Lombardy, which were directed, not entirely, but primarily, against heresy, for those looking to enhance his image as a specifically anti-heretical saint.

[154] Reltgen-Tallon, 'L'historiographie des Dominicains du Midi', p. 399.

who are wavering between heresy and Catholicism, and who have come to Dominic for advice; this story is repeated almost verbatim by Stephen of Bourbon.[155] The second sees Dominic saving one of a group of heretics from the pyre after having a premonition that he will convert. What is significant about this account is that Constantine tells us that it was Dominic himself who convicted the heretics.[156] Both these additions are included by Humbert in his *legenda*. Stephen of Salanhac, writing slightly later, makes this connection explicit in his gloss interpreting the signs around Dominic's birth. By the time of Bernard Gui's continuation of Stephen's *De quatuor in quibus* in the early part of the fourteenth century this image of Dominic as the first inquisitor was firmly established in the hagiographical tradition.[157]

The exact nature of Dominic's inquisitorial role is not always so clear or consistent in other Dominican texts of this period. No mention is made at all of the papal commission to the Order of the office of inquisition in the *Chronica ordinis*, for example, despite the fact that it demonstrates a general concern to record official progression and appointments of the order and to align itself with papal policy.[158] There appears to be some ambiguity, too, about the office of inquisition in Humbert of Romans' views on preaching. Humbert's *Liber de eruditione praedicatorum* aims very determinedly to confirm and defend preaching as the vocation of the Order.[159] Heresy may perhaps form part of the stimulus to this vocation, if the 'demons' that 'have applied themselves with great diligence and for a very long time to subjugating the whole world' can be understood in this way, but it remains only one reason in this chapter on the necessity of preaching and does not represent a vocation in itself.[160] Brett shows Humbert to be accepting of inquisition, but not uncritical.[161] He also points to Humbert's view that 'odious occupations' that cause hostility, such as 'the receiving of delegates, inquisitions, visitations, and other such matters of judgement', should be avoided by the preacher so as not to prevent his preaching having good effects.[162] Though Tugwell's observation that this does not necessarily refer exclusively to inquisitions of heretical

---

155 Stephen of Bourbon, *Tractatus* / Stephen of Bourbon, lib.1, pp. 34–5/165–6.
156 Constantine, MOPH 16, pp. 320–22.
157 Canetti, *L'invenzione*, pp. 253–5, 102–3.
158 The *Chronica ordinis* is appended to Reichert's edition of the *Vitae fratrum* in MOPH 1 (1896), 321–38.
159 S. Tugwell (ed. and trans.), *Early Dominicans, Selected Writings* (New York, 1984), p. 182.
160 'A longo tempore ad subjugandum sibi mundum totum'; Humbert, *Opera*, II, 377. Tugwell, *Early Dominicans*, p. 187.
161 E. T. Brett, *Humbert of Romans: His Life and Views of Thirteenth-Century Society* (Toronto, 1984), p. 166.
162 'Receptio compromissorum, inquisitiones, visitationes, et hujusmodi judicalia'. The phrase is echoed in another of Humbert's works, *Super constitutiones fratrum praedicatorum*: 'secundum est [impedimenta fructus animarum] officia odiosa, ut sunt inquisitiones, visitationes et correctiones violentae, exactiones testamentorum arbitrorum sententiae, ex quibus conturbatur frequenter hominum devotio ad fratres'; Humbert, *Opera*, II, 474, 36, cited by Brett, *Humbert of Romans*, p. 165.

depravity is of course true, these latter must surely still be covered by this list.[163]

At the same time other authors are very matter of fact, and indeed quite explicit, about the functions of, and their involvement in, the inquisitorial process. The Louvain Dominican Thomas of Cantimpré describes a heretic called Gilles Boogris driven into hiding by his fear that he will be discovered and burned by the Dominicans. Thomas casually remarks, almost as an aside, that this was at the time when 'they had made many climb upon the fire'.[164] As we saw above, several times in his *Tractatus* Stephen of Bourbon describes himself as an inquisitor and twice mentions his involvement in the trial and condemnation of a large group of 'Manicheen heretics'. William Pelhisson is even more forward, partly because inquisition is a much more central part of his narrative than it is for Stephen. William gives us the details of his involvement with no qualms whatsoever: 'Friar Arnold Catalan with Friar William Pelhisson ... making inquisition against heretics in Albi ... condemned Peter of Podiumperditum and Peter Bomacip, who were burnt alive'.[165] William can perhaps be placed within the southern tradition of Dominican writers that Reltgen-Tallon describes who were more able than were the northern, university-based Dominicans to reconcile their involvement in inquisition with the wider Dominican vocation, and indeed saw their work as forming a continuum with the original purpose of Dominic's early years.[166] The fact that both William and Stephen were themselves active inquisitors for many years may also have made it easier to reconcile inquisition with their vocation.

In general, though, there does seem to be a certain level of ambivalence in the Dominican representation of their actions in connection with heresy. Action against heretics is rarely emphasized and it is equally rare to find any specifically judicial element. What is emphasized instead is the 'zeal for souls' with which St Dominic is so frequently characterized, conversion and the good

---

[163] Tugwell, *Early Dominicans*, p. 324, n. 76.

[164] This story is from a moralizing treatise on bees composed between 1256 and 1263 by Thomas of Cantimpré, an itinerant Dominican from Louvain. The *Bonum universale* contains a large number of *exempla*, many of which – but not all – have been extracted and translated by Henri Platelle. According to Berlioz about a third have been omitted from Platelle's translation; none of the *exempla* that Berlioz adds appear to contain heresy. Thomas of Cantimpré, *Les exemples du Livre des Abeilles*, ed. and trans. H. Platelle (Turnhout, 1997); J. Berlioz, P. Collomb and M. A. Polo de Beaulieu, 'La face cachée de Thomas de Cantimpré. Compléments à une traduction française récente du *Bonum universale de apibus*', *AHDLMA* 68 (2001), 73–94 (pp. 269–70). Caldwell points out that inquisition itself functioned as a mode of piety within the Dominican's model of their apostolate, 'Peter Martyr: The Inquisitor as Saint', esp. p. 147.

[165] 'Frater Arnaldus Cathalanus et Frater Guillelmus Pelhisso in Albia faciebant inquisitionem ... contra hereticos, ubi Petrum de Podio Perdito et Petrum de Bono Mancipio condempnaverunt, qui vivi combusti sunt'; William Pelhisson, *Chronique*, p. 58; trans. (adjusted) W. L. Wakefield, *Heresy, Crusade and Inquisition in Southern France 1100–1250* (London, 1974), pp. 214–15.

[166] Reltgen-Tallon, 'L'historiographie des Dominicains du Midi', *passim*.

example of the brethren. Even in the story of Peter Martyr, which is full to the brim with heresy, there is no story concerning his action as an inquisitor – he debates with heretics, he is chosen by the pope to be an inquisitor, we are told that he pursues heretics, but see none of this described, and then he is martyred. Gerard of Frachet, though he describes Peter as an inquisitor, does not frame any of his encounters with heretics in the context of an inquisition; similarly account of the Martyrs of Avignonet. On the whole, in the edifying literature, where there is any action against heretics, inquisitorial or otherwise, there are no consequences for the heretics involved unless it is conversion or confutation. None of the heretical opponents in the various public debates that appear in these accounts are handed over to the secular arm; indeed, often any retribution or defeats that they may suffer are not through the agency of the Friars Preacher, but by divine intervention. They may leave defeated, or converted, but they are rarely seen to be punished by the Dominicans.[167]

Instead, the main arena for contact between the Dominicans and the heretics is nearly always that of debate or verbal confrontation. The various accounts of Diego of Osma's mission all recount the stories of St Dominic in private discussion with his heretical host and in public debate with the local heretics. Indeed, Dominic and his opponents, in the debate at Montréal, are so evenly matched that the judges are unable to decide between them; noticeable also is that both parties' arguments are in a written, text-based form.[168] Peter Martyr, too, is involved in debates, both in private with his heretical family, and in public with the heretical élite. We see him confront in debate a 'heretic of great ability and eloquence', as well as a Catholic bishop turned bad. He argues with his own family members, in a dispute based on written authorities: 'his uncle then tried to prove to him by authorities ... that the devil created these things, but, what was wonderful, [the child] turned all these authorities against him in such a fashion that he could find no way to resist him'.[169]

Heretics therefore serve as foils to the brethren to emphasize the importance of example, as well as preaching and debate, in the Dominican ethos. Outside the section that covers Peter of Verona, and one incident involving St Dominic, heresy appears in the *Vitae fratrum* in the context of stories which demonstrate, through visions and divine signs, the merit of individual brothers or the Order in general.[170] In separate stories two heretical Lombard

---

167 On this, see Caldwell Ames, *Righteous Persecution*, pp. 182–227.
168 Jordan, MOPH 16, pp. 33–4, 37–8; Tugwell, *Early Dominicans*, p. 54; Testimony of John of Spain, for canonization of St Dominic, in Tugwell, *Early Dominicans*, p. 75; Jordan, MOPH 16, p. 37; Tugwell, *Early Dominicans*, p. 54.
169 'Tunc patruus nisus est ei probare per auctoritates ... quod dyabolus ista creaverit ... sed mirum valde, quod ita omnes illas auctoritates contra eum convertit, quod in nullo potuit ei resistere'; *Vitae fratrum*, pp. 236–9.
170 The *Vitae fratrum* account of St Dominic is limited by the fact that it does not cover the same

women are converted after receiving visions of the Order as divinely appointed. A Provençal medic, led astray by the apparently greater piety of the Waldensians, returns to the faith again by virtue of a vision that shows this piety to be only superficial. Gerard's chapter on miracles wrought by the brethren contains several stories in which heretics are converted by the miracles' power.[171] Heresy, or rather the activity of the heretics, is presented as a stimulus to Dominican activity and for many of the Order's early recruits, such as Peter Martyr and a young Tuscan man, Florimund. The most obvious example of this function is the occasion on which Diego, in Jordan's account, draws a parallel between the heretics and the pseudo-apostles and persuades the Cistercian legates that the false sanctity of the heretics can be defeated only by a display of genuine holiness: 'chase off their feigned holiness with true religious life', exhorts Diego. 'The imposing appearance of the false apostles can only be shown up for what it is by manifest humility'. So they must lose their luxuries, and in this Diego leads the way himself.[172] The one story involving heretics that Gerard includes in his account of St Dominic revolves around the quiet and steadfast patience shown by the saint towards a heretic who has deliberately led him astray, through thorns and brambles, while he is on his way to the famous debate at Montréal. By his shining example, which is of course the point of the story, he is able to win the man over and convert him.[173] There is further mockery of St Dominic himself, in the *Libellus* and John of Mailly's account, all of which allows an opportunity for Dominic to demonstrate his forbearance, as well as his divine sanction, when such mockery is punished by miracles.[174] Likewise, in a story of a heretic who feigns possession to escape the attention of the inquisitors in Thomas of Cantimpré's *exempla* collection, the 'possessed' heretic pays no respect to St Acharius, and is duly punished.[175]

The representation of heretics, then, also plays a wider role in the construction of the Dominicans as legitimate successors to the apostolic life, and, in their turn, heretics are characterized predominantly by the insincerity of their appearance. The theme of false appearance is of course not peculiar to this material, but within the Dominican tradition, at least as it is presented in these texts, false appearance, and indeed the heretics more generally, serves to underline the Dominican claim to true piety; false appearance is therefore prominent in the representation and function of heresy in these texts.

In the *Libellus* account of Diego of Osma's journey to France a church

---

ground as the *legendae*, and so there is little material on the founder in general, and only one occasion in which heresy is involved.

171 *Vitae fratrum*, pp. 22, 183–4, 225–8, 193–5.

172 'Fictam sanctitatem vera religione fugate, quia fastus pseudoapostolorum evidento vult humilitate convinci'; Jordan, MOPH 16, p. 36; trans. Tugwell, p. 6.

173 *Vitae fratrum*, p. 68. For other examples of Dominicans enduring the mockery of heretics, see ibid. pp. 225, 240.

174 Jordan, MOPH 16, pp. 41–2; Tugwell, *Early Dominicans*, p. 55.

175 Thomas of Cantimpré, *Les exemples*, ed. and trans. Platelle, pp. 269–70.

council at Montpellier explains to Diego, when he enquires, that the local here-tics deceive the people by arguing and preaching and by 'examples of feigned holiness'.[176] John of Mailly, who produced an abbreviated version of Jordan's account, omits the arguing and preaching, and reports only the 'false appear-ance of virtue'.[177] A more elaborate rendering of the same theme can be found in one of the stories in the *Vitae fratrum*, in which Florimund, a young Tuscan adherent of the Cathars – here called the 'Albigensians' – discovers after years of membership that the true nature of the doctrine is dualist. A chance remark – as they are talking in the sun, one of his companions exclaims: 'see how Lucifer bestows his warmth upon us' – startles Florimund to such an extent that his companion asks: 'do you still not know that the devil created these visible things?' Florimund rounds up as many of his heretical companions as he can and asks why no one has told him of this belief, even though he has been with them for twelve years – an omission reminiscent of the differing levels of initiation that Raniero Sacconi describes. Florimund demands that they provide support for their doctrine and, when their arguments prove inad-equate, he decides he cannot accept this belief and looks for another; unsurprisingly he chooses Catholicism and becomes a Dominican, hence the story's inclusion here.[178]

The theme finds a characteristically arresting expression in the work of a now familiar Dominican, Stephen of Bourbon, who also employs this motif. He adapts a quotation from Matthew – 'they tear at their faces, that they may appear to others to be fasting' – to reinforce his point that heretics mislead people with the sophistry and duplicity of their words. Stephen's description of the Waldensians, 'displaying the appearance of holiness and faith', also includes the equally evocative though more literally intended description of a heretic who, 'like a Proteus, transformed himself'. The latter description refers rather to physical appearance, but also recalls the language of the Corinthians verse on the pseudo-apostles, often attached to heretics' false appearance.[179]

In these accounts the heretics function in much the same way as they do in

---

176 'Simulate sanctitatis exemplis'; Jordan, MOPH 16, p. 36.

177 Tugwell, *Early Dominicans*, p. 54.

178 'Ecce quomodo nos lucifer calefacit!'; 'nescis tu adhuc, quod dyabolus hec visibilia fecit?'; *Vitae fratrum*, pp. 184–6; trans. (adjusted) Conway, p. 161.

179 'Excoriant facies suas, ut videantur ab hominibus jejunantes'; 'speciem sanctitatis et fidei pretendentes'; 'quasi Proteus se transfigurabat'; Stephen of Bourbon, *Tractatus*, pp. 311, 293, and see below, p. 168. In the Württemberg Bible Society edition of the vulgate, the text of Matthew 6.16 runs thus: 'demoliuntur enim facies suas ut pareant hominibus ieiunantes'; *Biblia sacra iuxta vulgatam versionem*, ed. R. Weber et al., 2 vols. (Stuttgart, 1969), II, 1534. The Clementine version is: 'exterminant enim facies suas, ut appareant hominibus ieiunantes'; *Biblia sacra iuxta vulgatam Clementinam*, ed. A. Colunga and L. Turrado, 4th edn (Salamanca, 1965). 2 Corinthians 11.13–15. The Dominican Thomas of Cantimpré talks about heresy infrequently in his *exempla* collection, but those stories that he does include revolve around the familiar theme of deception and false appearance. As well as Giles Boogris, he also tells the story of a man named William Cornelius. Considered holy all his life because of his poverty, his deception was so effective that it was discovered only after

the *exempla* collections proper, as elements in a narrative rather than subjects in themselves. Their presence is dependent on their dissent in as much as it is their conversion that drives the force of the story: it is important that they are heretics, but the error that makes them heretics is not. With a few exceptions, heretics are generic in this hagiographical and biographical body of work, and it is their status as heretics that is significant. Belief makes only rare appearances and generally is simply one of the things that mark individuals out as 'heretics', the non-specific label used almost universally in these texts to describe those individuals.[180] In the widely focused *Vitae fratrum*, at least, heretics seem often to be present almost incidentally. Those heretics that feature as proof of the miracles of the brethren feature among other very similar stories which do not depend on the presence of heretics at all, and their inclusion seems to rely as much on their general presence in the world of the stories' authors as on the purpose of the stories themselves. That Gerard is not writing these accounts for himself, but editing contributions from brothers living all over Europe, suggests that to some extent heretics are included as a commonplace of contemporary life. But they more often tend to fulfil a similar *exemplum*-style purpose of illustrating the sanctity of Dominican notables.

Heretics are, among other things, the competition, and it is a contest being fought by both sides on the same criteria of piety and apostolic lifestyle. The fineness of the line between them is brought home by the fate of Franciscan missions from Italy in the early decades of the Order. One group of missionaries, who travel to the south of France, are asked by the locals if they are heretics. The Italian missionaries reply, in all innocence and a failure to understand the question, that yes, they are. The confusion is resolved in this case, but another group who travel to Germany and encounter the same situation are less fortunate.[181] For a Dominican identity that has competition and conflict with heretics so close to its core, the insistence on the falseness of the piety that

---

his death that he had believed that poverty destroyed all sin, as rust is destroyed by fire; Thomas of Cantimpré, *Bonum universale*, ed. and trans. Platelle, pp. 198–9.

180 The occasional differentiation of Waldensian heretics might suggest in these instances a corresponding use of 'heretic' to mean Cathar, in the southern French mode. Gerard of Frachet's text is less uniform in its presentation than the others by virtue of its nature as a collection, but most of the entries nonetheless use the term 'heretic' with little distinction.

181 Jordan of Giano, *Chronica fratris Jordani*, ed. H. Boehmer, Collection d'Études et de Documents sur l'Histoire Religieuse et Littéraire du Moyen Age 6 (Paris, 1908), pp. 5–6; translated in E. Gurney-Salter (trans.), *The Coming of the Friars Minor to England and Germany* (London, 1926), pp. 132–4. The dangers of the language barrier rear their head. The brothers spoke little German, and simply replied 'ja' to all questions asked of them, that method having initially proved effective. The luckier ones seem only to have lost their habits, but Jordan says that, from this point on, 'Germany was considered ... to be such a ferocious country that only those inspired by a longing for martyrdom would dare to return thither'. The unfortunate fate of the Franciscan brothers suggests that heretics were sufficiently common in both regions for all indeterminate wandering religious to be assumed to be heretics.

would otherwise give the heretics a claim on apostolic legitimacy is necessary to construct the Dominican version as different.

Across the whole range of these texts there is a strong impression of heresy as a contemporary phenomenon, which stems not only from the use of material that seems to address and describe events from memory or experience, but also from the fact that heresy often appears in the background as a common-place and sometimes un-remarked feature of contemporary life. Though the picture of heresy throughout these sources is varied, several constants seem to function in its representation, not least the theme of false appearance. Often, also, a connection to supernatural powers is made, either in terms of the power or origin of the heretics or in terms of their punishment.

In the context of edification and improvement more generally, stories of heresy and the lives of heretics, to a greater or lesser degree, seem to serve most often as plausible and effective cautionary elements, usually in the service of some wider point. The individual heretic, and not the heretical error or belief itself, forms the basis for, and usually the focus of, these discussions. Any edifying purpose is not aimed at the heretics themselves; rather, heretics are used as a tool for the improvement of others, something that rests in large part on their plausibility and familiarity as a feature of the contemporary land-scape. It is most obvious in the case of the *exempla* collections, but heresy also serves a similar function in the 'internal' Dominican texts, where the Order's historical involvement with heresy is not only reported but also used selec-tively in the creation of a Dominican identity.

The *Summae auctoritatum*, on the other hand, seem to be, and indeed are framed as, expositions of Catholic doctrine to be used for preaching to the faithful and for teaching basic elements of doctrine to the general populace, a policy that was certainly beginning to emerge in contemporary canon-legal provisions against heresy.[182] But they differ from our other edifying texts in a number of ways, most immediately in their lack of representation, due rather to their abbreviated nature, but more fundamentally in their concentration not on the figure and characteristics of the heretic but instead on points of heretical doctrine. The *Summae auctoritatum* appear to straddle the gap between defen-sive preaching and more proactive attack by being flexible enough to form sermons as easily as they supply material to the polemical tradition. Like the polemics, they tend to proceed against heresy first by refutation and then by defence and reinforcement of the Catholic faith, a pattern that the *Summae* resemble closely, their design allowing them to function both in an edifying role and as a more active form of the polemic approach for use in the debate arena that the Dominican and *exempla* traditions describe so often.

---

[182] See below, p. 97.

3

Who Walks in Shadow:
The Canon-legal Perspective

Quis in tenebris ambulet, quis in luce[1]

The representations of heresy that have been considered so far have all been located in what could loosely be termed a literary context; next to that material, a substantial corpus of legislation against heresy, which formed a distinctive anti-heretical tradition all of its own, was developing. Ultimately, in the mid thirteenth century, that tradition increasingly meant the documentary output of inquisition, but the texts produced by that process will be considered in their own right in the following chapter. This chapter will consider the representation of heresy within the wider tradition of canon law, through conciliar material and through the textbooks of canon law. The former group includes both the canons of the ecumenical councils and especially the canons of the various regional councils, in which many of the more specifically anti-heretical provisions were put in place. Next to the direct legislation must be placed the textbook material that provided the basis for the teaching of canon law, those collections of authorities that informed the wider under-standing of the law – namely Gratian's *Decretum* and the *Liber Extra* of Gregory IX. A systematic and exhaustive description of the vast legal context of heresy is not the purpose here – there will be no serious consideration of imperial or civil law, for example. Rather, the aim is to delineate the main features of the canon-legal treatment of heresy through an examination of those texts that either *are* the principal example of their genre or which can be taken as repre-sentative. To that end, we will begin with a brief panoramic view of heresy as it appears in the ecumenical decrees.

The ecumenical councils of the twelfth century show heresy and the control of heresy gradually gaining in prominence in the internal discussions of the church. Heresy had been a central concern of ecumenical councils since the early days of the Catholic Church, when Catholicism was itself crystallizing out of a variety of opinions and entering a phase of self-definition in which the

[1] Narbonne 43, canon 5, Mansi, XXIII, 357.

demarcation and ownership of true doctrine became the principal criteria for Christian identity.[2] For that reason, most of the early councils are directed specifically against one or more heretical groups: the first council of Nicaea addresses the Arian heresy, Ephesus deals with Nestorianism. The condemnation of heresy was usually accompanied by a statement of orthodox doctrine, the most notable example being the Nicene Creed.[3]

By the twelfth century the general councils were again beginning to devote increasing amounts of space to the re-emergent problem of heresy, their measures reflected in regional meetings and in those councils dedicated to specific individuals – the suppression of Abelard's writings at Sens in 1140, for example.[4] Like the early councils, anti-heretical canons are directed against named individuals, but, over the course of the century, condemnation of less specific groups, 'other schismatics and heretics', gradually becomes commonplace.[5] The 1139 Lateran council, repeating the sentence of Toulouse twenty years earlier, not only condemns 'those who, simulating a kind of religiosity, condemn the sacrament of the Lord's body and blood, the baptism of children' but also 'bind[s] up their defenders with the fetter of the same condemnation'.[6] The generalizing tone continues to grow in the lesser councils, such as Tours in 1163, and is developed more fully by the third Lateran council of 1179.[7] In its final, twenty-seventh canon, alongside a condemnation of mercenary groups,

---

2   R. A. Markus, 'The Problem of Self-Definition: From Sect to Church', in *Jewish and Christian Self-Definition*, ed. E. P. Sanders et al., 3 vols. (London, 1980), I, *The Shaping of Christianity in the Second and Third Centuries*, 1–15 (11–13). W. Bauer, *Orthodoxy and Heresy in Earliest Christianity* (London, 1972), chapter 7. On this process in the high medieval period, see J. Nelson, 'Society, Theodicy and the Origins of Heresy: Towards a Reassessment of the Medieval Evidence', in *Schism, Heresy and Religious Protest*, ed. D. Baker, Studies in Church History 9 (1972), pp. 65–77.

3   *DEC*, I, *Nicaea 1 to Lateran 5*: Nicaea 1 325, can. 8 p. 9, can. 19 p. 15; Constantinople 1 381, can. 6–7 pp. 33–5; Ephesus 431, pp. 40–74; Nicaea 2 787, can. 9, p. 146. Latin text originally published as *Conciliorum oecumenicorum decreta*, ed. J. Alberigo et al. (Bologna, 1962).

4   *DEC*, I: Lateran 1 1123, pp. 190–94, see can. 5 p. 190; Lateran 2 1139, pp. 197–203, see can. 30 p. 203; Lateran 3 1179, pp. 211–25, see can. 27 pp. 224–5. Lateran 4 is on pp. 230–71 of *DEC*, but references here will be to the García edition, *Constitutiones Concilii quarti Lateranensis una cum Commentariis glossatorum*, ed. A. García y García (Vatican City, 1981), see cans. 1–3, pp. 41–51. See earlier discussion by Maisonneuve, *Études*; Lateran 3, esp. pp. 133–9, Lateran 4, esp. pp. 229–33.

5   Gregory VIII in Lateran 1, can. 5, *DEC*, I, 190; Anacletus II in Lateran 2, '… ordinationes factas a Petro Leonis et aliis schismaticis et haereticis'; can. 30, *DEC*, I, 203. On Gregory VIII and Anacletus in the Lateran councils, see R. Foreville, *Latran I, II, III et Latran IV*, Histoire des Conciles Oecuméniques 6 (Paris, 1965), pp. 44–5, 73–4.

6   'Eos autem qui religiositatis speciem simulantes, Domini corporis et sanguinis sacramentum, baptisma puerorum'; 'defensores quoque ipsorum eiusdem damnationis vinculo innodamus'; Lateran 2, can. 23, *DEC*, I, 202. Foreville, *Latran I, II, III et Latran IV*, pp. 86–8.

7   Fredericq, I, Toulouse 1119, no. 23, p. 29; Rheims 1148, no. 31, p. 33; Rheims 1157, no. 34, pp. 35–36; Tours 1163, no. 39, p. 39. Heretics are further specified, geographically, as 'Albigensian' in the title of the Tours canon.

the council focuses on a broad target: those 'whom some call the Cathars, others the Patarenes, others the Publicani, and others by other names'. Though still named, this is now an enemy of much greater numbers, spread through Gascony, the regions of Albi and Toulouse 'and in other places'.[8] It is also in the third Lateran council that refinements to the degrees of heretical involvement are first made, as it is here that the categories of *defensores* and *receptatores*, already present in a limited form in the second Lateran council, and in some of the regional meetings, begin to appear in earnest in the language of the councils.[9] Over the course of the twelfth century church councils are increasingly instituting measures against a heresy that is located in a wider, less defined group than the named sects of earlier canons. Without doubt, though, the most significant shift in the ecumenical treatment of heresy comes with the fourth Lateran council and the advent of the pontificate of Innocent III.

From the beginning of his reign in 1198 Innocent placed the fight against heresy at the forefront of his policy. In 1199 he issued the famous decretal *Vergentis in senium*, and the Albigensian crusade was launched under his auspices in 1209; Innocent was 'a pope known to be anxious about the growth of heresy'.[10] His determination to purge Christian society of heresy reached its legislative apex in the great council of 1215.[11] According to García, the marked juridical tone of this council was due in large part to Innocent the canonist, and though the precise authorship of the canons themselves is uncertain, the importance of Innocent's personal influence in their composition is indisputable.[12]

No longer tucked away in the recesses, heresy and its repression are granted pride of place at the very beginning of the fourth Lateran canons, and it is these canons that continue to represent the main ecumenical treatment of heresy throughout the thirteenth century.[13] The next serious attention paid to

---

[8] 'Alii Catharos, alii Patrinos, alii Publicanos, alii aliis nominibus vocant'; 'et aliis locis'; *DEC*, I, 224.

[9] Foreville, *Latran I, II, III et Latran IV*, pp. 146–7.

[10] Nelson, 'Religion in "Histoire totale": Some Recent Work in Medieval Heresy and Popular Religion', *Religion* 10 (1980), pp. 60–85 (p. 73).

[11] C. Morris, *The Papal Monarchy: The Western Church from 1050–1250* (Oxford, 1989), pp. 442–51.

[12] A. García y García, 'El concilio IV de Letrán (1215) y sus comentarios', *Traditio* 14 (1958), 484–502 (p. 486); for a useful discussion of the authorship of the canons, see García, *Lateran 4*, pp. 5–11. A concise overview of the composition and authorship of the commentaries written on the council can be found in A. García y García, 'The Fourth Lateran Council and the Canonists', in *The History of Medieval Canon Law in the Classical Period, 1140–1234: from Gratian to the Decretals of Pope Gregory IX*, ed. W. Hartmann and K. Pennington (Washington D.C., 2008), pp. 367–78.

[13] The two general councils that were held during the thirteenth century in Lyons, outside the reach of imperial influence, have little to say on the matter of heresy, beside the condemnation of Frederick II by the first of these councils in 1245, in which suspicion of heresy is only one of four charges levelled at Frederick by the bull of deposition. The attachment of this

heresy by the canons of an ecumenical council comes with the council of Vienne, in 1311–12, which likewise opened with a doctrinal decree, and condemned, among others, the Templars and the Beguines.[14] The anti-heretical provisions of the fourth Lateran council, however, and indeed those of the third, continued to be influential throughout the thirteenth century and beyond, both in their own right, owing to their wide manuscript distribution, and as a result of their inclusion in the section of the *Liber extra* that deals with heresy.[15]

Overall, the fourth Lateran constitutions define heresy in a very broad and generalized way. The second canon of the council condemns Joachim of Fiore's treatise against Peter Lombard point by point and defends the Lombard's Trinitarian doctrine in the same fashion. In its aim, this canon resembles those heresiarch-specific condemnations of early councils, and the brief denuncia-tion of the 'most perverse doctrine of the impious Amalric' is certainly in this mould, but the canon as a whole differs in its content in giving a rich descrip-tion and exposition of the errors and doctrine involved, so much so that it can perhaps also be seen as an extension of the creed that constitutes the first canon.[16] It also stands in contrast to the general and all-encompassing condem-nation of heretics in the third. This canon, which constitutes the council's main provision against heresy, gives its subject no name, and no body of errors is described or addressed. Heresy is defined here not by what it is, but by what it is not: namely, the creed that forms the opening constitution of the council.

For the first time since late antiquity the 1215 council sets forth a full and clearly defined statement of faith and, like previous creeds, its formulation can be seen to be in part motivated and determined by heresy and the need to draw lines of distinction.[17] The underlying presence of heresy in the fourth Lateran statement of faith, 'regarded as fully authoritative by subsequent

---

condemnation to the council proper is not entirely secure, and its promulgation seems to have been limited. Introduction to council in *DEC*, I, 274–7. Bull of deposition is at I, 278–83. There is nothing on heresy in Lyons II, though its statement of the doctrine of the procession of the Holy Spirit insists that it proceeds from Father and Son, but not from two principles: *DEC*, I, can. II.1, p. 314. On Frederick II see H. Wolter and H. Holstein, *Lyons I et Lyons II*, Histoire des Conciles Oecuméniques 7 (Paris, 1966), pp. 17–26. On political uses of heresy, see A. Patschovsky, 'Heresy and Society: On the Political Function of Heresy in the Medi-eval World', in *Texts and Repression*, ed. Bruschi and Biller, pp. 23–41.

14 Vienne 1311–12, *DEC*, I, 360–401; error condemned on p. 361; p. 374; *Ad nostrum* is on pp. 383–4. On Beguines, see W. Simons, *Cities of Ladies: Beguine Communities in the Medieval Low Countries, 1200–1565* (Philadelphia, PA, 2001). On Vienne and *Ad nostrum*, see R. Lerner, *The Heresy of the Free Spirit in the Later Middle Ages* (Berkeley, CA, 1972), pp. 78–84; J. Leclercq, *Vienne*, Histoire des Conciles Oecuméniques 8 (Paris, 1964), Beguines and *Ad nostrum*, pp. 159–61, Templars, pp. 63–88, *passim*.

15 According to García, the Lateran 4 constitutions are extant, either in whole or in part, in 64 manuscripts: García, *Lateran 4*, p. 20; Introductions to councils in *DEC*, I, 207–10, 228–9.

16 García, *Lateran 4*, p. 47.

17 Morris, *The Papal Monarchy*, p. 448.

synods', is easily discerned.[18] Error, especially that of the Cathars, has shaped the form and substance of the Catholic doctrine: like the *Summae auctoritatum*, a negative image of Catharism emerges from reading the articles set out here. The opening description of God as maker of all things visible and invisible, itself present in earlier creeds as a response to dualism, has been extended in a way that seems intended to counter specific Cathar claims about the nature of creation: 'one principle of all things, creator of all things, invisible and visible, spiritual and corporeal ... created from nothing both spiritual and corporeal creatures, that is to say angelic and earthly'. The statement that 'the devil and other demons were created by God naturally good' is similarly suggestive, and there are other parts of the statement of faith which, again, seem to answer heretical tenets directly: 'all of them will rise with their own bodies', for example, or 'not only virgins and the continent but also married people find favour with God'.[19]

Other intellectual disputes and errors have also left their mark on the formulation of this constitution. The legacy of the various Eucharistic debates of the previous two centuries means that Aristotelian language is used in the creed of the Eucharist, which is 'changed in substance', 'under the forms of the bread and wine', the first time non-Biblical language had been included in the decrees of the universal church.[20] The concerns over Trinitarian doctrine raised by the teaching of Joachim of Fiore, though treated in the second canon, also spill over into the creed. In fact, the first canon of the fourth Lateran council provides a neat answer for most of the doctrinal errors of its time.[21] And this is, of course, the point. Heresy is defined specifically by the creed, as the opening line of canon three explicitly states: 'we excommunicate and anathematize every heresy raising itself up against this holy, orthodox and catholic faith which we have expounded above'.[22] In moving away from outlawing specific errors, and presenting a series of points which define error by exclusion, Lateran four makes heresy generic, doctrinally specific only in the negative, defined by its external status and undifferentiated within itself. The same shift

---

[18] Ibid., p. 512.

[19] 'Unum universorum principium, creator omnium invisibilium et visibilium, spiritualium et corporalium ... de nichilo condidit creaturam spiritualem et corporalem, angelicam videlicet et mundanam'; 'Diabolus enim et demones alii a Deo quidam natura creati sunt boni'; 'omnes cum suis propriis resurgent corporibus'; 'non solum autem virgines et continentes, verum etiam coniugati ... placentes Deo'; García, *Lateran 4*, pp. 41–3; trans. *DEC*, I, 230–31. See comparison of Lateran 4 with Nicene and Constantinopolitan creeds in Foreville, *Latran I, II, III et Latran IV*, pp. 276–9.

[20] 'Sub speciebus panis et vini'; 'transsubstantiatis'; García, *Lateran 4*, p. 42; trans. *DEC*, I, 230. Morris, *The Papal Monarchy*, p. 512.

[21] Foreville, *Latran I, II, III et Latran IV*, pp. 283–5.

[22] 'Excommunicamus igitur et anathematizamus omnem heresim extollentem se adversus hanc sanctam, orthodoxam et catholicam fidem, quam superius exposuimus'; García, *Lateran 4*, p. 47; trans. *DEC*, I, 233.

that renders heresy general, however, also demands that error be understood and dealt with in terms of these articles: that is, as a point of doctrine.

Unlike previous councils the fourth Lateran dispenses with names entirely in its general condemnation of heretics and instead denounces 'all heretics whatever names they may go under. They have different faces indeed but their tails are tied together.'[23] The above phrase is drawn directly from *Ad abolendam* and from Innocent's own decretal, *Vergentis in senium*, parts of which legislation go into the make-up of this canon.[24] It is a characterization that reflects the fact that all error is now defined by the same rejection of Catholic doctrine, although the connection between these heretics is their pride, not their belief. Like heresy, heretics are generalized and no differentiation is made between different groups. The fourth Lateran treatment of heresy represents a movement from the brief, reactive, problem-specific articles of previous councils to a universal condemnation of all heresy, defined here by opposition to a now more clearly defined orthodoxy.

Regional councils

While the ecumenical constitutions were church-wide and concerned with doctrinal definitions, it was in the regional church councils that much of the practical and legal regulations for action against heresy were set out, and a significant proportion of the body of laws that gradually came to comprise the procedure of inquisition were also introduced by their canons. According to Dossat's overview of the development of inquisitorial law, after 1255, during the pontificate of Alexander IV, conciliar activity was practically nil and for the most part inquisitors were left to conduct their business under their own supervision.[25] He also observes that on the whole, Alexander's output with regard to heresy did little more than reproduce earlier material; for Dossat, the period of real development was during the reign of Gregory IX, 1227–41.[26] Arnold identifies two phases to the accumulation of inquisitorial legislation, though he emphasizes that there is continuity between them and that the two periods are not entirely exclusive. The first, driven by considerations arising out of the crusade, he places between 1227 and 1235. His second phase, between 1236 and 1254, is characterized by the emergence of a coherent and complete system, with different types of adherence to heresy properly defined and categorized.[27]

---

23 'Universos hereticos quibuscumque nominibus censeantur, facies quidem habentes diversas, set caudas ad invicem colligatas'; García, *Lateran 4*, p. 47; trans. *DEC*, I, 233.
24 *Vergentis in senium*, García, *Lateran 4*, p. 49, lines 38–49; the council of Verona and *Ad abolendam*, García, *Lateran 4*, p. 50, lines 64–75.
25 Dossat, *Crises*, p. 195.
26 Dossat, *Crises*, p. 108.
27 J. H. Arnold, *Inquisition and Power: Catharism and the Confessing Subject in Medieval Languedoc* (Philadelphia, PA, 2001), pp. 33–8.

From that period of activity, from the cluster of regional meetings that were held in the south of France and Tarragona, will be drawn the councils to be used here: the councils of Narbonne, in 1227, Toulouse, in 1229, Béziers, in 1232, an important meeting at Tarragona in 1242, Narbonne again in 1243, another at Béziers in 1246, Valence, in 1248, and the 1254 council of Albi.[28] These are the councils that formed the core of authorities for contemporary commentators and which were central to the construction of anti-heretical canon law.

A large proportion of the anti-heretical canons promulgated by the regional councils are concerned mainly to make provision for correct procedure – and very quickly this means inquisition – to ensure the legal obligations of secular authorities and to lay down guidelines for punishment. The council of Toulouse, reiterating the provisions of the earlier council of Avignon, requires that each priest investigate heresy in his area, along with two or three laymen 'of good opinion', and that this inquiry be ongoing; it is joined by the provision that the secular lord of an area and his bailiffs are also to inquire after heresy in their jurisdiction.[29] This first lay inquiry into heresy is reiterated in 1246 at Béziers, and both are repeated by the council of Albi in 1254.[30] Despite the importance of the laity in the initial stages of inquiry, and, post-conviction, in not supporting heretics once they have been identified, the church is careful to reserve to itself the right to label heretics: 'no one is to be punished as a believer or a heretic unless he has been judged a believer or a heretic by the bishop of that place, or by another ecclesiastical person who has the power to do so'.[31] The measures taken by all of these councils, with the exception of the council of Tarragona, deal either with the initial seeking of heretics by the local clergy or the lord of the area or with their treatment after conviction.[32] They are aimed squarely at the repression and control of the heretic, and of the several categories of individual that are attached to him, through differentiation and punishment according to those categories.

The different 'categories' of supporters, which indicated different grades of

---

[28] Mansi, XXIII: Narbonne 1227, 19–26; Toulouse 1229, 191–204; Béziers 1232 (dated 1233 in Mansi, see Dossat, *Crises*, p. 109), 269–78; Tarragona 1242, 553–8; Narbonne 1243 (dated 1235), 353–66; Béziers 1246, 689–704; Valence 1248, 769–80; Albi 1254, 829–52. Full text of Tarragona constitutions in Selge, *Texte*, pp. 50–59. For council of Albi, 1230, see O. Pontal, *Les statuts synodaux Français du XIIIe siècle*, 4 vols. (Paris, 1971–95), II, 8–33. We shall pass gratefully over the issue of *Vox in Rama*, at Mainz in 1233, Mansi, XXIII, 321–8. See earlier discussion of these councils by Maisonneuve, *Études*, pp. 287–307.

[29] Avignon, 1209, canon 2, Mansi, XXII, 785–6, repeated at Montpellier, 1224, canon 46, Mansi, XXII, 950; Toulouse, 1229, canons 1 and 3, Mansi, XXIII, 194.

[30] Béziers 43, canon 1, Mansi, XXIII, 691; Albi 54, canons 1 and 4, Mansi, XXIII, 832–3.

[31] 'Ne aliquis ut credens vel haereticus puniatur, nisi per episcopum loci, vel aliquam personam ecclesiasticam, quae potestatem habeat, fuerit credens vel hereticus judicatus'; Toulouse, canon 8, Mansi, XXIII, 195.

[32] Albi 1230 for example, canon 14, charges all Catholics 'ad hereticos fugandos'; Pontal, *Les statuts synodaux*, II, 12.

involvement and guilt, as noted above, began to appear in the twelfth century and entered universal church legislation in the second and third Lateran councils. It was during the course of the thirteenth century, however, that they acquired their more precise meanings, as they came to be used in the context of inquisition, though the exact boundaries between them remained problematic for inquisitors throughout this period.[33] In all the conciliar material considered here, however, these groups remain distinct from the heretic proper.

The definition of 'heretic' given by the key council of Tarragona is very brief: 'heretics are those who persevere in their error'. Heretics are defined always in terms of belief, characterized as holders of error, and also by obstinacy in that error. Indeed, obstinacy appears at least as frequently as error in the definition of a heretic. The first council of Béziers orders that all who are obstinate in their refusal to undergo their punishment – that is, who will not wear their crosses – are to be considered as heretics.[34] Further, the first canon of this council, which states that 'heretics and their believers, supporters, their receivers and defenders, are to be excommunicated every Sunday', then goes on, now omitting heretics deliberately from this list, to say that if one of 'aforesaid believers, supporters, receivers and defenders', having been warned and excommunicated by name does not return to their senses, if they impede the inquisition, or remain stubborn in their refusal to make restitution within forty days of excommunication, then they should be punished as 'heretics', since it is just such perseverance in and defence of error that make a heretic, and that in this instance effect a shift in status from follower to leader. This canon is repeated by the second of the councils held at Béziers.[35]

'Heretics' thus established at the top of the list and slightly apart, the other categories are then listed relative to the heretics, the holders of belief. As with many aspects of anti-heretical procedure, it is not until the council of Tarragona in 1242 that the terminology that describes the supporters of heretics is explicitly defined in the conciliar legislation in a systematic way. The methodical and comprehensive nature of the Tarragona constitutions can be attributed to the presence at the council of the Dominican and renowned canon lawyer Raymond of Peñafort, compiler of the decretal collection that appeared under Gregory IX's name, and a former Master General of his order.[36] This is the only time in these councils that we see outlined in practical

---

33 The councils of Narbonne in 1227, canon 15, Mansi, XXIII, 24–5; Toulouse in 1229, canon 1, Mansi, XXIII, 194–6; Béziers in 1232, canon 1, Mansi, XXIII, 270–71.

34 'Heretici sunt, qui in suo errore perdurant'; Béziers 32, canon 4, Mansi, XXIII, 271.

35 'Haeretici et eorum credentes, fautores, eorum receptatores et defensores, singulis diebus Dominicis excommunicantur'; 'praedictorum credentium, fautorum, receptatorum et defensorum'; 'cum perseverantia et defensio erroris in talibus hominem faciat haereticum judicari'; Béziers 32, canon 1, Mansi, XXIII, 270, Béziers 46, canon 8, Mansi, XXIII, 693–4. Note, a town can also be suspected of heresy: 'villa suspecta de haeresi habeatur'; Toulouse, canon 10, Mansi, XXIII, 196.

36 Raymond was elected Master General in 1238, a post he resigned two years later, see M.

legal terms what is meant by the labels that are elsewhere used without definition, and it is to Tarragona that commentators repeatedly return; as such, they
will be used as a guide to understand the broader ideas at work.

What is immediately striking about the definitions of the different types of
follower is the extent to which they are almost entirely based on specific
actions. Most of the categories are relatively self-explanatory, with the exception of the *credens*, which carries a degree of ambiguity. Someone is 'suspected
of heresy' who has heard the preaching or reading of the heretics, prayed with
or kissed them, or who believes them to be 'good men'. Next are 'celatores'
and 'occultatores', concealers and hiders; a distinction of intention is made
between the former, those who see heretics and do not reveal them, and the
latter, those who make a conscious choice before the fact not to reveal heretics.
'Receptatores', or receivers, are those who knowingly receive heretics into
their house twice or more, and give them hospitality. 'Defensores', defenders,
knowingly defend heretics by word or deed. A supporter of heretics, or
'fautor', is really a general term for those guilty of any or all of the above, or of
providing any other help or advice. None of these lesser grades of heretical
involvement are characterized by an error of belief, but are defined primarily
by, and in terms of, physical actions and behaviour.

What also emerges from the above definitions is the emphasis, made
continually in these councils, on the individual supporter's awareness of the
heretic's status as a heretic. Punishment falls on those who have knowingly,
scienter, defended, supported or believed in heretics, or made the conscious
choice to hide them. In a broader way, the same emphasis on awareness
underlies the prominence of suspicion in the councils, since the rumour and
local reputation that was the basis for the launch of an inquisition, similarly
implies a degree of understanding. Such knowledge must come primarily
from the public announcement of the names of heretics and supporters at the
reading of the ban of excommunication which is to be held every Sunday and
feast day, according to the already quoted provision of the 1246 council at
Béziers, as well as canon two of the same council: 'if anyone has been
convicted or has confessed this [knowingly allowing heretics to live on land],
let him be denounced publicly and by name throughout the duration of his
excommunication'.[37] Given that, from the council of Toulouse onwards,
everyone is required at the age of discretion formally to abjure heresy, at least

---

Brundage, *Medieval Canon Law* (London, 1995), pp. 222–3; *SOPMA*, III, 283; *Dictionnaire de
spiritualité, ascetique et mystique: doctrine et histoire*, 17 vols. in 21 (Paris, 1937–95), XIII,
190–91.

[37] 'Si quis autem de hoc convictus fuerit vel confessus, tamdiu excommunicatus nominatim et
publice nuncietur'; also 'haeretici et eorum credentes, fautores, eorum receptatores et
defensores, singulis diebus Dominicis excommunicantur'; quoted above p. 95, n. 35, Béziers
46, canon 2, Mansi, XXIII, 692. Provision for public reading of excommunications by name is
also made at Béziers 46, canon 8, Mansi, XXIII, 693, and Albi 54, canon 19, Mansi, XXIII, 837.
Penances for heretics in the first canon of Narbonne 43 are very public.

in theory, there can be no legal grounds for not knowing that heresy is condemned by the church, whether the mechanics behind it are understood or not.[38]

Increasingly, though, provision is made for the general populace to be taught the articles of the Catholic faith. Education in correct doctrine first appears as an anti-heretical measure, along with public excommunication, in the second council at Béziers, where it is stated that priests are to teach the articles of faith on a Sunday and that boys are to be instructed in the faith. The council of Albi in 1254 repeats this and adds that the faith is also to be explained when people take their oath to abjure heresy and uphold the Catholic faith.[39] The formal record of such an oath is a part of the shrewd use made by inquisitors of their written records as a weapon in the control of heresy and undoubtedly there is a deterrent factor at work here, but there is also a concern to educate and an idea perhaps that heresy is fostered by ignorance. There is, in a negative way reminiscent of the fourth Lateran council, a construction of heresy that is doctrinal in nature, though it is only hinted at here, and of lay understanding and subsequent recognition of heresy in terms of error and not merely as a list of names. What this also serves to highlight, however, is again the fact that the focus of these regulations is almost never on heresy itself. Instead, they address the people involved in it, and the canons of the provincial councils rarely, if ever, address heretical belief in anything other than the most generic form. Though 'error' and 'heresy' are both mentioned they are never described, nor are their content or nature expounded.[40] They appear primarily as a condition of the heretic, whose status is defined by error, obstinately held and defended.[41] Intention is important to the definition of the lesser grades, but belief is not.

The partial exception to this rule are the 'credentes', who seem at times to occupy a sort of limbo between proper heretics and the lesser grades, and, like the obstructive and the obstinate, can be subject to a shift in status. The council of Tarragona's definition of the 'believer' is even more cursory than that of the 'heretic': 'believers, in fact, in the said heresies are similarly to be called heretics'.[42] Yet *credentes* are not included in the penance assigned to heretics by the canons of this council. At Narbonne, in the following year, heretics and *credentes* are consistently equated in terms and in punishments. The general pattern though, before Tarragona, and indeed after the Narbonne council, is to place the *credentes* with the *fautores*, *defensores* and *receptatores*, in a bloc separate from the heretics, as we saw in the first canon of the 1232 council of Béziers.

---

38 Toulouse, canon 12, Mansi, XXIII, 196. Repeated at Albi, canon 11, Mansi, XXIII, 835.
39 Béziers 46, canon 7, Mansi, XXIII, 693 and Albi 54, canons 17, 12, 18, Mansi, XXIII, 835–7.
40 Except on one occasion, in the Tarragona canons, where a very brief example of Waldensian error is given; Selge, *Texte*, p. 51; Tarragona, Mansi, XXIII, 554.
41 'Cum perseverantia et defensio erroris in talibus hominem faciat haereticum judicari'; Béziers 32, canon 1, Mansi, XXIII, 270, Béziers 46, canon 8, Mansi, XXIII, 693–4.
42 'Credentes vero dictis heresibus similiter heretici sunt dicendi'; Selge, *Texte*, p. 51; Tarragona, Mansi, XXIII, 553–4.

The early council of Toulouse at times includes the *credentes* in the treatment of heretics, but there is no place for them in the provision for renunciation of error and so no real equation on the grounds of belief.[43] That they occupy both states reflects the fact that the legal status of convicted *credens* is equivalent to that of a heretic, while the criteria on which an individual is judged as a *credens* are of the same quality as any other grade – that is, based on a relationship to heretics. The blurring of the boundary between heretic and follower in the case of the *credens* is also in part the result of evolving ideas of the role of intention and discernment in broader discussions of criminality, particularly pertinent here in the realm of occult crime. All of which means that the *credens* is the most fluid of all the categories of heretical supporter, which is one reason why questions on the exact nature of the *credens* continue to dominate the legal consultations sought by inquisitors in this period. Despite this overlap, for a follower to be regarded *ut hereticus* nevertheless implies an understanding of heretic as a distinct category, and, as a general rule, heretics and supporters stand apart, distinguished by error on the one hand and action on the other.

The Narbonne council of 1243 states that heretics or *credentes* who avoid their penance 'openly show their impenitence and false conversion'.[44] Although the categorization of suspects depends on actions, statements such as the above would seem to suggest that these actions are seen to betray an inner allegiance or condition. The relationship between action and belief will be examined further in the next chapter, but one aspect of this idea needs to be noted here: namely, that though the inner condition of these groups is not ignored, neither is it prominent, nor connected to religious belief in any way except, again, occasionally in the case of *credentes*. Indeed, the ultimate characteristic and definition of each of these lesser grades is that they are categorized not by their connection to heresy, but to heretics: they are defenders, supporters, receivers of heretics. Most tellingly, even *credentes* are usually believers of heretics, and not of heresy, not of the error itself.

It is not only by definition that heretics are differentiated from the other grades of involvement, but also by the punishment and penances that are prescribed. Prison is the most common penance imposed on convicted heretics, though at times its punitive function appears more conspicuous: according to the council of Toulouse heretics who confess spontaneously are to receive penance, while only those who confess from fear can expect to be imprisoned. Later councils deny freedom to all converts, penitent or otherwise: a necessary measure, according to one council, because the conversion of

---

[43] Toulouse, canons 17 and 10, Mansi, XXIII, 198, 196. For a useful treatment of this pattern, see Arnold, *Inquisition*, pp. 37–47.

[44] 'Sic suam impoenitentiam, fictamque conversionem aperte ostendunt'; Narbonne 43, canon 10, Mansi, XXIII, 359; a similar thing in canon 11, for relapses. Tarragona's provision for the exhumation and cremation of dead heretics' bones perhaps also highlights the reliance on exterior signs to prove the guilt of someone whose interior condition is beyond recall; Selge, *Texte*, p. 56.

many heretics is false.[45] A more structured system of punishment and penance is introduced into the conciliar material by the council of Tarragona. Here, 'heretics, persevering in their error' are to be given up to the secular arm and prison is retained as a penitential measure. *Perfecti haeretici*, or fully fledged heretics – that is, the heretical élite – if they wish to convert, must be prepared for perpetual imprisonment.[46] The treatment is very brief in comparison with the penances handed down for the other levels of involvement. Even *credentes* are given much more opportunity to do penance outside prison, despite the fact that, according to the definitions given by this council, their legal status is the same as *heretici*.

Other punitive measures are imposed by these councils on those convicted as 'heretics' beyond a system of penance, and are again different from the treatment of lesser grades. Like the social exclusion imposed by a prison sentence, these measures also segregate heretics legally and politically. The disinheritance of heretics and their families that was introduced by Innocent III in *Vergentis in senium* is reinforced in the regional meetings. Heretics, and those suspected of being heretics, are barred from public office by the 1227 council of Narbonne, although these provisions are revised in later councils, and *heretici* are cut off from the more inclusive approach taken to the lesser grades.[47]

Heretics are therefore represented as different from the other groups, distinguished by the presence of belief, the brevity of treatment given to them, and by the physical and legal exclusion from the main body of believers that the sentence incurs.[48] The councils assume an identification and trial process that is happening elsewhere, taking for granted the labelled individual, a characteristic of the conciliar representation of the heretic that we can see also to some degree in the ecumenical treatment. For the lesser grades of involvement Tarragona's outlines provide the necessary information for conviction, but in the case of the heretic, so clearly demarcated by his error, there is no informa-

---

45 Toulouse, canons 10, 11, 15, Mansi, XXIII, 196–7. 'Unde ne per tales, sub ficta conversionis specie, catholicae fidei professores perniciosius corrumpi contingat'; Arles, canon 6, Mansi, XXIII, 338.

46 'Haeretici perseverantes in errore'; Tarragona, Selge, *Texte*, pp. 51–2. This is perhaps one reason why becoming an inquisitor was so appealing for converts like Raniero. Provisions were added in the council of Narbonne 1243 to allow those charged with heresy to enter religious orders, with special permission from the Pope, Narbonne 1243, canon 18, Mansi, XXIII, 361.

47 Narbonne 27, canon 16, Mansi, XXIII, 25. 'Credentes et fautores hereticorum, seu defensores eorum' are forbidden from buying the office of bailiff; Béziers 32, canon 3, Mansi, XXIII, 270. Selge, *Texte*, pp. 57–9, Tarragona, Mansi, XXIII, 556–7, *formae poenitentiarum*.

48 The term 'vested heretics', *heretici vestiti*, is also used to describe these individuals: Narbonne, canon 16, Mansi, XXIII, 25, Toulouse, canon 10, Mansi, XXIII, 196. Tarragona also has 'perfected heretics'; Selge, *Texte*, p. 52, Tarragona, Mansi, XXIII, 555. See also below, p. 124, n. 44, and pp. 201–2 on these terms.

tion here that would allow his identification, no description of error. They remain generic figures, only occasionally referred to by specific group names, though it is important to be aware that although 'heretic' is more often than not a general term, it can at times also be understood to refer specifically to the Cathars. Such a use is visible where 'heretics' are in direct contrast to another group, usually the Waldensians.[49]

In a regulation designed for general application such a generic type is necessary: the case-specific treatment lies in the emphasis placed on the discretion of the judge and inquisitor by those councils that speak more directly to their inquisitorial operatives: that is, those of Tarragona and Narbonne. Tarragona appeals to the discrimination of its judges in phrases such as 'the discerning judge' and 'let the judge beware'. More explicitly, Narbonne outlines the importance of discretion and prudence to the Dominicans that it addresses, telling them that they should impose penances 'according to their discretion ... carefully and prudently', so that the way of life of the guilty is corrected or at least 'that they are able to show, who walks in shadow, who in light; who is truly penitent, who falsely converted'. Perhaps most telling, the canons of this council admit that discretion should 'make up for what cannot easily be understood by writing'.[50] The gap left by the councils here will be discussed later. What matters as far as the regional councils are concerned is that the representation of heresy that they contain consists of a variety of actions that are performed in relation to heretics which have only an oblique basis in error, and that they diffuse a typology of heretical support and a vocabulary with which to describe it.

Textbooks

Concordia discordantium canonum[51]

Gratian's *Concordia discordantium canonum*, better known as the *Decretum*, became the standard canon-law textbook of the high medieval law schools and was so widely adopted in the decade or so after its compilation that its appearance is now generally taken to mark the beginning of the 'classical' era of canon law.[52] The exact dating of the *Decretum* is disputed; although it has in

---

49 For the general use of heretics as synonymous with the Cathars in Languedoc, see J. Duvernoy, 'L'acception: 'haereticus' (iretge) = 'parfait cathare' en Languedoc au XIIIᵉ siècle', in *The Concept of Heresy*, ed. Lourdaux and Verhelst, pp. 198–210.

50 'Secundum discretionem ... caute et provide'; 'valeat apparere, quis in tenebris ambulet, quis in luce; quis vere sit poenitens, quis ficte conversus'; 'suppleatque discretio, quod scripto non posset facile comprehendi'; Selge, *Texte*, pp. 53, 55, Tarragona, Mansi, XXIII, 555, 558. Narbonne 43, canons 5 and 16, Mansi, XXIII, 357, 361.

51 Friedberg, I, *Decretum magistri Gratiani*. Lenherr's edition of C.24 q.1 has also been consulted, in Lenherr, *Gratian*, pp. 18–56.

52 Brundage, *Medieval Canon Law*, pp. 48–9 and n. 7, citing G. Le Bras, C. Lefebvre and J. Rambaud, *L'âge classique, 1140–1378: Sources et théorie du droit* (Paris, 1965).

the past been placed somewhere in the region of 1140, as a result of the work of Anders Winroth we now know that the *Decretum* was compiled in two stages. The first recension was put together probably in or just after 1138, and was less than half the size of the substantially larger second recension, which was produced by 'Gratian two', who may or may not have been the same person, at some point before 1158; for the sake of convenience, we will refer to the author or authors of this text simply as 'Gratian'. It was the longer, second recension that came to represent the standard version used in later centuries.[53] For this reason, it matters less for this study what differences there are between the original and later versions in their treatment of heresy, as, by the thirteenth century, the longer version would have been the one that contemporaries would have known and used.[54]

As its title suggests, the *Concordia discordantium canonum* is constructed according to dialectical principles, a feature that made it very useful for teaching and which was one of the main reasons that it was adopted so broadly. It is arranged over three parts: part one deals with specific topics and is divided into *distinctiones*; part two presents sample *causae*, or cases, and then answers the various questions that they raise; the third part, the *Tractatus de consecratione*, is concerned with sacramental and liturgical law.[55] Accompanied by Gratian's own remarks, or *dicta*, the *Decretum* sets out within this framework a collection of various canons, drawn from conciliar and decretal material and especially from writers of the early church, in order to explore and resolve contradictions in the canon-legal corpus.

The *Decretum* was compiled a century before our period of study, but its continued primacy in the study of canon law in this and following centuries makes it crucial to the law of our period. Its influence can be seen throughout the constitutions of the fourth Lateran council, for example, and the specific influence of its provisions on heresy in particular is clear in the level to which later canon-legal texts on the subject continue to refer to the authority of these *causae* as their starting point.[56] The *Summa de poenitentia* of Raymond of Peñafort relies heavily on the *Decretum* throughout its treatment of heresy, despite having been revised by Raymond in the same year that he completed the compilation of the *Liber extra*.[57] The *Decretum* also provided the main

---

53 Winroth uses 'Gratian two' to refer to the compiler of the second recension, while making it clear that this may not necessarily be a different individual from 'Gratian one'; A. Winroth, *The Making of Gratian's* Decretum (Cambridge, 2000), pp. 122, 136–8, 135.

54 The first recension of C.24. q.3 omits canons 3, 8, 9, 10, 11, 13–25, 30–38 and 40 – twenty-seven out of a total of forty. Winroth argues, in his chapter on this *causa*, that although the argument may become more coherent, the meaning remains the same. The canons added to *causa* twenty-four do not add anything qualitatively to the content, but they do affect the proportion of space given to obedience as a factor. Winroth, *Gratian's* Decretum, Appendix, pp. 218–20, pp. 34–76.

55 Brundage, *Medieval Canon Law*, pp. 47–8, and appendix, pp. 190–94.

56 For the use of the *Decretum* in the constitutions of Lateran 4, see García, *Lateran 4*, pp. 12–15.

57 *SOPMA*, III, 285.

source for one of the most influential legal consultations on the subject of heresy, written in the 1250s by Gui Foulques, and its significance is by this time so entrenched that Gui is able to refer to sections of the *Decretum* by nothing other than the relevant number. Perhaps the most meaningful example that can be given here, though, is that in the mid-century gloss to the new collection, Gregory's *Liber extra*, the majority of the commentary for its section on heresy is given over to references to the *Decretum*.

Most of the material on heresy in the *Decretum* occurs in two of the *causae* that make up the second part of the work: *causa* twenty-three and *causa* twenty-four. As with the other *causae*, they begin with an outline of a hypo-thetical situation from which all the questions that make up the *causa* are then derived.[58] For *causa* twenty-three Gratian posits a situation in which several bishops have fallen into heresy and are beginning to compel the Catholics around them to follow suit. When their heresy is discovered military action is ordered against them. Gratian's questions centre on the church's status in rela-tion to heretics and the majority of them concern the legitimate use of force: the fact that the bishops are heretical is not immediately important to the ques-tions that follow except as a device to allow the discussion of the use of force against others. In this *causa*, question four, 'whether punishment is to be imposed', and question seven, 'whether heretics should be stripped of their own property and [any] church property [they happen to possess]? And whether they who possess heretical goods are said to possess alienated property', contain the most material on heretics specifically.[59]

Causa twenty-four opens with a complementary scenario: a bishop, having fallen into heresy, deprives others of their office and marks them with the sentence of excommunication. After his death he is convicted of heresy and condemned, together with his followers and their households. The consequent situation affords Gratian an opportunity to examine problems that arise with regard to the status of the accused, rather than of those taking action against him, as in twenty-three: that is, whether or not a heretic can deprive others of office; whether a sentence of excommunication can be passed after death; and how such a sentence should affect the rest of the individual's household. It is this third question that has the most to say about heresy as a subject in its own right.

The questions that Gratian seeks to answer in these two *causae* are often tangential or unconnected to heresy itself: discussion of heresy is not the aim of the argument. Rather, like the *exempla* collections, heresy appears in the *Decretum* within the boundaries set up by the hypothetical cases and the signif-

---

[58] Winroth, *Gratian's* Decretum, p. 34.

[59] 'An vindicta sit inferenda'; 'an heretici suis et ecclesiae rebus sint expoliandi? Et qui possident hereticis ablata an dicantur possidere aliena'; C.23 q.4, Friedberg, I, 899–928; C.23 q.7, Friedberg, I, 950–53. The summary of question four is taken from the introduction to the whole *causa*, 889.

icance of the content of these sources is subject always to the progression of Gratian's dialectical argument. Therefore, some canons, though not referring to heresy in their content, are nonetheless framed as pertinent to it, while others that talk specifically about heresy are presented as proving something unconnected.[60] It is only in the last part of twenty-four that heresy is the subject of the questions as well as the material. In the earlier parts of *causa* twenty-four, and also in most of twenty-three, heresy forms much of the substance of the sources, but is more a part of the background to the discussion of other issues.

Gratian on the whole used very little new material in the construction of his text, preferring instead to rely on more established sources, and these two *causae* are no exceptions.[61] A glance at the sources of the canons shows the overwhelming presence of the works of the Fathers, especially Jerome and, in *causa* twenty-three particularly, Augustine, as well as the writings of the early popes, whose work makes up a good proportion of the material in *causa* twenty-four. Although the presence of heresy in the structure of the text suggests that the questions it raised were not without contemporary relevance, the use of early material colours the background picture of heresy that is gained from reading these canons, a picture that was born out of a context very different to that of the *Decretum*.

Underlying much of this early material are heresies held and expounded by heretics who are on more level terms with their Catholic counterparts than the heretics of Gratian's time, who can correspond with leading Catholic figures on points of doctrine and the validity of the church's persecution of their group.[62] Augustine seems to regard heretics as a stimulus to learning and good teaching, in the mode of Paul's teaching on the necessity of heresies.[63] Augustine's arguments in his letter to Petilianus are perfect material for Gratian's discussion of the legitimate use of force, within which this excerpt falls, but they present at the same time an informed exchange between two opponents writing within the same tradition as each other. Learning is also associated with the heretics that these texts describe, whether in a straightforward remark, such as Ambrose's use of the term 'heretical teacher' in his commentary on Luke, or in a more developed description.[64] The parts of Petilianus' letter that are reproduced within Augustine's are of the same character and form. But the sense of academic enquiry is twisted: Leo I claims that

---

60 For example, C.23 q.1 c.4, C.23 q.3 c.3 and 4, Friedberg, I, 892, 897, as opposed to, e.g. C.23 q.4 c.25, Friedberg, I, 910–11.

61 Winroth, *Gratian's* Decretum, p. 139.

62 C.23 q.1 c.4, Friedberg, I, 897; q.4 cc.7, 38, 40, Friedberg, I, 900, 917–18, 920–21; q.5 c.3, Friedberg, I, 930.

63 'Cum interrogant nos ea, que nescimus, sic discutiamus pigriciam, et divinas scripturas cupiamus … Hii autem Deo probati sunt, qui bene possunt docere'; C.24 q.3 c.40, Friedberg, I, 1006.

64 'Preceptor hereticus'; Lenherr, *Gratian*, p. 25; C.24 q.1 c.26, Friedberg, I, 976.

they are made masters of error when, on finding the way to truth difficult, they turn to their own selves instead of the authority of the prophets, the apostles or the evangelists – 'what indeed is more iniquitous than to have a taste for impious things and not to believe in wise men and teachers?'[65] And it is harmful, according to Jerome's description of heretics, who 'often oppress churchmen through their sophisms and dialectical arts'.[66] That background picture nonetheless reflects the definition given in *causa* twenty-four that heresy results from an understanding of the Scripture that is different from that which the Holy Spirit demands.[67]

The most important section of the *Decretum*, as far as heresy itself is concerned, is that made up by the last parts of *causa* twenty-four, where the nature of heresy becomes the primary focus and subject of Gratian's discussion. The last two sections of question three are the part of the *Decretum* that deals specifically with the position of heresy in law, and would therefore be the first port of call for anyone looking for a canon-legal treatment of the subject. As a result, several of the canons became central to subsequent treatments of heresy. They are contained in section four 'what is the difference between schism and heresy, and who are heretics, and how many are the sects of heretics', and section five, 'who in fact, should properly be called "heretics"'.[68]

These are two groups of texts that attempt a definition of heresy. Section four comprises two extracts from Jerome, the first of which outlines the difference between heresy and schism, the former being distinguished from the latter by the possession of 'perverse dogma', which precipitates the separation from the church.[69] The second excerpt from Jerome is a definition of heresy, 'so called from the Greek "choice"', though one that quickly becomes a definition rather of the heretic: one who chooses a teaching, 'disciplinam', that seems better to him, 'anyone, therefore, who understands Scripture other than in the sense the Holy Spirit requires'. Section five is much longer, made up of twelve canons, but it continues without pause to discuss the problem of definition: Jerome's view of heresy is followed immediately by two extracts from Augustine on the same subject. The first defines the heretic more straightforwardly as one who 'begets or follows false or new opinions'.[70] This is refined by the

---

65 'Quid autem iniquius est quam inpia sapere, et sapientoribus doctoribusque non credere?'; C.24 q.3 c.30, Friedberg, I, 998.

66 'Quod sophismatibus suis et arte dialectica sepe opprimant ecclesiasticos'; C.24 q.3 cc.36, 33, Friedberg, I, 1000, 999.

67 C.24 q.3 c.27, Friedberg, I, 997–8.

68 'Quid intersit inter scisma at haeresim, et qui sint heretici, et quot sint hereticorum sectae?'; 'qui vero proprie dicantur heretici'; C.24 q.3 cc.26–39, Friedberg, I, 997–1006.

69 C.24 q.3 c.26, Friedberg, I, 997.

70 'Heresis grece ab electione dicitur'; 'quicumque igitur aliter scripturam intelligit, quam sensus Spiritus sancti flagitat'; 'falsas ac novas oppiniones gignit vel sequitur'; C.24 q.3 cc.27, 28, Friedberg, I, 997–8.

second, which emphasizes carefully that it is only the defence of error that makes a heretic: one who fails to reject his error even after the second admonition.

The following five contributions, from Popes Urban and Leo and one more each from Augustine and Jerome, are really just variations on the two main themes established by the first four canons. It is the possession of dogma, or error, that is the primary defining attribute of the heretics, who are consistently and exclusively identified by the fact, if not often the content, of their error. Beside error is the emphasis on obstinate belief in that error. According to Augustine's definition, those who, once corrected, return to the correct belief must not be considered heretics.[71] The same theme of not only wrong but obstinate belief is developed in the following canons, where defence either of one's own error or of the error of others is added to the requirements for heretical status: 'those who will not amend their dogmas, but persist in defending them, are heretics', and 'he who defends the errors of others is more damnable than these ... he is to be called not only a heretic, but also a heresiarch'.[72]

The remainder of this section is made up of four canons on relations between the clergy and heretics and the legitimacy of their condemnation, and the final canon, the longest by far of the extracts presented here, is lifted from Isidore's *Etymologies*. An already widely circulated text, the inclusion here of this excerpt from Isidore's section on heresy extended its influence even further and cemented its place at the heart of the legal idea of heresy. The long canon that Gratian derives from this source is a list of the names of sixty-eight different heresies. For each one is provided the derivation of the name, from either the author or the cause of the error, as well as one or occasionally two lines that describe the principal error of the sect: for example, 'the Origenists began with their founder, Origen; they say that the Son cannot see the Father, nor the Holy Spirit see the son'. The error given is nearly always doctrinal, occasionally behavioural, but remains, as it does in the formal definitions, the identifying characteristic of heretics.[73]

The authorities that make up the last part of *causa* twenty-four, and the ideas that they embody, remain the principal starting point for canon-legal thought on heresy into and beyond the mid thirteenth century, though they do not necessarily remain static. Canons thirty-one and thirty-two, those that extend the theme of obstinacy in defence introduced by Augustine, were

---

71 C.24 q.3 c.29, Friedberg, I, 998.

72 'Qui ... dogmata emendare nolunt, sed defensare persistunt, heretici sunt'; 'qui aliorum errorem defendit multo est dampnabilior illis ... non tantum hereticus, sed etiam heresiarcha dicenda est'; C.24 q.3 cc.31, 32, Friedberg, I, 998–9.

73 'Origeniani Origene auctore exorti sunt, dicentes, quod non possit Filius videre Patrem, nec Spiritus sanctus Filium'; C.24 q.3 c.39, Friedberg, I, 1001–6; trans. (adjusted) Isidore of Seville, *The Etymologies of Isidore of Seville*, trans. S. A. Barney et al. (Cambridge, 2006), p. 177.

among those that were added to the original by the second redaction.[74] Parallel, perhaps, to the increasing concern with control that is evident in the conciliar literature, the refusal to be corrected has grown in significance in the time between the two redactions, and the trajectory continues into the next century. The ordinary gloss written through the first half of the thirteenth century further emphasizes the theme to the point where the role of obstinacy in the definition of heretic, and in the delineation of the boundary between heretic and non-heretic becomes central to the reading and interpretation of these canons.[75]

It is worth noting, in this connection, the tone taken by the *Decretum* toward repression. Much of *causa* twenty-three deals with the legitimacy of the use of force, and it is within this discussion that the repression of heresy falls, of which the overwhelming impression, from the sources chosen but also from Gratian's framing of them, is of an emphasis on correction and conversion over punishment.[76] The question which discusses repression is summed up by Gratian with the conclusion that 'punishment should be imposed not through the love of punishment itself, but from zeal for justice; not for the expression of hatred but the correction of wickedness'.[77] The attitude of the *Decretum* toward heresy would be left behind to some extent, but the texts which made up the collection, and in particular those of the latter sections of *causa* twenty-four, continued to be central to the idea of heresy, carrying with them that double-edged definition of error and obstinacy that is so familiar. Once the four texts that make up the definition of heresy are brought together in the *Decretum* they appear frequently as a bloc in later writings: Raymond of Peñafort's *Summa de poenitentia*, for example, written in 1224–6 and revised in 1234, opens its section 'of heretics and their supporters' with a summary of the above definitions by Augustine and Jerome, together with some others that Raymond has harvested from other parts of the *Decretum* that pertain to sacramental error.[78] Similarly, Isidore's list of heresies, extracted from its context

---

[74] C.24 q.3 cc.31, 32, Friedberg, I, 998–9.

[75] Gloss to 'dixit apostolus', Gratian, *Decretum divi Gratiani, totius propemodum iuris canonici compendium, summorum que pontificum decreta atque praeiudicia, una cum variis scribentium Glossis et expositionibus* (Lyons, 1560), col. 1403. See also *Corpus Juris Canonici* (Rome, 1582) via <http://digital.library.ucla.edu/canonlaw/>, directed by H. Batchelor, H. A. Kelly et al.

[76] For example, one of the extracts taken from Augustine's work: that severe measures, or 'medicine', undertaken by the church are for correction, 'karitatis freneticum ligare, lethargicum stimulare, ambos amare. Ambo offenduntur, sed ambo diliguntur'; C.23 q.4 c.25, Friedberg, I, 910–11. See also C.23 q.4 c.37, Friedberg, I, 916–17; C.23 q.5 c.1, Friedberg, I, 928; rather less tolerant in C.23 q.4 c.39, Friedberg, I, 919.

[77] 'Vindicta est inferenda non amore ipsius vindictae, sed zelo iusticiae; non ut odium exerceatur, sed ut pravitas corrigatur'; C.23 q.4 dpc.54 (or 53, 54 is a *palea*), Friedberg, I, 928.

[78] 'De haereticis et fautoribus eorum'; Raymond of Peñafort, *De poenitentia, et matrimonio* (Rome, 1603, repub. Farnborough, 1967), pp. 38–45. Dates from *SOPMA* III, 285. See also discussion at pp. 190–1.

and brought to the fore, is a constant, if not always explicit, presence in anti-heretical thought from this point on. However their meaning is understood or manipulated, this set of texts continues to inform and underpin all subsequent legal discussions of heresy.

Decretales Gregorii IX

Partly as a result of the *Decretum*, which had the effect of highlighting lacunae and defects in the corpus, canon law developed at a greater rate after the middle of the twelfth century and much new material was produced, mainly in the form of the papal letter. After the pontificate of Alexander III, during which the output of these documents increased exponentially, they were collected systematically over time into compilations. The five *Compilationes* were used alongside the *Decretum* until Gregory IX commissioned his confessor, Raymond of Peñafort, to gather and reconcile all the relevant material produced since the *Decretum* into one new collection. The decretal collection known as the *Decretales Gregorii IX*, or the *Liber Extra*, was published in 1234, and soon took up a place next to the *Decretum* at the centre of legal education.[79]

Its organization is more straightforward than that of the *Decretum*; the new material is collected, in chronological order, under descriptive titles that are arranged within five books. In the fifth book, title seven, *de hereticis*, contains the *Liber Extra*'s material on heresy, sandwiched between titles on Jews and Saracens on the one hand, and Schismatics on the other, placing heretics among the confirmed enemies of the Catholic church.[80] Not all the material collected here is new: there are also additions from the same writers of the early church that Gratian draws upon: Augustine, Gregory and other early popes. However, the majority of the texts that make up the *Liber extra*'s treatment of heresy were written against heresies which, as Pope Lucius III has it, 'began to break out and spread in modern times', and reflect a much more recent tradition of anti-heretical legislation than that represented in the *Decretum*, including the condemnation of Cathar heretics in canon twenty-seven of the third Lateran council and the whole of the fourth Lateran's third canon.[81]

Next to the Lateran provisions this title also includes two of the most important decretals to be issued against heresy. *Ad abolendam* was first promulgated in 1184 by Lucius III, in conjunction with Frederick I. Here were formally instituted both the practice of episcopal inquisitions into heresy and the obligations of support for the process and penalty from the secular authori-

---

79 Brundage, *Medieval Canon Law*, pp. 53–5; P. Landau, 'The Development of Law', in *The New Cambridge Medieval History*, vol. 4, c.1024–c.1198, ed. D. Luscombe (Cambridge, 2004), pp. 113–47 (pp. 132–5).

80 Friedberg, II, *Decretalium collectiones*, 778–90.

81 'Modernis coepit temporibus pullulare'; X 5 7.9, Friedberg, II, 780.

ties, although the exact nature of the punishment was left unspecified.[82] The other, Innocent III's decretal *Vergentis in senium*, issued at Viterbo in 1199, for the first time formally identified heresy with the secular crime of treason. The introduction of this principle of Roman law into the ideas both of heresy and of papal power thus provided the justification for sentences of confiscation and death.[83] The other decretals in this title include some short contributions from Gregory himself and two more from Innocent III, *Si adversus nos*, which removed notarial and legal support from heretics, and another that proscribed non-licensed preaching. These two, together with *Vergentis in senium*, and the fourth Lateran constitution, make Innocent the most represented authority in this title.[84] In terms of the way in which the decretals represent heresy, the texts that followed *Ad abolendam* and *Vergentis in senium* share and indeed borrow so much of their language from the latter two that an examination of these two decretals can be considered representative of much of this material.[85]

With one eye on the past, Lucius's decretal begins with a trope that would provide a minor theme for several later works on heresy: the heresies of 'modern times' standing in contrast to those that had gone before was a small but hereafter recurring motif of anti-heretical writing that also appears to have set the tone for Innocent's slightly apocalyptic opening to *Vergentis*. A more powerful theme, of heretics as deceptive and operating under a false appear-

---

[82] X 5 7.9, Friedberg, II, 780–82. Maisonneuve, *Études*, pp. 151–6; Arnold, *Inquisition*, p. 31. The late Roman penalty of burning was first prescribed for heretics by Pedro II's Gerona ordinance of 1198; Nelson, 'Religion in "Histoire totale"', p. 73.

[83] X 5 7.10, Friedberg, II, 782–3. Arnold, *Inquisition*, p. 31; M. Lambert, *The Cathars* (Oxford, 1998), pp. 92–5; Maisonneuve, *Études*, pp. 156–8, 278. According to Maisonneuve, although the use of Roman law in canonical tradition was not new – started by Gratian, and employed by Huguccio, who likened heresy to theft, and by Lucius III – in using it to prove this particular point Innocent was also concerned to support ideas of pontifical theocracy. Lansing frames Innocent's redefinition of heresy as treason in terms of a response to Cathar presence in the papal states: C. Lansing, *Power and Purity: Cathar Heresy in Medieval Italy* (Oxford, 1998), p. 6. On *lèse majesté* in *Vergentis* see W. Ullmann, 'The Significance of Innocent III's Decretal "Vergentis"', in *Études d'histoire du droit canonique dediées à Gabriel le Bras* (Paris, 1965), I, 729–41. Frederick II also threw his weight behind the repression of heresy, which is central to the Constitutions of Melfi, or *Liber Augustalis*, that he issued in Sicily in 1231, parts of which were later incorporated into a letter written to the authorities of northern Italy by Innocent IV. Frederick's text accepts the equation of heresy and treason established by Innocent III and draws on all the language and imagery employed by the papal decretals, emphasising in particular the hidden nature of the heretics and the poisonous truth that lies beneath. *Liber Augustalis, or, Constitutions of Melfi promulgated by the Emperor Frederick II for the Kingdom of Sicily in 1231*, trans. J. M. Powell (Syracuse, NY, 1971); Mansi, XXIII, 586–9; A. Piazza, '"Affinché ... costituzioni di tal genere siano ovunque osservate". Gli statuti di Gregorio IX contra gli eretici d'Italia', in *Scritti in onore di Girolamo Arnaldi, offerti dalla Scuola nazionale di studi medioevali*, ed. A. Degrandi et al. (Rome, 2001), pp. 425–58 (pp. 451–4).

[84] X 5 7.11, 12, Friedberg, II, 783–7.

[85] The glosses to the later decretals also refer back to these two texts with some regularity.

ance, is then introduced into the text through the use of a series of words to do with falsehood and by the invocation of Scriptural references: 'having the appearance of piety, but, as the apostle has said, denying its power'.[86]

Using the same citation, Innocent also describes heretics in terms of deception and pretence, as 'having the appearance of piety'; the heretic, 'cloaked in the appearance of religion ... both deceives many simple people, and seduces some astute ones'.[87] Innocent's decretal is generally much richer, rhetorically, than Lucius's. In its first third in particular the language is full of words and images that convey ideas of pollution and corruption. There are several strands to this, and ideas of a ruined harvest – 'the cornfields bring forth tares, or rather are polluted', in which 'the wheat dries, and fades into chaff' – serve next to the vocabulary of disease and poison to characterize their subject. Heresy is 'like cancer', 'creeping imperceptibly wider in secret', or is the 'the poison of the Babylonian dragon in a golden chalice', both of which images are also used to reinforce the idea of false appearance that is inherent in the *species pietatis* quoted above and is continued throughout Innocent's text. Several animal forms are also employed by Innocent to characterize the heretics that are damaging the vine and the grain, some traditional – the wolves and the little foxes – some less so, such as moths.[88] The themes and images of corruption and false appearance, in particular the appearance of piety, are picked up and reproduced throughout the subsequent decretals.

Beyond the imagery and powerful language there is a broader construction at work, of the general and undifferentiated heresy against which most of the new material in this title directs its condemnation and prohibitions. *Ad abolendam* defends the unity of the church against the falsehood of heretics by the issue of a universal condemnation of 'all heresy, by whatever name it may be called'.[89] Although a selection of names follows this sentence, including the Cathars and the Poor of Lyons, the phrase, and the idea, became a standard refrain in later works. The idea is also reinforced by *Vergentis*, which paints heretics as united in their falsehood, but it is in the fourth Lateran constitution that it finds its fullest expression, in the excommunication of canon three that defines its subject in reference to the creed of canon one, in what amounts to a universal condemnation of a heresy made uniform through exclusion.

The heresy of these texts is now about deception and danger. False appearance sits at the centre of that, but the impression is also conveyed by the more

---

86 'Sub specie pietatis virtutum eius, iuxta quod ait Apostolus, abnegantes'; X 5 7.9, Friedberg, II, 780, from II Timothy 3. 5. The 'falsitas' of heretics is a theme of the opening part of the decretal: 'falso nomine', 'in ipsis falsitatis', 'professio falsitatum'.

87 'Habentes ... speciem pietatis'; 'dum palliata specie religionis et multos decipit simplices, et quosdam seducit astutos'; X 5 7.10, Friedberg, II, 782.

88 'Segetes in zizania pullulant, vel potius polluntur'; 'triticum arescit, et evanescit in paleas'; 'sicut cancer'; 'amplius serperet in occulto'; 'virus draconis in aureo calice Babylonis'; X 5 7.10, Friedberg, II, 782.

89 'Omnem haeresim, quocunque nomine censeatur'; X 5 7.9, Friedberg, II, 780.

urgent sense of concern about heresy as a problem that is evident in the contemporary texts and in the choices from the older authorities. The focus is less on error and more on control and disobedience. The growth in the role of obstinacy continues and is entrenched and extended by the prohibitions on unlicensed preaching. It continues that development that we saw begun in the councils of the twelfth century toward greater control of heresy and presents a much more polemical and repressive approach than the more measured and detached view of the *Decretum*.

One point of comparison that has been frequently made between the two collections is the difference in tone evident when the texts are placed in conjunction with each other. Gone is the corrective attitude dominant in the *Decretum*, and in its place there is an emphasis on punishment and eradication. The more coercive stance permeates the whole of title seven, including the older material that makes up the first six, short chapters. The extracts chosen from the early authors for the *Liber extra* all embody a similar, less forgiving position to the newer material. It is interesting to note on this point the difficulty that the decretists had with this development. While Raymond of Peñafort seems to have taken the same line as Innocent, that heresy could be considered as treason, Maisonneuve demonstrates very clearly the ways in which other commentators on *Vergentis* took issue with the harsh nature of the disinheritance of heretics and points to the comparison that they made with an equivalent but more even-handed article of Roman jurisprudence. Initially drawn by Johannes Teutonicus, the comparison was carried to a fuller conclusion by both Vincent of Spain and Tancred, who openly came out in favour of the latter, more lenient precedent.[90] Sensitivity to this issue is also visible in occasional comments in the gloss on the *Decretum*. Augustine's quotation from the hundred and first Psalm, 'the man that in private detracted his neighbour, him did I persecute', is glossed 'we are able to pursue [heretics] openly, not in secret'. Later, when Augustine repeats Paul's words from first letter to the Corinthians, that an evil man should be delivered to the devil 'for the destruction of the flesh, that the spirit may be saved', the gloss adds 'just as we deliver heretics to the authorities'.[91]

Whatever scholarly opinions surrounded the changes represented by these laws, however, the difference in approach to the repression of heresy also resulted in a difference in the way that heresy itself was represented. The texts of the earlier compilation always portray the heretic as the outsider, the non-Catholic element. In canons nine, ten and eleven of the first question of

---

90 Maisonneuve, *Études*, pp. 277–86.

91 'Detrahentem secreto proximo suo, hunc persequebar'; 'manifeste vos possumus persequi, non latenter'; 'possem quidem dicere ipsum satanam omnibus malis hominibus esse peiorem, cui tradidit Apostolus hominem in interitum carnis; ut spiritus sit salvus in die Domini Iesu', based on I Cor 5. 5; 'sicut nos tradimus hereticos principibus'; C.23 q.4 c.40, Gratian, *Decretum divi Gratiani ... cum variis scribentium Glossis*, 'h' and 'k', col. 1302.

causa twenty-four Gratian seeks to answer the question of whether or not a heretic (and this extends more broadly to the excommunicate in general) can deprive others of orders, a question more concerned with the status and authority of the clergy than with the heresy itself. The implication that the process of answering this question has for the heresy involved is primarily that heretics, being excommunicate, are characterized by an outsider status. They are something apart from and outside of the Catholic Church, but it is made clear that this is through their own agency.[92] The theme of the heretic as outsider in fact dominates the tone of this question as a whole.[93] In this much, the two collections are very similar, but where in the *Decretum* there is a sense that these individuals have removed themselves from the church by virtue of their error and through their own choice, the twelfth- and thirteenth-century texts that make up the *Liber extra* treatment, and the fourth Lateran constitution especially, are proactive in excluding heresy and its adherents on Catholic terms, an emphasis that is reinforced by the gloss, which throughout defines heretics as those not observing what the church deems to be correct. Heretics are now outside because the church has put them there.

Connected to this is a greater emphasis on the figure of the heretic in the *Liber extra*, to the exclusion of heresy as error. The doctrinal nature of the heretic's status and the choice of erroneous belief that were so strong in the earlier text are now largely absent, and a heretic in the texts of the *Liber extra* is defined by the judgement and sentence of the church, not the false doctrine and misapplied learning of Gratian's collection. Here the heretic is even more 'ready-made': no space is given to identification or definition, and the primary business is with the treatment of heretics. Part of this increased emphasis on the figure is a result of the extension of the range of the subject, which now also includes the various categories of followers, who are even more divorced from the error than the heretics appear to be, being described and condemned purely in terms of their affiliation to the heretics. Individual holders of a heterodox belief are no longer the location of the heresy discussed by these sources and collections, and the focus of the canon-legal treatment of heresy is now concentrated on a much wider range of involvement.

To try to draw some of these threads together: the twelfth-century conciliar view progressed toward a representation of heresy that was increasingly general, though it remained based on the actions of those involved. At an ecumenical level in particular this meant that by our period, in the constitutions of the fourth Lateran council where heresy was defined by exclusion from Catholic doctrine, all heresies were now included under one, very general understanding of the term, though at the same time that shift also

---

92 'Quo a nobis separamini'; C.24 q.1 c.38, Friedberg, I, 982; Lenherr, *Gratian*, pp. 51–2. Also Friedberg, I, 982, Lenherr, *Gratian*, pp. 52–3.

93 C.24 q.1 cc.9–11, Friedberg, I, 969; Lenherr, *Gratian*, pp. 26–7.

demanded that this understanding be based in articles of faith. A similar development can be seen in the treatment of the heretic figure, always the real subject of conciliar action, but now increasingly undifferentiated. Heretics are also more numerous: a growing emphasis can be seen in the council of Tours and in the third Lateran council on the spread of heretics through different lands, which becomes wider still at Verona in the *Ad abolendam* decree that describes heretics in 'in most parts of the world'.[94]

As the heretic becomes more generic the group surrounding him becomes increasingly differentiated with the gradual accumulation of other categories of involvement.[95] The subject of anti-heretical legislation becomes more diverse, including a range of other figures defined by their actions toward and relationship to heretics. In turn, the heretics themselves seem to take on the function of a focal point for the status of these categories and, in many places, especially in the regional councils, they are often not the main subject of the measures being put in place. Like the texts of the *Liber extra*, the regional councils pay almost no attention to doctrinal error. Arnold has described the very physical nature of the search for heresy in this period of legislation, which concentrates more on finding heretics than discovering error.[96] For all that, neither do these councils spend much of their time talking about heretics proper; they are concerned primarily with the practical process of finding them and limiting their support. In common with that of the decretals and the ecumenical councils, the regional treatment of heretics seems based on a similar idea of a generalized heretic. Though here it is perhaps the focus on actions, and on dismantling their social and political network of support, that produces this effect, the underlying idea must be the same.

There is a great deal of similarity between the ecumenical council view and that of the *Liber extra*, not least because the latter contains significant parts of the former, but also as a result of the inclusion of so much of Innocent III's work. It is perhaps important to note in this context that the individual decretals were not, as the ecumenical constitutions were, universally binding, but were directed at particular groups or regions, a fact that some decretists, mentioned above, used to delimit the theoretical application of the confiscation laws.[97] The inclusion of these texts in the *Liber extra*, however, meant that the ideas contained in them were widely diffused. One of the more significant of these ideas was the equation of heresy with public crime – in particular, that of treason. The punitive and increasingly harsh measures taken against here-

---

[94] 'Plerisque mundi partibus'; X 5 7.9, Friedberg, II, 780; trans. E. Peters (ed. and trans.), *Heresy and Authority in Medieval Europe: Documents in Translation* (Philadelphia, PA, 1980), p. 170.

[95] Arnold sees the use of the term 'heretic' in these councils as more polemical than technical. Arnold, *Inquisition*, p. 38.

[96] Arnold, *Inquisition*, p. 36.

[97] Maisonneuve, *Études*, pp. 281–2.

tics by the councils echo the more coercive attitude of the newer legislation embodied in Gregory's new textbook.[98]

Where does this leave the *Decretum*? It has already been made clear that this text continued to play a central role in canon-legal thought throughout our period. Much use was made of the constituent parts of its discussion of heresy, in particular the definitions and the list of heresies from Isidore, but perhaps, at least in the majority of the anti-heretical legislation that we have looked at, the texts that make up the collection were not used with the same purpose for which Gratian included them.[99] The predominantly doctrinal view of heresy is absent, though implicit in the fourth Lateran constitution. Certainly the tone of correction seems to have been left behind, although some commentators and canonists, as Maisonneuve suggests, tried to strike a more restrained note.[100] The canon-lawyer Gui Foulques, who will be discussed in the next chapter, seems to have embodied this more nuanced approach in his consultation, very popular with inquisitors, which addressed the categories of guilt. With this in mind, let us now turn to look at the sharp end of this legislation, as manifested in the products of inquisition.

---

98 An example of 'the close links between academic legal theory and legal practice during this period' described by Landau, 'The Development of Law', p. 132.

99 The influence of this section of Isidore would also have been reinforced by its independent diffussion as part of this very popular text; see below, p. 181, n. 101.

100 Maisonneuve, *Études*, p. 286.

4

High is the Heart of Man: Inquisition Texts

Altum est cor hominis et inscrutabile[1]

Although the organized repression of heresy had its foundations in the legislation of the twelfth and early thirteenth centuries, the formal practice of inquisition into heretical depravity was put in place during the pontificate of Gregory IX. The use of the old legal method of *inquisitio* for the investigation of heresy had been introduced and adapted by Innocent III. Unlike the traditional method of *accusatio*, which depended on proactive witness testimony, an inquisition allowed the judge to act on his own authority, on the basis of *fama*. An ideal tool for investigating a hidden crime, it quickly became the normal form of procedure against heresy.[2] Several of the regional councils, in particular those at Narbonne in 1227 and Toulouse in 1229, were central to this process, but the official beginnings of inquisition can be found in the bull *Ille humani generis*, first issued in 1231, and the decretal *Excommunicamus*, also of 1231.[3]

In the context of repression, inquisition into heretical depravity, as it was always called, came to embody a highly specialized expertise and developed an impressive documentary tradition that was its ultimate source of power.[4] Each stage of the process of an inquisition produced documentary records, from the initial abjurations and confessions to records of the depositions and the sentences and penances imposed, which were carefully collected and preserved. Together, these records produced a profile of the levels of heresy in a region, and, even if a deponent knew nothing, that fact was still recorded

---

[1] Foulques, *Consilium*, q.9, p. 196.
[2] Dossat, *Crises*, p. 107; *Dictionary of the Middle Ages*, ed. J. R. Strayer, 13 vols. (New York, 1982–9), VI, 478–9.
[3] Dossat, *Crises*, pp. 105–18.
[4] On this idea, see J. H. Arnold, *Inquisition and Power: Catharism and the Confessing Subject in Medieval Languedoc* (Philadelphia, PA, 2001); J. B. Given, *Inquisition and Medieval Society: Power, Discipline and Resistance in Languedoc* (Ithaca, NY, 1997); and T. Scharff, 'Schrift zur Kontrolle – Kontrolle der Schrift', *Deutsches Archiv für Erforschung des Mittelalters* 52 (1996), 547–84.

and their statement could be used against them if it later turned out to be false. The importance of these records was lost neither on their creators nor on the people whose lives they detailed; staff with access to the inquisitors' archives were limited in number and reports of attempted or successful theft of inquisition registers demonstrate an awareness of their significance among the populace.[5] Though survival of these records is now patchy, some impression of the efficiency and thoroughness that inspired such anxiety can be gained from the organization of a typical register: the manuscript of the Carcassonne register contains a table of all the deponents before the inquisitor, arranged by location.[6] Within the register itself, a marginal note corrects the record of one deponent who added to his confession: it is a working and accessible record of a population's involvement in heresy.[7]

Beside those texts stemming directly from the inquisition process – that is, registers of depositions and of sentences – the business of inquisition also generated ancillary texts; it is at this time that we begin to see the appearance of the inquisitors' handbook, as well as new legal consultations on the subject of heresy. These latter two categories of texts, together with the registers of the inquisition process itself, constitute the majority of the written product of inquisition, and it is with these that this chapter is concerned.

As with the previous two chapters, the lines of division between one set of texts and another are not always rigid or easily discernible, and there is a certain amount of overlap between some of the inquisition texts and the legal material of the previous chapter: the canons of several of the councils, for example, especially Tarragona and Toulouse, were often included as legal consultations in document collections. This chapter is, however, concerned with only one specific and specialized aspect of the legal repression of heresy – the texts designed solely and specifically for the legal inquisition of heresy, rather than the general legal texts of the previous chapter.

Legal consultations

The legal consultation, essentially a response by a lawyer or lawyers to questions asked on a given topic, was not a form exclusive to the practice of inquisition, but as lists of questions, asked of legal experts by those engaged in the repression of heresy, our consultations tell us some part of what it was that inquisitors wanted to know. Although requested by particular individuals and occasionally referring to very particular cases, they were nonetheless copied and used by others where their questions and answers were more widely applicable.

---

5 Given, *Inquisition and Medieval Society*, pp. 26–8.
6 See below, p. 122.
7 Douais, *Documents: Textes*, p. 244, n. 1; p. 273, n. 4.

Consultation of John of Bernin[8]

Sent in 1235, by John, then papal legate for the repression of heresy in the Narbonne area, to the Dominican prior for Provence, Romeo.

Consilium peritorum Avinionensium quo declaratur qui dicuntur credentes[9]

A short but significant text, this consultation was written in 1235 by the Dominican prior and four lawyers at Avignon as a response to an enquiry from the Dominican William of Valence and two other men, who were seeking advice on the different types of guilt.

Consultation of Peter Collemieu[10]

Written probably in 1246 by Peter, who was bishop of Albano and cardinal legate between 1243 and 1246. It is distinct from another consultation by the same author to the inquisitors of Lombardy.

Consilium peritorum super quibusdam dubitabilibus propositis et solutis[11]

The *Consilium peritorum* is an anonymous consultation of the mid thirteenth century which Dondaine suggests may come from the same place as the Avignon opinion.

Consilium domini Guidonis Fulcodii[12]

This consultation, written around 1255–6 by the French lawyer and counsellor to Louis IX of France, Gui Foulques, was, according to Dondaine, the most frequently copied of all the great consultations of the thirteenth century, in part by virtue of the authority conferred upon it by its author's later elevation to the holy see, as Pope Clement IV, in 1265. It exists in two versions, though of the same redaction, the shorter of which omits the prologue, the list of questions and the responses to the first and third of those questions.[13] Gui also

---

8   BAV MS Vat. Lat. 3978, fol. 26ra–b. See Dondaine, 'Manuel', p. 142.

9   Patschovsky and Selge, *Quellen*, edition of text on pp. 50–54. Text is also in BAV MS Vat. Lat. 3978, on fols. 25ra–25va. See Dondaine, 'Manuel', pp. 141–2.

10 Dossat, *Crises*, pp. 348–9. Text is also in BAV MS Vat. Lat. 3978, fols. 28vb–29ra. See Dondaine, 'Manuel', p. 143.

11 BAV MS Vat. Lat. 3978, fols. 25va–26ra; Dondaine, 'Manuel', p. 142. There is a reference to torture here: 'minetur eis tormenta et eos duris questionibus submissuros'.

12 *Consilium Guidonis Fulcodii de quibusdam dubitacionibus in negocio inquisicionis*, in 3978 fols. 21rb–25ra; ed. in Foulques, *Consilium*. Dossat believes that the consultation was written just after the reinstatement of the Dominican inquisition in Languedoc, c.1256: Dossat, *Crises*, p. 199. For biographical details of Foulques see Dossat's article in Cahiers de Fanjeaux, 'Gui Foucois, enquêteur-réformateur, archevêque et pape (Clément IV)', *CF* 7 (1972), 23–57.

13 Dondaine, 'Manuel', pp. 184–5.

produced other, much smaller, consultations, notably in 1259/60, while he was archbishop of Narbonne, as well as a letter to the Dominican provincial of France in 1267 on the subject of heresy.[14]

To look generally at these consultations is to realize that they are for the most part concerned not with the heresy itself but with inquisition; one of Gui Foulques's smaller consultations is entirely concerned with questions of inquisitorial authority.[15] Many of the questions asked are to do with the jurisdictional and procedural aspects of the office, and either have little to say on their ultimate subject of inquiry or assume it to be an accomplished fact, and are concerned with issues to do with, for example, the legal status of convicted heretics. Where they do ask questions about heresy they tend to be on technical points and are overwhelmingly concerned with the divisions between the different grades of guilt, the different categories of follower outlined by the regional councils. From the two *Consilia peritorum* and the consultation of John of Bernin, to the canons of the councils of Tarragona in 1242 and Narbonne in 1243, to the consultations of Collemieu and Foulques, the same sorts of questions are asked: what is a *credens*? How does one distinguish between different grades? The predominance of such questions, and the legal construction of heresy that follows from dealing with it in this context, means first that heresy is presented in a way that is very like that of the regional councils – mainly physical and external – and that this in turn has implications for the manner in which the heretic himself is constructed.

John of Bernin's consultation of 1235, written early in the life of the papal inquisition, while very short and concerned really with procedural issues, provides a clue to the way in which the information on heresy in these texts should be understood. Bernin tells Romeo that he should require deponents to confess publicly, 'according to the quality of guilt'.[16] This phrase is echoed a decade later in Peter Collemieu's longer text, which states that deponents should be punished 'according to the quality of transgression' and that, 'according to the quantity and quality of transgression, they are to be punished with the penalty for relapses'.[17] The main principle of engagement with heresy is a concern to establish the precise quality of guilt. In practical terms it means that what descriptions and treatments of heresy these texts do present tend to revolve around the definition of different categories of involvement and of the boundaries between them.

The *Consilium peritorum Avinionensium quo declaratur qui dicuntur credentes*, as its title would suggest, answers really only one question: what is a *credens*?

---

14 In BAV MS Vat. Lat. 3978 fols. 78[ra–rb]; 78[rb–va]. See Dondaine, 'Manuel', pp. 151–2, no. 15 (d) and (e).
15 BAV MS Vat. Lat. 3978, fol. 78[rb–va].
16 'Secundum qualitatem culpe'; BAV MS Vat. Lat. 3978, fols. 26[rb], 29[ra].
17 'Secundum qualitatem delicti'; 'iuxta quantitatem et qualitatem delicti pena relapsis debita puniantur'; Dossat, *Crises*, p. 349.

The first criterion for this status is, rather unsurprisingly, a demonstrable belief in the heretics – in this case, Waldensians. Apart from their belief, the Avignon lawyers define a *credens* in terms of their actions towards heretics, in some cases with actions such as *visitare* or *recipere* that elsewhere tend to warrant a different and lesser category: a *credens* will have confessed to heretics, eaten with them, been taught by them, visited them or heard their preaching, or received them or done them favours.[18]

At the other end of the scale, both in terms of chronology and of detail, the consultation of Gui Foulques, the fullest and most detailed of these consultations, nonetheless presents a similar picture. Foulques's consultation again devotes much of its space to answering questions on the authority of inquisitors, but there are also questions devoted to a variety of categories: *fautores, receptatores, defensores*. Each of these categories is defined wholly in terms of actions. The only exception to this pattern in Foulques's text, as in the Avignon text, is in his definition of a *credens*, which begins with belief in heretics but then continues as a series of actions.[19] The prevalence of actions in the inquisition view of heresy has been noted often in studies of the texts that emerge from the process, and the legal consultations, like the regional councils to which they are in many ways similar, share that preoccupation.[20] The definitions they give rest almost exclusively on behavioural criteria, on measurable and perceivable actions, something reflected even in the names given to the different categories.

The predominant position given to actions in the identification of the guilty is not something that has escaped the attention of Gui Foulques either, however, who spends several lines in justifying the use of exterior facts in the demonstration of interior condition:

> For a presumption about disposition is to be made from external acts, as is argued *XXXII, q. V*, Qui vidit, C. De dolo, *l*. Dolum. Truly it makes no difference whether someone conveys their will through words or deeds (*ff. De l. et de se. con. l.* De quibus), for we can deny and confess not only by mouth but also by deed (*XI, q. III*, Existimant), and this applies to those deeds in which error is expressed, as above.[21]

---

18 Patschovsky and Selge, *Quellen*, pp. 51–2.

19 Foulques, *Consilium*, pp. 196–200.

20 P. Biller, '"Deep is the Heart of Man, and Inscrutable": Signs of Heresy in Medieval Languedoc', in *Text and Controversy from Wyclif to Bale: Essays in Honour of Anne Hudson*, ed. H. Barr and A. M. Hutchison, Medieval Church Studies 4 (Turnhout, 2005), p. 270 and *passim*.

21 'Nam ex factis exterioribus presumitur de affectu ut ar[guitur] XXXII, q. V, *Qui vidit* (C. 22 q. 5 c. 13, Qui viderit; Friedberg I, 1136), [et] C. *De dolo*, l *Dolum* (Cod. 2. 20 (21). 6; *Codex Justinianus*, ed. P. Krueger, Corpus Iuris Civilis 2, 12th edn (Berlin, 1959) p. 109). Nec enim refert utrum dictis an factis quis voluntatem suam insinuet ff. *De l[egibus] et de se[natus] con[sultis]*, l. *De quibus* (Dig. 1. 3. 32; *The Digest of Justinian*, ed. T. Mommsen and P. Krueger, trans. A. Watson, 4 vols. (Philadelphia, PA, 1985) I, 13). Nam negare et confiteri possumus non solum ore sed etiam facto XI, q. III, *Existimant* (C. 11 q. 3 c.84, *Existimant*; Friedberg, I,

On this basis evasion of penance can be considered a good sign of a false confession, while a further cautionary note warns the reader that, contrary to what many have written, actions performed under the influence of some familial or monetary obligation do not a *credens* make.[22] It is ultimately the interior condition that such signs indicate, and not the signs themselves, that Gui sees as the ultimate basis for a conviction.

A useful way of thinking about this gap, between action and inner state, has been suggested by Arnold in the context of the regional councils constitutions. He posits that contemporary ideas of literacy and understanding meant that, in the case of the unlettered, access to the individual's interior condition could be gained only through actions and, as a result, 'inquisitorial discourse constructs a particular relationship between "action" and "belief": the former functioning solely as a sign of the latter'.[23] As far as the consultations themselves are concerned Biller has used Gui Foulques's in particular to illuminate the concentration on external matters that we find in the legal material generally, linking it to a wider debate in legal thought about the use of actions as proofs. He shows Gui Foulques once again taking a more measured line than contemporary legislation, in particular that of the council of Narbonne, which took actions as clear evidence of guilt. Foulques counsels instead that motive must also be taken into account.[24]

The latter point is a key to what is going on here. The analyses by Arnold and Biller mean that we can feel secure in understanding that the inquisitors' interest in actions was as signs of inner state, but if we look again at the quotation from Gui Foulques above we see that it is not belief that is being sought, but intention. The consistent emphasis that we saw in the councils on these actions being done *scienter* would reinforce this, and the impression is strengthened further by the provisions of the Tarragona council. In answer to the question of whether suspects should be considered as believers Raymond answers no, 'unless he is so learned or discerning that he cannot put forward [the plea of] ignorance'. Similarly, no one is to be judged a heretic or a *credens* 'unless he is so literate or discerning that he cannot be in any way excused on the grounds of simplicity or ignorance'. In both cases, the ultimate decision is left to the discretion of 'a discerning judge', but the fact that a person is thought to have the capacity to understand the implications of their action, is either literate or discriminating, will tell against any denial of guilt.[25]

---

666). Et hoc dico de hiis factis in quibus error exprimitur sicut supra', Foulques, *Consilium*, p. 196. For the canon and Roman law cited here by Foulques, see Biller, 'Deep is the Heart of Man', p. 278, n. 28, and Foulques, *Consilium*, p. 196, nn. 58–61.

22 Foulques, *Consilium*, p. 200.

23 Arnold, *Inquisition*, pp. 44–7, 152. See also on this issue A. Cazenave, 'Aveu et contrition. Manuels de confesseurs et interrogatoires d'inquisition en Languedoc et en Catalogne (XIIIᵉ–XIVᵉ)', *Actes du 99e Congrès National des Sociétés Savantes* 1 (1977), 333–52 (esp. p. 337).

24 Biller, 'Deep is the Heart of Man', pp. 270–73, 277.

25 'Nisi adeo esset litteratus vel discretus, quod non posset ignorantiam praetendere'; 'nisi

The only point at which belief has a role in the determination of categories is in the definition of the *credens*, which would at least seem to grant the consultation picture of heresy an element of devotional existence, but the belief referred to here is not as straightforward as that. The *credens* is, after all, not a believer of heresy, but of heretics: in the same terminology as the church councils, both Gui Foulques and the anonymous author of the *Consilium peritorum super quibusdam dubitabilibus* refer to them as *credentes hereticorum*.[26] Even where they are believers of errors, those errors are firmly attached to, and mediated by, heretics: they are *credentes hereticorum erroribus*. Belief in heretics, belief in their errors or belief in their condition as good men are, according to the *Consilium peritorum Avinionensium*, one and the same.[27] That equation has the effect of rendering the error of belief as a single article, the belief in the otherwise unspecified errors of unspecified heretics, and means that the nature of those errors is immaterial. Although, as Arnold demonstrates, the question of belief undoubtedly remained a problematic one for inquisitors, it was in this way at least made into a question that was universally applicable. The fault lies in the fact of belief, not the error of it, and can therefore be answered in the single question, 'did you believe the heretics, or what they said?' A distinction is being made here between a relationship to error, which defines the heretic, and a relationship to a person, which defines the *credens*, and indeed all the lesser grades of guilt. In fact, Foulques himself emphasizes the importance of exactly this distinction in the case of *defensores*, distinguishing between those who defend error – that is, heretics – and those who defend people.[28] In this way, then, believing, or believing incorrectly, which is what we would usually understand heresy to be, and what Gui Foulques defines it as, is here transformed into one more verb in the list of culpable actions.

The other effect of the distinction that these texts draw between error and person is to separate the 'heretic' from the larger group, reflecting the similar

---

adeo litteratus sit et discretus quod nullatenus per simplicitatem vel ignorantiam valeat excusari'; 'quod arbitrio discreti judicis duximus reliquendum'; Selge, *Texte*, pp. 53, 57. On the ethics of intention in scholastic thought, and development of this in theology and law, see M. L. Colish, 'Early Scholastics and the Reform of Doctrine and Practice', in *Reforming the Church before Modernity: Patterns, Problems and Approaches*, ed. C. M. Bellitto and L. I. Hamilton (Aldershot, 2005), 61–8 (esp. p. 64).

[26] BAV MS Vat. Lat. 3978, fol. 25va, other grades also attached, fol. 25vb; Foulques, *Consilium*, p. 196.

[27] 'Credere quippe Valdensibus vel credere ipsorum erroribus vel credere ipsos bonos homines, pro eodem dixerunt firmiter se habere'; Patschovsky and Selge, *Quellen*, p. 51.

[28] Foulques, *Consilium*, p. 199. A similar distinction is made by Damasus's gloss to the third canon of the fourth Lateran council: 'istud loquitur in receptoribus et defensoribus hereticorum, non de ipsis hereticis'; García, *Lateran 4*, p. 420. On Damasus see also A. García y García, 'The Fourth Lateran Council and the Canonists', in *The History of Medieval Canon Law in the Classical Period, 1140–1234: from Gratian to the Decretals of Pope Gregory IX*, ed. W. Hartmann and K. Pennington (Washington D.C., 2008), pp. 367–78, especially pp. 374–6.

distinction made in the church councils and canon-legal textbooks. The heretic is the object of all the verbs that designate guilt, or as the paradigm by which others will be judged.[29] Despite Collemieu's injunction that 'inquisition is to be made for the ... investigation of *hereticos perfectos*', almost no provision is made for this eventuality.[30] There is some overlap with the *credentes*, with whom they are sometimes associated, in such statements as 'they are not believers, nor heretics, but supporters', though it is for this reason that the ever-cautious Gui Foulques emphasizes that the charge of *credens* is a serious one, and should not be made lightly.[31] Otherwise the heretic is an outside figure, with little real presence except as the focal point for the actions of the followers and as the locus of the error and ritual, distinguished from others by their relationship to error. Though occasionally differentiated by name, as the Waldensians sometimes are, and though we can probably assume that 'heretics' usually indicates Cathars in the southern French tradition, with error reduced to a label, heretics are doctrinally homogenous.

What we see here, then, is heresy not as a series of beliefs, but as a series of actions, all revolving around an abstracted figure. The virtue of this, from a legal point of view at least, is that, as such, heresy and all its characteristics become generic and, because dependent on actions and devoid of doctrinal content, universally applicable. This is not the idea of heresy that derives from a theological standpoint; where 'heresy' is used here, it has a general sense which encompasses all the actions and levels of involvement relating to the heretics and their errors. Although Gui Foulques employs legal authorities as a theologian might use Scripture, heresy in these texts is a legal error, not a doctrinal one: it is a crime and is talked about in these terms, described here and elsewhere in terms of the equations made in canon law with secular crimes of treason and theft.[32]

The product of inquisition

We now leave behind our consultations, with their advice on the correct process of inquisition, and move to those texts generated by the process itself, the depositions of witnesses before the inquisitors and the sentences and penances imposed upon them. For this period, though we have some records from northern Italy, much of what survives represents inquisitions that were

29 'Velut hereticos condemnandos'; Foulques, *Consilium*, p. 196.
30 'Inquisitionem faciendam pro ... investigandum hereticos perfectos'; Dossat, *Crises*, p. 349.
31 'Non sunt credentes nec heretici sed fautores'; Foulques, *Consilium*, p. 196. Gui Foulques is always careful to draw a line between heretics and others where there is a danger of confusion, and emphasises several times that the seriousness of a charge of heresy should mean that judgements ought always to err on the side of caution.
32 The description in the anonymous *Consilium peritorum super quibusdam dubitabilibus* is that 'omnes criminosi et infames in heresi crimine admittuntur etiam principes criminis sicut in crimine lese maiestatis'; BAV MS Vat. Lat. 3978, fol. 26[ra].

carried out in the south of France, a survival that is due in large part to the mission of Doat in the seventeenth century.

Penances of Peter Cellan[33]

The penances imposed on the deponents before Peter Cellan's inquisition in the Quercy region in the years 1241–2 survive in volume 21 of the Doat collection. They are extremely short and abbreviated, though Duvernoy believes this to be their original form, given the length of the other documents reproduced in the same volume.

Depositions before Carcassonne inquisitors[34]

The whole of volume 23, as well as part of 24, of the Doat collection is taken up with the depositions made before the Carcassonne inquisitors Ferrier, Pons Garin and Peter Durand between 1243 and 1245.

Sentences of Bernard of Caux and John of St-Pierre[35]

The sentences passed by 1244–8 in Toulouse by these two inquisitors, who were also responsible for writing the *Ordo processus narbonensis* considered in the next section, are edited by Douais in the text volume of his *Documents*, along with the depositions given before them against one Peter Garcias in 1247.

Register of a Carcassonne notary[36]

A collection of penances from 1250–58, and some interrogatories from 1250–67, again edited by Douais.

Depositions before Toulouse inquisitors[37]

The 25th Doat volume reproduces the later depositions before Renous of Plassac and Pons of Parnac at Toulouse between 1272 and 1278.

---

[33] Duvernoy, *Quercy*. On Cellan and his sentences see J. Feuchter, *Ketzer, Konsuln und Büßer: die städtischen Eliten von Montauban vor dem Inquisitor Petrus Cellani (1236/1241)*, Spätmittelalter, Humanismus, Reformation 40 (Tübingen, 2007).

[34] Doat 23–4.

[35] Douais, *Documents: Textes*, 1–89; pp. 90–114, are depositions against Peter Garcias taken from Doat 24.

[36] Douais, *Documents: Textes*, pp. 115–301.

[37] P. Biller, C. Bruschi and S. Sneddon (ed.), *Inquisitors and Heretics in Thirteenth-Century Languedoc: Edition and Translation of Toulouse Inquisition Depositions 1273–82*, Studies in the History of Christian Tradition 147 (Brill, 2011), with thanks.

Tuscan records[38]

A selection of Florentine depositions, sentences and penances from the time of Dante were edited by Felice Tocco as an appendix to his work on the Divine comedy, the first nineteen of which, dated 1244–76, provide a useful Italian source of inquisition records.

Tuscan formulary and Orvieto Register[39]

Two sets of documents are edited by Mariano d'Alatri: the first is a formulary, used in Tuscany and Umbria. The date of its use is hard to ascertain; the manuscript is fourteenth-century, but the documents that comprise it, where they are dated, are from the 1240s and 1250s. Several of these documents find their way into the inquisitors' manual in MS Vat Lat 3978 (see below). The second group of texts is the *Liber inquisitionis* of Orvieto, a register of the sentences imposed by the inquisitors Ruggero Calcagni in 1239 and 1249 and brother Giordano in 1263.[40] According to Lansing, the marginalia of the manuscript suggest that it was kept as a treasury document.[41]

Before looking at these texts in detail it is important to note the difficulties that they present to the historian. These difficulties, which have been brought to light in a succession of studies, most notably by Herbert Grundmann and Grado Merlo, and more recently by Caterina Bruschi, relate principally to the processes by which these documents were produced. The stages of translation through which they passed, from vernacular to Latin, from oral to written, and from the first person to a third-person narrative, mean that their apparently smooth texture is in fact composed of several layers. This multi-layered structure naturally poses a variety of problems when trying to reach the 'truth' that they contain about heresy, not least the danger of circularity – namely, that the information contained by the records is the information that the inquisitors asked for. It is important to be aware in this context that what appears to be a spontaneous confession is usually in fact rendered as such from a list of closed questions and their answers.[42]

---

38 Tocco, edition of documents pp. 34–60 (pp. 61–78 contain further documents too late for this study).

39 D'Alatri, *Orvieto*, edition of documents pp. 171–338.

40 Parts of the formulary are also in BAV MS Vat. Lat. 3978, fols. 32ra–32rb, 34vb–35ra, 50va–51rb, 53ra–54ra.

41 C. Lansing, *Power and Purity: Cathar Heresy in Medieval Italy* (Oxford, 1998), p. 27.

42 For a succinct and helpful summary of these problems and processes, see Biller, 'Deep is the Heart of Man', pp. 267–70. See also H. Grundmann, 'Ketzerverhöre des Spätmittelalters als quellenkritisches Problem', *Deutsches Archiv für Erforschung des Mittelalters* 21 (1965), 519–75, repr. in Grundmann, *Ausgewählte Aufsätze*, I, 364–416; G. G. Merlo, *Eretici e inquisitori nella società piemontese del Trecento: con l'edizione dei processi tenuti a Giaveno dall'inquisitore Alberto de Castellario (1335) e nelle Valli di Lanzo dall'inquisitore Tommaso di*

Further to this, it is also worth noting that these documents were not intended to be read in the same way as the other sources that have been considered here: they were not a text, but a record. Of course their interest in this context is still as a record, though of the ideas and constructs used by those involved in their creation, rather than an individual's involvement with heresy, but they are also to some degree being treated as 'texts' in the source-critical sense and, as Arnold suggests, examined for their language and the rhetoric to which that language is harnessed.[43]

One more point must be mentioned in the context of this chapter: though there are variations in the content of the information between the documents of different regions, in the names given to heretics, for example, or in the proportion of male to female heretics that appear, the type of information that is sought, the pattern of the questions and the essential framework of the documents remain the same. Indeed, most of the variations in this genre would seem to result more from differences between inquisitors than any regional peculiarities.

Unsurprisingly, there are several similarities between the representation of heresy that we find in these inquisition documents and that which emerges from the reading of the consultations and the regional council material. Perhaps the biggest similarity lies in the role played by the heretic in the scheme of guilt and involvement, although there is also a disparity here in that the inquisition documents, built around real, named individuals and the details of their networks and itineraries, present a much fuller and more immediate picture of the heretics themselves than do the legal and conciliar texts. We will look first at the picture of heretics that the inquisition materials provide before moving on to look more closely at the role that they play.

As with the other legal texts that we have looked at, there is in the inquisition material a layer of heretics proper, a level of involvement that is not only higher than that of the others, but somehow apart from them, a distinction achieved most obviously through the terminology used to describe them. The Orvieto register stands out among these texts for the ornate and almost polemical language with which it describes heretics, employing a great deal of fairly standard imagery, but, for the most part, heretics are distinguished firstly by their name. Though all the deponents may be involved in 'heresy', only the élite and the obstinate become 'heretics'. The label is usually further refined by the use of terms such as *heretica induta* or, occasionally, the Cathar term *boni homines*. The Italian records use *heretici consolati* with some frequency; the Tuscan register sometimes also makes this a noun, *consolati*, to stand for heretics proper, though, interestingly, in this collection of texts, there seems occasionally to be a distinction drawn between heretics and consoled

---

Casasco (1373) (Turin, 1977); C. Bruschi, '"Magna diligentia est habenda per inquisitorem": Precautions before Reading Doat 21–26', in *Texts and Repression*, ed. Bruschi and Biller, pp. 81–110.

[43] J. H. Arnold, 'Inquisition, Texts and Discourse', in *Texts and Repression*, ed. Bruschi and Biller, pp. 63–80 (p. 63).

heretics: 'certain heretics, three or four, of whom two were consoled'.[44] The Italian sources also use the term 'Patarine' interchangeably with 'heretic', in contrast to the southern French records, which use either 'heretic' or 'Waldensian'.[45] There is also, in the Tuscan records, one rogue use of 'Manichee'.[46]

The descriptions of these heretics and their lives given by the deponents and, on occasion, the heretics themselves, though directed by the questions of the inquisitor, create a detailed picture in which several aspects remain constant. Not least of these is the pastoral activity of the heretics. Their preaching and their administration of sacrament and ritual to their followers is an omnipresent element in the depositions, apparent in the background of all the testimony here. Indeed, the southern French heretics are extremely mobile, moving frequently between houses and also, from time to time, back and forth to nearby Lombardy, where conditions seem to have been more favourable.[47] Lombard connections are noticeable in the earlier Carcassonne records of Bernard of Caux and of the Carcassonne notary, but are far more prominent, perhaps unsurprisingly, in the registers of Renous of Plassac and Pons of Parnac, which are filled with depositions from a time when many of the Cathars had fled the south of France for the relative safety of Lombardy.[48] As has been made well known by specialists on the theme of women and heresy, a number of the active élite are female: they are not frequent, but they can be found in all our sources, especially perhaps in the Tuscan records.[49] Doat 23 contains one long deposition from Arnaude, who had been a 'consoled' heretic for many years; even in Peter Cellan's brief penances there is mention of female heretics preaching and of a Waldensian sister expounding Scripture.[50]

Exposition itself is rarely mentioned, and equally rarely described, though the depositions against Peter Garcias, which even include the supporting Scriptural authorities, are a marked exception to this. There is, however, a faint but fairly continuous presence of heretical books to be found in these docu-

---

44 'Quidam heretici, tres vel iiij, ex quibus erant duo consolati'. 'Vested heretic', for example: Douais, *Documents: Textes*, p. 28, Doat 23, fol. 48ᵛ; 'good men', for example: Doat 23, fol. 119ʳ, d'Alatri, *Orvieto*, pp. 202, 249, Tocco, pp. 36, 35, 43, 50. For the use of term 'perfects', see below, pp. 201–2.

45 D'Alatri, *Orvieto*, e.g. pp. 228, 213. Tocco, e.g. pp. 36, 43.

46 Tocco, p. 58.

47 On mobility and itinerancy see C. Bruschi, *The Wandering Heretics of Languedoc* (Cambridge, 2009).

48 Inquisitorial interest in geographical movement: Douais, *Documents: Textes*, p. 265; Doat 25, e.g. fols. 12ʳ, 90ʳ; in Lombard connections: Douais, *Documents: Textes*, pp. 33, 287; Doat 25, e.g. fols. 13ᵛ, 131ᵛ, 39ᵛ–40ʳ, 91ᵛ, 44ᵛ. Dyas goes to northern Spain to hear heretics, Doat 23, fol. 71ʳ. Such movement was not limited to the heretics; one Arnold Richier of Narbonne also left for fear of the inquisition, see testimony of Peter Daide, Doat 23, fol. 140ʳ.

49 Tocco, e.g. p. 38; d'Alatri, *Orvieto*, pp. 306, 318, 265. Also in Douais, *Documents: Textes*, p. 70.

50 Tocco, p. 38; Doat 23, fols. 2ᵛ–49ᵛ, female heretics administer medical aid; fol. 72ᵛ. Douvernoy, *Quercy*, pp. 78, 214, 152, 246.

ments. One deposition of Doat 25 records the possession by heretics of books not only in the vernacular, but also in Latin, of which they also seem to be making copies. The deponent who provided this information was supposedly guarding the books for the heretics, a situation that, apart from ritual, is the most common context in which we find books. Interestingly, the same deponent claimed also to have studied the books and formed his (heretical) belief on the basis of what he read in them, though this may simply be a more literary version of the 'nobody taught me; I thought it up myself' dodge that deponents sometimes use to avoid implicating others.[51] What is never, or almost never, recorded is the content of the books mentioned, or, for that matter, of the sermons that the deponents attended.[52] What does emerge is a picture of a highly mobile and, above all, organized group with its own hierarchy composed of the 'deacons' and 'bishops' who make appearances from time to time, and which was still strong in the south of France even mid-century: Peter Cellan's register of penances records an occasion on which seventy heretics were present in one house, and, by the time of the register surviving in Doat 25, the Cathars still appears to have an fairly sophisticated hierarchy in place.[53]

Despite this apparent success heretics are also shown as hidden, and many of their activities are undertaken in secret. The hiding place is a well-established topos in the Catholic representation of heresy; heretics or their meetings are often located underground, in a 'den' or 'lair', an image associated with ideas of heresy as an infection or pollution and enshrined in anti-heretical legislation, in which edicts of the councils demand that the physical places of heresy be destroyed. In this way it is also present in the sentences of inquisition. An Orvieto sentence decrees that the house of the condemned is to be razed to the ground as a 'squalid refuge that was a den of perfidies'.[54] In a similar way the Orvieto formulary condemns a house as a 'perpetual refuge of filth, where at times there was a den of heretics'.[55]

The *latibulum* constructs a physically hidden heresy, in parallel to the hidden moral condition that we have seen emphasized elsewhere, but there is also a layer of hiddenness that is more straightforwardly to do with avoiding persecution. Indeed, for all its traditional resonance, the *latibulum* itself could nonetheless be a real enough place. The deposition of Austorga of Rosenges is largely taken up with descriptions of moving and hiding various heretics from

---

[51] Use of books (vernacular) Doat 25, fol. 197ᵛ (Latin) fols. 198ʳ, 199ʳ. Peter Daide, Doat 23, fols. 128ʳ, 129ᵛ, 138ʳ. Douais, *Documents: Textes*, p. 281. D'Alatri, *Orvieto*, formulary, pp. 186, 181.

[52] Preaching: Doat 23, e.g. fols. 73ᵛ, 133ᵛ, but throughout; d'Alatri, *Orvieto*, pp. 176, 215, 230, 231, Patschovsky and Selge, *Quellen*, p. 57; inquisitorial interest in words of Waldensian preaching, Doat 25, fol. 197ʳ.

[53] Duvernoy, *Quercy*, p. 102; Doat 23, fols. 2ᵛ–49ᵛ; heretical deacon, Doat 25, fols. 12ᵛ, 13ʳ–ᵛ; as established church, Doat 25, fol. 132ʳ–ᵛ; visible hierarchy Tocco, pp. 41, 51.

[54] 'Receptaculum sordium que fuit latibulum perfidiorum'; d'Alatri, *Orvieto*, p. 213.

[55] 'Perpetuum receptaculum sordium, ubi fuit aliquando latibulum hereticorum'; Tocco, p. 181.

the late 1220s onwards, but it contains one detail of particular interest, in which Austorga describes hiding two *hereticae* in her home. One heretic, already in residence, would not eat without her *socia*, and so Austorga found the heretic's companion and led her to her house, where 'she opened a certain little door and went in to the other heretic, and she placed both heretics in a large cask'.[56] As extraordinary as that sounds, some further explanation can perhaps be found in the later deposition of her neighbour, Arnold of Bonhac, whose wife sees heretics hiding in the cellar of the Rosenges's house, 'where there is a certain "cell"', testimony that seems to suggest a specialized heretic-hiding facility beneath Austorga's house.[57]

If the hiddenness is real, then, in the French material, a change is visible over time: Arnaude of Lamothe's descriptions of her early life as a Cathar include the presence of several publicly maintained Cathar houses, something also found in Dyas of Deyme's testimony; in both cases these date from the first decade of the thirteenth century. In the later phase of her heresy, however, after a brief return to the Catholic faith, Arnaude spends most of her time as a 'Good Woman' moving covertly between different hiding places, often located in woods.[58]

Despite the covert nature of southern French heresy toward the middle of the century it is nonetheless also possible to find disputations in this region. Undoubtedly one of the most entertaining of Douais' *Documents pour servir à l'histoire de l'inquisition* are those depositions before Bernard of Caux and John of St-Pierre of a group of Franciscan friars who appear to have taken it in turns to hide in the rafters of their house in order to eavesdrop on a dispute between one of their number and a local *credens*.[59] That dispute was conducted in private, but there are also many witnesses to public debate in Cellan's register, not only between heretics and Catholics but between different heretical groups as well, and one witness before the inquisitors at Toulouse remembers a local cleric, later burnt for heresy, arguing with the mendicant preachers over the consecration of the host.[60] As in the polemics, a similar picture emerges from

---

56 'Aperuit sibi hostiolum quoddam et intravit ad alia hereticam et reposuit ambas hereticas in quodam dolio'; Doat 24, fol. 2ᵛ.
57 'Ubi est quoddam clusellum'; Bibliothèque municipale, Toulouse, MS 609, fol. 200ʳ. A similar small underground hiding-place is described in the deposition of Arnaude of Lamothe, who hides 'subtus terram in quadam domuncula per unum mensem'; Doat 23, fol. 22ᵛ. The classic account of heretics' hiding places in Languedoc is in J. Guiraud, *Histoire de l'inquisition*, 2 vols. (Paris, 1935–8), II, chapter 3.
58 Doat 23, public Cathar houses: fols. 3ᵛ, 13ʳ; wood-dwelling in later phase of life, e.g. fol. 22ᵛf; public houses in Dyas's testimony, fol. 71ʳ. Peter Daide's deposition also often shows heretics in the woods, e.g. fol. 131ʳ. See also Douais, *Documents: Textes*, p. 252. In Bernard of Caux and John of St-Pierre's register condemned heretics are on several occasions visible through the depositions of their followers, roaming around, still at large despite their conviction. Douais, *Documents: Textes*, pp. 61, 72.
59 Douais, *Documents: Textes*, pp. 90–114.
60 Duvernoy, *Quercy*, for example pp. 56, 64, 68, 78, 96, 102, 112; Doat 25, fol. 42ʳ.

the Italian sources: a witness before the Orvieto inquisition testifies that 'he saw Patarenes in Cremona, talking and disputing',[61] and another Tuscan deponent claims to have witnessed a heretic 'disputing about heresy with the notary William' – the latter situation, a northern Italian layman engaged in dispute with heretics, recalls those polemics written by Salvo Burci and George.[62]

There is, coming through these depositions, a picture of active and organized heretical groups, but although there are also suggestions of heretical learning in, for example, the presence and use of books, and of the heretics' apparently disputative nature, there is little information that would give a fuller picture and very rarely is there any detail of the errors behind this learning. The level of detail that the depositions provide about the movements of heretics and connections between them and their followers is a result of the interest of the inquisitors in obtaining information about the local network that can be used to control and dismantle it. A large part of inquisition is indeed about police work, and it is information of this sort that makes up the vast proportion of the content of these sources.[63] The main agenda of the interrogations visible in these depositions, therefore, seems to be the acquisition of information – names, dates and contacts – that will allow the removal of material support from the heretical networks. That agenda is visible quite clearly in the penalties that the registers record: it is noticeable in Peter Cellan's penances, for example, that those who receive the harshest penalties are those who have provided property or land for the heretics' use. Gaubert Sicard of Courande, who allowed the Cathars to keep a 'hereticated house' on his land, for which the heretics paid him, seems to have had little more to do with them other than to bring them their groceries; nonetheless he is sent to exile in Constantinople, it would seem indefinitely.[64] Similarly, the Orvieto sentences are almost entirely material in their nature, dealing out confiscation and disinheritance, but very little in the way of crosses and pilgrimage.[65] If we look ahead to one of the inquisitors' manuals, the *Ordo processus narbonensis* regards deprivation of goods as the most effective remedy against heresy: 'we cause the goods of heretics, the condemned and the imprisoned as well, to be confiscated, and we insist that this be done, as we are duty bound to do. It is in this way that heretics and believers are particularly confounded.'[66]

---

[61] 'Vidit patarenos in Crimona [*sic*] loquentes et disputantes'; d'Alatri, *Orvieto*, p. 231.

[62] 'Disputantem de heresi cum Guilielmo notario'; Tocco, p. 51. See also discussion of debate above, pp. 22–4.

[63] Biller, 'Deep is the Heart of Man', pp. 268–70. See also A. Roach and P. Ormerod, 'The Medieval Inquisition: Scale Free Networks and the Suppression of Heresy', *Physica A* 339 (2004), 645–52.

[64] 'Hereticata domus'; Duvernoy, *Quercy*, p. 126.

[65] D'Alatri, *Orvieto*, pp. 223, 226; Douais, *Documents: Textes*, pp. 6, 250; d'Alatri, *Orvieto*, p. 249.

[66] 'Bona hereticorum tam dampnatorum quam immuratorum publicare facimus et compellimus ut debemus, et per hoc est quod specialiter confundit hereticos et credentes';

Only some parts of heretical activity are therefore recorded here – that is, the actions that determine involvement. The names of those who were present at rituals are sought and noted, and details of the ritual itself are included in as much as they determine the level of adherence – if you were at the adoration did you also bend your knee; did you say bless?[67] Attendance of heretical sermons and debates are a mark of guilt, but the contents of those sermons are not. Peter Daide is asked not about the subject of the sermons he heard, only about the fact of his, and others', attendance.[68] While a picture of heretics does emerge from these sources, in some ways in spite of the direction of the questioning, the actual construct of the heretic is similar to that of the consultation material: heretics remain in some ways in the background and, although they are more common in some registers than in others, they are only occasionally the deponent before the inquisition. Mostly heretics are a constant but more or less distant presence, as the axis around which activities and guilt revolve, including, for many deponents, belief: there is only one penance among those in Cellan's register that includes any reference to error, a condensed and abbreviated version of Cathar doctrine which contains very little else above the usual belief in the salvific abilities of sect and heretics.[69] Heretics are most often the object of those verbs that the consultations and councils use to define guilt and which separate heretics from the raft of their supporters and believers.[70]

In light of this we can now turn to look more closely at the representation of heresy in the inquisition texts, and what relationship this representation has with that of the consultations in particular. At a broad level, one similarity has already been highlighted, that which lies in the role played by the heretic in relation to the wider group. There is, as noted, a technical distinction between the heretics and the followers who make up the majority of the depositions, a distinction that is made in two main places, the first and most obvious of which has been described: the terminology used to describe them. The position of these heretics relative to the other deponents and, more importantly, to error, sets them further apart from the rest. As in the other legal sources, believers are never believers of error, but of heretics and the error of heretics.[71] Heretics are once again the medium between error and believer, and, once again, the only blurring of this line is the overlap of *credens* with heretic, in line with the legal injunction to inquisitors that believers of heretics' errors are to be considered, in legal terms, *ut heretici*. They are equated in the abjuration

---

Selge, *Texte*, p. 76; trans. W. L. Wakefield, *Heresy, Crusade and Inquisition in Southern France 1100–1250* (London, 1974), p. 257.

67 Details of ritual: Duvernoy, *Quercy*, p. 124; Doat 25, fols. 50^v, 162^r; Tocco, p. 59.

68 Doat 23, e.g. fol. 133^v.

69 Duvernoy, *Quercy*, p. 108.

70 Doat 23, fol. 133^v; Douais, *Documents: Textes*, pp. 6, 250; d'Alatri, *Orvieto*, p. 249.

71 For example: Tocco, pp. 51, 58; d'Alatri, *Orvieto*, p. 212; Douais, *Documents: Textes*, pp. 12, 21, 192.

given by the Tuscan formulary and Cellan's penances also present them as a group.[72]

The distinction that is drawn in the legal material though, and in the language of the inquisition documents, is not always maintained in the treatment received by the few heretics that are brought before the inquisitors. What sentences we have for 'vested' or full heretics record a penance or punishment that seems remarkably similar to that imposed on the lesser grades. Huguette, and Bernarde of Rou, for example, two *hereticae perfectae*, are given penances by Peter Cellan that are hardly different from, and in some cases rather less severe than, those received by followers, although their punishment is distinguished from that of the lesser grades by the imposition of crosses.[73] Nevertheless, in the Carcassonne register, we find a 'vested' heretic in among a list of believers and followers, given the same sentence without apparent distinction.[74] Similarly, the Orvieto book gives a sentence for a 'consoled heretic', which imposes the same, albeit harsh, punishment on her as on many others who are not so labelled.[75]

More interesting, while the sentences are inconsistent in their discrimination between heretic and follower, one of the few depositions that we have of a 'vested' heretic betrays no difference in approach or interest in the inquisitors' interrogation. The long deposition of Arnaude of Lamothe, a heretic for over thirty years in the south of France, contains no detail of error at all. Arnaude is not questioned about belief, and the questions she is asked are precisely those that are asked of everyone else, the only difference being that she is the object, rather than the subject, of the normal actions: not did you adore any heretics, but did anyone adore you?[76] Although there is a distinct layer of heretics that are nominally separate from the other deponents, what that seems to mean, principally, is someone who has undergone the ritual of initiation, who has 'made herself a heretic'.[77] The name is also to be applied to those who have relapsed, or refused to do their penance, in which case they can be sentenced 'as a heretic'. The term 'heretic' is understood, in other

---

[72] 'Quod hereticos et credentes eorum tot posse meo persequar et tam eos quam eorum fautores'; d'Alatri, *Orvieto*, pp. 177, 275, 296. 'Fugerunt heretici et credentes qui ibi erant'; Duvernoy, *Quercy*, p. 94.

[73] Duvernoy, *Quercy*, pp. 260, 262. Huguette and Bernarde are both sent to Puy, St-Gilles, Santiago de Compostela, St-Denis, and the shrine of St Thomas in Canterbury, and are also given crosses, one for life, the other for five years. This is the same penance – minus the crosses – that is that is given to several followers, such as Raimunda, wife of Bosolens, Duvernoy, *Quercy*, p. 180. Some followers are sent to Constantinople for years on end. On Cellan's sentences see Feuchter, *Ketzer, Konsuln und Büßer*, chapter 6. In contrast, see Tocco's collection, which includes a sentence for a heretic, Bona, who is condemned to the stake: Tocco, pp. 38–9.

[74] Douais, *Documents: Textes*, p. 28.

[75] 'Hereticam consolatam'; d'Alatri, *Orvieto*, pp. 245, 256.

[76] Doat 23, fols. 2ᵛ–49ᵛ.

[77] 'Fecit se haereticam'; Doat 23, fol. 129ᵛ. Similarly, 'fecit se Valdensem'; fol. 139ʳ.

words, as a made thing, either through the actions of ritual or the action of inquisition, and so, in the context of inquisition documents, even heretical status can be signalled in terms of a tangible action. That differentiation between heretic and *credens* is borne out by Vincent of Spain's gloss to the fourth Lateran constitutions, which explains *credentes* as those 'who do not yet openly profess any sect'.[78] So it is that Peter Garcias, who appears, in his dispute with the Franciscan brothers, to hold full heretical beliefs, and even to be living a semi-heretical, ascetic lifestyle, cut off from his wife, can still be called a *credens*.[79]

All of which is not to say, however, that inquisitors were not interested in error; we can see that there are a few occasions on which they do use question lists that are built around known heretical errors to interrogate a deponent, though the deposition of one heretic in Tocco's collection, for example, seems to be little more than a checklist of standard errors.[80] Although for the most part heretical errors do not have much more presence beyond that of a label in these depositions, as something attached to heretics, and any 'belief' on the part of the follower is either mediated by heretics or is little more than a statement of spiritual belief in salvific qualities of the sect, occasionally we are given depositions that contain nothing but error. The case of the Franciscan depositions against Peter Garcias, which provide the content of his argument and the ensuing debates in great detail, are the best example of such depositions. Aside from the Garcias case, of the collections that we have looked at here, some of most error-based interrogations can be seen in depositions contained in the 25th Doat volume. Several of these are unusual in being given not by Cathar believers or followers of a known sect, but by individuals who seem to have held, so Wakefield suggests, independently unorthodox ideas, 'materialistic or rationalistic explanations of natural phenomena', that the corn grows because of the earth and not the power of God.[81] The structure of the questions here, for example – 'asked if he had ever said that even if the body of Christ was as big as a mountain, the clerics would have devoured it long since' – make it clear that they have been drawn from the testimony of another witness or witnesses, though it is also worth noting that the usual questions of when, how often, and who else was there still follow each article.[82] The consequent depositions record a great deal

---

78 'Qui nondum profitentur sectam aliquam'; García, *Lateran 4*, p. 291.

79 Douais, *Documents: Textes*, pp. 90, 109, 95.

80 Tocco, pp. 35–6.

81 W. L. Wakefield, 'Some Unorthodox Popular Ideas of the Thirteenth Century', *Medievalia et humanistica* n.s. 4 (1973), 23–35 (pp. 25–6). Doat 25, fol. 22ᵛ. See also P. Biller, 'Cathars and the Material World', in *God's Bounty? The Churches and the Natural World*, ed. P. Clarke and T. Claydon, Studies in Church History, 46 (Woodbridge, 2010), pp. 89–110.

82 'Interrogatus si dixerat unquam quod si corpus Christi esset ita magnum sicut unus mons clerici comedissent illud diu est'; Doat 25, fol. 21ʳ⁻ᵛ.

more information than usual on the precise nature of belief, in contrast to the regulated documentation of external markers, and the reason for this no doubt lies in the irregularity of these ideas, the deviance from the normal range of systematic belief that inquisitors knew, or expected, those markers to convey.[83]

If we look in the same volume at the deposition by and against Fabrissa of Limoux we can see a similar thing happening: again, unusually, there is a level of detail in the report of error, and, even more unusually, the depositions of her neighbours against her are preserved in the same register. It is these depositions that form the starting point for the inquisitors' interrogation. Fabrissa clearly has a firm grasp of at least the principal errors of the Cathar sect and, like the deponents above, is asked about several very specific statements drawn from other depositions, such as whether she had ever said to a pregnant woman that she had the devil in her belly. The inquisitors do not, however, ask her to give further details of these errors, but rather to say whether or not she did actually say or think them.[84]

The pattern of these depositions suggests that where error does have some presence in these depositions, however exceptional, the inquisitors' interest in it is not investigative: where any detail of error appears it is as part of an interrogation based on *fama* and not as part of a theological examination. Even the Garcias depositions follow the same pattern of using witness statements to build a question list that will establish guilt, and the detailed nature of these statements is perhaps attributable to the equally unusual fact that the deponents are mendicant friars. The reported error is used as a marker and the usual auxiliary questions are added. Perhaps the non-standard errors of the 'materialists' are afforded more space than usual, but interrogations based on unusual errors are not seeking an explanation of the errors from the deponent any more than question lists that repeat established articles of error – only assent or denial to a series of articles. Error is a present and integral part, but is not what inquisitors are looking for in these interrogations.

A focus on actions and on information which sees even heretical status defined in terms of measurable actions makes the picture of heresy that we find in the depositions overwhelmingly a thing of ritual and of presence. Arnaude's deposition is filled with details of where she went, what rituals she performed, what others did for her, and, in each case, who was there at the time. For the heretics, as well as for the supporting cast, heresy is a fuller version of that list of verbs that constitute the culpable actions outlined in the consultations, and deponents are charged with *crimen hereseos*, or *crimen heresis*, which the Tuscan formulary glosses as including 'whether believing in the errors of heretics, or receiving them, or giving them any sort of help,

---

[83] Doat 25, fols. 20ᵛ–5ᵛ; fols. 226ᵛ–8ᵛ.
[84] Doat 25, fols. 37ᵛ–53ʳ.

counsel or favour, or transgressing in any way whatsoever with regard to this crime'.[85]

All these examples are taken from documents that were not intended for public reading. Sentences, on the other hand, were pronounced and carried out publicly.[86] Between the documents produced by those two processes there was a significant gap in the information included. The case of Austorga of Rosenges, mentioned above, is one of those relatively unusual occasions on which there are both a confession and a sentence surviving for the same deponent. Her sentence, which is a group sentence that includes many other deponents, is brief and to the point. She and the others saw, adored and believed the errors of heretics, and, after having abjured heresy, then did all those things again. They all received a penance of perpetual incarceration. Behind this short condemnation are various depositions, including one of her own – the Rosenges family were, according to Douais, notorious for their involvement in the affairs of heretics, and Austorga seems to have been caught out at least three times – all of which provide a detailed and complex picture of involvement. None of that detail or complexity is transmitted to the public sentence.[87] The collections of sentences are really the main public face of the inquisition process to which we have access.

Both Italian registers contain a single sentence that lists the specific errors of the deponent.[88] The sentence collection of Bernard of Caux and John of St-Pierre also contains one sentence that describes, though in no great doctrinal or theoretical detail, the errors in question. It is neither the earliest nor in any other way significantly different.[89] The inclusion of such details in one or two sentences seems odd, especially when they are hardly prominent in the depositions themselves, but they can perhaps be explained as public safety announcements. Whether or not an action was undertaken 'knowingly' is, as we have seen, a recurrent concern in the legal texts that we have looked at, and it appears to have been equally important for those interrogating

---

85 'Sive credendo hereticorum erroribus, sive ipsos receptando, sive quodlibet auxilium, consilium et favorem prestando, sive quoviscumque modo circa crimen huiusmodi delinquendo'; d'Alatri, *Orvieto*, p. 172.

86 'Lecta lata et publicata fuit dicta sententia … in pleno populo marum et mulierum dicte civitatis ad hec convocato'; d'Alatri, *Orvieto*, p. 213.

87 Sentence in Douais, *Documents: Textes*, no. II, pp. 3–5, p. 4, n. 2; see also p. 97, n. 1. Deposition by Austorge in Doat 24, fols. 1r–7v. See also depositions by Arnold of Bonhac, Toulouse, MS 609, fol. 200r, Peter Fogasset of Caraman, Doat 23, fol. 325v, Aymersens of Cambiac, Doat 22, fol. 239v, cited by Douais, *Documents: Textes*, p. 98, n. 1. Aymersens's deposition before Ferrier and Peter Durand in Doat 24 comes two years before her sentencing by Bernard of Caux and John of St-Pierre in 1246, but already she admits here to having been caught and abjured once before, by the inquisitors of Toulouse some years earlier. At that point she claims to have been a *credens* for sixteen years. The events described by Arnold of Bonhac must have occurred only months after her 1244 deposition.

88 D'Alatri, *Orvieto*, pp. 318–20; Tocco, pp. 35–7.

89 Douais, *Documents: Textes*, p. 71.

deponents.[90] Sure enough, the Tuscan records cite the public reading of sentences as a good reason to disregard any attempt to claim ignorance of heretical status on the part of the deponent.[91] A knowledge of what inquisitors meant by heresy can be seen in the case of the deponent who, on meeting some heretics, apparently questioned them about their dualist doctrine. The heretics promptly denied this, and ascribed it instead to vicious rumours started by the Catholics. Such a denial perhaps suggests the restriction of secret knowledge, but it also points to an uninitiated member being able to put his finger on what it was that made the heretics doctrinally wrong or different. One man can even be seen in the Quercy register to want to compare the two sects; having visited the Waldensians, he then 'went to the heretics, wishing to test which were better, Waldensians or heretics'.[92] Though it is equally probable that the origin of either man's knowledge would be someone like Fabrissa, a source of local and neighbourly knowledge, perhaps the seeming use of inquisition vocabulary by deponents is not only a result of rewriting by the agents of the Catholic church, but also of exposure to inquisition method and language in its public aspects, and in court. There are even places in which a counter-tradition can be discerned: an awareness of how to avoid difficult answers, a tradition that we know from other sources to have existed and which can perhaps be seen behind the illustrations of heretical sophistry under interrogation that are presented by Stephen of Bourbon and the Pseudo-David of Augsburg.

It is clear, then, that the list of actions that define heresy in the councils and in the consultations also define the picture of heresy that the inquisition material presents; the same ideas determine what questions are asked and what information recorded. Overall there is little concern with heresy as doctrinal error. Further, the scheme of actions in the registers also includes heretics, who are also now indicated by actions that function as markers of guilt. Little distinction is made in these documents between the treatment of heretics and lesser categories, or indeed between members of different heretical groups, with the exception of the élite: depositions usually begin with the question did you see heretics *or* Waldensians, and certainly people appear to have been able to distinguish. The same vocabulary, though, the same list of actions, is applied to almost everyone else, and the same actions seem to result in the same label for followers of both groups. Heresy here is a crime, or at least is in the process of becoming one. We can see in the consultations especially that actions are considered at least to some extent as shorthand for an interior condition, although in the registers the weight given to details of actions and physical presence by the inquisitors' questions can perhaps also be seen to rest

---

[90] Duvernoy, *Quercy*, e.g. p. 54; Douais, *Documents: Textes*, p. 4; d'Alatri, *Orvieto*, p. 222.
[91] Tocco, p. 53.
[92] 'Ivit ad hereticos, volens temptare qui essent meliores, Valdenses vel heretici'; Duvernoy, *Quercy*, p. 146. *Meliores* is Duvernoy's correction of *milieres*. See also above, p. 23, n. 40.

on a desire to remove the material basis, as the conciliar legislation instructs. The process behind these records nevertheless turns an error of belief into an error of action.

Inquisitors' handbooks

Que scripto facile non possent comprehendi

Handbooks for inquisitors were a young tradition in the mid thirteenth century, developing alongside the process of inquisition. Unlike the conciliar and consultation material, the handbooks represent a private body of knowledge passed from inquisitor to inquisitor, and written by them to be ancillary to the process of inquisition. We owe our appreciation of their importance to the work of Dondaine, who highlighted the central role of the previously under-used inquisitors' manual in the development of the inquisition process and in our understanding of it.[93] Part of a broader trend in the production of manual literature which had emerged and gathered speed with the success of the mendicant orders, inquisitors' manuals were procedural, 'how-to' books that grew alongside the new process being formed in the constitutions of church councils and the tribunals taking place across southern France and northern Italy. Dondaine saw the manual as developing in stages out of collections of texts and identified several distinct phases in the evolution of the form, though the range and variety of the material means that the distinctions between his different stages are not always clear. Beginning with the earliest *manuels sans formulaire*, manuals then acquire supplementary material to become *manuels avec formulaire*, all of which is ultimately integrated into coherent *traités raisonnés*. In our period the manual is still at an early stage of development according to Dondaine's scheme. Beside the manuals there are other texts, handbooks aimed at informing the inquisitor about other aspects of inquisition beside process.

The principal concern of all these texts is the communication of information: information about heretics on the one hand, and about the repression of heresy – that is, inquisition – on the other. There are a number of different elements common to these texts as a group, providing different types of ancillary information: as well as procedural material there are formularies, models of documents to be produced; technical information, descriptions of the office of inquisition and how to best conduct the tribunal, as well as explanations of inquisitorial powers – this becomes more common as legislation increased in volume and the process gathered momentum and expertise; and substantive information, descriptions of heretics, their errors and their customs. The different types of information were combined in a variety of ways in different handbooks and this is in part what makes them such a diverse group of texts.

93 Dondaine, 'Manuel', pp. 85–6.

Some are concerned with only one element: the *Ordo processus Narbonensis* deals only with information about the process of inquisition; Raniero Sacconi does not discuss it at all, but instead treats the errors and customs of different heretical groups. Others are compilations of materials that collect together official texts and consultations with the formularies of procedure. Given that the boundaries between the different types are so fluid, the term 'handbook' will be used here in a general sense to refer to all the texts.

Ordo processus Narbonensis[94]

Written in 1248/49, by the inquisitors Bernard of Caux and John of St-Pierre, this is one of the earliest examples of the inquisitors' manual.[95] It is extant in only one manuscript, in Madrid, but is referred to by several later authors.[96]

Summa de Catharis et Pauperibus de Lugduno[97]

The *Summa de Catharis et Pauperibus de Lugduno*, which the explicit dates to 1250, details the beliefs of the Cathars, their various churches and the writings of John of Lugio; information on the *Pauperes de Lugduno* is relegated to a short section at the end of the work.[98] Its author, Raniero Sacconi, born in Piacenza near the beginning of the thirteenth century, reverted to Catholicism after seventeen years as a Cathar. In 1245, under the influence of Peter of Verona, he became a Dominican friar and later, between 1254 and 1259, inquisitor for his native Lombardy. He describes himself as a former 'heresiarch' and, though it is unclear whether by this he means that he was one of the higher members of his sect, the fact that he seems privy to the higher levels of knowledge that he describes as restricted, and that he also uses the term heresiarch of John of Lugio, elder son and bishop of the Albanenses, might suggest that this was the case.[99] According to Šanjek, the *Summa de Catharis et Pauperibus de Lugduno* is still extant in over fifty manuscripts.[100] The *Summa* survives in two forms: in its

---

94 Selge, *Texte*, pp. 70–77; trans. Wakefield, *Heresy, Crusade and Inquisition*, pp. 250–58. See also Dondaine, 'Manuel', pp. 97–101.

95 Dondaine attributed this text to William Raymond and Peter Durand, but this has been superseded by Dossat's ascription to the two named above, Dossat, *Crises*, p. 167. See also Arnold, *Inquisition*, p. 243, n. 2, and in 'Inquisition, Texts and Discourse', p. 65, n. 10, and Wakefield, *Heresy Crusade and Inquisition*, p. 250.

96 See Dondaine, 'Manuel', p. 101.

97 Raniero Sacconi, *Summa*, pp. 31–60; trans. Wakefield and Evans, *Heresies*, pp. 329–46. Also printed in *Un traité néo-manichéen du XIIe siècle. Le Liber de duobus principiis suivi d'un fragment de rituel cathare*, ed. A. Dondaine (Rome, 1939) (reprint of the Martène and Durand edition). See Rottenwöhrer, I.i, pp. 64–6.

98 Dondaine, 'Manuel', pp. 132, 149, 166. The authenticity of the Waldensian section was called into question by Gieseler according to Dondaine, *Un traité néo-manichéen de XIIIe siècle*, p. 59, n. 32.

99 Raniero Sacconi, *Summa*, pp. 44, 52, 59, 57.

100 Raniero Sacconi, *Summa*, pp. 39–41.

original, discrete state, and as a part of another treatise into which it was imported around 1260, that of the Anonymous of Passau. The opening of the text suggests a descriptive or discursive work on the opinions of the Cathar and Waldensian sects, rather like that given by Stephen of Bourbon, and to some extent that is what is presented, but Raniero seems unable to contain his text within the framework he sets out. Instead, the text ranges away from the description of beliefs to provide also descriptions of way of life and behaviour, as well as accounts of the history and development of the different groups of the sort that we start to see appearing in later inquisitors' manuals. Raniero also shows concern to make clear the different geographical distinctions of the heretical churches and the corresponding doctrinal peculiarities.

MS Vat. Lat. 3978[101]

One of Dondaine's *manuels avec formulaire*, contained, along with various other anti-heretical materials, in Vatican Latin manuscript 3978, a manuscript of the second half of the fourteenth century which looks like a collection for inquisitors; beside the manual it contains official texts, formularies and treatises, including extracts from Moneta, Raniero, the Pseudo-David of Augsburg and the *Disputatio* – in fact, a large proportion of the texts that we have looked at. It is designed as a work of reference: each section is clearly numbered and a corresponding list of contents is provided at the beginning of the text; marginal notes and rubrics allow easy navigation between the different sections: all the reference tools introduced in the late twelfth and thirteenth centuries to render a text searchable.[102] The manual itself is a compilation of texts and documents, French in origin, though it also exists in a later Italian version.[103] Dondaine dates the manual to shortly after 1265, given the propensity of collections generally to include the most recent material and the date of the newest document in the collection, the reissue of Frederick II's anti-heretical legislation by Clement IV in 1265. Dossat follows Dondaine, dating the manual to 1266 and placing it firmly in the context of the southern French inquisitions, but Dondaine also raises the possibility that the 1265 document may have been added later – it is missing from another version of the manual – and this suggestion is seconded by Riccardo Parmeggiani. Following the same logic as Dondaine, he therefore dates the manual to the next latest item that it contains, the consultation of Gui Foulques, of *c.*1255.[104]

---

101 BAV, MS Vat. Lat. 3978.

102 M. A. Rouse and R. H. Rouse, *Authentic Witnesses. Approaches to Medieval Texts and Manuscripts* (Notre Dame, 1991), pp. 193, 221–2.

103 In BAV MS Vat. Lat. 2648, see Dondaine, 'Manuel', pp. 106–7, 154–67.

104 Dondaine, 'Manuel', p. 107, n. 68; the Constitutions of Frederick are missing from Vat. Lat. 4265. Dossat, *Crises*, pp. 196–9, and 'Gui Foucois', pp. 33–4. Parmeggiani sees the collection in MS 3978 as a key work in the development of the manual and believes that, in its original format, it probably did not contain the 1265 bull, arguing instead that the inclusion of

MS Vat. Lat. 3978 probably represents the earliest surviving example of its kind.[105]

Anonymous of Passau

The compilation known as the Anonymous of Passau is a large and composite work that is directed at various enemies of the church, mainly the Jews, but also the antichrist and heretics, and which incorporates a version of Raniero Sacconi's *Summa de Catharis et Pauperibus de Lugduno* so completely that it can also be considered an extension of the *Summa*'s manuscript survival.[106] Patschovsky's study of self-references within the compilation suggests that the compiler was a Dominican who had been an inquisitor in the diocese of Passau during the 1260s.[107] The large numbers of manuscripts that survive of this text show that it quickly became popular, but they have also made a definitive version of the work very hard to establish. The Anonymous of Passau has a complex manuscript tradition and is extant in at least two recensions, if not more – Patschovsky shows that the earlier version in fact exists in many different forms. Moreover, Nickson argues that one later version, also known as the Pseudo-Reinerius, is in fact a shortened version of the anti-heretical sections of the original and itself exists in two versions, having been further abbreviated in a second redaction.[108] The later recensions cannot really be dated more securely than 1270–1300, but ultimately reproduce the earlier text. The text has, unsurprisingly, never been edited in its entirety; a selection was published by Gretser originally in the seventeenth century and reprinted several times since, and some parts have also been edited by Patschovsky and by Nickson. In the light of the complex and fragmentary nature of what has been edited, and the consequent difficulty of identifying which version is represented by each edition, in the following the work is cited without distinguishing between the different recensions.

---

decretal material was a later Italian development from the two-part French style of manual, which included consultations and formularies only; R. Parmeggiani, 'Un secolo di manualistica inquisitoriale (1230–1330): intertestualità e circolazione del diritto', *Rivista Internazionale di Diritto Comune* 13 (2002), 229–70 (pp. 257–8, 237–46).

[105] Dondaine, 'Manuel', pp. 106–7, 140–54; on the existence of one possible earlier manuscript, see Biller, 'Deep is the Heart of Man', p. 279.

[106] Dondaine, 'Manuel', p. 173.

[107] A. Patschovsky, *Der Passauer Anonymus. Ein Sammelwerk über Ketzer, Juden, Antichrist aus der Mitte des 13. Jahrhunderts*, Monumenta Germaniae Historica Schriften 22 (1968), pp. 78–89.

[108] M. A. E. Nickson, 'The "Pseudo-Reinerius" Treatise, The Final Stage of a Thirteenth Century Work on Heresy from the Diocese of Passau', *AHDLMA* 62 (1967), 255–314 (pp. 256–60).

De inquisitione hereticorum[109]

Attributed by Preger, rather precariously, to the German Franciscan David of Augsburg, but certainly written by an inquisitor or by someone working closely with inquisitors, this text is a manual dealing with the Waldensian heresy and its inquisition from the second half of the thirteenth century. It is extant in at least two recensions, identified by Dondaine, of which the order of precedence is uncertain, though Dondaine believes the Short recension to be the earlier text. It is generally thought that the short text is of French origin, and the longer German, but there are also arguments for a German origin for both. The Short recension is reproduced entirely in the Long, with the exception of its initial and the final three chapters, which seem to have been added, and the Long recension includes additional chapters and reorganizes the shorter text to some degree. According to Dondaine it is only the shorter of the two that appears in the collections designed for inquisitors.[110] A precise dating of this text is very difficult, but there are signs that point some of the way. Two definite facts present themselves: first is a reference to the conflict between emperor and pope in which Frederick (II) is described as 'late'; Frederick died in 1250. Secondly, there is a reference to 'St. Peter OFP', who was killed in 1252 and canonized in 1253. This, then, gives a solid *terminus post quem* of 1253. What may also possibly be helpful is that the added chapter at the beginning of the Short recension is a highly condensed version of the account of Waldensian origins given by Stephen of Bourbon in the *De septem donis de Spiritus Sancti*. The preface is missing from the Dublin manuscript of this recension, however, and though Esposito, following Quetif and Echard, suggests that the following twenty-four sections of the *De inquisitione* are in part adapted from Stephen's work the only apparent similarities lie in two parallel pieces of the sample interrogation. Given the difficulty of dating the composition of Stephen's unfinished work, sometime between 1250 and 1261, any dependence on the *De septem donis* does not narrow the date range for the *De inquisitione* very helpfully.[111]

---

109 Short recension: Pseudo-David, *De inquisitione*. Long recension ed. by Preger, Pseudo-David.

110 Dondaine, 'Manuel', p. 93.

111 M. M. Esposito, 'Sur quelques écrits concernant les hérésies et les hérétiques aux xiie et xiiie siècles', *Revue d'Histoire Ecclesiastique* 36 (1940), 143–62 (p. 159); J. Quétif and J. Echard (ed.), *Scriptores Ordinis Praedicatorum recensiti, notisque historicis et criticis*, 2 vols. (orig. Paris, 1719–21, reprinted New York, 1959), I, 191.ii-192.ii. The similarity appears limited. Stephen's account of Waldensian errors is very limited and brief, and is followed by an account of his experience, and then of Cathar errors. The sample interrogation contains two pieces that are similar; one question: 'Credis Christum de Virgine natum, passum, resurrexisse et ascendisse in coelum? Respondit alacriter, Credo' is in Stephen given as: 'cum queritur: "Credis Christum natum, passum, etc.?" Respondent: "Bene credo" vel "firmiter credo", id est firmam vel bonam habeo credenciam', here referring to plural speakers, and not specifically Waldensians but heretics generally. A similar response also, where the *De inquisitione* heretic says '"Simplex homo sum et illiteratus, nolite me capere in

Explicatio super officio inquisitionis[112]

A manual written either for or by the Franciscan inquisitors of Tuscany, which appeared sometime between 1262 and 1277. It reprises the structure of the *Ordo processus narbonensis*, though in a fuller and more detailed form. The similarity between the two texts led Dondaine to suggest a direct borrowing of the French text by the author of the *Explicatio*, a suggestion reinforced by the fact that the Ordo directly follows the *Explicatio* in what was then thought to be the only manuscript. The dependence has been confirmed by Parmeggiani, who also identifies a second manuscript.

Tractatus de hereticis[113]

Although the surviving copy of this work is anonymous, we know, through the work of Dondaine, that it was written by the Lombard inquisitor Anselm of Alessandria. It was begun by Anselm around 1267 and he continued to add to it throughout his career until 1279; it survives in only one manuscript, in the National museum of Hungary in Budapest. The manuscript also contains a copy of the *Summa de Catharis et Pauperibus de Lugduno* of Anselm's fellow inquisitor, Raniero Sacconi, inserted incongruously into Anselm's text in a way that leads Dondaine to believe that it is the result of scribal accident. Dondaine sees Anselm's handbook as complementary to Sacconi's text, providing as it does information on the Concorezzensan schism much as Raniero does for the Albanensan church.[114]

The opening words of the *Explicatio super officio inquisitionis* establish three constituent parts to the office of inquisition: 'the laying out of statutes, the inquisition of heretics and believers, and the defining or imposition of punishments'.[115] Those elements, the citation, examination and sentencing of heretics, together comprise the essential purpose of inquisition, and are what the inquisitors' handbooks address between them, though the manner in which

---

verbis meis"', Stephen's claims '"Ego sum homo simplex, talis et talis, et nescio istas questiones"'. Both of these look like independent expressions of the same ideas. Pseudo-David, *De inquisitione*, col. 1790; Stephen of Bourbon, *Tractatus*, p. 313. On the dating of Stephen's text, see above, p. 60.

112 Biblioteca Casanatense, Rome, MS Cas 1730, fols. 134–43. On the *Explicatio*, see Dondaine, 'Manuel', pp. 101–4, to which add Parmeggiani, 'Un secolo di manualistica inquisitoriale', pp. 234–6 and n. 22, who identifies a second copy.

113 Anselm of Alessandria, *Tractatus*. See Rottenwöhrer, I.i, pp. 98–9.

114 Dondaine, 'La hiérarchie II, III', pp. 239–40. It is possible that Anselm used Raniero's *summa* as a model for his own, at least in part; we certainly know that he made use of it; Anselm of Alessandria, *Tractatus*, p. 315.

115 'Negotium tibi commissum a domino papa qui inquisitor es heretice pravitatis principaliter tria continet, scilicet statutorum positionem, hereticorum et credentium inquisitionem et penarum taxationem sive impositionem'; MS Cas 1730 fol. 134ra.

they do so varies. The *Explicatio* and the *Ordo processus* both do so explicitly by outlining procedure, describing the role of the inquisitor and providing what almost amounts to a script for him to follow. The earliest of these texts, the *Ordo processus narbonensis*, is a 'manual' proper, in the sense that it provides instructions for new inquisitors on how to conduct an inquisition from beginning to end by means of a set of examples and instructions of how to proceed, technically, that together create a schematic view of the tribunal. The interrogatory that it includes is a list of the verbs that appear in the consultation material which build a profile of guilt: did you see heretics; when, and where; how many and who with; did you hear their preaching, or receive them; lead them; eat or drink with them; give them anything; perform administrative tasks for them; keep anything for them; accept the peace from them; adore them, or bow your head, bend your knee, say 'bless'; were you present at their rituals; did you confess to or accept penance from Waldensians, or have any other association with them; make any agreement to hide the truth, or know of anyone who did; and, finally, do you believe in them or their errors?

The later *Explicatio* uses the *Ordo processus'* material and in particular its structure to talk about the process of inquisition in a similarly schematic, though much fuller, way, developing in particular the discussion of the powers and legal status of the inquisitor. It also includes a version of the same question list for *credentes* as well as a different list designed specifically for *heretici consolati*, which is directed much more to doctrinal questions. The discussions of office and process that make up these two texts also appear in the others to some extent, though it is not their majority part, and the *Summa de Catharis et Pauperibus de Lugduno*, indeed, has no such material at all. The compiler of the Anonymous of Passau text includes some pieces that tell his readers how to recognize sects from outward signs, as well as the way to examine a heretic and how to punish them.[116] There are also brief sections that discuss inquisitorial procedure. Anselm's text also contains some items on procedure that are similar to those of the *Ordo* – a brief interrogatory and two formulae – and has a section, later borrowed by Bernard Gui, on the proper exercise of the office of inquisition. Of these other texts, the Pseudo-David's text is the only one that presents an even balance between procedural information and the descriptions of heretics that make up most of Raniero, Anselm and the Anonymous.

MS Vat. Lat. 3978 is a different sort of text both from the procedural discussions of the *Ordo* and the *Explicatio* and from the descriptive, substantive material of the more treatise-like handbooks. Instead, rather like Stephen of Bourbon's text, it provides something more like raw material for inquisition. The texts that this manual contains fall into two parts: consultations and formulary. The consultations include all those that we looked at in the first

116 Anonymous of Passau, pp. 272–4. See also Nickson, 'The "Pseudo-Reinerius" Treatise', pp. 285–6.

part of this chapter, by Gui Foulques, Peter Collemieu, John Bernin and the two sets of lawyers. They are joined by the canons of the councils of Narbonne and Béziers, from 1243 and 1246. The formulary itself is made up of sample documents drawn from real inquisition registers. Many of these documents were also used in the Tuscan formulary edited by d'Alatri and in the later Italian collection know as the *Libellus*.[117] The reproduction of material from different countries obviously has important implications for the history of the office, but several points can also be made here about the texts themselves. The fact that records from different inquisitions, and indeed different regions, could be copied and adapted as formulae by other inquisitors means that, though they were the product of the inquisition of a particular individual in a particular place, they could as easily be applied to any other deponent who fitted the same criteria, and that the ideas of heresy they contained were not isolated but general and transferable. It also reinforces the impression given by reading the legal material that the lists of actions, and the questions that derive from them, were intended to fit deponents into a predetermined structure of guilt, and that the idea of heresy they were based on was of a series of actions that stood at a remove from the interior state that they represented. All of which is a rather long-winded way of saying that these ideas were self-perpetuating and the inquisition texts reflexive.

The interaction is not only between inquisition documents. As the sentences and depositions reflect the ideas of the consultations, here is another level of reflexivity, in the inquisitors' manual, which contains both. MS Vat. Lat. 3978 is an example of what Petrucci calls a coherent collection of texts: it was written, copied and used as a connected and coherent whole, its 'value and function result from its completeness and reciprocity'.[118] This means that the consultations and the depositions are part of the same coherent idea; that the depositions feed off each other, and off the consultations, and the collection as a whole reflects a legal idea of heresy.

It is to legal texts, too, that the tone of the more straightforward manuals, the *Ordo processus* and the *Explicatio*, bear the closest resemblance, not least in their concentration on actions, but also in their focus on the follower. It is noticeable that the question lists position the deponent consistently as a follower of heretics, all the questions try to establish the relationship of the deponent to heretics and the texts as a whole appear to focus less on the heretics proper, as the other texts do, and more on the lesser categories of involvement. Where belief in error is mentioned, in the condemnation or at the end of the question list, it is, as with our legal consultations, one of list of active markers of guilt, and again attached to a somewhat disembodied heretic: the

---

117 Parmeggiani, 'Un secolo di manualistica inquisitoriale', p. 243.
118 A. Petrucci, *Writers and Readers in Medieval Italy: Studies in the History of Written Culture*, ed. and trans. C. M. Radding (New Haven, CT, 1995), pp. 14–18.

sentence of the *Ordo processus* condemns its subject as a heretic 'because he believed in the errors of heretics'.[119] This is not to say that it does not provide for real heretics, but that the use of the term seems to reflect the abstracted idea of otherness that the other legal texts employ.

In contrast to this, the other handbooks spend most of their time in describing the errors and rituals of the heretics and providing sections on topics such as how to proceed against heretics, how to recognize supporters, how to use prison and fear as a coercive method, how to interrogate heretics and how to avoid bad judges. The Pseudo-David, for example, focuses much more clearly on the practical business of inquisition and the difficulties that come with it. Most of the advice of the *De inquisitione* pertains to the inquisition of heretics specifically. Little attention is shown to the lesser grades, other than how to pick them out of a crowd, and they only appear to be catered for in the Pseudo-David's awareness that a *credens hereticorum* is to be judged as a heretic in law.[120] The Anonymous of Passau and Anselm similarly concentrate on heretics as the subject of interrogation, though the sample interrogations are less concerned with verbal wrangling than the Pseudo-David and, in Anselm's case, they are a little more concerned with error.

MS Vat. Lat. 3978 perhaps tells us more about the inquisitors' ideas of inquisition than of heresy. As Dondaine points out, the texts that make up the formulary are neatly and helpfully arranged in order of the inquisition process, from the general sermon to the exhumation of dead heretics. These are the things that an inquisitor needed to know: the legal process and the legal definitions of both his office and the subject of his enquiry. It has already been pointed out that much of the information in the consultations that is not to do with the office is to do with the finer grades of guilt, the complicated legal definitions that the inquisitors found difficult. They clearly wanted all their legal information in one place, a 'library without a library'.[121] Unlike the more treatise-like handbooks, there is little information on heresy and lots on inquisition. The first two groups of inquisition texts, the consultations and the depositions, are represented by the 3978 manual, but the handbooks and their information are neither included nor apparently relevant. Again the reflexive nature of the depositions and consultations is significant here. If the legal ideas of the consultations shape and are shaped by the questions that govern the depositions, and therefore by the information that these questions elicit, then the material that makes up the handbooks is not drawn from this source, and does not reflect that legal idea of heresy.[122]

---

119 'Quia hereticorum erroribus credidit'; Selge, *Texte*, pp. 71–2, 75.
120 Pseudo-David, *De inquisitione*, cols. 1787–8.
121 Dondaine, 'Manuel', pp. 106–8; Petrucci, *Writers and Readers in Medieval Italy*, p. 8.
122 The authors of the handbooks seem in part to have used other texts as source material, whether that was other Catholic texts or books written by the heretics themselves. We have seen that Raniero uses a book by John of Lugio and that Anselm had a copy of the *Secretum*;

If the formulae for examination and interrogation make no provision for a detailed investigation of error, or at least for records that might contain that type of information, why are these handbooks written by inquisitors for one another and in what way do they support the inquisition of heretical depravity? It is noticeable that, in the procedural material, nearly all of the forms given are for those parts of the tribunal that require a publicly given announcement. Perhaps it is to supplement and support those parts of inquisition that are hard to describe in writing, as the *Ordo processus* has it, in the brief but pregnant phrase: 'we do various other things, indeed, in the process and in other matters which cannot easily be reduced to writing'.[123] Or perhaps it is more to do with information, for the inquisitors to know, as the Pseudo-David suggests, how to identify and treat heretics and their followers – 'evil cannot be avoided unless it is known'.[124]

What do inquisitors want to tell each other about heresy to supply and reinforce those parts of inquisition that procedure does not cover? Raniero opens his short text with a simple comparison: 'although at one time sects of heretics were numerous, by the grace of Jesus Christ they have been almost completely destroyed; yet two major ones are now found'.[125] With these few lines Raniero places his subject in an historical frame; it is very brief, but he later adds more detail, describing recent events in Cathar history as a background to the schism in the Albanensan church. The first impulse of these texts is to provide, however briefly, a historical background for the sect in question. Like Raniero, the Anonymous of Passau draws a comparison between the relative numbers of heresies old and new. The Passau text in fact opens with three theoretical chapters on the difference between the Catholic church and heretical sects and on the causes of heresy, but the fourth chapter, the first to begin describing the heretics themselves, echoes Raniero's opening lines. 'On the sects of ancient heretics' deals with older heresies very briefly, and only to say that the many – he gives the number as seventy – have now been reduced to four, of which

---

Anselm of Alessandria, *Tractatus*, pp. 318–19. They also appear to gather information from the heretics at first hand: Anonymous of Passau, p. 264; Pseudo-David, *De inquisitione*, col. 1790; and Stephen of Bourbon, *Tractatus*, pp. 293–4.

[123] 'Plura quidem et alia facimus in processu et aliis, que scripto facile non possent comprehendi'; Selge, *Texte*, p. 75; trans. (adjusted) Wakefield, *Heresy, Crusade and Inquisition*, p. 257.

[124] 'Malum non vitatur nisi cognitum'; *Brevis simmula*, p. 114. An explanation of ritual and of the doctrine behind it is shown to be necessary by some practical advice from Anselm: 'bene facerent consolamentum etiam si paries vel murus vel fluvius esset in medio; et ideo diligenter cavendum est quando habemus aliquos suspectos ne cathari infirmantibus appropinquent, vel etiam domibus in quibus detinentur'; Anselm of Alessandria, *Tractatus*, pp. 313–14.

[125] 'Cum secte hereticorum olim fuerint multe, que omnino fere destructe sunt per gratiam Ihesu Christi, tamen due principales modo inueniuntur'; Raniero Sacconi, *Summa*, p. 42; trans. (adjusted) Wakefield and Evans, *Heresies*, p. 330.

heresies 'none is more dangerous to the church than [the sect of] the Leonists'. The next chapter, on modern heretics, focuses on the Waldensians and begins with an outline of the origins of the Waldensian sect, though it does not name Valdes himself.[126]

The pattern is repeated in Anselm and the Pseudo-David, both of which begin with a potted history of the sect in question. Anselm does this more thoroughly than the others and prefaces his account of the Cathar churches of Italy by tracing their historical and geographical spread from the ancient Manicheans and from Bulgaria via the north of France to the south and Italy – as Barber points out, this section makes Anselm one of the few western writers of this period to attempt to investigate the history of the Cathars himself.[127] The Pseudo-David similarly begins with an account of Waldensian origins, though the first paragraph, which traces the sect to Valdes, was a later addition by a different author; the original account, now the second section, instead describes the origins of the sect in Lyons and the actions of 'certain simple laymen'. The Pseudo-David also has echoes of the contrast between old and new that Raniero and the Anonymous of Passau draw. These heretics, whom he later calls the heretics of modern times, 'mix with the errors of ancient heretics those of their own invention'.[128]

So, all the texts open with a historical perspective in some form. There are two aspects to this, the most straightforward of which is the provision of some account of the origins of the sect in question at or near the beginning of the text. Alongside this is the comparison between heresies of the ancient world and those of modern times and their relative numbers. The heresies of the old world are apparently taken from an Isidorean model of heresy, that model which is contained in the *Decretum* and which names a large number of sects, an abbreviated version of which is tacked onto the end of Anselm's treatise. The influence of this idea can be seen in the Anonymous of Passau's later description of other sects, in which he uses Isidore's practice of deriving their names from their author or their cause.[129]

Two elements of the sects' make-up form the principal concern of all four texts and the focus of the majority of their material: the errors of the heretics, and their behaviour and customs. For Raniero, this is the whole of his subject.

126 'De sectis antiquorum hereticorum'; 'non est pernicior Ecclesie quam Leonistarum'; Anonymous of Passau, p. 264; Pseudo-David, *De inquisitione*, cols. 1777–8. Peter Martyr also makes direct comparisons of modern heresies in terms of which is the most dangerous, Kaeppeli, 'Une somme', pp. 331–2.
127 Dondaine, 'La hiérarchie II, III', pp. 308–9; M. Barber, *The Cathars: Dualist Heretics in Languedoc in the High Middle Ages* (Harlow, 2000), p. 27. On the wider significance of the history given by Anselm, see P. Biller, 'Northern Cathars and Higher Learning', in *The Medieval Church*, ed. Biller and Dobson, *passim*.
128 'Quidam simplices laïci'; 'antiquorum hereticorum errores suis adinventionibus miscuerunt'; Pseudo-David, *De inquisitione*, cols. 1777–8, 1779, 1788.
129 Anonymous of Passau, p. 272.

He begins with a brief outline of the main Cathar errors before moving on to a detailed description of their sacraments and their ecclesiastical structure and of the doctrine that lies behind each of these. He then breaks the structure down into individual churches – and not just roughly divided by types of dualism, but sixteen distinct groups, each with separate names and separate, though overlapping, doctrines. Raniero's text presents us with a picture of Catharism as a highly structured and hierarchical movement, with an organization that is common to all the groups, and though Raniero points out where certain groups, usually the Albanenses, differ from the rest, this also serves to highlight that otherwise these structures are shared.[130] Raniero's treatment of the Waldensian sect is very brief, but, like his account of the Cathars, is nevertheless based on the principal divisions in the sect, with one chapter devoted to the Poor of Lyons and one to the Lombard branch.[131]

In a way very similar to the *summa* of his colleague, the doctrinal differences between the Cathar groups, including the schism in the church of Concorezzo, provide the framework for Anselm's description of Cathar errors, which comprises much of his first section. They are also the basis for his treatment of the Waldensians, which is more extensive than Raniero's. Like Raniero, Anselm imparts his information without judgement or comment and makes no attempt to engage with the error, but merely to describe it, and his reserved approach continues in his treatment of heretical custom, which preserves one of the most detailed descriptions that we have of the Cathar ritual of *consolamentum*. There is an emphasis on ritual and formalized behaviour in this text, and, alongside the *consolamentum*, Anselm describes in similar detail the disposition of penance, Cathar behaviour at table and even the secret question that they use to determine whether they are among friends: '"is this a crooked stick?"'[132]

The Anonymous of Passau is similar again. It also devotes a lot of space to error, not least because of its inclusion of Raniero's text, though this is also the only material that it has on heretical custom or hierarchy. The chapter on modern sects, which is really only about the Waldensians, includes a long

---

[130] Raniero Sacconi, *Summa*, pp. 43–9.

[131] Three segments on the Waldensians were sometimes copied into manuscripts directly after Raniero's text, presumably to remedy the deficiency of his text on this subject. They continue in the same vein, providing information on the errors, with some attention to differences, and details of Waldensian customs and sacraments. See Dondaine, 'Manuel', p. 150, no. 11. BnF MS Lat. 14983, fols. 46–54. They also follow Raniero's text in BAV MS Vat. Lat. 3978, fols. 58va–59rb.

[132] 'Est hoc lignum tortum?'; Anselm of Alessandria, *Tractatus*, pp. 313–17. The 'crooked stick' in question presumably refers to a person present. The Anonymous of Passau also describes the use of the 'crooked stick' code, used to determine if they are among friends, here given as '"Cavete, ne inter nos sit lignum curvum"'. The difference in phrasing in this account, and the German words that form the coded reply, suggest similar usages among heretics in different regions, rather than textual borrowing: Anonymous of Passau, p. 264.

descriptive list of their errors. The subsequent chapter, on the names of sects, again describes different groups in terms of their error, but again there is no polemic or invective, merely report.

The *De inquisitione* launches into a description of errors in the first chapter and directly after the historical account, as the Passau text does, and then goes on to spend most of the descriptive part of the text giving details of the characteristics and character flaws of the heretics. The middle parts of the Pseudo-David are in fact given over to a description of behaviour that is more polemically directed than the other handbooks, describing their methods of learning and preaching and their associations with rich women, apparently in order to condemn them; the Pseudo-David does make some attempt at even-handedness in clearing the Waldensians of any sexual misconduct, but only to then lay the charge at the feet of the Cathars.[133] There is none of the description of ritual and formalized behaviour given in the other three texts. In fact, it is really only the Italian texts that want to talk about lifestyle – the Anonymous of Passau contains information on this aspect only by virtue of containing also Raniero.

In describing the structural composition of these texts, the contrast in style between the texts of the Pseudo-David and the Anonymous of Passau on the one hand and the detached work of the two Italian inquisitors on the other may already have become apparent. Raniero and Anselm are mostly concerned to describe and inform, and, while the other two are also designed to provide information, that information is not imparted without comment, and the difference in tone affects the pictures of heresy that the two pairs project. Common themes run through all four portrayals of heresy, but they are differently realized, in part through the rhetorical tone employed by the non-Italian texts, in particular the Pseudo-David.

The theme of division in the representation of heresy in the handbooks has already been highlighted. It is a characteristic that is fundamental to all of the texts except the Pseudo-David, who seems not to see much distinction at all between heretical groups and even cites the death of Peter Martyr of Verona as evidence against the Waldensians.[134] Like the polemics, also all Italian productions, the division of heresy provides the structure of Anselm and Raniero's texts. For the Anonymous of Passau, however, the differentiation of the heretics' sect is one of the markers of their error: despite the claim shortly afterwards that modern heretics have been reduced to only four groups, the tenth sign of the church's superiority 'is the integrity of faith. For it is not divided, but one. But there are more than seventy sects of heretics' – the same number that he later gives for the ancient sects.[135] And this is the general pattern

---

133 Pseudo-David, *De inquisitione*, cols. 1782–5.

134 Pseudo-David, *De inquisitione*, col. 1785.

135 'Est integritas fidei. Non enim est divisa, sed una. Sed hereticorum plus quam LXX sectae sunt'; Anonymous of Passau, p. 263.

between the two pairs: the rhetorical images and ideas of the Anonymous of Passau and the Pseudo-David echo more practical representation in the Italian treatises.

The deceptive and false nature of heretics is the pervading theme of the *De inquisitione*, which places a consistent and indeed predominant emphasis on the difference that lies between the appearance of the Waldensians and the inner reality. It underlies the Pseudo-David's juxtaposition of the modern heretic, who does not declare his heresy openly, and his ancient counterpart.[136] The theme is partly developed through the repeated use of terms related to disguise and deception: the image of a cloak is used often.[137] It is stated several times that the Waldensians claim to be the true successors of the apostles and early saints and that they presume to take on the role of the church through pride, an idea that is taken up and expanded on in the long recension, where, 'like a monkey' the heretics think themselves to be the successors of the apostles.[138] The holiness of the heretic is affected, however; it is a 'cloak of sanctity'. Twice heretics are compared to wolves in sheep's clothing, though more obliquely on the second occasion, and this is reinforced with oppositions: they 'praise continence', but yield to their desires 'with burning lust'.[139] Indeed, the sample interrogation is given over in its entirety to the demonstration of the deceptive nature of heretics. It would seem that the main objection that the author has to this secrecy is that it results in the deception of the simple, although he also has something to say about lack of church presence and the effect of ignorance.[140] Ultimately, though, it is the fact that the heretics of modern times hide their errors so effectively that makes them so difficult to find and to defeat, and which means that, for this author at least, the secrecy of heretics is the justification for inquisition. It is precisely that secret nature that justifies, even necessitates, the existence of the inquisitor, whose role it is to see through the affected piety.[141]

---

136 The juxtaposition occurs as part of the chapter on examining heretics in the Short recension, Pseudo-David, *De inquisitione*, col. 1788, but is elevated to the introduction of the Long recension, and expanded upon: Preger, Pseudo-David, p. 204.

137 Pseudo-David, *De inquisitione*, cols. 1779, 1782, 1783, 1788, 1790.

138 'Sicut enim symea'; Preger, Pseudo-David, p. 211. The heretics as monkeys imitating the true church comes from Cyprian. William of Auxerre also uses it: *Summa aurea*, ed J. Ribailler, Spicilegium Bonaventurianum 16–19, 4 vols. in 6 (Paris, 1980–87), IV, 376, lib.IV, tract.XVI, cap. iv.

139 Pseudo-David, *De inquisitione*, cols. 1782, 1792. 'Continentiam laudant, sed urente libidine, concedunt ei satisfieri debere quocumque modo turpi, exponentes illud apostolicum melius est nubere quam uri [I Cor 7. 9], quod melius sit quolibet actu turpi libidini satisfacere, quam intus in corde tentari: Sed hoc valde tenent occultum, ne vilescant'; col. 1779.

140 Pseudo-David, *De inquisitione*, cols. 1780, 1781, 1782, 1783, 1785, 1786, 1788, 1790.

141 The Pseudo-David also advocates in several places the use of secrecy and deception in the apprehension of heretics: 'vulpes enim astutae sunt subtili astutia capiendae'; Pseudo-David, *De inquisitione*, cols. 1784, 1787, 1788.

The device of false appearance is also used in the Anonymous of Passau, in, for example, the first description of the sect of the 'Leonists', who 'have a great appearance of piety', though it features less prominently than in the *De inquisitione*.[142] The false appearance of the Waldensians manifests itself in several places, such as their fictitious attendance of church and participation in Catholic ritual: 'falsely they go [to church]; they offer, they confess, they take communion, but all falsely'.[143] Similarly, a demonstration of their verbal evasion and misdirection is included in a list of signs by which heretics can be recognized, but false appearance is only partly a rhetorical device here and also suggests a genuine concern for concealment.[144]

The Anonymous of Passau is in some ways closer to the view of heretical deception that we find in the Italian texts. In the latter, although glimpses of a former openness can be seen in Anselm's account of their historical existence, his portrayal of heretics shows a similarly hidden group, but this hiddenness appears less as a function of their deceptive nature and more as a practical consequence of their persecution by the church. Like the Anonymous of Passau, heretics, in this case Cathars, attend Catholic feasts only to avoid scandal and, as noted, have a coded way of inquiring whether they are among friends which points to a covert existence. They also have ways to disguise the truth of their words, 'when they wish to conceal their error', though Anselm gives this none of the polemical value that the *De inquisitione* ascribes to such characteristics. The heretics' vision of themselves in this world, as seen through Anselm's account of their ritual, is, ironically, as sheep among wolves; '"from now on you will be among us, and deep down [you will be] in this world like a sheep among wolves"'.[145]

Raniero also has something to say about the practicality of the Cathars' maintenance of an outward pretence, here not so much of holiness, but of Catholic ritual, once again 'to avoid scandal among their neighbours'. Interestingly, what Raniero adds to this picture is deception and concealment of error within the sect itself. The errors of John of Lugio, which are recalled here in detail, are kept secret, according to Raniero: 'this John and his associates do not dare to reveal to their believers the errors described, lest their own believers desert them on account of these novel errors'. More generally, a wider distinction is drawn by this former Cathar across the sect between the initiated and the lower levels of adherents, who are characterized in fact as 'simple'. 'All the Albanenses ... held the beliefs described above', Raniero tells

---

142 'Magnam habet speciem pietatis'; Anonymous of Passau, p. 264.
143 'Ficte vadunt, offerunt, confitentur, communicant, sed totum ficte'; Anonymous of Passau, p. 266, repeated later, p. 272.
144 Anonymous of Passau, pp. 272–4.
145 Anselm of Alessandria, *Tractatus*, pp. 313, 316–17. 'Quando vult cooperire errorem suum'; 'a modo eris inter nos et penitus in hoc mundo sicut ovis in medio luporum'; Anselm of Alessandria, *Tractatus*, pp. 312, 314; trans. Wakefield and Evans, *Heresies*, p. 364.

us, 'except the simpler people, to whom particular points were not revealed'. Again, if any Cathar denies the above errors then the inquisitor can safely consider 'that he utters lies in hypocrisy, which is a characteristic of the Cathars ... unless perhaps that person be someone simple or a novice among them, for to many such they do not reveal their secrets'.[146]

The distinction that Raniero makes between the initiated and the simple highlights a third common theme in the handbooks, though one that also presents a stronger and more pointed contrast between the picture that the two Italian inquisitors put forward and that of the other two texts. In the course of Raniero's account of his errors John of Lugio emerges as an educated and literate man. He makes use not only of Scriptural proofs but also of arguments that are redolent of natural philosophy, and he even shows some familiarity with Roman Law.[147] Raniero's source for his discussion is the book written by John of Lugio himself, 'a large volume of ten quires, a copy of which I have. I have read it through and from it have extracted the errors cited above'.[148] Anselm too is in possession of a heretical book, which he calls the 'Secret' of the Concorezzenses, the text that we know as the Secret Supper, or *Interrogatio Iohannis*, though he seems unimpressed by the heretics' Latinity, quoting the rubric from the text '"this is the *Secret* of the heretics of Concorezzo ... full of errors"' and adding drily 'and also of bad Latin'.[149] Nonetheless, the description by both Raniero and Anselm of a Catharism that produces texts and distinguishes between its different groups on a doctrinal basis projects the view of a reasonably literate group of people, at least in the higher levels of the hierarchy.[150]

That straightforward and detailed picture of an educated group of heretics stands in direct contrast to the picture that we find in the Pseudo-David and the

---

[146] 'Propter scandalum uicinorum suorum vitandum'; 'dictus Iohannes et eius complices non audent revelare dictos errores credentibus suis, ne ipsi credentes discedant ab eis propter hos novos errores'; 'Predicta opiniones tenebant omnes Albanenses'; 'exceptis simplicioribus quibus singula non revelabantur'; 'quod ipse in ypocrisi mendacium loquitur, quod est proprium Catharorum ... nisi forte fuerit homo simplex vel novicius inter eos, talibus enim multis illorum secreta minime reuelantur'; Raniero Sacconi, *Summa*, pp. 47, 57, 52, 59; trans. (adjusted) Wakefield and Evans, *Heresies*, pp. 334, 343, 338–9, 345.

[147] See also *Disputatio*, p. 4 and n. 6. Moneta, *Adversus catharos*, Moneta, p. 23, also possible use of Aristotle, p. 83. Raniero Sacconi, *Summa*: Lugio using whole bible, pp. 53, 56; perhaps natural philosophy, p. 54; Roman Law p. 54.

[148] 'Quoddam volumen magnum X quaternorum, cuius exemplarium habeo et perlegi et ex illo errores supradictos extraxi'; Raniero Sacconi, *Summa*, p. 57; trans. Wakefield and Evans, *Heresies*, p. 343.

[149] '"Hoc est secretum hereticorum de Concorezzo portatum de Bulgaria plenum erroribus", et etiam falsis latinis'; Anselm of Alessandria, *Tractatus*, p. 319; trans. Wakefield and Evans, *Heresies*, p. 371. A very similar description can be found in an extant copy of the original text, and would presumably have been added by someone connected with inquisition: see also Wakefield and Evans, *Heresies*, p. 465 and n. 79, p. 776.

[150] If further proof of heretical literacy were needed, Raniero himself was a heretic only five years before writing his *summa*.

Anonymous of Passau. The old topos of the heretic as illiterate and stupid runs through these two texts, especially in the *De inquisitione*. Heretics are referred to or described in similar terms to the uneducated masses, as 'laymen', or *simplices*, and their error as 'unread' and 'foolish'. Such descriptions do not fit with the picture that emerges from the descriptions both give of heretics that are often in some way either literate or educated: their masters are still referred to in the same terms as those of the orthodox church, *doctores*, *magistri*; there is some suggestion that they use rational arguments, and are accused of interpolating Augustinian texts with their own rites and heresies; they own or use books, and there is reference to debate, and to some conflict via text; and, even if they are not literate, they are also said to know parts of the Scripture by heart, though in a vernacular form.[151] Though described as illiterate, the heretics that the Pseudo-David attacks likewise seem educated and well equipped. What is interesting in this text, though, is that in the Pseudo-David we also see the heretics constructing themselves in the same terms. In the dialogue between heretic and examiner the heretic says 'if you wish to interpret all I say other than in a sound and simple way, then I do not know how I ought to respond. I am a simple man, and illiterate, do not trap me in my words.'[152] Here the simplicity becomes another part of the deceptive and artificial exterior of the heretic and reinforces the idea that the heretic disguises himself as the wolf among the sheep. To this end, the lengthy dialogue that is reproduced as an example of pitfalls in interrogation is more an elaborate game of verbal logic than an attempt to disprove theological errors, and there is little discussion of points of belief, except where they serve to illustrate avoidance.

A similar, though less pronounced, tension lies between the use of a topos of illiterate heretics and the underlying picture of heresy in the Anonymous of Passau. Of the seven causes of heresy that this text lists, the first three are connected with learning; the last four are causes located within the Catholic Church. The first seems to indicate that heretics are learned people: heresy results from seeking after the glory of the church Fathers. The second two, however, portray the heretics as foolish, teaching and learning without proper study, and, more pointedly, using vernacular texts and expounding the Scripture wrongly because 'they are illiterate laymen'. At the same time, the author says later on that he has counted up the schools of the heretics from various inquisitions that he has attended, of which schools he then provides a list.[153] As in the *De inquisitione*, the heretic once again seems to purposely construct his own simplicity: 'he pretends he is simple ... or he pretends he is foolish'.[154]

---

151 Pseudo-David, *De inquisitione*, cols. 1787, 1789,1780,1784, 1788, 1780, 1781.
152 'Si omnia quae dico vultis aliter interpretari quam sane & simpliciter, tunc nescio quid debeam respondere. Simplex homo sum & illiteratus, nolite me capere in verbis meis'; Pseudo-David, *De inquisitione*, col. 1790.
153 'Sunt laici idiotae'; Anonymous of Passau, pp. 263–4.
154 'Simulat se simplicem ... vel simulat se stultum'; Anonymous of Passau, p. 266.

The handbooks of Raniero and Anselm, and of the Pseudo-David and the Anonymous of Passau, two Italian, one certainly German, the other possibly, seem to build their description of their subject from a set of common elements. Though the content varies and their respective approaches range from the highly polemical attitude of the *De inquisitione* author to the reticent tone of Anselm and Sacconi, they all follow, basically, a generic pattern in their description, beginning with a historical sketch, followed by characteristics of the sect, error and custom or behaviour, though not necessarily in that order. The differences in tone are in large part explained by the fact that they were written within different currents of the anti-heretical tradition. In the case of the topos of the illiterate heretic at least, this was a stereotype that had a longer life in the German-speaking regions of Europe than in France and Italy, and which tended to be used against the Waldensians where it did survive in the south.[155] The rather matter-of-fact impression of heretical learning that the Italian texts present, on the other hand, which they share with the polemical material, reflects the greater degree of lay literacy in Italy at this time, as well as the condition of heretical literacy specifically.[156] Something that they all share, though, and which is worth noting briefly, is the way that the information about the sect is presented as the attributes and characteristics of heretics. Where the polemical texts, which also to some degree present their reader with information on the doctrinal nature of the heresy, tend to anchor this in a rather abstract, rhetorical 'heretic' figure, these handbooks, particularly the Italian ones, ground all their description firmly in much more concrete figures.

Though he provides details about the lives and errors of the modern heretic, the Pseudo-David's vision of a successful interrogation still rests on the information generated by the standard procedural, action-based questions: the deponent revealing the extent of their involvement in heresy and, more particularly, the involvement of others.[157] If heresy is a crime of actions and the process of inquisition is aimed at the collection of information about those actions and the networks they comprise, then the handbooks generate and perpetuate that process and the documents that sustained it. To do so requires not only models and procedural material but also the understanding of the inquisitors' legal position and the categories of guilt provided by the consultations. But the inquisitors also want to know about error beyond the legal categories and grades, and they spend time sharing knowledge about belief and lifestyle, privately, with no immediate application to the documentary process of the tribunal. The different types of information necessarily function together in the different arenas of the inquisition tribunal. That all these types

---

[155] On this, see P. Biller, 'The *topos* and Reality of the Heretic as *illiteratus*', in Biller, *The Waldenses*, pp. 169–90.

[156] Paolini, L., 'Italian Catharism and Written Culture', in *Heresy and Literacy*, ed. Biller and Hudson, pp. 83–103 *passim*.

[157] Pseudo-David, *De inquisitione*, col. 1792.

of information came eventually to be incorporated into later manuals confirms that. What is clear, though, is that the procedural material is based on an idea of heresy that derives from legal sources and developments. The more substantive material, deriving from text and experience in the field, reflects a broader idea and suggests a layer of inquisition to which the records do not provide access. In any case, the material that inquisitors need from legal and official sources does not appear to be the same as what they want to tell each other.

5

De heresi

Quid faciat hereticum et quid sit hereticus[1]

The picture of heresy that we receive from texts is a construction of orthodox commentators, rather than a straightforward description. This has been a given since the introduction and entrenchment of the text-critical methods that revealed the different filters at work and the distortions that result from them, particularly in those texts produced in the context of a tribunal. Heresy is of course, by definition, always relative, but what recent work has shown is that its representation in text is a major part of how that otherness is created and maintained, even if the precise meaning or significance of that representation – from what is it built and to what end – is debated. Once layers of distortion are identified in a text, however, there is a tendency to peel them away in an eagerness to see what lies beneath, and there is a danger that, in doing so, the significance of the layers themselves is disregarded; and, perhaps, the assumption that they are so easily removable is itself questionable. The purpose in looking at a broad cross section of texts is to understand, rather, what those layers are and how they work: how the constructions relate to each other, how they are combined and whether something can be said about the ideas and preoccupations of the writers as visible in texts.

The themes that we will look at are themselves in many ways interconnected, but for the sake of clarity the general construction of heresy has been divided here into three main areas. At the end of the chapter we will consider the most basic level of the construct, the meanings of the terms 'heresy' and 'heretic'. Before that, there will be an examination of the role played by ideas of number in the representation of heresy. First, though, we will look at the figurative construction of heresy – that is, the way in which our authors use the various commonplaces and rhetorical devices of the anti-heretical tradition.

---

[1] Peter Lombard, *Sententiae in IV libris distinctae* xiii.2, ed. I. Brady, Spicilegium Bonaventurianum 4, 2 vols. in 3 (Grottaferrata, 1971–81), II, 314.

Figurative construction

Since Grundmann, most historians of heresy have written with an awareness of the operation of what he labelled the 'topos' of the heretic within the anti-heretical corpus. His analysis of the rhetorical patterns used by authors writing about heresy in the Middle Ages outlined several elements in an idea that he saw stretching from the eleventh century to well into the fifteenth. Beginning with pride, he said, heretics were further characterized by their secrecy, their wolf-like hiddenness and deceptive appearance. While these elements applied to all heretics regardless of differences between them, diversity was nonetheless introduced through one of the most important parts of the topos, that of the little foxes.[2] That the imagery and representation of heresy was governed by rhetorical norms is now taken for granted; as an idea it has been influential in a number of studies, notably Lerner's and Cohn's, and several subsequent historians have addressed the different commonplaces directly. Like Grundmann, his pupil Alexander Patschovsky also sees a broad idea of heresy that encompassed all heretics, characterized by metaphors of idolatry, monstrosity and poison.[3] Beverly Kienzle, as part of her work on the Cistercians, has in a similar way outlined four rhetorical patterns in the anti-heretical tradition of the twelfth century – demonization, pollution, threat to social order and apocalypticism – which all converge to portray heretics in general. Within these patterns she points to a series of polarities and recurrent images, again: the foxes, serpents, dogs, wolves and tares, all of which combine to create a vocabulary of hostile rhetoric.[4] The patterns and commonplaces of figurative construction in the mid thirteenth century material share some of these themes, but reading the texts together also shows a different set of preoccupations and a different use of the same images, which suggests that the topos is neither as static nor as singular as Grundmann describes it.

Some texts are more involved with the development of the topos than others. The inquisition records and the canons of the regional church councils do not compete well here with the rich language of the *exempla* or the treatises, or even of the larger councils and decretals, but there are nonetheless several themes that are so widely spread that they warrant examination. The focus here will not be so much on the many stock phrases that recur with varying frequency in the anti-heretical tradition; the image of the dog returning to eat its own vomit, which so 'preoccupied medieval commentators', employed often in the context of relapse, for example.[5] Rather than those stand-alone

---

2 Grundmann, 'Typus', esp. pp. 98–100.
3 A. Patschovsky, 'Heresy and Society: On the Political Function of Heresy in the Medieval World', in *Texts and Repression*, ed. Bruschi and Biller, pp. 23–41 (p. 39).
4 B. M. Kienzle, *Cistercians, Heresy and Crusade in Occitania, 1145–1229. Preaching in the Lord's Vineyard* (York, 2001), p. 215.
5 J. E. Salisbury, 'Human Animals of Medieval Fables', in *Animals in the Middle Ages*, ed. N. C. Flores (New York and London, 1996), 49–66 (p. 56).

phrases, the concern here will be more with the most prominent and most coherent of those elements employed in the construction of heresy, which form deliberately structured schemes of representation, namely: false appearance, corruption and, of course, the little foxes.

Foxes

The association between heretics and foxes as a topos, widespread in our texts, provides a good place in which to begin an examination of the commonplaces at work in the description of heresy, thanks to its clearly defined nature and imagery and to the fact that something quite definite can be said about its history. After the lion, the fox was the second most popular animal in exemplar literature – in large part because of Reynard – and was renowned for its cunning, though for some writers it was also a dirty creature.[6] Grundmann saw the fox as one of the most prominent images used to describe heretics in medieval Biblical exegesis, more prominent indeed than the perhaps more obvious Pauline passage on the necessity of heretics among the faithful.[7] Certainly, in anti-heretical writing of the twelfth century, the fox in the vineyard was the leitmotiv of the Cistercian tradition that dominated the church's response to the newly emergent heresy.[8] The image rests on the verse in the Song of Songs in which the spouse says to her beloved 'catch us the little foxes that destroy the vine', where the little foxes are interpreted as the heretics, the vine the Catholic Church.[9] The association was given particular emphasis and impetus by St Bernard's sixty-fifth and sixty-sixth sermons on the Song of Songs, written after his anti-heretical mission of 1143.[10]

Such an interpretation was attached to this verse long before Bernard's time, not least by Augustine, and by Irenaeus of Lyons in his treatise against heretics.[11] The twelfth-century gloss on the Bible, begun by Anselm of Laon, however, made it contemporary and direct; although it is not extensive, the Ordinary Gloss for this passage clearly indicates how it is to be understood. The interlinear reads for *capite*, 'the voice of Christ against heresies', that is the

---

6 Ibid., pp. 53–4, 61.

7 I Corinthians 11.19: 'Nam oportet et haereses esse, ut et qui probati sunt manifesti fiant in vobis'; H. Grundmann, 'Oportet et haereses esse. Das Problem der Ketzerei im Spiegel der mittelalterlichen Bibelexegese', in *Archiv für Kulturgeschichte* 45 (1963), 129–64, Italian trans. by O. Capitani, in *L'eresia medievale*, ed. O. Capitani (Bologna, 1971), pp. 23–60.

8 As described by J.-L. Biget, '"Les Albigeois": remarques sur une dénomination', in *Inventer*, ed. Zerner, pp. 219–55 (p. 236), and especially by B. M. Kienzle, 'Tending the Lord's Vineyard: Cistercians, Rhetoric and Heresy, 1143–1229. Part 1: Bernard of Clairvaux, the 1143 Sermons and the 1145 Preaching Mission', *Heresis* 25 (1995), 26–61.

9 'Capite nobis vulpes parvulas quae demoliuntur vineas'; Song of Songs 2.15.

10 Bernard of Clairvaux, *Opera*, ed. J. Leclerq, C. H. Talbot, H. M. Rochais, 8 vols. (Rome, 1957–77), I, xvi.

11 This according to D. Iogna-Prat, trans. G. R. Edwards, *Order and Exclusion: Cluny and Christendom Face Heresy, Judaism, and Islam (1000–1150)* (Ithaca, NY, 2002), p. 127, n. 20.

vulpes, 'schismatics and heretics who are crafty, and make themselves seem humble'. The marginal gloss reinforces this, promoting not only preaching and example but active defence: 'it is not enough ... unless we correct those who are erring'.[12] At various other points in the *Glossa ordinaria*, where other Biblical foxes are interpreted to mean heretics, it is almost always in direct reference to this passage – foxes elsewhere in the Bible are heretics because of the interpretation of the verse in the Song of Songs. Another, slightly later, commentary on the same book, by Alain de Lille, is equally explicit about this connection: 'by foxes, which are deceitful creatures, living in dens in the ground, are to be understood heretics; for vines, are to be understood the Church ...; capture for us, that is for our welfare destroy, foxes, that is heretics; little, on account of their frailty'.[13]

Despite the longevity of the tradition, however, it was undoubtedly Bernard's use of the passage and the weight that he put on it in his condemnation of heretics that led to the general adoption of the fox imagery in the years that followed. 'What shall we do with those foxes, the most malicious of all, who would rather inflict injury than win a victory in open fight?' 'Indeed, when a vine has been spoilt this is a sign that a fox has been there.'[14] His sermons on the Song of Songs enjoyed an extremely wide diffusion: there are more than 100 manuscripts extant from the twelfth and early thirteenth century.[15] After these sermons were written the frequency with which the little foxes appear in anti-heretical literature increases dramatically, not least because it was the Cistercians who provided much of the twelfth-century material on heresy. The tradition of fox imagery, then, Cistercian in the principal form in which it is inherited by the thirteenth century, is continued in our period and extended, in one specific way (to which we will return shortly), and also to a more general association between heretics and foxes.

---

12 'Vox Christi adversus haereses'; 'schismaticos et haereticos qui callidi sunt, et se humiles fingunt'; *parvulas* because 'in ipso initio fraudis, ne maiores effectae amplius noceant'; 'non sufficit ... nisi etiam errantes corrigamus'; *Biblia sacra, cum glossis ... Nicolai Lyrani postilla & moralitatibus, Burgensis additionibus & Thoringi replicis*, 6 vols. (Lyons, 1545), II, Song of Songs 2.15, 'Capite nobis vulpes parvulas' interlinear, and marginal gloss 'c'.

13 'Per vulpes, quae sunt fraudulenta animalia et in speluncis terrae habitantia, intelliguntur haeretici; per vineas, Ecclesiae intelliguntur ... capite nobis, id est destruite ad nostram utilitatem, vulpes, id est haereticos, parvulas, propter imbecillitatem'; Alain de Lille, *Compendiosa in cantica canticorum ad laudem deiparae virginis mariae elucidato*, PL 210, 51–110 (71A).

14 'Quid faciemus his malignissimis vulpibus, ut capi queant, quae nocere quam vincere malunt?' 'Et quidem recens vastatio vineae vulpem indicat affuisse'; Bernard of Clairvaux, *Opera*, II, Sermon 65, 173, 175; in translation, *On the Song of Songs*, trans. K. Walsh and I. M. Edmonds, 4 vols., Cistercian Fathers Series 4, 7, 31 and 40 (Kalamazoo, MI, 1971–80), III, Sermon 65, 180, 185.

15 St Bernard of Clairvaux, *Opera*, I, xxiii–xxxi. See also P. Biller, 'William of Newburgh and the Cathar Mission to England', in *Life and Thought in the Northern Church, c.1100–c.1700: Essays in Honour of Claire Cross*, ed. D. Wood, Studies in Church History, Subsidia 12 (Woodbridge, 1999), pp. 11–30 (pp. 14–15).

The thirteenth-century writers still make explicit use of the whole quotation; the Pseudo-David text still speaks of heretics in terms of 'the sly foxes, demolishing the vine of the lord'.[16] A 1257 letter to Raniero Sacconi from Pope Alexander IV describes the purpose of the inquisitorial office as to ensure 'that the root of heretical iniquity be cut off, and that the vine of the Lord – once the little foxes have been exterminated that destroy it with their perverse teeth – may bear forth the fruit of Catholic purity', a sentiment echoed almost verbatim by a later sentence from the Orvieto register.[17] The added prologue to the *Brevis summula* evokes this tradition to explain its purpose as a preventative tool against heresy by quoting the Song of Songs passage directly, and even glosses the foxes as 'heretical wickedness laying waste to the church'.[18] However, while these examples are unambiguous in their reference, the association between the activity of heretics and this Biblical passage is by this time so ingrained that we can also see several places in which the 'vine' is used almost as a shorthand. The etymology of St Dominic's name provided by the Ferrandi *legenda* and by the Golden Legend plays on the idea of the saint as 'custos Domini' of various things, including 'the vine of the Lord of Hosts', an association made more explicit by Ferrandi's later description of the heretics in Languedoc that 'were demolishing the vine of the Lord of Hosts'.[19] Here, the allusion is to a tradition now so fully absorbed by anti-heretical rhetoric that a reference to the 'vine' is alone enough to conjure the necessary associations, even in the canons of a church council: 'heretics and their believers and supporters strive to demolish the vine of the Lord of Hosts'.[20]

If the vine has become generalized, so too have the foxes. If 'heretics' can be, as in the above cases, used in place of 'foxes', the reverse is also true, and several of our texts use *vulpes* synonymously with *heretici*. Jacques de Vitry uses *vulpeculae* in this way on more than one occasion.[21] It is noticeable that

---

[16] 'Vulpes astutae vineam Domini demolientes'; Pseudo-David, *De inquisitione*, col. 1791; also col. 1788 'vulpes enim astutae sunt subtili astutia capiendae'.

[17] 'Radix iniquitatis haeretice succidatur, et vinea Domini, exterminatis vulpeculis, que perversis morsibus demoliuntur eandem, fructus afferat Catholice puritatis'; T. Ripoll (ed.), *Bullarium ordinis ff. praedicatorum*, 8 vols. (Rome 1729–40), I, 427 no. 24 (1257). 'Ex commisso nobis inquisitionis officio letiferam pestem pravitatis heretice radicitus extirpare de medio populi christiani et exterminare vulpeculas de vinea Domini Sabaoth que perversis moribus demoliuntur eandem'; d'Alatri, *Orvieto*, pp. 227–30.

[18] 'Hereticas pravitates ecclesiam devastantes'; *Brevis simmula*, p. 114.

[19] 'Vinee Domini Sabaoth'; 'vineam Domini Sabaoth demolirentur'; Jacobus de Voragine (Iacopo da Varazze), *Legenda Aurea*, ed. G. P. Maggioni, 2nd edn, 2 vols. (Florence, 1998), II, 718; Peter Ferrandi, *Legenda sancti Dominici*, ed. M. H. Laurent, MOPH 16, pp. 219, 222.

[20] 'Haeretici eorumque credentes atque fautores nituntur vineam Domini Sabaoth demoliri'; Narbonne 1243, can. 16, Mansi, XXIII, 361.

[21] Jacques de Vitry, *The Historia occidentalis of Jacques de Vitry. A Critical Edition*, ed. J. F. Hinnebusch (Fribourg, 1972), p. 146; Vitry, Crane, p. 9, no. xxvi. Humbert of Romans uses foxes to label heretics at least once: 'vulpium Samsonis'; Humbert, *Opera*, II, 452. The author of the second life of Anthony of Padua also frequently uses fox imagery in reference to

echoes of the Song of Songs terminology remain, through the diminutive *vulpeculae*. The foxes in the vine represent, in our texts, a general inheritance of imagery from the twelfth-century work of the Cistercians and the glossators.

To this generalized use of the fox imagery a new layer is added at the turn of the century by Innocent III's 1199 decretal *Vergentis in senium*. Next to a continued and undiluted use of the Song of Songs imagery, in phrases such as 'the moth in the flower, and the foxes in the fruit labour to destroy the vine of the lord', and 'to capture the foxes that demolish the vine of the lord', the rich rhetoric of Innocent's prose introduces this device: 'against such small foxes, having different appearances, but tied together by the tails'.[22] The source for this new element is ultimately the passage in Judges in which Samson 'went and caught three hundred foxes, and coupled them tail to tail, and fastened torches between the tails'.[23] Unlike the Song of Songs foxes, the Judges verse has no interpretation in the Ordinary Gloss that connects these verses to heretics or heresy in any way. The gloss for the eightieth Psalm, however, does just that: 'therefore Samson tied the tails of the foxes ... foxes are the deceitful, especially heretics', an interpretation which is echoed in other commentaries that draw on the same source as the Gloss – that is, Augustine.[24] In several places, Augustine interprets Samson's foxes in Judges as heretics, often connecting this explicitly to the foxes of Solomon.[25]

As St Bernard's commentary made a previous tradition current for his period, so Innocent's *Vergentis* takes a precedented association and places it firmly in the contemporary frame of reference for the discussion of heresy, especially through the direct juxtaposition with the theme of the previous century, a construction further reinforced by the decretal's later inclusion in the treatment of heresy in the 1234 *Liber extra*. Like the vine, because heretics were so generally synonymous with foxes, the two types of fox are easily interchangeable. Thomas Agni, in his life of Peter Martyr, says that he 'sought after and scattered Samson's foxes' in the context of his inquisitorial office, here neatly combining shorthand references to both traditions.[26] The conjoined tails also become a discrete element in their own right, in legal language especially.

---

heretics: L. de Kerval (ed.), *Sancti Antonii de Padua vitae duae quarum altera hucusque inedita* (Paris, 1904), pp. 219–21.

22 'In flore tinea et vulpes in fructu demoliri vineam Domini moliuntur'; 'capere vulpes demolientes vineam Domini'; 'licet autem contra vulpes huiusmodi parvulas, species quidem habentes diversas, sed caudas ad invicem colligatas'; X 5 7.10, Friedberg, II, 782.

23 'Perrexitque et cepit trecentas vulpes, caudasque earum iunxit ad caudas, et faces ligavit in medio'; Judges 15.4–5.

24 'Ideo Samson caudas vulpium colligavit ... Vulpes sunt insidiosi, maxime haeretici'; Remigius, *Enarrationes in psalmos*, PL 131, 575.

25 For example: Augustine, *De Samsone, Sermones ad populum, V, sermones dubii*, CCCLXIV, PL 39, 1639–43, 1641.

26 'Simpsonis vulpeculas perquirebat & dissipabat'; *Acta sanctorum*, April 3, 29, 686–719, *vita Scripta per Thomam de Lentino coævum*, col. 695F; like the Orvieto register, here using foxes to refer to the object of inquisition.

The anti-heretical third canon of the fourth Lateran council uses the image without specific reference to the foxes: 'all heretics, whatever names they may go under [here combining this tag-line from *Ad abolendam* with the *Vergentis* rhetoric], they have different faces indeed, but their tails tied together'.[27] A similar sublimated usage is employed again by Gregory IX in a statement that also reinforces the combination of the inherited vocabulary of Lucius III and Innocent and which was itself reproduced by Gregory's successor in a general letter 'to all the faithful' in which he excommunicates 'all heretics … whatever names they may go under, they have different faces indeed, but their tails tied together'.[28] The topos of foxes, or rather of heretics, joined at the tail seems to be very firmly implanted in legal terminology by middle of the thirteenth century.[29]

The Judges imagery promulgated by *Vergentis in senium* is adopted in a similar way by two inquisitors in our period to indicate the essential sameness of different types of heretics. The *De heresi* section of the fourth book of Stephen of Bourbon's collection of *exempla* uses the image of Samson's foxes in this way; the heretics are 'tied together in their posterior parts by their tails, because they are all intent on one thing, fighting the church, like Samson's foxes'.[30] An even fuller version of this prefixes Stephen's account of a heretical meeting in which none of the parties can agree on correct doctrine: 'they are like Samson's foxes, in Judges, who had their tails tied together and different faces, because they have allied aims in attacking the faith of the church … among themselves they quarrel, and against us they all combine'.[31] There is a further extension of this idea in the Anonymous of Passau, which uses the other side of this implication to characterize the subject as essentially divided. We will return to this theme shortly; what is interesting here, and what further underlines the level to which this has been assimilated into the anti-heretical

---

[27] 'Haereticos universos, quibuscumque nominibus censeantur facies quidem diversas habentes, sed caudas ad invicem colligatas'; García, *Lateran 4*, p. 47; trans. *DEC*, I, 233. The substitution of 'facies', where *Vergentis* has 'species', to describe the variety of the heretics' appearance is perhaps explained as an allusion to, or slippage from, the torches, *faces*, of the Biblical passage.

[28] 'Ad omnes fideles': 'Excommunicamus … universos haereticos … quibuscunque nominibus censeantur, facies quidem habentes diversas, sed caudas adinvicem colligatas'. Though it is directed against all heretics, like Lucius III's decretal, Gregory takes the precaution of providing a selection of names: 'universos haereticos, Catharos, Patarenos, Pauperes de Lugduno, Passaginos, Iosephinos, Arnaldistas, Speronistas, et alios, quibuscunque' etc. X 5 7.13, X 5 7.15, Friedberg II, 787; 789; Mansi, XXIII, 583.

[29] Gregory IX still uses the original vines and foxes in *Ille humani generis*.

[30] 'Sunt coadunati sive colligati ex parte posteriori in caudis quia omnis tendunt ad unum quia intendunt impugnare ecclesiam ut vulpes sampsonis qui habebant facies diversas colligatas caudas'; Oxford, Oriel MS 68, fol. 218va–vb, BnF MS Lat. 14599 fol. 234ra.

[31] 'Sunt similes vulpibus Samsonis, de quibus Judicum, qui habebant caudas colligatas et facies divisas, quia intenciones habent conjunctas ad impugnandum fidem Ecclesie, … inter se dissident, et contra nos omnes conveniunt'; Stephen of Bourbon, *Tractatus*, p. 278.

canon, is the fact that in the latter example, and indeed also in the previous example from Stephen of Bourbon, though it purports to be the Judges passage, the text quoted by the Anonymous of Passau is in fact that of Innocent's decretal, and of its later extension in subsequent legislation: 'Just as it is read in the book of Judges: that Samson's foxes had different faces, but were tied together by the tails: so heretics are divided into sects among themselves, but are united in their attack on the church.'[32]

To the threat embodied in and expressed through the earlier Song of Songs foxes is now added another layer, the unified nature of that apparently plural threat, represented by the Judges foxes. The older strand remains, and is indeed so ingrained as to be almost incidental in places, and to allow the easy and natural assimilation of the newer layer, though the function of the latter is more active, and perhaps more pointed, than the vine imagery. Though the Orvieto register and the council of Narbonne, as we have seen, continue to employ Solomon's foxes, rather than Samson's, in the legal material and the inquisitors' manuals Innocent's foxes have been adopted as a motif and a device. What has perhaps already been noticeable here, in comparison with the trend of the previous century or so, is that, as a motif, foxes are almost completely absent from the polemic of the thirteenth century.

False appearance

Our polemical sources do not, in fact, as a whole, deal in 'rhetorical' attacks on heretics, unsurprising if one thinks of the aloof scholarship of Moneta of Cremona. In general, they prefer to employ a sort of adjectival invective, attached usually to the direct address and accompanying the refutation, rather than comprising it. Nonetheless, where there is a level of rhetorical construction in the polemics it is most likely to rest upon the topos of the false appearance of the heretic. That idea is, in fact, the most common across the whole of our corpus of texts in its frequency and certainly in its distribution, a frequency matched only by the running theme of corruption, but far more concentrated and sharply drawn than the latter, in places drawing that older idea into some sort of superstructure. While the foxes are largely absent from the polemical material, the more complex set of imagery that surrounds the idea of false appearance makes up most of what little figurative representation the polemics do employ. In fact, one of the richest expressions of the idea can be found in the Pseudo-James Capelli, who stands alone among the polemi-

---

32 'Sicut in Iudicum libro legitur: quod vulpes Sampsonis facies diversas habebant, sed caudas sibi invicem colligatas: sic haeretici in sectis sunt divisi in se, sed in impugnatione Ecclesiae, sunt uniti'; Anonymous of Passau, p. 264. Compare this to the Biblical passage: 'perrexitque et cepit trecentas vulpes, caudasque earum iunxit ad caudas, et faces ligavit in medio', to which it bears little relation, and to *Vergentis*, and later legislation: 'licet autem contra vulpes huiusmodi parvulas, species quidem habentes diversas, sed caudas ad invicem colligatas', and 'facies quidem diversas habentes'.

cists in his colourful language, and who provides a useful way in to the exploration of this idea.

The Pseudo-James' chapter on heretics' abstinence from meat and eggs opens with these pointed words:

> Since no truth supports the pernicious traditions of the heretics, they therefore season them with the flavour of simulated virtues, so that the pleasing sweetness of honey makes the hidden poison less perceptible. They have indeed the appearance of piety, but, bearing as they do the rapacity of wolves underneath a sheep's skin, they do not have the virtue of holiness. ... In fact their religion is shown to be false ... For they may use a cloak of good works to recommend false doctrine.[33]

Present here are most of the principal images and terms associated with this idea of a pretended outward form, which we can look at before we move to consider the wider aspects of this theme. Much of the general vocabulary used to convey false appearance can be found here: the cloaking of a real agenda, usually with words, here with good deeds; the simulation, whether of piety or of religion. Noticeable as well here is the underlying venom of the heretics' true nature.[34]

The Pseudo-James' contrast between the outer pretended piety and the inner reality of heretics as wolves in sheep's clothing combines the two main Scriptural images that form part of the basis of the topos. The first, the ravening wolves, is taken from the warning of Matthew's gospel to beware false prophets: 'beware of false prophets who come to you in the clothing of sheep, but inwardly they are ravening wolves. By their fruits may you know them.' False prophets, and the ravening wolves, are all understood to refer 'particularly to heretics' by the Ordinary Gloss.[35] The Gloss further explains that those wolves and pseudo-prophets are 'covered with the clothing of piety', an allusion to the other Scriptural image that underlies the Pseudo-James' construction. The *species pietatis* that the sheep's clothing affords the

---

[33] 'Quum nulla veritas hereticorum perniciosas traditiones subsequatur ideo eas quodam simulatarum virtutum sapore condiunt ut per dulcedinem mellis quem placet, minus sentiatur venenum quod latet; habent quidem speciem pietatis sed sub ovina pelle luporum rapacitatem gestantes sanctitatis virtutem non habent ... Illorum quippe religio falsa esse ostenditur ... Nam ipsi ut bonorum operum palliatione falsam doctrinam commendent'; Capelli, *Adversus haereticos*, p. clxxxvi.

[34] On the history and use of this theme as a whole, see J. H. Arnold, *Inquisition and Power: Catharism and the Confessing Subject in Medieval Languedoc* (Philadelphia, PA, 2001), pp. 63–5.

[35] 'Attendite a falsis prophetis qui veniunt ad vos in vestimentis ovium, intrinsecus autem sunt lupi rapaces. A fructibus eorum cognoscetis eos'; Matthew 7.15, *Biblia sacra, cum glossis*, II, Matthew 7.15, c and f. The passage is glossed: 'specialiter de hereticis'. Heretics are also given as one reading of the thorns and thistles in this passage. Pseudo-prophets and pseudo-christs appear elsewhere in Matthew, at 24.24, and 'pseudochristi et pseudopropheti' are also in Mark 13.22. The gloss for this passage in Mark runs: 'unde melius de haereticis accipiendum, qui contra ecclesiam venientes, se Christos esse mentiuntur'; *Biblia sacra, cum glossis*, II, Mark 13.22, a.

wolves in the above extract is drawn from that passage of the second letter to Timothy, often invoked in the description of heretics, which describes the coming of evil men in the last days who lead others astray through false holiness or virtue, 'having an appearance indeed of piety, but denying the power thereof'.[36] Between them, these two sets of images and words form the basis for the idea of false appearance.

The author of the *Disputatio*, like the Pseudo-James, describes his opponent in terms of the contradictory realities of his inner and outer conditions, though in more idiosyncratic language: 'wretched hypocrites, who have ravaged your faces so that you may seem to be men who fast and are worthy: and [yet] you rather choose the sodomitic crime, sharing your beds with men!'[37] George is paraphrasing the words of Matthew's gospel here, to characterize the hypocrisy of his opponent as the Scriptural hypocrisy condemned by Christ, a usage that also occurs in the work of Stephen of Bourbon and of Peter Ferrandi. Just as often, George places the vocabulary of false appearance in the mouth of his heretical opponent, who accuses the Catholic speaker of using 'cloaked language', and the Catholic church of having both 'spot and wrinke, because there are there [in the Catholic church] adulterers ... and ravening wolves'.[38] In another example, the polemical treatise attributed by Kaeppeli to Peter Martyr states that the heretics refrain from meat and eggs because they say that it leads to sin, but 'this they do not believe, for all that they insist on it when in the presence of those they believe to be simple'. Like George, here is a picture of feigned appearance that does not necessarily depend on the received imagery, and one that adds another layer of pretence, directed specifically at the ascetic pretensions of heretics.[39] Moneta's text, however, more an academic refutation than an attack, does not use this or any of the other topoi to construct or attack his opponent. Even Salvo Burci, whose prose is the opposite of Moneta's in precision and in colour, uses this motif sparingly, describing 'all the depravity of heretics, who say [things] under the habit and appearance of religion'.[40] The polemical approach to heresy adopted by these texts has little need of rhetoric that is directed at the quality of their opponent when what they want to target is the content of their error.

In contrast stands the incidence of this motif in the church legislation, and subsequently the legal textbook of Gregory IX. Aside from a commentary on

---

36 'Quaedam pietatis veste tecti'; 'habentes speciem quidem pietatis virtutem autem eius abnegantes'; II Timothy 3.5.
37 'Tristes ypocrite, qui exterminatas habetis facies, ut videamini ieiunantes et honesti, et sodomiticum potius scelus eligitis, masculorum concubitores!'; *Disputatio*, p. 18.
38 'Palliato sermone'; 'maculam et rugam, quia sunt ibi adulteri, ... lupi rapaces'; *Disputatio*, pp. 56, 77.
39 'Istam non credunt, tamen allegant ipsam coram illis quos simplices existimant esse'; Kaeppeli, 'Une somme', p. 331.
40 'Omnis errecticorum pravitas, qui sub habitu et specie religionis dicunt'; Salvo Burci, *Suprastella*, pp. 252, 249.

the princes of Judea by Jerome, which connects heretics to sophistry and the dialectic arts, there is little of this imagery to be found in the *Decretum*, constituted, as it is, almost entirely from the writings of the Fathers and the early church. Gregory IX's *Liber extra*, on the other hand, is replete with the imagery and language that characterize this strand of rhetoric; not, it has to be observed, in the additions that it makes from the texts of antiquity and the church Fathers, but in its inclusion of the work of recent and contemporary popes. The new material in the *Liber extra* reflects a shift, in which false appearance is now a very prominent part of the canon-legal idea of heretics.

Several of the twelfth-century church councils contain references to false appearance in their treatment of heretics. As early as the 1119 council of Toulouse heretics were condemned as 'eos qui religionis speciem simulantes'. The canons of the council of Rheims in 1157 similarly describe 'Manicheans' operating 'under the appearance of religion', deceiving the simple, in particular the *mulierculae* of the second letter to Timothy. The danger to the 'simple' stands in direct relation to the level of secrecy in the heretic's behaviour again at Tours: 'the more it creeps in secret, the more grievously the vine of the lord is destroyed in the simple'.[41] Noticeable is the prominence of the *species* image from Timothy discussed above; here it is a 'species religionis' and not 'pietatis', though in fact the gloss for this verse gives 'religionis' as an explanation of 'pietatis'. With Lucius III's *Ad abolendam*, however, the use of that verse to describe the nature of heretics is made explicit in direct quotation: those who preach without a mission do so 'having the appearance of piety, but, as the apostle has said, denying its power'.[42]

While that image is entrenched by the beginning of the thirteenth century, the broad theme of the false appearance of heretics is really brought to the fore by the output of Innocent III, in particular, again, by *Vergentis in senium*. The following quotation makes clear how strongly that decretal emphasizes false appearance, framed in the language of Timothy:

> They are the innkeepers who mix water with wine, and offer the poison of the Babylonian dragon in a golden chalice to drink, having, according to the Apostle, the appearance of piety, but inwardly denying its virtue ... thus far the deadly plague could not be destroyed, but rather, just like cancer, was creeping imperceptibly wider in secret, and now may openly spread abroad the poison of its wickedness, while, cloaked in the appearance of religion, he who had not been the disciple of truth, now made master of error, both deceives many simple people, and seduces some astute ones.[43]

---

[41] 'Sub specie religionis'; 'quanto serpit occultis tanto gravius Dominicam vineam in simplicibus demolitur'; Fredericq, I, 29, 35–6, 39.

[42] 'Sub specie pietatis virtutum eius, iuxta quod ait Apostolus, denegantes'; X 5 7.9, Friedberg, II, 780; trans. E. Peters (ed. and trans.), *Heresy and Authority in Medieval Europe: Documents in Translation* (Philadelphia, PA, 1980), p. 171.

[43] 'Hi sunt caupones, qui aquam vino commiscent, et virus draconis in aureo calice Babylonis propinant, habentes, secundum Apostolum, speciem pietatis, virtutum autem eius penitus

The emphasis on hiddenness, poison and disguise is continued in similar terms in the other documents by Innocent included in the *Liber extra*; in his letter to the king of Aragon: 'you set up light as shadows, and shadows as light' and 'not with the wine of remorse, but with the poison of the dragon', once again held in the 'golden chalice of Babylon'.[44] On the usurpation of the preaching office by heretics: 'since vice enters secretly under the appearance of virtue, and the angel of Satan imitates and transforms himself into an angel of light', and again 'truly under the pretence of truth you fall into the pit of error and under the appearance of virtue into the snare of vices'.[45] Innocent places false appearance at the centre of his construction of heretics, tied firmly to the Scriptural vocabulary of Timothy and Corinthians, and it is an attitude continued by his later successor Gregory IX, not only in the document which forms chapter fourteen of this title, also on the usurpation of preaching, which repeats verbatim Innocent's language of chapter twelve, but also in the decretal *Ille humani generis* of 1231, in which Gregory reprises most of the themes and images of *Vergentis in senium*.[46]

We can see this language enter also the great ecumenical council of Innocent's reign. Though the seduction of the simple and the infirm had characterized heretics in the previous Lateran council, the third canon of the 1215 meeting quotes directly from Timothy in its portrayal of its subject: 'some, having the appearance of piety, but (as the apostle has said), denying its power'. The inserted words may indicate a quotation from *Ad abolendam*.[47] By the 1230s not only has the language of Innocent's anti-heretical legislation become the standard mode for papal output in Gregory's decretals, it is reflected also in the secular law of the emperor, in the *Liber Augustalis*, which uses much the same vocabulary, as well as many wolves and lots of snakes, making false appearance one of the foremost traits of heretics in anti-heretical legislation.

The canon-legal tradition seems once again to set the tone in terms of the language used to discuss heresy, but the predominance of the theme of false

---

abnegantes ... nondum tamen usque adeo pestis potuit mortificari mortifera, quin, sicut cancer, amplius serperet in occulto, et iam in aperto suae virus iniquitatis effundat, dum palliata specie religionis et multos decipit simplices, et quosdam seducit astutos, factus magister erroris, qui non fuerat discipulus veritatis'; X 5 7.10, Friedberg, II, 782. The last phrase paraphrases C.24 q.3 c.30, Friedberg, I, 998.

44 'Ponitis lucem tenebras et tenebras lucem'; 'non enim vino compunctionis, sed felle draconis'; 'aureo calice Babylonis'; X 5 7.11, Friedberg, II, 783–4.

45 'Quum vitia sub specie virtutum occulte subintrant, et angelus Satanae se in angelum lucis simulat et transformat'; 'ne sub praetextu veritatis in foveam decidatis erroris et sub specie virtutum in laqueam vitiorum'; X 5 7.12, Friedberg, II, 784–7.

46 'Ne vitia sub specie virtutum occulte subintrent'; X 5 7.14, Friedberg, II, 789, a repetition of Innocent in X 5 7.12. *Ille humani generis* repeats most of the rhetoric of *Vergentis*, dominated by theme of deception and false appearance.

47 'Nonnulli sub specie pietatis virtutem eius (iuxta quod ait Apostolus) abnegantes'; García, *Lateran 4*, p. 50.

appearance throughout the anti-heretical corpus of this period – and it is the prevailing theme of the topos at this time – is a result not simply of rhetoric but of the role it plays. In the legal material it is often used in connection with usurpation and competition. So it is in the other texts, especially those which relate to a preaching context, at one remove or another. The function of the text in the context of confrontation with heretics and heretical ideas shapes the preoccupation of the topos with a theme that undermines the enemy and promotes the legitimacy of the Catholic speaker. False appearance is the dominant construction among the *exempla* collections in particular, where the deceptive nature of the heretic lies at the centre of many of the stories they tell about heresy. The *exempla* build their picture of false appearance using some of the same passages employed to such great effect in the legislation: Caesarius of Heisterbach refers to heretics as 'ravening wolves' and believes Matthew's warning about the pseudo-Christs and pseudo-prophets to have been fulfilled in the Amalricians.[48] References to these Scriptural motifs are sometimes more allusive than specific, and the *exempla* writers also generalize the basic images, so that the wolves, like the foxes, are on their own enough to recall the associations of those motifs. That indirect use is at work in Jacques de Vitry's automatic labelling of heretics as *lupi* in his *exempla*, even where there is not then any explicit development to false appearance.[49] Here the association with heretics interacts with a wider tradition of the Scriptural wolf imagery, which is used generally to signify those who cannot be trusted with the fate of the simple.[50] Wolves and all their connotations are, though, only one element of a prevalent idea of false appearance that is often built into the fabric of these stories, and if false appearance occurs with some frequency in the *exempla* cited, of Caesarius and Jacques, in the *Tractatus de diversis materiis* it is unavoidable.

The basic tenor of Stephen of Bourbon's treatment of heretics, and this is something that functions at both a background and a foreground level, is a criticism of their deception of the simple, Stephen's ultimate audience. Heretics approach the simple 'wishing to pervert [them], by disguised appearance'.[51] Consequently, the pretence of the heretics' outward persona runs as a prominent image through much of what Stephen has to say about them, though it is an image located as much in their false speech as in their appearance. A Waldensian heretic, while literally disguised, 'transfiguratus', is also deceptive in his 'sophistical words'. Stephen's concern with the 'sophisms' and 'the duplicities of words' employed by heretics is such that, as we have seen, it occupies a large part of his 'how to spot a heretic' section, and here that

---

[48] Caesarius, *Dialogus*, I, 296, 305, quoting Matthew 7.15 and 24.24.
[49] Vitry, Greven, p. 57.
[50] The wolf that eats the sheep it should be guarding is used by Odo of Cheriton, for example, to signify corrupt priests: Salisbury, 'Human Animals', p. 56.
[51] 'Cupientes pervertere eum, dissimulato habitu'; Stephen of Bourbon, *Tractatus*, p. 277.

concern, elsewhere focused on the simple, is extended to the deception also of the learned. Indeed, the sophistry of heretics forms another layer of the false appearance topos. The same anxiety – that heretics are capable of misleading not only the simple but also the learned – also occurs in *Vergentis in senium*: the heretic 'both deceives many simple people, and seduces some astute ones'.[52] The *Decretum*, likewise, includes a warning from Jerome that heretics 'often oppress churchmen through their sophisms and dialectical arts'.[53] This aspect of the motif is the form in which it features in the inquisitors' manuals, particularly in the Anonymous of Passau and even more so in the Pseudo-David of Augsburg. In the latter text, as in Stephen's text, it is employed primarily in the context of the seduction of the simple by heretics, alongside the wolf imagery of Matthew. Once their deception has succeeded in perverting their audience, then, as in Stephen's story of the bird catcher heretic, their errors can be introduced or revealed. An emphasis on this type of false appearance parallels the inquisitors' concerns with the deception not only of the simple but, more immediately, of the tribunal, and the obstruction of truth.

If we turn again to the extract that we looked at from the Pseudo-James at the beginning of this section, we can notice that the context in which this diatribe occurs – and it is by far one of the most extended attacks in this text as a whole – is that of the Cathars' ascetic diet. Peter Martyr also expends a large amount of energy defending the consumption of meat and eggs. A similar level of self-denial is described by the Pseudo-David for the Waldensians, with a similar level of contempt: 'certain heretics afflict themselves with fasts and vigils and suchlike, because without such things they cannot acquire for themselves the reputation of holiness among simple people, nor deceive [them] through the fiction of simulation'.[54] The connection here between false appearance and elements of an apostolic lifestyle is something that we have seen before, in the Dominican edifying texts, and one that perhaps forms its own sub-tradition within the wider topos of deception. We have seen that this is often employed in Dominican texts in connection with preaching or fasting, aspects of apostolicity where mendicant friars, and indeed the preaching church generally, would be in direct competition with the heretics in the public perception of the two groups. St Dominic competes explicitly on this level for the allegiance of a noble household by fasting more convincingly than the Cathar 'Good Men' who are staying there.[55] The abstinence of the heretics

---

52 'Verba sophistica'; Stephen of Bourbon, *Tractatus*, pp. 279–80. 'Sophismatibus'; 'verborum duplicitatibus'; Stephen of Bourbon, *Tractatus*, p. 288. 'Multos decipit simplices, et quosdam seducit astutos'; X 5 7.10, Friedberg, II, 782.

53 'Quod sophismatibus suis et arte dialectica sepe opprimant ecclesiasticos'; C.24 q.3 c.33, Friedberg, I, 999.

54 'Quidam tamen haeretici affligunt se jejuniis & vigiliis & hujusmodi, quia sine talibus non possunt apud simplices nomen sibi sanctitatis acquirere, nec decipere simulationis figmento'; Pseudo-David, *De inquisitione*, col. 1780.

55 Ferrandi, *Legenda*, MOPH 16, pp. 225–6, 228.

in this story is characterized by Dominic's hagiographer Ferrandi, in the same words used by the author of the *Disputatio*, as the false piety of the hypocrites described by Christ during the sermon on the mount: the heretics 'they ravage their faces, in order to appear to people as men who fast'. In contrast to this excess, Dominic practises abstinence not to gain the praise of others but to lead the faithless away from error and back to the love of the Catholic Church.[56]

The theme of false appearance is prominent in Dominican literature, apparently as a foil to the Friars Preacher, to emphasize their true example and preaching, and in part an element of the construction of their identity. We can look to this perhaps as one of the motives behind the strong presence of this element in Stephen's writing, who also uses a version of the Matthew verse 'they tear at their faces, that they may appear to others to be fasting' to illustrate their hiddenness, the third of his four signs by which 'heretics especially are specified'.[57] The false sanctity of one of his more realistic heretics, Alberea, is indeed connected explicitly to her abstinence from meat and animal products.[58] There are echoes in this last point of Grundmann's observation, in his analysis of the false appearance motif, that saintliness had to some degree become in itself a mark of heresy. The author of the Anonymous of Passau is able to suggest asceticism as a method by which heretics could be recognized, using Paul's words in the second letter to the Corinthians, the same transfiguration of evil into an angel of light used by Innocent in the letter quoted above.[59]

However, it is perhaps also possible to see behind this construction a background and mundane reality to these concerns. In the course of their description of the Cistercian legates that Diego met on his mission in the Languedoc, Stephen, as well as the accounts of the story in Peter of les Vaux-de-Cernay and the various *legendae* of St Dominic, all also relate that the heretics use the opulent life of the churchmen against them in their perversion of the Catholic faithful. In his introduction to the story Stephen makes this point succinctly: 'they do not have a stronger argument for the defence of their error and the subversion of simple people than the bad examples of Catholics and especially of prelates'.[60] Stephen spins this into a criticism of the heretics, who resort to this line of attack when they run out of other, better arguments. As Diego understood, however, the ability to exhibit and control the appearance of piety was the arena in which the church and the heretics were competing – what

---

56 'Exterminant quippe facies suas, ut videatur hominibus ieiunantes'; ibid., p. 226. See above, p. 85.
57 'Excoriant facies suas, ut videantur ab hominibus jejunantes'; 'heretici maxime denotantur'; Stephen of Bourbon, *Tractatus*, pp. 311, 307.
58 Stephen of Bourbon, *Tractatus*, p. 149.
59 Grundmann, 'Typus', pp. 101–2; Anonymous of Passau, p. 272.
60 'Non habent forcius argumentum ad defensionem erroris sui et subversionem simplicium quam exempla mala catholicorum et maxime prelatorum'; Stephen of Bourbon, *Tractatus*, pp. 213–14.

Arnold refers to as 'semiotic warfare' – and it recurs as a concern in the Dominican literature.[61] Ferrandi, in his life of St Dominic, expresses exasperation at the heretics' appearance: 'what person, even a wise one, would not be taken in at first by such people? Who would not reckon them most holy?' The nobles' admiring reaction to the superior display of fasting and prayer of Dominic and his companion – 'truly these are good men' – prompts the beginnings of a return to the Catholic faith.[62]

Outside the hagiographical traditions of the Order it is clear that this is indeed a major problem facing the Dominicans. The manual written for his brother preachers by the master general Humbert of Romans highlights the problem, complaining of heretics who will travel widely to visit their followers and who collect alms to support the poor and lure people to their faith. Peraldus similarly claims that the illiterate cannot believe that the dignity of the church resides in men of evil life, who make easy targets for heretics' accusations.[63] That heretical asceticism was indeed making a strong impact on the 'simple', as these sources seem to fear, might be confirmed by the words of one deponent before the inquisition, who believed that the heretics were good on account of their continued fasting.[64]

The idea of false appearance therefore had a larger existence than its purely rhetorical expressions. Further, the descriptive elements of the inquisitors' handbooks present a layer of deception in the appearance of heretics that is unconnected to any outward show of piety; rather, it is to do with the practical reality of heretics' lives. While Stephen of Bourbon's story of the sophistical Waldensian revolves around the deception exercised by the heretic, the man nonetheless also walks 'transfiguratus', in disguise, dressed as a crossbowman. The comparison that Stephen draws between another senior Waldensian and Proteus is based on the fact that, when he is captured, the man is found with the trappings, 'indicia', of many different trades. These he had used to disguise himself as, variously, a pilgrim, a penitent, a cobbler, a barber, a reaper – all occupations that would allow him the freedom of movement necessary to meet with and administer to his followers. If he was sought under

---

61 Arnold, *Inquisition*, p. 65. Arnold points out that even the habits of the Order were perceived as an imitation of Cathar dress.

62 'Quis vel sapiens in prima fronte non deciperetur a talibus? Qui eos non sanctissimos reputaret?'; 'vere isti homines boni sunt'; Ferrandi, *Legenda*, MOPH 16, p. 225.

63 Humbert, *Opera*, II, 471. Peraldus's text is cited from the website maintained by Siegfried Wenzel, who is one of a team preparing a new edition of the *Summa de vitiis*: William Peraldus, *Summa de vitiis* VIII.xxxii <http://unc.edu/~swenzel/peraldus.html> (accessed 8 January 2011).

64 Duvernoy, *Quercy*, p. 234. In contrast, Duvernoy, while discussing abstinence – as distinct from fasting – talks of the relish taken by Cathars in 'delectable foods' and points to many occasions observed by followers of their being given fine salmon, fine trout, fish pasties and so on: J. Duvernoy, *Le Catharisme: La religion des Cathares* (Toulouse, 1976), pp. 177–8, 177, n. 52.

one disguise, he would transform himself into another. That both men felt the need to conceal their identity in public might remind us of the account given by both Anselm of Alessandria and the Anonymous of Passau of the 'crooked stick' code used by the Cathars to determine whether or not they were among friends.[65] A further degree of hiddenness is visible in the communication of heretical belief. Raniero tells us that there are some beliefs that are not taught to the lesser grades, and this seems to be borne out by the author of the Peter Martyr treatise, who is insistent on the 'secrets' of the heretics: 'this is one of their secrets and this pestilence they have stolen from the Saracens', or 'this error they drew from the heresy of the Manichees and is one of their arcane secrets'. He also reports this speech as the opinion of the heretics on the subject of transmigration of souls: 'I shall disclose to you our most secret secret, which few even from our *consolati* know.'[66] The *Vitae fratrum* story of the Tuscan youth Florimund, who discovered the dualist nature of the Cathar sect only after several years of membership, will be remembered here.

Whatever the reality of their piety, then, there is certainly a level below the rhetoric in which heretics, rather than being deceptive, are simply hidden. If we look back to the twenty-seventh canon of the third Lateran council, we can find a comparison of Cathars to other heretics in terms of their hiddenness:

> The damnable perversity of [those] heretics whom some call the Cathars, others the Patarenes, others the Publicani, and others by other names, has grown so strong, that they now they do not practise their wickedness in secret, as others do, but proclaim their error publicly and draw the simple and weak to agree with them.[67]

Two things are significant here, the first of which is the ongoing concern for the deception of the simple that runs through the whole of this topos of appearance. The other point that needs to be noted is that there is an idea of multiple heretical groups, of which secrecy is apparently the normal condition. The Cathars, on the other hand, are able to preach openly because they are strong, presumably as a result of the support of the nobles, given that this

---

65 'Transfiguratus ad modum alicuijus balistarii'; Stephen of Bourbon, *Tractatus*, p. 280. 'Aliquando quidam maximus inter eos fuit captus, qui secum ferebat multorum artificiorum indicia, in que quasi Proteus se transfigurabat: si quereretur in una similitudine et ei innotesceret, in alia se transmutabat'; Stephen of Bourbon, *Tractatus*, p. 293. The Pseudo-David also describes Waldensians moving around in disguise: Pseudo-David, *De inquisitione*, col. 1781. For the 'crooked stick', see above, p. 146.

66 'Hoc est unum de suis secretis et hanc pestilentiam subriperunt a Saracenis'; 'hunc autem errorem traxerunt ab heresi manicheorum et est illud unum de suis secretis archanis'; 'tibi secretam secretissimam nostram, quam pauci etiam ex nostris consolatis sciunt'; Kaeppeli, 'Une somme', pp. 324, 330, 331.

67 'Haereticorum, quos alii Catharos, alii Patarinos, alii Publicanos, alii aliis nominibus vocant, invaluit damnata perversitas, ut iam non in occulto sicut aliqui nequitiam suam exerceant, sed suum errorem publice manifestent et ad suum consensum simplices attrahunt et infirmos'; *DEC*, I, 224.

canon is addressed primarily against abuse of secular power in the region of southern France.

If that picture is then compared to the legislation that grows out of the regional councils around the process of inquisition, which maintains a constant emphasis on the hiding places and *latibula* of heretics, we can perhaps suppose that the increasing prevalence of the false appearance topos in our period is connected to the increasing necessity for heretics to be hidden, as well as to the need for the Catholic Church to gain the upper hand in the continuing competition over the contested rhetoric of ascetic piety.

Corruption

The last aspect of the rhetorical construction that we will consider here is that of corruption, which here includes ideas both of infection and disease and of poison and pollution. These had been long-standing elements of the anti-heretical tradition already by the time our texts were written, as a quick glance at the patristic texts that make up the twenty-fourth *causa* of the *Decretum* easily demonstrates. Heretics are a contaminant 'who have polluted communion'. One extract from Augustine sets up an opposition between health and correct belief on the one hand, and 'pestilential and fatal dogmas' on the other. Another, from Jerome, draws a different medical parallel, which likens heresy to a putrid limb that must be removed to restore the health of the body.[68]

In our sources notions of corruption, medical or otherwise, are for the most part used in a far more generic way, in terms of the common vocabulary used to describe heresy rather than in more complex constructions. A generalized vocabulary of corruption and infection is employed in the description of heresy in what at times seems to be an almost inadvertent manner. Heresy – the 'tares' which 'in everything corrupt faith' – corrupts or infects wherever its action is described: the 'land of the Albigensians' is 'infected land'.[69] The *Liber inquisitionis* of Orvieto, which has perhaps the richest language of all the inquisition records considered here, makes quite frequent use of that general connection in its sentences. Here, again, heresy is depicted as 'deadly plague', while the accused refuse the cure of penance.[70]

It is worth taking a closer look at one aspect of the inheritance of the specifically medical aspect of this theme, which appears in the patristic literature

---

68 'Qui pollutam habent conmunionem'; 'pestifera et mortifera dogmata'; C.24 q.3 cc.31, 16, 36, Friedberg, I, 998, 995, 1000.

69 'In omnibus fidem corrumpunt'; *Disputatio*, p. 4, also p. 66. 'Terram albigensium ... terram infectam'; Stephen of Bourbon, *Tractatus*, p. 79; a priest is also 'perversus ab hereticis, ita exemplo suo infecit parrochiam suam'; p. 215. 'Zizania'; 'monachus: in tantum enim Albiensium error invaluit, ut brevi intervallo temporis infecerit usque ad mille civitates'; Caesarius, *Dialogus*, I, 300, 301.

70 'Letiferam pestem'; 'tanquam proprie vite hostes medicum et medelam'; d'Alatri, *Orvieto*, e.g. pp. 221, 227.

included by the *Decretum*. The treatment of heresy as disease and the corresponding role of the Catholic Church as medic together formed a concept that understood the church's relationship to sin in general in terms of the physician–patient relationship, where sin was disease, the sinner patient, and the church stood in imitation of Christ as *medicus*.[71] Originally borrowed by the Fathers from the pagan philosophers, in the writing of our period the idea remained current: in the prologue to his *Summa contra gentiles* Aquinas draws a parallel between himself, or the wise man, promoting truth and refuting error, and the medic, promoting health and defeating illness.[72]

According to several scholars of earlier heresy, in fact, disease was the most prominent characterization of heresy in the pre-inquisition period. Lobrichon sees two standard commonplaces in eleventh-century representations of heresy: as a putrid limb, with echoes of Jerome, and as a plague from elsewhere.[73] Moore takes this further and suggests a deliberate parallel between the representations of heresy and leprosy in the twelfth-century material, though incidence of direct comparison seems uncommon. Ziegler's analysis of the relationship between ideas of medicine and religion in this period would suggest, rather, that the 'medicalization' of religious language really began in general only at a later date, in the latter half of the thirteenth century, and *specialized* medical vocabulary became attached to erroneous belief and heresy even later.[74] Certainly, in our material there are general terms of disease, to do with plague and infection, and it is perhaps this underlying assumption, of heresy as infection, that to some extent informs the concern shown by the regional legislation on heresy to eradicate all physical locations in which heretics or heretical rites have been present or carried out. Reference to more explicitly medical terms, however, such as Salvo's warning to his 'dearest brothers' to 'beware of these lepers', is rare, and not developed.[75]

Jacques de Vitry manages nicely to combine our various elements in one *exemplum* about a family of women 'corrupted by heretical disease', one of whom tries to ruin her daughter with 'the venom of her perfidy', and who appears after her death as a 'cursed old woman, fetid and most foul'.[76] Jacques

---

71 See, for example, R. Arbesmann, 'The Concept of "Christus medicus" in St Augustine', *Traditio* 10 (1954), 1–28; D. W. Amundsen, 'Medicine and Faith in Early Christianity', *Bulletin of the History of Medicine* 56 (1982), 326–50.

72 J. Ziegler, *Medicine and Religion c.1300: The Case of Arnau de Vilanova* (Oxford, 1998), pp. 179–82. Aquinas, *SCG*, I.ii [2]; trans. Pegis et al., I, 61.

73 G. Lobrichon, 'Arras, 1025, ou le vrai procès d'une fausse accusation', in *Inventer*, ed. Zerner, pp. 67–85 (p. 67).

74 R. I. Moore, 'Heresy as Disease', in *The Concept of Heresy*, ed. Lourdaux and Verhelst, pp. 1–11 (pp. 2–4, 5, 9). Ziegler, *Medicine and Religion*, p. 275.

75 'Fratres karissimi, cavete vobis ab istis leprosis'; Salvo Burci, *Suprastella*, p. 16. More general, 'pestilencia verba ... qui in sordibus est sordescat adhuc'; Capelli, *Adversus haereticos*, p. cxii. 'Pestiferam scilicet haereticorum progeniem et falsas eorum doctrinas'; Kerval (ed.), *Sancti Antonii de Padua vitae duae*, pp. 219–20.

draws pollution out into an extended connection between heretics and foulness: heretics remain unaware of their own 'stench', while they see the small
faults of others as great. If we turn to look at an extract from Caesarius's
Dialogus, we will see this theme at work, here once again in the context of false
appearance:

> Two men, simple in dress, but not in heart, ravening wolves rather than sheep
> ... pretending the deepest piety. They were pale and wasted, they walked bare-
> foot, they fasted every day; there was never a night when they were absent
> from solemn matins in the cathedral, nor would they accept from anyone more
> than the most meagre food. When by such hypocrisy they had gained the good-
> will of all the people, then and not till then, they began to pour forth their hid-
> den poison.[77]

Caesarius's words here are reminiscent of Stephen of Bourbon's bird catcher,
and of the extract from the Pseudo-James, quoted at the beginning of the last
section, where the sweetness of honey disguises the taste of the poison
beneath. If the falseness of the heretics' apparent piety is the most prominent
topos at work in our texts, then the broad idea of corruption and venom to
some extent functions in this context as the underlying nature that that façade
conceals.

As with all our themes, corruption has its own attendant animal image. The
connection between the deception of heretics and the venom underlying their
outward form is reiterated and developed further by their portrayal as snakes,
and the frequency with which heretics' words or presence are characterized by
either venom or poison is related to the similarly frequent invocation of their
snake-like nature. The snake is the only animal imagery that features with any
real frequency in the polemics, though even then it is only in two of the texts.
The *Disputatio* and the *summae* of Moneta of Cremona and Peter Martyr maintain their general avoidance of this type of construction throughout. The
author of the Pseudo-James text, though, makes use of this imagery in his
descriptions of the heretics as 'pouring forth the deadly poison of depraved
heresy'.[78] They are, the author tells us in language that echoes once again that
of *Vergentis*, 'crafty serpents; innkeepers mixing water with wine'.[79]

---

76 'Heretica pestis corruptis'; 'corrumpere'; 'veneno perfidie sue'; 'vetula maledicta fetida et
turpissima'; Vitry, Greven, p. 57, no. 96, p. 58, no. 98. See also: Stephen of Bourbon,
Tractatus, p. 25. The fetid smell of a burning heretic, 'abhominabilis fetor', and 'quam
fetidus ipse esset et horror eius'; Stephen of Bourbon, lib.1, p. 114. A smelly cat which shows
the 'posteriorum turpitudinem': Stephen of Bourbon, *Tractatus*/lib.1, pp. 34–5/165–6.
77 'Duo homines, non mente, sed habitu simplices, non oves, sed lupi rapaces ... summam
simulantes religiositatem. Erant autem pallidi et macilenti, nudis pedibus incedentes, et
quotidie ieiunantes; matutinis sollemnibus ecclesiae maioris nulla nocte defuerunt, nec
aliquid ab aliquo praeter victum tenuem receperunt. Cumque tali hypocrisi totius populi in
se provocassent affectum, tunc primum coeperunt latens virus emovere'; Caesarius,
Dialogus, I, 296; trans. Scott and Swinton Bland, I, 338.

If the Pseudo-James makes much of this motif, then this is an image that the author of the *Liber suprastella* takes to its highest expression. Comparing the heretics to the ancient serpent who 'with clever words seduced the heart of innocence', Salvo tells us that from this '[ancient] serpent, these little serpents, that is heretics, have their doctrine'. To dispel any remaining ambiguity he clarifies for those who 'wish to see clearly if the doctrine of these heretics is from Satan'.[80] The heretic as snake image is one that he reuses from time to time in address – 'Oh serpentine heretics' – but the idea of heretics as venomous generally – 'Oh heretics, full of poison' – is also one that he develops: 'they are like a scorpion, because the scorpion flatters with the tongue, and then with the tail applies venom ... venom, that is, false doctrine'.[81] Salvo's heretical opponent also lays a similar charge at the feet of the Catholics, calling the Roman church 'prostitute and nest of serpents and beast' and 'nest of the serpent'.[82]

Apart from making a straightforward equation between snakes and heretics, the Pseudo-James also sees a serpentine source and quality for the heresy they maintain, which comes 'out of the breasts of serpents ... of their viperous opinions'.[83] The serpent is also cited as a source of error by the normally reticent Raniero Sacconi during his discussion of Cathar sacraments, in a phrase made all the more unsavoury by the aridity of Raniero's usual style: their penance 'is false and vain, deceptive and poisonous ... the poison of error which they have sucked from the mouth of the old serpent'.[84] Again, heresy is venom, and the ultimate source serpentine, the snake in the last two instances standing as a figure for the devil. The connection that our authors make at times between heretics and the devil often occurs in the context of this snake

---

78 'Pravae heresis letiferum virus diffundant', or 'venenata lingua delatrat'; Capelli, *Adversus haereticos*, pp. cxi, cxxxvi. Corruption of Scriptures: 'congruentes intellectibus ex scripturis venenatis excerpunt morsibus et locustarum more subitum habentes volatum et deciduum virencia quoque sanae intelligencia corrudunt et se atque fautores suos ad eternae dampnationis ariditatem perducunt'; Capelli, *Adversus haereticos*, p. civ.

79 'Calidi serpentes caupones aquam vino miscentes'; Capelli, *Adversus haereticos*, p. clxxxvi.

80 'Cum ingeniosis verbis seduxit cor innocentie'; 'a quo serpente isti serpentini, scilicet herretici, habent istam doctrinam'; 'vultis videre manifeste si doctrina istorum herreticorum [*sic*] est a Sathane'; Salvo Burci, *Suprastella*, p. 64.

81 'O erretici serpentini'; 'o erretici veneno pleni'; 'sunt tanquam scorpio, quia scorpio blanditur lingua et postea ponit venenum cauda ... venenum scilicet falsam doctrinam'; Salvo Burci, *Suprastella*, pp. 88, 144, 64. Also: 'isti sunt illi heretici quos dixit Apostolus ad Thimotheum attendentes spiritibus erroris et doctrinum demoniorum', p. 64.

82 'Meretricem et nidum serpentium et bestiam'; 'nidus serpentis'; Salvo Burci, *Suprastella*, pp. 70, 15.

83 'Ex serpentinis pectoribus ... eorum vipereas oppiniones'; Capelli, *Adversus haereticos*, p. xlii.

84 'Falsa est et vana, deceptoria et venenosa ... Erroris namque venenum, quod ex ore antiqui serpentis biberunt'; Raniero Sacconi, *Summa*, p. 44; trans. Wakefield and Evans, *Heresies*, pp. 331–2. A similar view of heresy as the suggestions of the devil can be seen with some frequency in the inquisition register of Orvieto.

imagery, though it is really only in Caesarius's collection that the devil features consistently in the characterization of heretics.[85]

For Grundmann, the topos of the heretic was a largely static motif, already established by the eleventh century and remaining largely unchanged until the fifteenth, with only a small variation between different authors. The commonplaces of language and imagery that Grundmann identified as the topos, and which provided a common stock of vocabulary and images from which authors could draw, are all present in the thirteenth-century texts, and are distributed through texts as diverse as the canons of church councils and the *exempla* collections, though not always to the same effect. The main themes of that topos crystallized around vivid animal images – of the fox, the wolf and the serpent – drawn ultimately from Scripture. However, while our authors were able to rely on a shared and standard set of figurative devices neither the form nor the function of those devices remained static. Although some elements in the figurative tradition were already well-established, particularly ideas of corruption and disease that had been used in the representation of heretics since the patristic era, a layering and accumulation can be seen to have taken place over time, particularly in contrast with the period immediately preceding ours, most obviously perhaps in the image of the foxes that had so dominated the Cistercian anti-heretical tradition of the previous century.

By the time our texts are being written, the little foxes among the vines – derived from the Ordinary Gloss on the Song of Songs and promoted by the work of Bernard of Clairvaux – have become ingrained to the point where the individual elements of the idea can stand independently and still represent the whole. The metonymic form in which Solomon's foxes survived provided a foundation for the introduction and dissemination, through *Vergentis in senium* and subsequent legislation, of Samson's foxes. The use of that Judges verse introduced a duality of division and unity into the topos of the heretic, which reinforced and coincided with wider notions of number and cohesion and was absorbed rapidly into the anti-heretical tradition alongside the original *vulpeculae*.

While the imagery of heretics as foxes is modified, there are more significant changes at work here. Where the foxes had provided the leitmotiv of the Cistercian-led polemic of the previous century, in thirteenth-century polemic it is a minor presence where it is present at all. The polemical sources are in fact curiously reticent about their use of this type of construction. Although it is not absent, and though it appears more strongly in the Pseudo-James and the *Liber suprastella*, for the most part any invective that these texts direct towards heretics is restricted to incidental remarks. By contrast, in the case of the foxes,

---

85 On the association of heretics with the devil, see K. U. Tremp, *Von der Häresie zur Hexerei: 'wirkliche' und imaginäre Sekten im Spätmittelalter*, Monumenta Germaniae Historica, Schriften 59 (Hannover, 2008).

it is the papal output that leads the way in the development and formation of the anti-heretical rhetoric of this period, not least the writings of Innocent III.

More significant is the shift away from the foxes and toward false appearance as the principal element of the topos. The growth and spread of the latter theme in our period makes it by far the most widespread and the most developed aspect of this level of construction. The two-sidedness of heretics, the disparity between their outer persona, characterized by false prophets and wolves, and their inner condition, which has the quality of corruption and the character of snakes, build a picture of a hidden nature and a false holiness. The theme was particularly prominent in Dominican literature, such as the *exempla* collection of Stephen of Bourbon, and especially in the accounts of the early years of the Order and its founder saint; in that hagiographical tradition false appearance played a role both in the construction of the heretics of the story and in constructing the Order itself through juxtaposition with those heretics. The function of false appearance in these texts seems to have been born, at least in part, out of the interaction of early Dominican preachers with heretics in the south of France, and their competition for the devotion of the laity through the superior holiness of their lifestyle. The prominence of false appearance in the Dominican material suggests a new dominance in anti-heretical writing, and that while the legal rhetoric may have driven changes in the language used, the core of the topos now reflected not Cistercian but Mendicant concerns.

Again, though, there is a layering of the construction here. To the Scriptural and polemical elements of false appearance is added a kind of practical hiddenness that seems to reflect a heretical lifestyle of disguise and secrecy, and which is apparently drawn from observation and experience. The position of false appearance as the dominant element in that construction was perhaps more broadly reflective of the changing nature of heresy and the increasing role of inquisition in the church's response to it. A connection to the post-crusade, post-inquisition reality of heresy suggests itself here in the move from fox to wolf. In the first place, it is easy to see an association between their generally hidden nature and an increasing need to be secretive in the face of a renewed campaign of repression by the church. The aspect of hiddenness and secrecy that runs through the theme is surely the counterpart of the more active seeking out of heretics by the church, and the subsequent practical need for heretics to be hidden, especially after the 1230s – something that we can see behind all the deposition accounts of night-time journeys and secret meetings. That campaign, which put heresy at the front of the church's agenda, can perhaps also be seen reflected in the predominance of the wolf and a more acute sense of the danger of heresy.[86]

Overall, the complex of commonplaces and images that made up the topos

---

[86] L. Kordecki, 'Making Animals Mean: Speciest Hermeneutics in the *Physiologus* of Theobaldus', in *Animals in the Middle Ages*, ed. Flores, pp. 85–102 (p. 97).

is almost entirely concerned with the characterization of the heretic – that is, with the condition of the figure – and as such is applied without distinction, regardless of error.[87] Unlike the trend of the preceding century, in which anti-heretical polemic led the way in the development of rhetorical devices, figurative construction does not, on the whole, feature strongly within the polemical texts, and what new developments there were in the basic form of the topos often occurred rather in the texts that were generated by the preaching environment or in the central legislation of the church, particularly in the writing of Innocent III.

The figurative imagery of the anti-heretical tradition was, then, not fixed in its expression. Though the component elements of the tradition may have remained relatively stable, the role of those elements, or the emphasis that they received, appears to have changed according to their contemporary application. Rather than dictating the way in which the texts could represent their subject, the elements of the topos were instead drawn on and adapted to suit the purpose of the text and the function to which it would be put.

Number

The updated papal version of the fox imagery that is drawn from the book of Judges constructs heretics in two ways: as plural, and as united against the church. Throughout our sources the ideas of number that the fox topos reflects are a consistent feature of the construction of heresy, comprising several interconnected elements.

Contemporary with the appearance of the renewed fox imagery of Innocent's *Vergentis in senium*, Alain de Lille's introduction to his *De fide catholica contra hereticos* was also portraying the 'heretics of our times' as unified, drawing together different errors, where those heretics of the past had created new dogma from nothing:

> We read that formerly, in fact, various heretics at various times dreamed up various and contradictory dogmas, which we know were condemned by public edicts of the universal Church. In our times, however, new heretics – or should we say old and inveterate heretics? – in the process of aging are drawing dogmas from various heresies and constructing them into one general heresy: as it were, using many idols to construct one idol, many monsters to construct one monster. It is as though from many poisonous herbs they brew up one general poison.[88]

---

87 Grundmann, 'Typus', p. 105.
88 'Olim vero diversi haeretici diversis temporibus, diversa dogmata et adversa somniasse leguntur, quae generalis Ecclesiae publicis edictis damnata noscuntur: nostris vero temporibus, novi haeretici, imo veteres et inveterati, veterantes dogmata, ex diversis haeresibus, unam generalem haeresim compingunt, et quasi ex diversis idolis unum

This passage from Alain is directly comparable to Innocent's imagery: both portray modern heretics as united against the church, but Alain's view differs in that it sees the various heretical groups as one doctrinally coherent entity, as singular in their nature, rather than in their position or purpose.

Alain's remarks here have been read as representative of an important stage in the development of the idea of heresy in the thirteenth century. Michel Lauwers sees this passage, and Alain's stance as a whole, as a departure from a previously dominant patristic view of heresy, which saw it as a plural entity that needed to be catalogued. Alain, in Lauwers' view, made heresy singular, a general heresy of which individual heresies were part.[89] That is undoubtedly what Alain meant, and certainly there was at this time a shift to a view of contemporary heresy that included more material drawn from recent experience and literature, and that was moving away from the reliance on models of early heresy for details of doctrine and custom. How much Alain's idea of a singular heresy is at work in our sources, however, is less certain.

A more useful perspective, at least with regard to the mid thirteenth century texts, is to be found in Patschovsky's view of this passage from the *De fide*. Patschovsky uses the above passage to illustrate what he sees as a stable pattern in the idea of heresy throughout these centuries: that, though they gave them different features, Catholic writers of this period viewed all forms of religious deviance as the same, characterized by the same things (idolatry, monstrosity, poison) – what he calls the 'internal coherence of non-Catholic world'.[90] We can see that principle at work in several of the texts that we have used, either in description or in classification. Stephen of Bourbon and the Pseudo-James Capelli both place heretics together with other groups external to the Catholic faith, as the latter author has it, with Saracens and other men 'who are damned' or 'straying ... from the unity of the Catholic faith'.[91] Stephen's stated aim at the beginning of his *De heresi* section is to 'test and approve our faith through comparison with other sects' – a group that includes Saracens.[92] In the legal field, the *Liber extra* again treats heresy in the same context, locating it, as we saw, among sections concerning Jews, Saracens and Schismatics. The principle that Patschovsky sees in Alain's text, that all enemies of the church can be considered as a whole, seems indeed to inform these examples. However, it is less easy to find references to the specific unity

---

idolum, ex diversis monstris unum monstrum; et quasi ex diversis venenatis herbis unum toxicum commune conficiunt'; *PL* 210, 307–8.

[89] M. Lauwers, '*Dicunt vivorum beneficia nichil prodesse defunctis*. Histoire d'un thème polémique (xie–xiie siècles)', in *Inventer*, ed. Zerner, pp. 157–92 (p. 185).

[90] Patschovsky, 'Heresy and Society', pp. 38–40.

[91] 'Qui dapnantur [*sic*, r. dampnantur]'; 'ab unitate catholicae fidei ... aberrantes'; Capelli, *Adversus haereticos*, pp. vi, cxii.

[92] 'Probat et approbat fidem nostram per collacionem ad alias sectas', Stephen of Bourbon, *Tractatus*, p. 275.

of heretics that Alain talks about, with one main exception, the topos of the little foxes, which seems to echo Alain's text at least in part.

One of the clearest expressions of the new layer of the foxes topos outside Innocent's writing we have seen already, in the Anonymous of Passau. For the latter author, the lack of unity among heretics is a proof of their error. In contrast to the integrity of the Catholic faith, which 'is not divided, but one', the number and *differentiation* of heretical sects is held up as a sign of the Catholic Church's legitimacy: 'there are more than seventy sects of heretics'.[93] The idea of division is here suggestive of unity in so far as the depiction of that division as a flaw would imply a potential for unity, a view of heresy as one big generic whole. The author later does just that, drawing directly on the imagery of Innocent's bull to say that 'thus heretics are divided among themselves into sects, but in attacking the church, they are united'.[94]

The duality of the idea of division and unity is visible again in a more condensed expression in Stephen of Bourbon's text: his statement that 'among themselves they quarrel, and against us they all combine', like the above example from the Anonymous of Passau, is drawn from Innocent's use of that same passage in Judges. Stephen goes further, to illustrate his point with an *exemplum* that depicts a meeting of heretical delegations come together to settle an internal dispute. Portrayed in a deliberately ludicrous manner, each delegation tries to prove the veracity of their version of their heretical faith, each repeating the same assertions, each failing to reach an accord. The 'man of understanding' from whom Stephen has this story assures him that many have come back to the Catholic faith as a result of this dissension.[95] Later, he repeats this idea, saying that 'they are joined or tied together in their posterior parts by their tails, because they are all intent on one thing, fighting the church, like Samson's foxes who had different faces but were tied by the tails'.[96] Stephen uses the image of the foxes as at once divided and united for polemical effect: the story of the arguing heretics he uses to prove that the Catholic faith is true and that heresy is to be confounded, the true faith confirmed in the hearts of the faithful. The second example is the sixteenth item in Stephen's list of heretics' evil qualities.[97]

---

93 'Non enim est divisa, sed una'; 'haereticorum plus quam LXX sectae sunt'; Anonymous of Passau, p. 263. Andrew of Florence also contrasts the divisions of the heretics against the unity of the true church; Andrew of Florence, *Summa contra hereticos*, ed. G. Rottenwöhrer, Monumenta Germaniae Historica, Quellen zur Gesistesgeschichte des Mittelalters 23 (Hannover, 2008), pp. 111, 115, 116.

94 'Sic haeretici, in sectis sunt divisi in se, sed in impugnatione Ecclesiae, sunt uniti'; Anonymous of Passau, p. 264.

95 'Inter se dissident, et contra nos omnes conveniunt'; Stephen of Bourbon, *Tractatus*, pp. 278–9.

96 'Sunt coadunati sive colligati ex parte posteriori in caudis quia omnis tendunt ad unum quia intendunt impugnare ecclesiam ut vulpes sampsonis qui habebant facies diversas colligatas caudas'; Oriel MS 68, fol. 218va–vb, BnF MS 14598, fol. 234r.

97 Stephen of Bourbon, *Tractatus*, pp. 275, 278–9.

While it is perhaps rather unfair to have used Alain in this way, who surely did not intend his work to be read as the principal view of his period, his text provides us with a useful way into some of the ideas at work in our texts. And elements of Alain's view of heresy can in fact be seen at work in our texts as part of Patschovsky's wider unity of enemies of the church and also, in places, as a body united against church. The unity that does exist among heretics is not, however, specifically doctrinal in nature, as it is in Alain's text, and whether or not his view was, as Patschovsky suggests, representative of the only or even the dominant view of heresy, at least in the mid thirteenth century, is less certain. In our sources, in fact, it seems not to be the case, for two main reasons: firstly, that where uniformity among heretics is a part of the construct it is as a result of something other than doctrinal unity; and, secondly, that plurality and division are equally if not more present in the texts' depiction and representation of their subject.

Unity, or perhaps more correctly uniformity, is something that we have encountered before in the constructs of heresy that our sources present, most prominently in the texts designed for edification and in the anti-heretical legislation of the first half of the century. In the edifying literature there is a sameness that derives from the function of the heretics within that material. All the heretics that appear in those hagiographical and exemplary texts are, with a few exceptions, invariably portrayed in the same way: nameless, and doctrinally indeterminate. They are all described in the same terms and serve the same function, in the same way that the authors of our texts apply the different topoi of the anti-heretical tradition without regard for any differences between groups.

In the legal material uniformity derives from a different cause. Previous legislation by the 1163 council of Tours appears to have prefigured Alain's comments to some degree, where it states that 'from various parts they gather in one den, pressed together, and having no cause to linger in the one dwelling except for a consensus of error'.[98] However, after Tours, a type of uniformity emerges in the representation of heresy by the church councils that is different to that described by Alain, and in the next century, after the 1215 council, there is nothing of that sentiment to be found. Instead, in a formulation that begins with the decretal *Ad abolendam*, heresy is unmistakeably plural, but for all that is regarded as one in the eyes of the church, as a negative image. Though not immediately influential in political or legal terms, this decretal was effective in shaping subsequent ideas of heresy.[99] *Ad abolendam*'s idea reached its most condensed and neat expression in *Vergentis in senium*, as examined at the beginning of this chapter.[100] With Innocent III's fourth Lateran council heresy became a firmly homogenous entity in as much as the canons of that council defined heterodox opinion by opposition to a unified and closely delineated

---

[98] 'De diversis partibus in unum latibulum crebro conveniunt et praeter consensum erroris nullam cohabitandi causam habentes in uno domicilio commorantur'; Fredericq, I, 39.
[99] Maisonneuve, *Études*, p. 155.
[100] X 5 7.10, Friedberg, II, 782.

Catholic doctrine, which effectively denied autonomy to the individual error; the unity of the faith excluded them all equally.

In the regional councils, and within the higher levels of legislation as well, is another level of uniformity, which applies to the grades of guilt assigned to the heretics and their different followers, and which therefore translates also into the documents produced by the inquisition process. Each of the levels below heretics proper can be applied as equally to a follower of the Cathars as to a Waldensian follower, and the only place in which any differentiation occurs is in the upper reaches, where doctrine and direct contact with belief are at work. Even there, once condemned, all heretics are essentially the same, a legal status that creates the otherwise undifferentiated mass that can be seen in the majority of the legislation. Our previous examination of the regional councils made it clear that the heresy that they address is a previously defined and identified entity, that there is no engagement with the error and that they deal almost entirely with the treatment of heretics after conviction. The difference between Alain's text and both general and regional councils is that where Alain's sameness derives from the heretics' own agency, the Lateran canon and the councils make heresy uniform only by virtue of doctrinal or legal exclusion, and it is this latter idea that is the more common in the texts of our period.

Though different types of uniformity emerge, ultimately, in all of the examples that we have looked at here, that uniformity would seem to arise from the removal of error, not the amalgamation of it. What unity there is in our sources, in fact, applies to the common nature of figures and groups, while the unity of doctrine that Alain stresses is not present in any large way. The more common appearance of uniformity in the representation of heresy is less a part of an idea of heresy than of the church's relationship to it; there is not so much a unity of heresy as a homogeneity of heretics.

Let us return then to the foxes, and look at the other side of that construct – namely, the degree to which heresy is represented in terms of plurality and of division. The idea of division could be used in a polemical way, as we saw, in juxtaposition to the unity of the Catholic Church and as a clear mark of the heretics' error. The examples looked at above have been used recently by Peter Biller to illustrate a widespread idea of sects as many and divided, between each other and within themselves. That idea he sees as reinforced by the Scriptural foxes, but emanating ultimately from the use and diffusion of Isidore's *Etymologies*. In the section on heresies the *Etymologies* presents a proliferation of heretical sects, naming around seventy groups and providing for each one a derivation of the name, from either author or cause, along with a one-line description of the major error. Already a widely known text as a result of the 'swift and extensive' diffusion of the *Etymologies*, the availability of the heresy section became even wider with its inclusion in the *Decretum*.[101] It is worth

---

[101] P. Biller, 'Goodbye to Waldensianism?', *Past and Present* 192 (2006), 3–33, (pp. 31–2). Isidore of Seville, *Etymologiae*, VIII.v, 'De haeresibus Christianorum', ed. W. M. Lindsay, 2 vols.

noting here that the formula that ends that list, which declares that 'although they disagree with each other, differing among themselves in many errors, they nevertheless conspire with a common name against the church of God', looks rather like the combination of heretics found in Innocent III's model.[102]

Isidore's text, easily accessible and easily borrowed, in what Dondaine calls an 'erudition à bon marché', is cited in several of our texts, notably those written by or for inquisitors.[103] Anselm of Alessandria, at the end of his handbook, before the list of heretical elect, provides an adapted form of Isidore's list that names forty-seven sects, to which he adds 'boundless others, for instance the Cathars, Waldensians, Speronists, Circumcisors, Arnaldists'.[104] Though his *De heresi* section describes the errors of 'the heretics of our times, that is the Waldensians and the Albigensians', Stephen of Bourbon also makes reference to Isidore's list. He recounts information given to him by a heretic concerning the heretics of Milan, who, according to Stephen's source, number 'seventy sects, divided among themselves and against each other'. After listing several of these, Stephen enjoins any reader that may want to learn more about their divisions and diversity to read Isidore's *Etymologies*, since 'one may find there the names of a good sixty-seven or sixty-eight sects, which were before these times', and gives an exact reference to the extract's location in the *Decretum*.[105] The Anonymous of Passau gives the same number for modern heretics, over seventy, that he later gives for the ancient sects on the basis of Isidore's list.[106] The principle enshrined in that list can be seen working also in the Anonymous of Passau' later description of other sects, in which he uses this rule for deriving their names from their author or their cause.[107]

None of these authors appear to see any great incongruity in using or adapting Isidore's list of ancient heretical sects to include or describe those of their own time. In fact, some of our contemporary writers were aware of and made reference to the disparity between what they saw of the heresy of their

---

(Oxford, 1911), unpaginated. C.24 q.3 c.39, Friedberg I, 1001–6. For the spread of the *Etymologies*, see L. D. Reynolds (ed.), *Texts and Transmission: A Survey of the Latin Classics* (Oxford, 1983), pp. 194–6.

[102] 'Dum in se multis erroribus divisae invicem sibi dissentiunt, communi tamen nomine adversus ecclesiam Dei conspirant'; C.24 q.3 c.39, Friedberg I, 1006; trans. Isidore of Seville, *The Etymologies of Isidore of Seville*, trans. S. A. Barney et al. (Cambridge, 2006), p. 178.

[103] Dondaine, 'La hiérarchie II, III', p. 252.

[104] 'Aliorum infinitorum, sicut et catharorum, valdensium, speronistarum, circumcisorum, arnaldistarum'; Anselm of Alessandria, *Tractatus*, pp. 323–4.

[105] 'Hereticis nostri temporis, scilicet Valdensibus et Albigensibus'; 'septemdecim sectas a se invicem divisas et adversas'; 'et inveniet ibi bene sexaginta septem vel octo nomina sectarum que jam precesserunt tempora hec'; Stephen of Bourbon, *Tractatus*, pp. 279–81. There are in fact sixty-eight heresies named in the *Decretum* extract as marked out by Friedberg's edition, but, as anyone who has tried to count the number in Isidore itself knows, that number is very hard to pin down.

[106] Anonymous of Passau, p. 263.

[107] Anonymous of Passau, p. 272.

own times and that depicted in the patristic descriptions that made up their anti-heretical inheritance, this most often in the arena of number. Those authors position their subjects firmly in the context of the presentation of the heretical past that they found in their source material – there were many, now there are few: 'the sects of heretics were more than seventy, all of which by the grace of God have been destroyed, apart from the sects of the Manichees, the Arians, the Runcarii and the Leonists'.[108] The concern to contrast past times still contains a view of sects as several, and where Alain saw a break with the past others appear to see a difference only of number. Some authors, as Raniero did above, mark a reduction in numbers, while for others the situation is becoming relatively worse: 'Alas! that there should be so many heresies in the church today' laments the Novice in Caesarius's collection of *exempla*.[109] There is even an apocalyptic tone to the preface to the *Disputatio* in which the proliferation of heretics is a mark of the end of days and the Patarines are only one of many groups:

> As the world moves toward decline and dangerous times impend, wherein many persons depart from the faith and form a sect of perdition, gathering followers who are itching to hear them, every faithful person – insofar as God allocates to him a measure of faith – ought to rise up against those heretics who are called Patarines.[110]

Instead, there is a level of continuity between the inherited ideas of the heresies of the past and the new heretics, who, according to the Pseudo-David, 'with the errors of ancient heretics they mix those of their own invention'.[111] As we saw, Stephen and Anselm use the Isidore extract as a list to be added to, a process that has elsewhere been described as 'the yoking of experience with the authority of written texts'.[112] The inherited models of heresy are not discarded, but neither are our authors dependent on them for their material. That independence can be seen not only in the models that our texts use but also in the sources that they draw upon. Moneta draws a history of the Cathars within a framework that juxtaposes the Catholic and Cathar 'churches' directly

---

108 'Sectae hereticorum fuerunt plures quam LXX quae omnes, per Dei gratiam deletae sunt, praeter sectas Manicheorum, Arianorum, Runcariorum et Leonistarum'; Anonymous of Passau, p. 264.

109 'Heu quod tot hodie haereses sunt in ecclesia'; Caesarius, *Dialogus*, p. 300.

110 '*Vergente ad occiduum mundo* et *instantibus periculosis temporis*, quibus multi discendentes a fide configunt sibi *sectam perditionis*, congregantes sibi discipulos *prurientes auribus*, unusquisque fidelis, prout divisit sibi dues mensuram fidei, in illos hereticos debet insurgere, qui Patarini vocantur'; *Disputatio*, p. 3.

111 'Antiquorum haereticorum errores suis adinventionibus miscuerunt'; Pseudo-David, *De inquisitione*, col. 1779. The Pseudo-David also sees a difference in openness – that modern heretics are hidden, where in the past heretics held their error openly: see above, p. 145, n. 128.

112 Kordecki, 'Making Animals Mean', p. 96.

when discussing the origin of the Cathars. That origin he roots in the traditions of Pagans, Jews and Christian apostates, putting together an unusual collection of antique names, including Pythagoras and the *Saducaei*, as well as Mani, and portraying the Cathars as constructing a faith consciously from diverse elements of other error.[113] Mani remains as a feature of Cathar origins from the borrowed anti-Manichaean texts of Augustine, as had been the trend in the previous century, but he is no longer alone, and the Isidorean author/heresy model is rather lost in this collection of names.

In fact, the obligation that Isidore's text brought with it – that a sect should be named for its author, or at least for its cause – had perhaps always presented a problem for the historical view of heresy. Valdes is included in the potted histories of the Waldensian sect, or his town of origin, Lyons, in those texts that call them Leonists, and the academic heresies such as those of Amalric and Joachim, at the turn of the century, also have their authors and their correspondingly derived name. For Catharism, though, the idea of the grand heresiarch has disappeared to some extent, although Mani is sometimes still named. Aquinas still uses 'Manicheans' in a modern context to mean modern dualists, in statements such as 'this theory survives to this day among heretics, the Manicheans for example'.[114] The difficulty for contemporary authors of finding an author for this particular group may in part account for the adoption of the Manicheans, or the Patarines, as a model, or even for the continued application of the general term 'heretics'.[115] In any case, Moneta is alone among the polemicists in trying to present a history of the sect, but the same concern can be seen to operate in the inquisitors' handbooks of Anselm, the Anonymous of Passau and the Pseudo-David. In none of these texts, though, do the authors rely any longer on that inherited tradition for information about the details of the error or the custom of the sect, and the historical link to the antique past is sometimes included in such a way that it functions almost a topos in itself.[116]

Similarly, the expectation that heresy should be plural, that there would be several sects, appears not to have been left behind, but to have remained and been adapted. *Ad abolendam*, as we saw, addressed 'the depravity of various heresies, which in many parts of the world in modern times has begun to spring up', and this plurality can be seen at work throughout many of our

[113] 'Quod Ecclesia Romana a Christo velut capite sumpsit exordium, nunc unde Catharorum Ecclesia originem duxerit ostendamus'; Moneta, *Adversus catharos*, p. 411.

[114] 'Quidem opinio usque hodie apud haereticos manet, quorum Manichei'; Aquinas, *SCG* II.lxxxiii, [140]; trans. Pegis et al., II, 274.

[115] On the origin of the name 'Patarine', see Patschovsky, 'Heresy and Society', pp. 27–31.

[116] On academic authors using 'Manichei' contemporaneously, see P. Biller, 'Northern Cathars and Higher Learning', in *The Medieval Church*, ed. Biller and Dobson, pp. 25–53 (pp. 25–6, 28–30, 45–7). See also C. M. Kurpiewski, 'Writing Beneath the Shadow of Heresy: the *Historia Albigensis* of Brother Pierre des Vaux-de-Cernay', *Journal of Medieval History* 31 (2005), 1–27 (pp. 3, 25, n. 146).

texts.[117] The explicit to the third of Douais' *Summae auctoritatum* directs the texts against Manicheans, Patarines and heretics, as well as 'Passagians' and 'The Circumcised', and many other heretics. The fourth of his *Summae* is more conservatively aimed at the Patarines alone, but within the text it still regards the latter as one among several.[118]

There is a tendency, then, in particular in the manual material, to regard and represent 'heresy' as plural and, as part of that plurality, to portray it in terms of the mutual division that forms the other half of the fox imagery, sometimes in a semi-polemical fashion. Connected to this, to a greater or lesser degree, is the representation of the internal divisions of the sects in question. Stephen of Bourbon's description of the attempts made by the Lombard heretics to convince each other of the legitimacy of their different opinions is a typically entertaining and acute illustration of his argument, but it also appears to represent a fairly realistic portrayal of the heresy of that region. Native Salvo Burci similarly describes the efforts of the various Cathar groups of the north of Italy to reconcile their differences and unite under a common faith, devoting much energy and expense, to no avail – proof, says Salvo, that 'they are not the church of God', quoting in support Luke's gospel, that 'every kingdom divided against itself is brought to desolation'. Like Stephen, Salvo tells us that the scandal caused by these factions has caused many to turn from the heretical sects to the Roman church, and Salvo similarly uses this piece of information to invite criticism.[119]

That internal division is, however, much more an integral part of Salvo's conception of heresy in the rest of his text than it is for Stephen. Though not always in a consistent pattern, Salvo's text addresses, as well as the Waldensians, the errors of the Italian Cathars, dividing his treatment along the lines of their different factions according to what their individual peculiarities of belief might be and how that pertains to the point that he is trying to make. In fact, Biller sees this idea of division as potentially a more important formal idea than unity in the way that these texts construct heresy, and, as he points out, it functions as the organizing principle for many of Salvo's compatriots.

The most obvious examples of such organization are of course the two Italian handbooks by Raniero Sacconi and Anselm of Alessandria. As we saw in an earlier chapter, the structure of Raniero's text is based specifically upon the differences between the Italian Cathar churches and includes a first section that covers beliefs and practice held in common, followed by detailed chapters on the separate beliefs of each of the main factions. Apart from the organiza-

---

117 'Diversarum haeresium pravitatem, quae in plerisque mundi partibus modernis coepit pullulare'; X 5 7.9, Friedberg, II, 780.
118 'Tangit manifestissime sectam Patarinorum, cum inter ceteras hereses illa sola sit hunc salvatorem inficians'; Douais, *La somme*, p. 73 [IV]. *Vox in Rama* also addresses itself against new heretics that are 'inter diversas haeresum species'; Mainz, 1233, Mansi, XXIII, 324.
119 'Non sunt Ecclesia Dei'; Salvo Burci, *Suprastella*, pp. 5–6. Luke 11.17.

tional structure, it is worth noting that Raniero's text also presents a Catharism divided along lines of wealth, age, geography, number, knowledge and level of initiation, a sort of structure of Cathar society as well as an institution.[120] Like Raniero's text, the handbook written by Anselm of Alessandria is to some extent structured around the differences between the Italian Cathar groups.

The frameworks of the polemical texts are also connected, however, at least in a small way, to this idea of division, as we have seen already for Salvo. While the *Disputatio* deals with only one Cathar church, Moneta's *Summa* is certainly divided into books that deal individually with different factions of the Cathars, though it rather generally only treats 'moderate' and 'absolute'. The Pseudo-James Capelli sits somewhere between those two. The text opens with a description of the principle divisions in the heresy of the Cathars, and in fact in its earlier parts it differentiates between absolute and moderate Catharism in the structure of its chapters. That structure falls away, but throughout there are occasional remarks that indicate an awareness of those divisions on the part of the author and, to some extent, demonstrate a framework dependent on the division of the sect, so that 'in this in fact they all agree', that 'others, dissenting from the aforesaid, believe' something different, or that 'opinions are diverse among them'.[121] It is possible to see many of the principal treatises of our period as being structured to a greater or lesser degree around the internal divisions or differentiations of their subject.[122]

Those internal differentiations run along purely doctrinal lines, as has already been described, a detail reinforced by the fact that, for each faction, the customs and rituals that are described are treated together and are for the most part common to all the different groups, as indeed are the hierarchical structures. The division that we are dealing with here seems different from that which was at work in the topos of division and unity as used in those texts examined earlier. Of course, the level of detail is much greater, as would be expected, but, more than that, it seems to be a matter for information only, drawn from experiential knowledge and observation. Division as a topos, however, is a two-sided thing, which deals with a plurality of sects and the division between them on the one hand, and on the other the relative unity between them when facing the Roman church. It is also often more explicitly concerned with the character of the heretics than with the basis of division.

Where that former construct of division occurs it tends to be in texts that

---

[120] Raniero Sacconi, *Summa*, pp. 47, 51, 48–9 (also the Waldenses on this basis, 59–60), 50–51; 44, 47, 52, 58.

[121] 'De divisione heresum catharorum qualiter, de principiis rerum inter se dissentientes garriunt tractaturi'; 'in hoc vero omnes consentiunt'; 'alii autem dissentientes a predictis credunt'; 'diverse inter eos sunt opiniones'; Capelli, *Adversus haereticos*, pp. i, xxvii, xxxviii, xxviii.

[122] Biller, 'Goodbye to Waldensianism?', p. 32.

originate in the north of Italy. The prevalence of heresy in that region is almost a commonplace in non-Italian texts, in the writings of Stephen of Bourbon, noted above, of Jacques de Vitry and of the chronicler of the Franciscan Order, Jordan of Giano.[123] As the Novice comments to Caesarius in the *Dialogus miraculorum*, he has heard that there are many heretics in Lombardy, to which the monk replies, yes, no wonder, when they have teachers in every town, who openly read the Scriptures and perversely expound them.[124] Within the Italian texts the complexity of that situation is fully revealed. Nearly all the *Summae auctoritatum*, for example, derive from south France or north Spain and have, so far as it can be distinguished, a fairly undifferentiated picture. The only one for which this is not true is the *Brevis summula*, the one among those texts that is certainly Italian in origin, and which is, in part, quite consciously structured in terms of division owing to its inclusion of a list that catalogues the different articles by Cathar group.

The third part of Douais' edition of the *Brevis summula*, which was reproduced more frequently than the other parts of the work, represents this division in its list of the different Cathar errors by placing the letters A, B or C beside each article to indicate which of the groups adheres to each belief.[125] All this proceeds with no intrusion or comment from the author. Although the *Brevis summula* is a composite work the texts that the compiler chose to include in his Bible similarly define the Cathars and the divisions between the various groups in purely doctrinal terms; the Albigenses (*sic*), Bagnolenses and Concorrezenses are different from each other because they believe different things and because they have inherited their belief from different sources, the Albigenses from 'Brugutia' (Drugunthia), and the latter two from 'Sclavenia et … Bulgaria'.[126]

While these Italian texts are immersed in an idea of heresy as an internally divided entity, none, save Salvo, make a polemical point of this fact. It is difficult to make a wide comparison on this point, as most of the texts in which the topos or descriptions occur come either from one place or the other – there is very little comparative polemic from France, for example – but the inquisitors' handbooks can be helpful here. Anselm and Raniero employ no invective on the basis of division or, indeed, on very much at all, despite the fact that their description of the Cathar churches places them on much firmer ground than the Anonymous of Passau's account of the Waldensians, which includes no information on a trans-alpine schism in the movement, even the brief account

---

123 Vitry, *Historia occidentalis*, ed. Hinnebusch, pp. 144–6; Jacques de Vitry, *Lettres de Jacques de Vitry (1160/70–1240), évêque de Saint Jean-d'Acre*, ed. R. B. C. Huygens (Leiden, 1960), Letter 1.34–54, pp. 72–3. E. Gurney-Salter (trans.), *The Coming of the Friars Minor to England and Germany* (London, 1926), p. 134.

124 Caesarius, *Dialogus*, I, 308.

125 *Brevis summula*, pp. 130–33.

126 Ibid., pp. 121–3.

in Raniero's text having been apparently removed.[127] The Pseudo-David of Augsburg, similarly, makes no point of criticizing the internal division of the Waldensians, although there are signs that the author was well aware of those divisions.[128]

There are, then, several connected and overlapping ideas about heresy and number, some to do with uniformity, some with division, and between them a fluctuating idea of heresy as either singular or plural in nature. The duality of the fox imagery represents quite neatly the different ideas of heresy at work, though they are not always at work in the same places. The unity of heretics that we saw in Alain's work in fact is relatively uncommon in our texts. Though the idea is operating in the background in several places, and heretics not only appear to be regarded in a broad sense as a part of a wider evil but are also represented as united against the church in the topos of the foxes, the unity that we see as part of that topos is not the unity of doctrine that Alain describes. Moreover, rather than moving away from their inherited views of heretics and heretical sects, these authors, though using patristic material less as a source for information, still use the ideas of heresy that they contain, but in a more independent way.

Far more common in our sources, where there is uniformity, is an idea of heretics as a homogenous mass precisely because connection with heretical doctrine has in one way or another been effectively removed from the construct of number. So, the heretics of the *exempla* collections are largely undifferentiated because their presence is, on the whole, subordinate to the narrative structure of the *exemplum* in which they feature. Their presence in those instances is dependent on their ability to function as a more or less specific evil, on their status as heretics, rather than on the root of that status. In a similar way, in parts of the legal material, particularly the regional council canons and some of the inquisition documents, the fact that the heretics mentioned were already labelled and convicted as such meant that their legal status as heretics made redundant any difference between them. In both cases it was the removal of error that allowed homogeneity, though in fact, in the case of the legal material, doctrinal difference was ultimately rendered irrelevant by the fourth Lateran council, whose opening creed made heresy uniform by exclusion. That homogeneity of different sects comes either as a result of the tightening of Catholic legislation or as the by-product of an ulterior didactic purpose, but it does not exclude the actual plurality of sects, while the importance of division in those texts that deal with error, most obviously the polemics and the manuals, means that they do not present a singular view either. Plurality as a commonplace of the idea of heresy is not superseded, but

---

[127] Anselm of Alessandria, *Tractatus*, pp. 323–4. The Anonymous of Passau nonetheless mentions connections with Lombardy: Anonymous of Passau, p. 266.

[128] 'Hoc autem quidam dicunt tantum per bonos fieri, alii autem per omnes qui verba consecrationis sciunt'; Pseudo-David, *De inquisitione*, col. 1779.

it is manipulated. Connected to the unity of the church as a mark of truth, division can function as a mark of error, but can also form part of the structure of the texts in question. Overall, it is this plural and divided image that is the more prevalent idea of heresy itself; homogeneity is more to do with the position of the church toward it. A deliberate part of the fox motif, all heresies were united against the church in a reinforcement of the doctrinal distinctness and, more important, the correctness of the Catholic Church through the enmity of outsiders.[129]

At no point, though, did our texts take a view of heresy as singular. While it may at times be homogenous, and in places said to be unified, underlying all that is always a presupposition of plurality; certainly it was never doctrinally singular. Even the fox topos, where mutual division functions as a mark of error, relies on a basic view of heresy as plural. If anything, heresy could perhaps be more plural in construction than it was in fact, through the use and adaptation of Isidore's list of heresies. A generally plural view of heresy also informed the role of division in the organization of the polemical texts and the inquisitors' handbooks, where real, doctrinal divisions between a variety of sects and among the factions of a sect – both Cathars and Waldensians – structured the texts' treatment of heresy.

It will have become clear that the various parts of this idea of number are not evenly spread across all our material. Internal division of the sect in question is central to and informs the structure of some of our texts – namely, the *Brevis summula*, two of four inquisition handbooks and the polemics, with the exception of the *Disputatio*, all of which are Italian texts. Our other sources, the legal material, inquisition documents and most of the exemplary and hagiographical texts, treat any division as invective and heresy in general as homogenous. Unlike the division of heresy presented by the former group, division as a flaw is to do with the characterization of heretics and not the description of the sect or the error. Where there is unity, or uniformity, whether it is rhetorical or legal, it is not connected to or describing heretical doctrine. The idea that heresy should be plural, though, appears to operate behind all of the texts.

The most immediate source of homogeneity, however, was what has been called by Markus, in the context of the early church, that 'ancient but inveterate habit of referring to [different sects and errors] by the blanket term "heresy"'.[130] In our period that habit is complicated by the fact that heresy and heretic are often used not only in a general way but also in specific reference, especially in the south of France, to the Cathars in particular. So far, though, we have considered 'heresy' to include whatever the sources label as such. For

---

129 R. A. Markus, 'The Problem of Self-Definition: From Sect to Church', in *Jewish and Christian Self-Definition*, ed. E. P. Sanders et al., 3 vols. (London, 1980), I, *The Shaping of Christianity in the Second and Third Centuries*, pp. 1–15 (p. 3).

130 Ibid., p. 5.

the most part, where a text has been addressed toward a particular sect, that heresy has usually meant the Cathars, although there is, as we have seen, a great deal of differentiation even within that group. However, that label of heresy, and of heretic, has a general use as well and is applied throughout our material, whether in reference to a specific individual or error or to a more nebulous and incidental evil; it is to that general application that we look now, and to what consistencies or patterns there may be in the use of these most basic terms.

Heresy and the Heretic

Paolini observed that an inquisitor's job was twofold. Because heresy presented him with both a criminal act and the results of sin, his response was conditioned as much by confessional practice as by legal principles.[131] Faced with an individual guilty of heresy, the inquisitor saw different ideas of heresy simultaneously, overlapping in the same place. In fact, inquisitors spent a great deal of energy in thinking about what heresy really was and what defined the boundaries between different classes of guilt, and sought and collected information of this type wherever they could – they were interested in thinking about what heresy was. The answer, to judge from the range of texts and discussions generated in the middle years of the century, seems to be that the idea of heresy with which they were engaging was made up of more than one aspect, or at least more than one set of assumptions.

There was a central idea of heresy, the dual formulation developed and promoted by canon-legal theory and summed up by the 1242 council of Tarragona as 'heretici sint qui in suo errore perdurant'. Though very brief, this short definition represents a crystallization of previous legal and theological ideas of the heretic. The importance of textbooks in the spread of ideas, and in particular of these central characteristics of heresy, is unmistakable. Those products of the 'text-book movement' of the high Middle Ages that rooted teaching and thought in common, inherited texts function much as the polemical texts did in the previous century, circulating and perpetuating a set of language.[132] Between them, the Ordinary Gloss and the *Sentences*, the *Decretum* and the *Liber extra*, provide a common base of reference for all our authors. The prominence of the legal collections in particular was clearly one reason why Innocent III's contribution to the rhetorical construct of heresy looms large, and explains the wide-ranging influence of the language and imagery of the legislation. In particular, it is the authorities that make up the *Decretum*'s

---

131 L. Paolini, 'Inquisizione medievali: il modello italiano nella manualistica inquisitoriale (XIII–XIV secolo)', in *Negotium Fidei: Miscellanea di studi offerti a Mariano D'Alatri in occasione del suo 80° compleanno*, ed. P. Maranesi, Bibliotheca Seraphico-Capuccina 67 (Rome, 2002), pp. 177–98 (pp. 192–3).

132 B. Smalley, *The Study of the Bible in the Middle Ages*, 3rd edn (Oxford, 1983), pp. 51–2.

definition of heresy that are fundamental to most discussions of heresy, not least because the same definition by Augustine, of the heretic as one who invents or follows false and new opinions, that is used in the twenty-fourth *causa* is also at the centre of Peter Lombard's definition. The idea of heretics contained within that quotation from Augustine must, by our period, have become firmly ingrained by virtue of its presence in both the standard legal and theological textbooks of the time.[133] This core principle remains stable, albeit refined and polished over time; the ways in which it is interpreted, however, vary according to circumstance and application. Overall, there are two broad frameworks for using the idea of heresy which understand the nature of the error being defended in different ways: either as a criminal action or as a set of beliefs.

The notion of heresy that permeates the practical legal sources for heresy – that is, the consultations, the depositions and sentences of inquisitions, and much of the material emanating from the lesser, regional councils – is one of actions and of externally measurable qualities. A series of different grades of guilt, ranging from believer to general supporter, they are all named and defined in terms of the actions that they involve. 'Heresy' in this context refers to any involvement in the activities that constitute the crime of heresy, in essence a graduated scale of association with 'heretics'. Within that scheme of culpable actions the heretic takes on a pivotal role as the centre of the activity that marked out the guilt of their followers; as the location of error. The *credentes* are, both in consultations and indeed in all the legal texts, believers of 'the errors of heretics'. It is this proximity to error that makes the *credens* liable to be judged as a heretic, if it can be shown that their belief was accompanied by a conscious choice and understanding. The precise nature of error itself is in this context immaterial; its quality as error is what matters, and belief in it is the culpable action.

The continuing emphasis on knowledge, or rather on whether or not a deed is done knowingly, in any case suggests that intention is more significant in this system than belief, and reflects the principal that heresy must be obstinate, must necessarily also be an erroneous act of will, a principle further defined by the parallel with secular crime, particularly the crime of treason. Foulques's description of *defensores* draws a careful distinction between the practical defence of another person – that is, the protection of heretics from the authorities – and the theoretical defence of error. It is only by the latter, deliberate defence of error that heretics or heresiarchs are made, and for this reason relapses – that is, individuals who return to their belief or their behaviour after having been warned and made aware of their error – are to be considered and judged 'as heretics'.[134]

---

133 Lombard, *Sententiae* IV.xiii.2, Brady, II, 314–15.
134 Questions 9 and 12, Foulques, *Consilium*, pp. 196–7, 199–200. See also p. 97 and n. 41.

The polemics, the *Summae auctoritatum* and a number of the inquisition handbooks, on the other hand, elaborate the basic idea of heresy differently. Rather than the fact of wrong belief established by the legal system, here it has the perhaps more conventional sense of theological error. 'Heresy', in this context, looks more like a coherent system of thought, a series of articles of belief. Where the legal texts flatten error, make it homogenous by exclusion in order to apply almost the same list of actions regardless of sect, the polemics and manuals and *Summae auctoritatum* are careful to distinguish even the finest lines of distinction between the doctrines of different groups and the level of differentiation between heresies.

The main starting point for the first of those two ideas, the criminal or legal idea of heresy, is naturally the twenty-fourth *causa* of the *Decretum*. The question begins with Augustine's heretic, defined firmly in terms of obstinate belief, but the authorities that Gratian then enumerates give greater weight to obstinacy as the principal identifier of a heretic, along with a more general lack of obedience to the authority of the church's teaching and commands. The role of obstinacy then comes to occupy the foreground even more in subsequent commentaries. The thirteenth-century gloss to the *Decretum* emphasizes a distinction between heretic and non-heretic made on the grounds of obstinacy, and heretics are firmly those 'who fall into error, and do not wish to be corrected'.[135] The concern that runs through the consultation and inquisition texts to establish intention on the part of the deponent, whether or not he or she had any awareness of the heretical status of their actions, is a response to the increasing importance of will and obedience in the contemporary reading of heresy, itself partly the result of the parallel development in canon law of the idea of culpability, in which guilt was seen to lie principally in the attitude and will of the individual.[136]

But while it reflects canon-legal thought of the period, the legal idea of heresy is also shaped by the practical business of repression for which it is designed. At the most immediate level the purpose of repression was to limit and remove material manifestations of heresy and the influence of heretics. The method by which this was achieved, or attempted – that is, the systematic sublimation of the inner state into a series of categorizable actions – was the product of the process, of the texts and ideas surrounding inquisition. The tendency of the legal material to construct heresy as homogenous can be explained in part as necessary in the context of the tribunal, in order that the criteria that define the crime be universally applicable.

This criminal version of heresy is a self-perpetuating system generated by a reflexive exchange between the legal consultations and textbooks on the one

---

135 'Qui in errorem cadunt, nec volunt corrigi: sunt inter hereticos deputandi'; C.24 q.3 c.29, Friedberg, I, 998; Gratian *Decretum divi Gratiani ... cum variis scribentium Glossis* (Lyons, 1560), description col. 1403.

136 M. Brundage, *Medieval Canon Law* (London, 1995), pp. 171–2.

hand, and the process of inquisition itself on the other, via the medium of formularies and inquisitors' handbooks, and that exchange determines the content of the depositions and the focus on actions, derived from the legal idea of heresy that the consultations contain. It was a standard practice of inquisition to produce question lists and formulas from pre-existing models, and the focus on actions produces interrogation questions that demand information on the facts and figures of heretical behaviour, though it is also fair to say that the need for such information in turn reinforces the focus on actions. The point here is that the system of proofs is established and reinforced within the context of repression built from the interaction of legislation and inquisition texts.

Augustine's definition is equally present in the theological idea of heresy developed in the dialectical texts and parts of the inquisitors' handbooks, but here it is the belief element that is given emphasis and significance. This is at least in part due to the trends in theological understanding of heresy, defined at the broadest level by the papal policy outlined in particular by Innocent III and the fourth Lateran council, which defined heresy in terms of doctrine and doctrine in terms of articles of faith, but it was further refined by academic discussion of the problem. Peter Lombard's reading of heresy, taken up by theologians, gives the central role to doctrine and interpretation, an emphasis that we have seen dominate the polemical response in this period and define the terms of debate as visible in those texts and in the *Summae auctoritatum*. So, while the Pseudo-James Capelli still characterizes his opponents in terms of their obduracy in the face of proofs both ecclesiastical and divine, his principal response to the heretics is in terms of their error, as defined in direct contrast to specific articles of faith: 'it is therefore clear that Jesus Christ assumed flesh and all who deny it are heretics and seducers', and 'all who prohibit marriage are divided from the faith'.[137]

Heresy is not only doctrinal in the polemics and the *Summae*; it is also intellectually driven and expressed. While the scholastic method with which our polemicists engage with their subject in itself constructs that subject as a doctrinal phenomenon, that construct appears to derive equally as much from the sources used by the polemics and various *summae*. Beneath the systematic refutations of the polemics lie the original source materials, as it were, the heretical texts that our authors tell us consistently that they are using and which their method would betray even if they did not. Drawn from heretical texts, as well as from debate and conversation with heretics, the heresy that these texts refer to, the system of thought, is apparently not of the texts' making, but of their sources'. Like the legal idea of heresy, the practical application of these texts, or the manner of their interaction with heresy or heretics,

---

137 'Patet igitur quod ihesus christus carnem assumpsit et omnes qui negant heretici sunt et seductores'; 'ergo omnes qui prohibent nubere a fide divisi sunt'; Capelli, *Adversus haereticos*, pp. cxxiii, cxxx, cxxi, clxxvi.

affects the content and shape of the idea of heresy they express. Where the application of a legal idea demands that it be self-generating and closed, the nature of those texts that deal in a more theological view makes room for variation and a more porous relationship with their subject. These texts, which are largely built within frameworks of exchange and debate, and which seem in places to be as much designed for verbal exchange as they are reproductions of it, are interested in belief and in engaging with it on a theological level, and this makes the idea of heresy that they contain more open to external sources. It is significant that most of the sources that deal with heresy in a more dialectical manner come out of a northern Italian context, a place where that two-pronged attack on heresy, through debate and preaching as well as through repression, would be necessary owing to difficulties of conducting inquisitions within this region.

It is in part the connection with function that drives the changes that can be seen over time. The term 'heresy' had carried with it that sense of unorthodox thought or belief which also informs the legal definition at least since the time of the early church, but within this use there were nonetheless differences in the extent to which that error was presented as theological or doctrinal in nature, or in the level of emphasis given to that doctrinal nature. That is to say, the degree to which heresy was perceived as a predominantly doctrinal phenomenon varied over time. In our period there are signs of an upswing in this perception, in line in fact with wider developments which underlie the notably doctrinal representation in our non-legal texts.

At the opening of the thirteenth century growing concerns over the connections between speculative philosophy and heresy had led the University of Paris to prohibit, in 1210, the use of Aristotle's natural works. It was similarly Peter the Chanter's belief that rash questions and the introduction of logical method into the study of theology would result in heresy.[138] The association between heresy and incautious intellectual inquiry continues in some places in our sources. In the earlier work of Caesarius of Heisterbach the monk warns his novice of precisely those dangers of intellectual curiosity in recounting the story of those heretics who provoked the Paris ban on Aristotle, the Amalricians. Less specific, but equally telling, is Caesarius's description of the learning of heretics in terms that suggest disputative behaviour and scholastic learning: of the prevalence of heretics in Lombardy he says 'they have their own masters in various cities, publicly reading [= lecturing upon] the scriptures and expounding them perversely'. A group of Catholic theologians go to visit the 'schools of a certain heresiarch'.[139] The connection can also be found in

---

[138] J. W. Baldwin, *Masters, Princes, and Merchants: the Social Views of Peter the Chanter and his Circle*, 2 vols. (Princeton, NJ, 1970), I, 99.

[139] 'Habent enim suos magistros in diversis civitatibus, aperte legentes, et sacram paginam perverse exponentes'; 'scholas cuiusdam heresiarchae'; Caesarius, *Dialogus*, I, 307–9; trans. Scott and Swinton Bland, I, 352–3.

the later compilation of the Anonymous of Passau and in all the accusations of heretical sophistry that are made throughout the anti-heretical corpus. Even Moneta of Cremona has enough reservations about some points of Aristotelian thought to include a short section on the errors they contain at the end of his anti-heretical treatise. However, the new wave of scholars at Paris, unconnected with the previously dominant circle of Peter the Chanter, began during the first decades of the thirteenth century to move towards a view of heresy, and of the response of the church to it, that led William of Auxerre to advocate the use of dialectic specifically to combat heresy.[140] The establishment of the University of Toulouse was similarly intended to combat the problem of heresy on an intellectual level.[141]

The significance of this generally literate and dialectic approach in a more narrowly defined anti-heretical context becomes clear when our polemical texts are considered next to those of the preceding period. The Catholic response to heresy moves away from what Iogna-Prat describes as the characteristically monastic, imprecatory approach of the twelfth century, in which the usual method had been to attack the heretics themselves, particularly on the basis of moral condition and personality, rather than to address the error in much detail at all.[142] By the mid thirteenth century this approach has been abandoned, and the idea of heretics as *illitterati* no longer seems to have any currency in the new polemic, where the discussion of interpretative error has taken the place of invective and more rhetorical constructs as the location of the polemical attack. More than this, heresy has come to be constructed as, and indeed received as, a coherent and systematic doctrine.

While the thirteenth-century polemics stand in contrast to their predecessors, this is in part because the heresy to which they were responding also stood in contrast to that which had gone before; error, or doctrine, was much less central to the anti-establishment heresies of the twelfth century.[143] Heretics of the mid thirteenth century, though, particularly the Cathars, were increasingly literate and were, moreover, entirely capable of using and producing academic texts. We can see heretics employing academic texts in various places – there is use of the *Decretum* and of the Ordinary Gloss by the Cathars in the *Disputatio*, for example, and use of the *Decretum* again by the Waldensians in the Pseudo-David of Augsburg.[144] Aquinas sees no difficulty

---

140 Baldwin, *Masters, Princes, and Merchants*, I, 107, Biller, 'Northern Cathars', p. 27.

141 Baldwin, *Masters, Princes, and Merchants*, I, 116.

142 On the approach taken by the *Contra Petrobrusianos* see above, p. 20 and n. 32.

143 J. Nelson, 'Society, Theodicy and the Origins of Heresy: Towards a Reassessment of the Medieval Evidence', in *Schism, Heresy and Religious Protest*, ed. D. Baker, Studies in Church History 9 (1972), pp. 65–77 (p. 74).

144 Use of the *Decretum, Disputatio*, p. 61. An apparent reference to a heretical gloss is made by the 'Catholic', p. 46. Cited by L. Paolini, 'Italian Catharism and Written Culture', in *Heresy and Literacy*, ed. Biller and Hudson, pp. 83–103 (p. 100), is corrected to 'bursa' by Hoécker, who suggests an oral rather than textual transmission. Cathar use of the Ordinary gloss is,

in locating the philosophical ideas of Plato in the doctrines of the Cathars: 'they side with Plato in saying that souls pass from body to body'.[145]

Background impressions from our other texts, particularly the edifying literature, provide a plausible context for such a picture, not least the corresponding picture of the heretics themselves as educated. Throughout most of our material this is achieved simply through the use of titles such as *magister*, with connotations ranging from teacher to master of the schools. Most convincing in this regard, though, is the presence that permeates the *exempla* collections, the Dominican literature and the inquisition registers. Here, not only are the heretics depicted frequently in debate – indeed, the heretics that appear in the *Lives* of St Dominic and Peter Martyr do so almost exclusively in that context – but there is also a consistent proximity to and use of books on the part of the heretical élite in a way that recalls Stock's model of a textual community. Though only a few originals survive today, the one-time existence of other books of heretical doctrine can be understood from the numerous references made to them by Catholic authors. The work of Bernard Hamilton, among others, has demonstrated from the books that do survive that they contain what can be considered to be a coherent belief system.[146] In terms of our texts, these books can be seen to contain a discussion of doctrine that requires the same in return. In fact, the codification and the progressively more intellectual nature of heresy, and the development of sharply defined, article-based Catholic doctrine, can be read as resulting, in part, from the interaction between the two systems.[147] It seems reasonable to assume that the processes that lay behind the development of Catholic doctrine in the new creed – the expansion of the schools and of speculative thought and, within that expansion, the increasing role of precisely those disputative tendencies that appear so prevalent among the heretics – were also responsible for the increasingly theological character of heresy. The impulse to treat heresy as an intellectual phenomenon and its repression as an intellectual exercise stems from a wider development of scholastic thought and practice, but that trend at the same time accounts for the character of the heretical texts themselves.

---

however, according to the arguments of Sarah Hamilton, visible elsewhere in the text; S. Hamilton, 'The Virgin Mary in Cathar Thought', *JEH* 56 (2005), 24–49 (pp. 39–41, 48). Pseudo-David, *De inquisitione*, col. 1780. Other possible use of the Ordinary Gloss by Cathars in Moneta, *Adversus catharos*, p. 279, and see Paolini, 'Italian Catharism', p. 98.

145 'Asserunt cum Platone, et eas de corpore ad corpus transire'; Aquinas, *SCG* I.ii, II.lxxxiii, [2, 140].

146 B. Hamilton, review of M. G. Pegg, *The Corruption of Angels*, in *American Historical Review* 107 (2002), 925–6.

147 G. Leff, *Heresy in the Later Middle Ages: The Relation of Heterodoxy to Dissent, c.1250–c.1450*, 2 vols. (Manchester, 1967); H. Fichtenau, *Heretics and Scholars in the High Middle Ages 1000–1200*, trans. D. A. Kaiser (University Park, PA, 1998), orig. pub. as *Ketzer und Professoren: Häeresie und Vernunftglaube im Hochmittelalter* (Munich, 1992); M.-H. Vicaire, 'Les Cathares albigeois vus par les polémistes', *CF* 3 (1968), 107–28.

The emphasis on interpretation that goes hand in hand with the theological idea of heresy therefore makes sense in this context as a response to competition from heretics able to expound and discuss Scripture on a relatively equal footing. A similar mechanism can be seen at work beneath the ways in which some of the texts talk about heretics, as distinct from ideas about heresy. In terms of both crime and belief system, the constructs of 'heresy' are to some degree independent of the figure of the heretic, generated and perpetuated as they are within and between texts. But the heretic is itself another facet to the idea of heresy underlying the texts, and 'heretic' has a broader meaning than simply a carrier for either legal or theological ideas about heresy, though it does serve that function. Straightforwardly, the heretic appears as a figure, a matter of fact presence in the texts. There is a range of focus or closeness that derives from the level of interest the text has in real individuals. In the polemical treatises and the *Summae auctoritatum*, where a 'heretic' appears it is as a much-reduced figure with little function beyond a token holder of the error under discussion, able to stand proxy for any opponent, whether written or encountered. At the other end of the scale, the legal texts and the records of inquisition appear to present a more concrete version of the figure, not least as a result of the greater number of 'real-life' heretics they include.

The representation used by the edifying literature suggests a similar background hum of heretical presence to that which also comes through in the inquisition depositions about the movements and networks of heretics. It is the familiarity that is generated by that presence that makes heretics so useful to the preacher. The defective moral condition of a figure which would have been recognizable to most of the preacher's audience makes the heretic a perfect vehicle for the moral of an *exemplum* or of an edifying tale of mendicant triumphs over evil.

However, the presence of heretics as a part of the contemporary fabric of social reality that allows such illustrative use also goes some way to explain the more constructed manner in which they appear in the *exempla* and the hagiography, which place them most often in a context of argument and debate. The competition that they present to the legitimacy and mandate of the mendicant orders, and the Dominicans in particular, predicated as it is on the true performance of the *vita apostolica*, defines the manner in which the texts respond. The heretic is therefore still defined by association with error – the *heretici* to whom Peter Martyr is related, his uncle and father, are those who try, 'per auctoritates', to prove heretical doctrine – but the error itself is adumbrated, and almost never related in detail.[148] Instead, looking at the *legendae* of St Dominic, most of the time heretics are distinguished primarily by false appearance. It is their moral condition and personal qualities that are at issue here. Stephen of Bourbon's long list of heretical qualities has almost nothing to

---

148 *Vitae fratrum*, p. 236.

say about their erroneous beliefs, describing aspects of the heretic that are not directly to do with the heresy itself: cunning, secrecy, deception. The elements of a topos, now for this reason strongly geared towards false appearance as its core theme, adhere to and construct the heretic. The threat of a rival focus for veneration, based on shared characteristics of holiness and erudition, means that in a mendicant-dominated idiom heretics are written as outsiders on the basis of falseness, generating the rhetorical construction of heresy and especially heretics in this period. This construct, though, remains largely independent of discussion of error.

The heretic is one more way of talking about heresy, but, much as the theological idea is concerned to challenge a heresy based on shared methods and texts, the construction of the heretic is also about the struggle to control and fully inhabit contemporary markers of legitimacy. If, as Stock suggests, it is possible to see what was understood by heresy through the means that were considered effective to combat it, then the different approaches taken across the range of mid-century texts suggest that there was more than one aspect to this view, and that heresy was not seen as a fixed and monolithic creature.[149]

Renato Rosaldo's criticism of *Montaillou* is directed principally at Ladurie's uncritical use of anthropological methods in his reading of Fournier's registers. But he also saw that, in failing to question the relationship of the deponent to his interrogator more closely – 'how can his data ("the direct testimony of the peasants themselves") have remained untainted by the context of domination ("the Inquisitor's register")?' – Ladurie had 'neatly liberated the document from the historical context that produced it.'[150] There is little risk of this approach being replicated now, in an historiographical environment in which text-critical, deconstructive readings are the norm, except that the concern to isolate and remove what is constructed, and the tendency to read the texts only for the agenda of those writing them, seems in places to be in danger of extending a similar distortion in the other direction, assuming a text manufactured within a closed and self-referential system, sometimes deliberately so. But a reading that sees the heresy represented in the Catholic tradition as entirely and deliberately constructed has to deny the range and variety of the surviving corpus of material in order to do so. The various texts may be responding to a central set of ideas, but the shared notions of heresy are made up of a wide range of different parts and the elements of tradition and the aspects of the idea of heresy that an author deploys depends on the function of his text. That is, the construction of heresy is determined more by the purpose

---

149 B. Stock, *The Implications of Literacy: Written Language and Models of Interpretation in the Eleventh and Twelfth Centuries* (Princeton, NJ, 1983), p. 107.

150 R. Rosaldo, 'From the Door of his Tent: The Fieldworker and the Inquisitor', in *Writing Culture: The Poetics and Politics of Ethnography*, ed. J. Clifford and G. E. Marcus (Berkeley, CA, 1986), pp. 77–97 (pp. 79, 81).

of the text and the function that it serves than by one overarching agenda, and, while the contents are affected by central ideas, they are not invented by them.

Moreover, the different ideas cohabit. The patterns of construction themselves reveal a great deal of interaction and exchange between the texts, not only within their own generic group, but often across the fluid and shifting boundaries between those groups. Nowhere is that clearer than in the inquisitors' handbooks. Both doctrinal and legal ideas are present at the vanguard of repression of heresy, in the minds of the inquisitors, and are represented in equal measure by the handbooks, even though the formula of inquisition neither provided for nor required the gathering of the detailed information of error that they contain. Interrogatories approach the subject from a position of knowledge, not of enquiry. Nevertheless, we have seen that detailed information about error was sought by inquisitors from heretical writings or from conversations beyond the tribunal with imprisoned or post-conversion heretics. Inquisitors' manuals, handbooks and the collections of texts that they used contain samples of nearly all our material; not only formulae and consultations that inform the inquisitor about the application of the series of markers of guilt that make up the crime of heresy, but also detailed information on the errors and customs of the different sects, even the different factions of each sect. Over time, and especially in the fourteenth century, differentiation and discussion of error would come to feature with increasingly frequency in the interrogations of inquisitors.

All of which suggests that we ought to be wary of looking for one view of heresy that proceeds from one approach or plan. If there is more than one part to the idea of heresy, and the writers who talk about it are able to use and adapt different elements as needed, then to read an overarching agenda ignores that variety while at the same time ascribing to Catholicism a unity and homogeneity that it cannot reasonably be said to have had. Even where that extreme interpretation is avoided the lack of comparison between types of writing leaves many of these accounts incomplete and privileges one agenda or reading. It also gives the impression that texts must belong to the ideas of one societal or institutional group or another regardless of the fact that often their authors belonged to and identified with several. The authors, many of whom fulfilled simultaneous functions, happily accommodate and shift between the different ideas. Stephen of Bourbon moves comfortably between homiletic, inquisitorial and polemical registers depending on what he wants his text to do, and chooses the elements that fit according to his purpose – he sees no contradiction between a detailed discussion of sectarian doctrinal errors and an undifferentiated heretic who provides a foil for his story.

If the broad view afforded by a comparison of sources allows us to see that there was more than one construction at work, though they were connected through fluid generic boundaries, then it also shows us that these were neither static constructs nor static texts, not in the topoi they used and not in their use of inherited material. What is apparent is a layering of the construction, both in terms of different types and motifs as well as the mixture of inherited ideas with new material from other texts, Catholic or heretical, and from material based in experience and observation of the contemporary people and movements the church labelled as heretical. Awareness of the traditional sources and rhetorical characteristics of these texts should not lead one towards epistemological pessimism. Our texts not only rely on a shared comprehension of the rhetorical and figurative mechanisms at work, but also on a common understanding of the reality of heresy, of the backgroundness of heretics, of what *mos hereticorum* meant. The large idea or concept of heresy that they embodied was a varied one, built from parts drawn from both tradition and experience. Ultimately, the balance of those parts, and the role that they came to play within the texts and the idea as a whole, was determined by their interaction with each other and with their context. If whistling to catch birds was a simile of deception, it was at the same time a real component of one Dominican's view of real contemporary preachers.

Appendix
Perfecti as a term to denote heretics

Although Peter of les Vaux-de-Cernay's chronicle famously referred to the Cathar élite as *perfecti* at the opening of the Albigensian Crusade, the use of the term *heretici perfecti* is in fact extremely rare in the records of inquisitions. The Tuscan formulary very occasionally uses *perfectus*. Peter Cellan also uses it, but rarely – only for female full Cathars, and then only in a minority of cases. A 1256 deposition by William Fournier of Toulouse, quoted by Belhomme, gives another example: 'the witness was and remains a *hereticus indutus et perfectus*'. However, Fournier's testimony is one of only a few examples that Arno Borst is able to give in his own footnote on this term, despite his extensive knowledge of inquisition material.[1] In fact, two very large collections of depositions, those before Renous of Plassac and Pons of Parnac in 1272–8 in Doat volumes 25 and 26, and the register of Toulouse MS 609, which between them cover a wide span of the mid thirteenth century and contain references to a huge number of *heretici*, offer not a single instance in which those heretics are described as *perfecti*.[2]

For the general reader, then, the widespread habit among modern historians of heresy of using 'Perfect/Perfects' as a noun to denote Cathar heretics creates an impression that is at odds with the infrequency with which it was used.[3] More, it conjures the modern sense of the word, of 'perfect' as 'best possible', 'flawless' or 'ideal'. High medieval usage of *perfectus*, though, would suggest that it was principally read and understood by readers and writers of Latin in this period in a different sense, as the past participle of *perficere*, to finish or complete, and was used in phrases like *opus perfectum*, a completed work. In the context of a person who was *perfectus*, something like 'fully

---

1 Peter of les Vaux-de-Cernay, *Hystoria albigensis*, ed. P. Guébin and E. Lyon, I, 13. D'Alatri, *Orvieto*, p. 180, here for a Waldensian heretic. For examples of Cellan's use of this term, see above, p. 130, n. 73. 'Ipse testis fuit et stetit hereticus indutus et perfectus'; A. Borst, trans. C. Roy, *Les Cathares* (Paris, 1984), pp. 175, n. 3, 268, citing M. Belhomme, 'Documents inédits sur l'hérésie des Albigeois', *Mémoires de la Société archéologique du Midi de la France* 6 (1852), 101–46 (p. 144).

2 For Doat, see above, p. 122. On Toulouse MS 609, see M. G. Pegg, *The Corruption of Angels: The Great Inquisition of 1245–46* (Princeton, NJ, 2001), p. 18.

3 Modern discussion of this issue includes: M. G. Pegg, 'On Cathars, Albigenses, and Good Men of Languedoc', *Journal of Medieval History* 27 (2001), 181–95; J. Théry, 'L'hérésie des bons hommes. Comment nommer la dissidence religieuse non vaudois ni béguine en Languedoc (XIIe-début du XIVe siècle?)', *Heresis* 36 (2002), 75–117.

fledged' would be the first sort of meaning that would come into the mind of the reader.

Thus, where the term *heretici perfecti* is used, it can mean nothing more specific than 'full' or 'complete' heretics – that is, the heresiarchs, teaching *magistri* or full initiate of any sect – without the narrow sense of 'Cathar heretics' with which it is often used. In that sense of initiation it corresponds more clearly with the more commonly used 'vested' or 'consoled' heretics. The clearest example of this non-sect specific usage comes later than our period, in the fourth part of Bernard Gui's *Practica*, where with customary clarity he distinguishes *perfecti* and *imperfecti* along these lines – the *imperfecti* here are the *credentes*.[4] In our period something similar can be seen in the Pseudo-David's use of *perfecti* to describe the Waldensian élite: 'some are called *perfecti*, and these are properly called *Poure Valdenses de Lyon*'. Stephen of Bourbon again appears to use the term to describe Waldensian heretics, as does Tarragona glossing *perfecti heretici* as '*Insabbatati*, or dogmatizers of their errors, or believers who have relapsed into [heretical] belief after having abjured or renounced heresy'. Humbert of Romans also uses the term in an apparently non-specific way.[5] Overall, what emerges from the mid thirteenth century material is a relatively infrequent use of *perfecti* to describe heretics, and a meaning, where it is used, that is probably nearer to that put forward by Gui – that is, not with reference to a particular group, but to heretics within any group who are fully fledged via the relevant ritual and who are, as it were, the clergy of that particular sect.

---

4 Bernard Gui, *Practica inquisitionis heretice pravitatis*, ed. M.-J.-C. Douais (Paris, 1886), p. 218.
5 'Quidam dicuntur perfecti, et hi proprie vocantur, *Poure Valdenses de Lyon*'; 'vel Insabbatati vel dogmatisantes eorum errores vel credentes relapsi in credentiam post abjurantam heresim vel renunciatam'; Pseudo-David, *De inquisitione*, col. 1781. Stephen of Bourbon, *Tractatus*, pp. 293–4. Selge, *Texte*, p. 52. Humbert, *Opera*, II, 471.

Bibliography

Unpublished primary works

Florence, Biblioteca Nazionale Centrale di Firenze
Conv. soppr. MS 1738
Oxford, Oriel College
MS 68
Paris, Bibliothèque nationale de France
Collection Doat 23; 24; 36
MS Lat. 174
MS Lat. 2584
MS Lat. 3656
MS Lat. 13151
MS Lat. 14598
MS Lat. 14599
MS Lat. 14927
MS Lat. 14983
MS Lat. 15970
Rome, Biblioteca Casanatense
MS Cas 1730
Toulouse, Bibliothèque municipale
MS 609
Vatican City, Biblioteca Apostolica Vaticana
MS Reg. Lat. 428
MS Vat. Lat. 3978

Published primary works

Acta sanctorum quotquot tot orbe coluntur, vel a catholicus scriptoribus celebrantur... 65 vols. in 67, new edn (Paris, 1863–1931).
Alain de Lille, *Compendiosa in cantica canticorum ad laudem deiparae virginis mariae elucidato*, PL 210, 51–110.
Alain de Lille, *De fide catholica contra haereticos sui temporis*, PL 210, 305–40.
Andrew of Florence, *Summa contra hereticos*, ed. G. Rottenwöhrer, Monumenta Germaniae Historica, Quellen zur Gesistesgeschichte des Mittelalters 23 (Hannover, 2008).
Anonymous of Passau, *<Tractatus>*, ed. J. Gretser, *Lucae Tudensis episcopi, scriptores aliquot succedanei contra sectam Waldensium* (Ingolstadt, 1613), pp. 262–75.
Anselm of Alessandria, *Tractatus de hereticis*, ed. A. Dondaine, 'La hiérarchie cathare en Italie II and III', *AFP* 20 (1950), 234–324.
Augustine, *Sermones ad populum, V, sermones dubii*, PL 39, 1639–43.
Bernard Gui, *Practica inquisitionis heretice pravitatis*, ed. C. Douais (Paris, 1886).

Bernard of Clairvaux, *On the Song of Songs*, trans. K. Walsh and I. M. Edmonds, 4 vols., Cistercian Fathers Series 4, 7, 31 and 40 (Kalamazoo, MI, 1971–80).

Bernard of Clairvaux, *Opera*, ed. J. Leclerq, C. H. Talbot and H. M. Rochais, 8 vols. (Rome, 1957–77).

Biblia sacra, cum glossis ... Nicolai Lyrani postilla & moralitatibus, Burgensis additionibus & Thoringi replicis, 6 vols. (Lyons, 1545).

Biblia sacra iuxta vulgatam Clementinam, ed. A. Colunga and L. Turrado, 4th edn (Salamanca, 1965).

Biblia sacra iuxta vulgatam versionem, ed. R. Weber et al., 2 vols. (Stuttgart, 1969).

Biller, P., C. Bruschi and S. Sneddon (ed.), *Inquisitors and Heretics in Thirteenth-Century Languedoc: Edition and Translation of Toulouse Inquisition Depositions 1273–82*, Studies in the History of Christian Tradition 147 (Brill, 2011).

Bonacursus, *Manifestatio haeresis catharorum quam fecit Bonacursus*, PL 204, 775–92.

Bozóky, E. (ed. and trans.), *Le livre secret des cathares*, Interrogatio Iohannis: *Apocryphe d'origine bogomile*, Textes, Dossiers, Documents (Série Annexe de la Collection Théologie Historique) 2 (Paris, 1980).

Caesarius of Heisterbach, *The Dialogue on Miracles: Caesarius of Heisterbach (1220–1235)*, trans. H. von E. Scott and C. C. Swinton Bland, 2 vols. (London, 1929).

Caesarius of Heisterbach, *Dialogus miraculorum*, ed. J. Strange, 2 vols. (Cologne, 1851, repub. Ridgewood, NJ, 1966).

Caesarius of Heisterbach: see also Hilka.

Chronica ordinis, ed. B. M. Reichert, *Vitae fratrum ordinis praedicatorum nec non cronica ordinis ab anno MCCII usque ad MCCLIV*, MOPH 1 (1896), 321–38.

Codex Justinianus, ed. P. Krueger, Corpus Iuris Civilis 2, 12th edn (Berlin, 1959).

Conciliorum oecumenicorum decreta, ed. J. Alberigo et al. (Bologna, 1962).

Constantine of Orvieto, *Legenda sancti Dominici*, ed. H. C. Scheeben, MOPH 16 (1935), 263–352.

Constitutiones concilii quarti Lateranensis una cum commentariis glossatorum, ed. A. García y García (Vatican City, 1981).

Corpus Juris Canonici (Rome, 1582) via <http://digital.library.ucla.edu/canonlaw/>, directed by H. Batchelor, H. A. Kelly et al.

d'Alatri, M., *L'inquisizione francescana nell'Italia centrale del duecento*, Istituto Storico dei Cappuccini, Bibliotheca Seraphico-Capuccina 49 (Rome, 1996).

Decrees of the Ecumenical Councils, ed. J. Alberigo et al., trans. N. P. Tanner, 2 vols. (London, 1990).

De heresi catharorum in Lombardia, ed. A. Dondaine, 'La hiérarchie cathare en Italie. I Le "De heresi catharorum in Lombardia"', *AFP* 19 (1949), 280–312.

The Digest of Justinian, ed. T. Mommsen and P. Krueger, trans. A. Watson, 4 vols. (Philadelphia, PA, 1985).

Disputatio inter catholicum et paterinum hereticum: Die Auseinandersetzung der katholischen Kirche mit den italienischen Katharern im Spiegel einer kontrovers-theologischen Streitschrift des 13. Jahrhunderts, ed. C. Hoécker, Edizione Nazionale dei Testi Mediolatini 4, Series I, 3 (Florence, 2001).

Douais, M.-J.-C. (ed.), *Documents pour servir à l'histoire de l'inquisition dans le Languedoc*, 2 vols. (Paris, 1900), II, *Textes*.

Douais, M.-J.-C. (ed.), *La Somme des autorités, à l'usage des prédicateurs méridionaux au XIIIe siècle* (Paris, 1896).

Douais, C., 'Les Hérétiques du Midi au XIIIe siècle: Cinq pièces inédits', *Annales du Midi* 3 (1891), 367–80.

Duvernoy, J. (ed.), Summula contra hereticos. *Un traite contre les Cathares du XIIIème siècle* (1987), at <http://jean.duvernoy.free.fr/>.

Eckbert of Schönau, *Sermones*, PL 195, 11–98.

Fredericq, P. (ed.), *Corpus documentorum inquisitionis haereticae pravitatis Neerlandicae*, 5 vols. (Ghent, 1889).

Friedberg, E. (ed.), *Corpus iuris canonici*, 2 vols. (Leipzig, 1879, repr. Graz, 1959).

Gerard of Frachet, *Lives of the Brethren of the Order of Preachers*, trans. P. Conway, ed. with notes and intro. B. Jarrett (London, 1955).

Gerard of Frachet, *Vitae fratrum ordinis praedicatorum nec non cronica ordinis ab anno MCCII usque ad MCCLIV*, ed. B. M. Reichert, MOPH 1 (1896).

Gratian, *Decretum divi Gratiani, totius propemodum iuris canonici compendium, summorum que pontificum decreta atque praeiudicia, una cum variis scribentium Glossis* (Lyons, 1560).

Gratian: see also Lenherr.

Gui Foulques, *Consilium Guidonis Fulcodii de quibusdam dubitacionibus in negocio inquisicionis*, ed. F. Lomastro Tognato, *L'eresia a Vicenza nel duecento. Dati, problemi e fonti* (Vicenza, 1988), pp. 193–203.

Gurney-Salter, E. (trans.), *The Coming of the Friars Minor to England and Germany* (London, 1926).

Hilka, A. (ed.), *Die Wundergeschichten des Caesarius von Heisterbach*, 2 vols. (Bonn, 1933–7), I, *Einleitung, exempla und Auszüge aus den Predigten des Caesarius von Heisterbach.*

Hugh Eteriano, *Contra Patarenos*, ed. B., J. and S. Hamilton, The Medieval Mediterranean: Peoples, Economies and Cultures, 400–1500 (Leiden, 2004).

Humbert of Romans, *Humberti de Romanis De dono timoris*, ed. C. Boyer, Corpus Christianorum, Continuatio Mediaevalis 218 (Turnhout, 2008).

Humbert of Romans, *Legenda sancti Dominici*, ed. A. Walz, MOPH 16 (1935), 355–433.

Humbert of Romans, *Opera de vita regularis*, ed. J. J. Berthier, 2 vols. (Rome, 1888–9, repr. Turin, 1956).

Ilarino da Milano (ed.), *Il 'Liber supra Stella' del piacentino Salvo Burci contro I catari e altri correnti ereticali*, in *Eresie medievali. Scritti minori* (Rimini, 1983), 205–367, orig. publ. in *Aevum* 16 (1942) 272–319; 17 (1943) 90–146; 19 (1945) 218–341.

Interrogatio Iohannis, see Bozóky.

Isidore of Seville, *Etymologiae*, ed. W. M. Lindsay, 2 vols. (Oxford, 1911).

Isidore of Seville, *The Etymologies of Isidore of Seville*, trans. S. A. Barney et al. (Cambridge, 2006).

Jacobus de Voragine (Iacopo da Varazze), *Legenda Aurea*, ed. G. P. Maggioni, 2nd edn, 2 vols. (Florence, 1998).

Jacobus de Voragine (Iacopo da Varazze), *The Golden Legend, Reading on the Saints*, trans. W. Granger Ryan, 2 vols (Princeton, NJ, 1993).

Jacques de Vitry, *Die Exempla aus den Sermones feriales et communes des Jakob von Vitry*, ed. J. Greven (Heidelberg, 1914).

Jacques de Vitry, *Die Exempla des Jacob von Vitry: ein Beitrag zur Geschichte der Erzählungsliteratur des Mittelalters*, ed. G. Frenken (Munchen, 1914).

Jacques de Vitry, *The Exempla or Illustrative Stories from the Sermones Vulgares of Jacques de Vitry*, ed. T. F. Crane (Ithaca, NY, 1894, repr. New York, 1971).

Jacques de Vitry, *The* Historia occidentalis *of Jacques de Vitry. A Critical Edition*, ed. J. F. Hinnebusch (Fribourg, 1972).

Jacques de Vitry, *Lettres de Jacques de Vitry (1160/70–1240), évêque de Saint Jean-d'Acre*, ed. R. B. C. Huygens (Leiden, 1960).

Jordan of Giano, *Chronica fratris Jordani*, ed. H. Boehmer, Collection d'Études et de Documents sur l'Histoire Religieuse et Littéraire du Moyen Age 6 (Paris, 1908).

Jordan of Saxony, *Libellus de principiis Ordinis Praedicatorum*, ed. H. C. Scheeben, MOPH 16 (1935), 1–88.

Jordan of Saxony, *On the Beginnings of the Order of Preachers*, ed. and trans. S. Tugwell (Dublin, 1982).

Kaeppeli, T., 'Une somme contre les hérétiques de S. Pierre Martyr (?)', *AFP* 17 (1947), 295–335.

de Kerval, L. (ed.), *Sancti Antonii de Padua vitae duae quarum altera hucusque inedita* (Paris, 1904).

Legendae S. Francisci Assisiensis I, Analecta Franciscana, sive Chronica aliaque varia Documenta ad Historiam Fratrum Minorum 10 (Quaracchi, 1941).

Lenherr, T., *Die Exkommunikations- und Depositionsgewalt der Häretiker bei Gratian und den Dekretisten bis zur* Glossa Ordinaria *des Johannes Teutonicus*, Münchener Theologische Studien 3, Kanonistische Abteilung 42 (St Ottilien, 1987).

Liber Augustalis, or, Constitutions of Melfi promulgated by the Emperor Frederick II for the Kingdom of Sicily in 1231, trans. J. M. Powell (Syracuse, NY, 1971).

Mansi, G. D. (ed.), *Sacrum conciliorum nova et amplissima collectio*, 53 vols. (Florence, 1759–1927, repr. Graz, 1961).

Moneta of Cremona, *Adversus catharos et valdenses libri quinque*, ed. T. A. Ricchini (Rome, 1743, repr. Ridgewood, NJ, 1964).

Oliger, P. L., 'Liber exemplorum fratrum minorum saeculi XIII (excerpta e cod. ottob. vat. 522)', *Antonianum* 2 (1927), 203–76.

Patrologia Latina, ed. J. P. Migne, 221 vols. (Paris, 1857–66).

Patschovsky, A. and K.-V. Selge (ed.), *Quellen zur Geschichte der Waldenser*, Texte zur Kirchen- und Theologegeschichte 18 (Gütersloh, 1973).

Peraldus, *Summa de vitiis* <http://unc.edu/~swenzel/peraldus.html>, website maintained by S. Wenzel et al.

Peter Cellan, *L'inquisition en Quercy: Le registre des pénitences de Pierre Cellan 1241–1242*, ed. J. Duvernoy (Castelnaud-la-Chapelle, 2001).

Peter Ferrandi, *Legenda sancti Dominici*, ed. M. H. Laurent, MOPH 16 (1935), 197–260.

Peter Lombard, *Sententiae in IV libris distinctae*, ed. I. Brady, Spicilegium Bonaventurianum 4, 2 vols. in 3 (Grottaferrata, 1971–81).

Peter of les Vaux-de-Cernay, *Hystoria albigensis*, ed. P. Guébin and E. Lyon, 3 vols. (Paris, 1926–39).

Peters, E. (ed. and trans.), *Heresy and Authority in Medieval Europe: Documents in Translation* (Philadelphia, PA, 1980).

Pontal, O., *Les statuts synodaux Français du XIIIᵉ siècle*, 4 vols. (Paris, 1971–95).

Pseudo-Praepositinus of Cremona, *The* Summa contra haereticos *Ascribed to Praepositinus of Cremona*, ed. J. N. Garvin and J. A. Corbett (Notre Dame, 1958).

Pseudo-David of Augsburg, *De inquisitione hereticorum*, ed. W. Preger, 'Der Tractat des David von Augsburg über die Waldesier', *Abhandlungen der bayerischen Akademie der Wissenschaften* 14 no. 2 (1879), 204–35.

Pseudo-David of Augsburg, *Thesaurus novus anecdotorum*, ed. E. Martène and U. Durand, 5 vols. (Paris, 1717) V, cols. 1777 C-1794 B.

Pseudo-James Capelli, *L'eresia catara. Appendice:* Disputationes nonnullae adversus haereticos. *Codice inedito Malatestiano del sec. XIII.*, ed. D. Bazzocchi (Bologna, 1920).

Raniero Sacconi, *Summa de Catharis et Pauperibus de Lugduno*, ed. A. Dondaine, *Un traité néo-manichéen du XIIe siècle. Le* Liber de duobus principiis *suivi d'un fragment de rituel cathare* (Rome, 1939).

Raniero Sacconi, *Summa de Catharis et Pauperibus de Lugduno*, ed. F. Šanjek, *AFP* 44 (1974), 31–60.

Raymond of Peñafort, *De poenitentia et matrimonio* (Rome, 1603, repr. Farnborough, 1967).

Remigius, *Enarrationes in psalmos*, *PL* 131, 572–7.

Ripoll, T. (ed.), *Bullarium ordinis ff. praedicatorum*, 8 vols. (Rome 1729–40).

Salvo Burci, *Liber Suprastella*, ed. Caterina Bruschi, Istituto Storico Italiano per il Medio Evo, Fonti per la Storia dell'Iitalia Medievale, Antiquitates 15 (Rome, 2002).

Šanjek, F. (ed.), 'Una "Summa auctoritatum" antiereticale (MS 47 della Bibiothlèque Municipale di Albi). Memoria di Raoul Manselli', in *Atti della Accademie Nazionale dei Lincei. 1: Classe di Scienze Morale Storiche e Filologiche*, Fasc. 6 (1985) 324–97, pp. 355–95.

Selge, K.-V. (ed.), *Texte zur Inquisition*, Texte zur Kirchen- und Theologe- geschichte 4 (Gütersloh, 1967).

Stephen of Bourbon, *Tractatus de diversis materiis praedicabilibus*, ed A. Lecoy de la Marche, *Anecdotes historiques, légendes et apologues tirées du recueil inédit d'Étienne de Bourbon, Dominicain du XIIIe siècle*, Société de l'Histoire de France, Publications 185 (Paris, 1877).

Stephen of Bourbon, *Tractatus de diversis materiis predicabilibus*, Corpus Christianorum, Continuatio Mediaevalis 124/124B, 2 vols. (Turnhout, 2002–6), I, *Prologus, prima pars, de dono timoris*, ed. J. Berlioz and J. L. Eichenlaub; III, *Liber tertius. De eis que pertinent ad donum scientie et penitentiam*, ed. J. Berlioz.

Thomas Agni de Lentino, *Legenda beati Petri Martyris*, in *Acta sanctorum quotquot tot orbe coluntur, vel a catholicus scriptoribus celebrantur* ... 65 vols. in 67, new edn (Paris, 1863–1931), April 3, 29, cols. 686–719.

Thomas Aquinas, *On the Truth of the Catholic Faith. Summa contra gentiles*, ed. A. C. Pegis et al., 4 vols. in 5 (New York, 1955–7).

Thomas Aquinas, *Opera omnia*, 25 vols. in 23 (Parma, 1852–73).

Thomas of Cantimpré, *Les exemples du Livre des Abeilles*, ed. and trans. H. Platelle (Turnhout, 1997).

Thouzellier, C. (ed.), *Un traité cathare inédit du début du XIIIe siècle d'après le* Liber contra Manicheos *de Durand de Huesca*, Bibliothèque de la Revue d'Histoire Ecclésiastique 37 (Louvain, 1961).

Tocco, F., *Quel che non c'è nella divina commedia. Dante e l'eresia, con documenti e con la ristampa delle questioni dantesche* (Bologna, 1899).

Tugwell, S. (ed. and trans.), *Early Dominicans, Selected Writings* (New York, 1984).

William of Auxerre, *Summa aurea*, ed J. Ribailler, Spicilegium Bonaventuriarum 16–19, 4 vols. in 6 (Paris and Grottaferrata, 1980–87).

William Pelhisson, *Chronique (1229–1244) suivie du récit des troubles d'Albi*

(1229–1244), Sources d'Histoire Médiévales publiées par l'Institut de Recherches et d'Histoire des Textes, ed. J. Duvernoy (Paris, 1994).

Secondary works

Altaner, B., *Der hl. Dominikus: Untersuchungen und Texte*, Breslauer Studien zur Historischen Theologie 2 (Breslau, 1922).

Amundsen, D. W., 'Medicine and Faith in Early Christianity', *Bulletin of the History of Medicine* 56 (1982), 326–50.

Arbesmann, R., 'The Concept of "Christus medicus" in St Augustine', *Traditio* 10 (1954), 1–28.

Arnold, J. H., *Inquisition and Power: Catharism and the Confessing Subject in Medieval Languedoc* (Philadelphia, PA, 2001).

Arnold, J. H., 'Inquisition, Texts and Discourse', in *Texts and Repression*, ed. Bruschi and Biller, pp. 63–80.

Arnold, J. H., 'The Preaching of the Cathars', in *Medieval Monastic Preaching*, ed. C. Muessig (Leiden, 1998), pp. 183–205.

Baldwin, J. W., *Masters, Princes, and Merchants: The Social Views of Peter the Chanter and His Circle*, 2 vols. (Princeton, NJ, 1970).

Barber, M., *The Cathars: Dualist Heretics in Languedoc in the High Middle Ages* (Harlow, 2000).

Bauer, W., *Orthodoxy and Heresy in Earliest Christianity* (London, 1972).

Belhomme, M., 'Documents inédits sur l'hérésie des Albigeois', *Mémoires de la Société Archéologique du Midi de la France* 6 (1852), 101–46.

Bériou, N., *L'avénement des maîtres de la Parole: la prédication à Paris au XIIIe siècle* (Paris, 1998)

Berlioz, J., '*Exemplum* et histoire: Césaire de Heisterbach (v.1180–v.1240) et la croisade albigeoise', *Bibliothèque de l'École des Chartes* 147 (1989), 49–86.

Berlioz, J., '"Les erreurs de cette doctrine pervertie …". Les croyances des Cathares selon le Dominicain et inquisiteur Étienne de Bourbon (mort. v.1261)', *Heresis* 32 (2000), 53–67.

Berlioz, J., '*Tuez les tous, Dieu reconnaîtra les siens'*: Le massacre de Béziers (22 juillet 1209) et la croisade contre les Albigeois vus par Césaire de Heisterbach* (Portet-sur-Garonne, 1994).

Berlioz, J., P. Collomb and M. A. Polo de Beaulieu, 'La face cachée de Thomas de Cantimpré. Compléments à une traduction française récente du *Bonum universale de apibus*', *AHDLMA* 68 (2001), 73–94.

Biget, J.-L., 'I catari di fronte agli inquisitori in Languedoc (1230–1310)', in *La parola all'accusato*, ed. J.-L. Biget, J.-C. M. Vigueur and A. Paravicini Bagliano (Palermo, 1991) pp. 235–51.

Biget, J.-L., '"Les Albigeois": remarques sur une dénomination', in *Inventer*, ed. Zerner, pp. 219–55.

Biget, J.-L., 'Un procès d'inquisition à Albi en 1300', *CF* 6 (1971), 273–341.

Biller, P., 'Cathars and Material Women', in *Medieval Theology and the Natural Body*, ed. P. Biller and A. J. Minnis, York Studies in Medieval Theology 1 (York, 1997), pp. 61–81.

Biller, P., 'Cathars and the Material World', in *God's Bounty? The Churches and the Natural World*, ed. P. Clarke and T. Claydon, Studies in Church History, 46 (Woodbridge, 2010), pp. 89–110.

Biller, P., 'The Cathars of Languedoc and Written Materials', in *Heresy and Literacy*, ed. Biller and Hudson, pp. 61–82.

Biller, P., '"Deep is the Heart of Man, and Inscrutable": Signs of Heresy in Medieval Languedoc', in *Text and Controversy from Wyclif to Bale: Essays in Honour of Anne Hudson*, ed. H. Barr and A. M. Hutchison, Medieval Church Studies 4 (Turnhout, 2005), pp. 267–80.

Biller, P., 'The Earliest Heretical Englishwomen', in *Medieval Women: Texts and Contexts in Late Medieval Britain. Essays for Felicity Riddy*, ed. J. Wogan- Browne et al. (Turnhout, 2000), pp. 363–76.

Biller, P., 'Goodbye to Waldensianism?', *Past and Present* 192 (2006), 3–33.

Biller, P., *The Measure of Multitude: Population in Medieval Thought* (Oxford, 2000).

Biller, P., 'Northern Cathars and Higher Learning', in *The Medieval Church*, ed. Biller and Dobson, pp. 25–53.

Biller, P., 'Through a Glass Darkly: Seeing Medieval Heresy', in *The Medieval World*, ed. P. Linehan and J. Nelson (London, 2001), pp. 308–26.

Biller, P., 'The *topos* and Reality of the Heretic as *illiteratus*', in *The Waldenses*, Biller, pp. 169–90.

Biller, P., *The Waldenses, 1170–1530: Between a Religious Order and a Church*, Variorum Collected Studies Series 676 (Aldershot, 2000).

Biller, P., 'William of Newburgh and the Cathar Mission to England', in *Life and Thought in the Northern Church, c.1100–c.1700: Essays in Honour of Claire Cross*, ed. D. Wood, Studies in Church History, Subsidia 12 (Woodbridge, 1999), pp. 11–30.

Biller, P., review of M. G. Pegg, *The Corruption of Angels*, *Speculum* 78 (2003), 1366–70.

Biller, P. and R. B. Dobson (ed.), *The Medieval Church: Universities, Heresy, and the Religious Life. Essays in Honour of Gordon Leff*, Studies in Church History, Subsidia 11 (Woodbridge, 1999).

Biller, P. and A. Hudson (ed.), *Heresy and Literacy, 1000–1530* (Cambridge, 1994).

Bird, J., 'The Construction of Orthodoxy and the (De)construction of Heretical Attacks on the Eucharist in *Pastoralia* from Peter the Chanter's Circle in Paris', in *Texts and Repression*, ed. Bruschi and Biller, pp. 45–61.

Borst, A., *Die Katharer*, Monumenta Germaniae Historica Schriften 12 (Stuttgart, 1953), French trans. by C. Roy as *Les Cathares* (Paris, 1984).

Boyle, L. E., 'Montaillou Revisited: Mentalité and Methodology', in *Pathways to Medieval Peasants*, ed. J. A. Raftis, Papers in Medieval Studies 2 (Toronto, 1981), pp. 119–40.

Brett, E. T., *Humbert of Romans: His Life and Views of Thirteenth-Century Society* (Toronto, 1984).

Brundage, M., *Medieval Canon Law* (London, 1995).

Brunn, U., *Des contestataires aux 'Cathares': discours de réforme et propagande antihérétique dans les pays du Rhin et de la Meuse avant l'Inquisition* (Paris, 2006).

Bruschi, C., '"Magna diligentia est habenda per inquisitorem": Precautions before Reading Doat 21–26', in *Texts and Repression*, ed. Bruschi and Biller, pp. 81–110.

Bruschi, C., *The Wandering Heretics of Languedoc* (Cambridge, 2009).

Bruschi, C. and P. Biller (ed.), *Texts and the Repression of Medieval Heresy*, York Studies in Medieval Theology 4 (York, 2003).

Caldwell, C., 'Peter Martyr: The Inquisitor as Saint', *Comitatus* 31 (2000), 137–74.

Caldwell Ames, C., *Righteous Persecution: Inquisition, Dominicans, and Christianity in the Middle Ages* (Philadelphia, PA, 2009).

Canetti, L., *L'invenzione della memoria: il culto e l'immagine di Domenico nella storia dei primi frati Predicatori*, Centro Italiano di Studi sull'Alto Medioevo, Biblioteca di 'Medioevo Latino' 19 (Spoleto, 1996).

Cazenave, A., 'Aveu et contrition. Manuels de confesseurs et interrogatoires d'inquisition en Languedoc et en Catalogne (XIIIe–XIVe)', *Actes du 99e Congrès National des Sociétés Savantes* 1 (1977), pp. 333–52.

Clanchy, M. T., *From Memory to Written Record. England 1066–1307*, 2nd edn (Oxford, 1993).

Cohn, N., *Europe's Inner Demons* (London, 1975).

Cohn, N., *The Pursuit of the Millenium*, 3rd edn (London, 1970, orig. 1957).

Colish, M. L., 'Early Scholastics and the Reform of Doctrine and Practice', in *Reforming the Church before Modernity: Patterns, Problems and Approaches*, ed. C. M. Bellitto and L. I. Hamilton (Aldershot, 2005), pp. 61–8.

d'Alatri, M., *L'inquisizione francescana nell'Italia centrale del duecento*, Istituto Storico dei Cappuccini, Bibliotheca Seraphico-Capuccina 49 (Rome, 1996).

d'Avray, D. L., *The Preaching of the Friars: Sermons Diffused from Paris before 1300* (Oxford, 1985).

Dictionary of the Middle Ages, ed. J. R. Strayer, 13 vols. (New York, 1982–9).

Dictionnaire de spiritualité, ascetique et mystique: doctrine et histoire, 17 vols. in 21 (Paris, 1937–95).

Dictionnaire de théologie catholique, 15 vols. in 30 (Paris, 1923–50).

von Döllinger, I., *Beiträge zur Sektengeschichte des Mittelalters*, 2 vols. (Munich, 1890).

Dondaine, A., 'Durand de Huesca et la polémique anti-cathare', *AFP* 24 (1959), 228–76, repr. in Dondaine, *Les hérésies et l'Inquisition*.

Dondaine, A., *Les hérésies et l'Inquisition, XIIe–XIIIe siècles: Documents et études*, ed. Y. Dossat, Variorum Collected Studies Series 314 (Aldershot, 1990).

Dondaine, A., 'La hiérarchie cathare en Italie. I Le "De heresi catharorum in Lombardia"', *AFP* 19 (1949), 280–312, repr. in Dondaine, *Les hérésies et l'Inquisition*.

Dondaine, A., 'La hiérarchie cathare en Italie II and III', *AFP* 20 (1950), 234–324, repr. in Dondaine, *Les hérésies et l'Inquisition*.

Dondaine, A., 'Le Manuel de l'Inquisiteur (1230–1330)', *AFP* 17 (1947), 85–194, repr. in Dondaine, *Les hérésies et l'Inquisition*.

Dondaine, A., "Saint Pierre Martyr: Études," *AFP* 23 (1953), 69–107.

Dondaine, A., *Un traité néo-manichéen de XIIIe siècle. Le* Liber de duobus principiis *suivi d'un fragment de rituel cathare* (Rome, 1939).

Dossat, Y., *Les crises de l'inquisition toulousaine au XIIIe siècle (1233–1273)* (Bordeaux, 1959).

Dossat, Y., 'Gui Foucois, enquêteur-réformateur, archevêque et pape (Clément IV)', *CF* 7 (1972), 23–57.

Douais, C. (ed.), *Documents pour servir à l'histoire de l'inquisition dans le Languedoc*, 2 vols. (Paris, 1900), I, *Introduction*.

Douais, C. (ed.), *La Somme des autorités, à l'usage des prédicateurs méridionaux au XIIIe siècle* (Paris, 1896).

Duvernoy, J., 'L'acception: 'haereticus' (iretge) = "parfait cathare" en Languedoc au XIIIe siècle', in *The Concept of Heresy*, ed. Lourdaux and Verhelst, pp. 198–210.

Duvernoy, J., *Le Catharisme: L'histoire des Cathares* (Toulouse, 1979).

Duvernoy, J., *Le Catharisme: La religion des Cathares* (Toulouse, 1976).

Esposito, M. M., 'Sur quelques écrits concernant les hérésies et les hérétiques aux xiie et xiiie siècles', *Revue d'Histoire Ecclesiastique* 36 (1940), 143–62.

Feuchter, J., *Ketzer, Konsuln und Büßer: die städtischen Eliten von Montauban vor dem Inquisitor Petrus Cellani (1236/1241)* (Tübingen, 2007).

Fichtenau, H., *Heretics and Scholars in the High Middle Ages 1000–1200*, trans. D. A. Kaiser (University Park, PA, 1998), orig. pub. as *Ketzer und Professoren: Häresie und Vernunftglaube im Hochmittelalter* (Munich, 1992).

Flores, N. C. (ed.), *Animals in the Middle Ages* (New York and London, 1996).

Foreville, R., *Latran I, II, III et Latran IV*, Histoire des Conciles Oecuméniques 6 (Paris, 1965).

García y García, A., 'El concilio IV de Letrán (1215) y sus comentarios', *Traditio* 14 (1958), 484–502.

García y García, A., 'The Fourth Lateran Council and the Canonists', in *The History of Medieval Canon Law in the Classical Period, 1140–1234: from Gratian to the Decretals of Pope Gregory IX*, ed. W. Hartmann and K. Pennington (Washington D.C., 2008), pp. 367–78.

Gilchrist, J., '*Simoniaca haeresis* and the Problem of Orders from Leo IX to Gratian', in *Proceedings of the Second International Congress of Medieval Canon Law* (1965), pp. 209–35, repr. in *Canon Law in the Age of Reform, 11th–12th Centuries* (Aldershot, 1993).

Given, J. B., *Inquisition and Medieval Society: Power, Discipline and Resistance in Languedoc* (Ithaca, NY, 1997).

Grabmann, M., 'Der Franziskanerbischof Benedictus de Alignano (†1268) und seine Summa zum Caput Firmiter des vierten Laterankonzils', in *Kirchengeschichtliche Studien P. Michael Bihl, O.F.M., als Ehrengabe dargeboten* ed. P. I. M. Freudenreich (Strasburg, 1941), pp. 50–64.

Grundmann, H., *Ausgewählte Aufsätze*, Monumenta Germaniae Historica, Schriften 25, 3 vols. (1976).

Grundmann, H., 'Ketzerverhöre des Spätmittelalters als quellenkritisches Problem', *Deutsches Archiv für Erforschung des Mittelalters* 21 (1965), 519–75, repr. in Grundmann, *Ausgewählte Aufsätze*, I, 364–416.

Grundmann, H., '*Litteratus-illiteratus*. Der Wandel einer Bildungsnorm vom Altertum zum Mittelalter', *Archiv für Kulturgeschichte* 40 (1958), 1–65, repr. in Grundmann, *Ausgewählte Aufsätze*, III, 1–66.

Grundmann, H., 'Oportet et haereses esse. Das Problem der Ketzerei im Spiegel der mittelalterlichen Bibelexegese', *Archiv für Kulturgeschichte* 45 (1963), 129–64, repr. in Grundmann, *Ausgewählte Aufsätze*, I, 328–63; Italian trans. by O. Capitani in *L'eresia medievale*, ed. O. Capitani (Bologna, 1971), pp. 23–60.

Grundmann, H., *Religiöse Bewegungen im Mittelalter: Untersuchungen über die geschichtlichen Zusammenhänge zwischen der Ketzerei, den Bettelorden und der religiösen Frauenbewegung im 12. u 13. Jahrhundert und über die geschichtlichen Grundlagen der deutschen Mystik* (Berlin, 1935; 2nd edn with Appendix, *Neue Beiträge zur Geschichte der religiösen Bewegungen im Mittelalter*, Hildesheim, 1961); trans. S. Rowan, *Religious Movements in the Middle Ages: The Historical Links between Heresy, the Mendicant Orders, and the Women's Religious Movement in the Twelfth and Thirteenth century, with the Historical Foundations of German Mysticism* (Notre Dame, 1995).

Grundmann, H., 'Der Typus des Ketzers in mittelalterlicher Anschauung', in

Kultur- und Universalgeschichte: Festschrift für W. Goetz (Leipzig–Berlin, 1927) pp. 91–107; repr. in Grundmann, *Ausgewählte Aufsätze*, I, 313–27.

Guiraud, J., *Histoire de l'inquisition*, 2 vols. (Paris, 1935–8).

Hamilton, B., 'Wisdom from the East: The Reception by the Cathars of Eastern Dualist texts', in *Heresy and Literacy*, ed. Biller and Hudson, pp. 38–60.

Hamilton, B., review of M. G. Pegg, *The Corruption of Angels*, *American Historical Review* 107 (2002), 925–6.

Hamilton, S., 'The Virgin Mary in Cathar Thought', *JEH* 56 (2005), 24–49.

Hudson, A., *The Premature Reformation: Wycliffite Texts and Lollard History* (Oxford, 1988).

Ilarino da Milano, 'Fr. Gregorio, O.P., Vescovo di Fano, e la "Disputatio inter catholicum et paterinum hereticum"', *Aevum* 14 (1940), 85–140.

Iogna-Prat, D., *Ordonner et Exclure: Cluny et la société Chrétienne face à l'hérésie, au Judaïsme, et à l'Islam 1000–1150* (Paris, 1998); trans. by G. R. Edwards, *Order and Exclusion: Cluny and Christendom Face Heresy, Judaism, and Islam (1000–1150)* (Ithaca, NY, 2002).

Jiménez-Sanchez, P., 'Le "Traité cathare anonyme": un receuil d'autorités à l'usage des prédicateurs cathares', *Heresis* 31 (1999 for 1996), 73–100.

Kaeppeli, T., 'Une somme contre les hérétiques de S. Pierre Martyr (?)', *AFP* 17 (1947), 295–335.

Kaeppeli, T. and E. Panella, *Scriptores Ordinis Praedicatorum Medii Aevi*, 4 vols. (Rome, 1970–93).

Kienzle, B. M., *Cistercians, Heresy and Crusade in Occitania, 1145–1229. Preaching in the Lord's Vineyard* (York, 2001).

Kienzle, B. M., 'Tending the Lord's Vineyard: Cistercians, Rhetoric and Heresy, 1143–1229. Part 1: Bernard of Clairvaux, the 1143 Sermons and the 1145 Preaching Mission', *Heresis* 25 (1995), 26–61.

Kordecki, L., 'Making Animals Mean: Speciest Hermeneutics in the *Physiologus* of Theobaldus', in *Animals in the Middle Ages*, ed. Flores, pp. 85–102.

Kurpiewski, C. M., 'Writing Beneath the Shadow of Heresy: The *Historia Albigensis* of Brother Pierre des Vaux-de-Cernay', *Journal of Medieval History* 31 (2005), 1–27.

Lambert, M., *The Cathars* (Oxford, 1998).

Landau, P., 'The Development of Law', in *The New Cambridge Medieval History*, vol. 4, *c.1024–c.1198*, ed. D. Luscombe (Cambridge, 2004), pp. 113–47.

Lansing, C., *Power and Purity: Cathar Heresy in Medieval Italy* (Oxford, 1998).

Lauwers, M., '*Dicunt vivorum beneficia nichil prodesse defunctis*. Histoire d'un thème polémique (xie–xiie siècles)', in *Inventer*, ed. Zerner, pp. 157–92.

Le Bras, G., C. Lefebvre and J. Rambaud, *L'âge classique, 1140–1378: Sources et théorie du droit* (Paris, 1965).

Leclerq, J., *Vienne*, Histoire des Conciles Oecuméniques 8 (Paris, 1964).

Leff, G., *Heresy in the Later Middle Ages: The Relation of Heterodoxy to Dissent, c.1250–c.1450*, 2 vols. (Manchester, 1967).

Lerner, R., *The Heresy of the Free Spirit in the Later Middle Ages* (Berkeley, CA, 1972).

Le Roy Ladurie, E., *Montaillou, village occitan de 1294 à 1324* (Paris, 1975).

Lobrichon, G., 'Arras, 1025, ou le vrai procès d'une fausse accusation', in *Inventer*, ed. Zerner, pp. 67–85.

Lobrichon, G., 'Le clair-obscur de l'hérésie au début du XIe siècle en Aquitaine: une lettre d'Auxerre', in *Essays on the Peace of God: The Church and the People in*

Eleventh-Century France, ed. T. Head and R. Landes, Historical Reflections/ Reflexions Historiques 14 (3) (1987), pp. 422–44.

Longère, J., *Œuvres oratoires de maîtres Parisiens au XIIe siècle: étude historique et doctrinale* (Paris, 1975).

Lourdaux, W. and D. Verhelst (ed.), *The Concept of Heresy in the Middle Ages (11th–13th C.)*, Mediaevalia Lovanensia, Series 1, Studia 4 (Louvain, 1983).

McGuire, B. P., 'Friends and Tales in the Cloister: Oral Sources in Caesarius of Heisterbach's *Dialogus miraculorum*', *Analecta Cisterciensia* 36 (1980), 167–247.

McGuire, B. P., 'Written Sources and Cistercian Inspirations in Caesarius of Heisterbach', *Analecta Cisterciensia* 35 (1979), 222–82.

McSheffrey, S., 'Heresy, Orthodoxy and English Vernacular Religion 1480–1525', *Past and Present* 186 (2005), 47–80.

Maisonneuve, H., *Études sur les origines de l'Inquisition*, L'Église et l'État au Moyen Âge 7, 2nd edn (Paris, 1960).

Manselli, R., 'Una "Summa auctoritatum" antiereticale (MS 47 della Bibiothèque Municipale di Albi). Memoria di Raoul Manselli', *Atti della Accademie Nazionale dei Lincei. 1: Classe di Scienze Morale Storiche e Filologiche* 6 (1985), 324–97.

Markus, R. A., 'The Problem of Self-Definition: From Sect to Church', in *Jewish and Christian Self-Definition*, ed. E. P. Sanders et al., 3 vols. (London, 1980), I, *The Shaping of Christianity in the Second and Third Centuries*, pp. 1–15.

Merlo, G. G., *Eretici e inquisitori nella società piemontese del Trecento: con l'edizione dei processi tenuti a Giaveno dall'inquisitore Alberto de Castellario (1335) e nelle Valli di Lanzo dall'inquisitore Tommaso di Casasco (1373)* (Turin, 1977).

Merlo, G. G., 'Il senso delle opere dei frati Predicatori in quanto "inquisitores hereticae pravitatis"', *Quaderni de Storia Religiosa* 9 (2002), 9–30.

Merlo, G. G., *Valdesi e valdismi medievali: itinerari e proposte di ricerca* (Turin, 1984).

Moore, R. I., *The Formation of a Persecuting Society: Power and Deviance in Western Europe, 950–1250*, 2nd edn (Oxford, 2007, orig. 1987).

Moore, R. I., 'Heresy as Disease', in *The Concept of Heresy*, ed. Lourdaux and Verhelst, pp. 1–11.

Moore, R. I., *The Origins of European Dissent* (Toronto, 1977).

Moorman, J., *A History of the Franciscan Order from its Origins to the Year 1517* (Oxford, 1968).

Morris, C., *The Papal Monarchy: The Western Church from 1050–1250* (Oxford, 1989).

Muessig, C., 'Les sermons de Jacques de Vitry sur les cathares', *CF* 32 (1997), 69–83.

Nelson, J., 'Religion in "Histoire totale": Some Recent Work in Medieval Heresy and Popular Religion', *Religion* 10 (1980), 60–85.

Nelson, J., 'Society, Theodicy and the Origins of Heresy: Towards a Reassessment of the Medieval Evidence', in *Schism, Heresy and Religious Protest*, ed. D. Baker, Studies in Church History 9 (1972), pp. 65–77.

Nickson, M. A. E., 'The "Pseudo-Reinerius" Treatise, The Final Stage of a Thirteenth-Century Work on Heresy from the Diocese of Passau', *AHDLMA* 34 (1967), 255–314.

Paolini, L., 'Inquisizione medievali: il modello italiano nella manualistica inquisitoriale (XIII–XIV secolo)', in *Negotium Fidei: Miscellanea di studi offerti a Mariano D'Alatri in occasione del suo 80° compleanno*, ed. P. Maranesi, Bibliotheca Seraphico-Capuccina 67 (Rome, 2002), pp. 177–98.

Paolini, L., 'Italian Catharism and Written Culture', in *Heresy and Literacy*, ed. Biller and Hudson, pp. 83–103.

Parmeggiani, R., 'Un secolo di manualistica inquisitoriale (1230–1330): intertestualità e circolazione del diritto', *Rivista Internazionale di Diritto Comune* 13 (2002), 229–70.

Patschovsky, A., *Der Passauer Anonymus: Ein Sammelwerk über Ketzer, Juden, Antichrist aus der Mitte des 13. Jahrhunderts*, Monumenta Germaniae Historica, Schriften 22 (1968).

Patschovsky, A., 'Heresy and Society: On the Political Function of Heresy in the Medieval World', in *Texts and Repression*, ed. Bruschi and Biller, pp. 23–41.

Patschovsky, A., 'The Literacy of Waldensianism from Valdes to c.1400', in *Heresy and Literacy*, ed. Biller and Hudson, pp. 112–35.

Pegg, M. G., *The Corruption of Angels: The Great Inquisition of 1245–46* (Princeton, NJ, 2001).

Pegg, M. G., 'On Cathars, Albigenses, and Good Men of Languedoc', *Journal of Medieval History* 27 (2001), 181–95.

Petrucci, A., *Writers and Readers in Medieval Italy: Studies in the History of Written Culture*, ed. and tr. C. J. M. Radding (New Haven, CT, 1995).

Piazza, A., '"Affinché … costituzioni di tal genere siano ovunque osservate". Gli statuti di Gregorio IX contra gli eretici d'Italia', in *Scritti in onore di Girolamo Arnaldi, offerti dalla Scuola nazionale di studi medioevali*, ed. A. Degrandi et al. (Rome, 2001), pp. 425–58.

Prudlo, D., *The Martyred Inquisitor: The Life and Cult of Peter of Verona ([martyred] 1252)* (Aldershot, 2008).

Quétif, J. and J. Echard (ed.), *Scriptores Ordinis Praedicatorum recensiti, notisque historicis et criticis*, 2 vols. (orig. Paris, 1719–21, repr. New York, 1959).

Reltgen-Tallon, A., 'L'historiographie des Dominicains du Midi: une mémoire originale?', *CF* 36 (2001), 395–414.

Reynolds, L. D. (ed.), *Texts and Transmission: A Survey of the Latin Classics* (Oxford, 1983).

Roach, A. P., *The Devil's World: Heresy and Society, 1100–1300* (Harlow, 2005).

Roach, A. and P. Ormerod, 'The Medieval Inquisition: Scale Free Networks and the Suppression of Heresy', *Physica A* 339 (2004), 645–52.

Roberts, P. B., 'The *Ars praedicandi* and the Medieval Sermon', in C. Muessig (ed.) *Preacher, Sermon and Audience in the Middle Ages* (Leiden, 2002), pp. 41–62.

Rosaldo, R., 'From the Door of his Tent: The Fieldworker and the Inquisitor', in *Writing Culture: The Poetics and Politics of Ethnography*, ed. J. Clifford and G. E. Marcus (Berkeley, CA, 1986), pp. 77–97.

Rottenwöhrer, G., *Der Katharismus*, 4 vols. in 8 (Bad Honnef, 1982).

Rouse, M. A. and R. H. Rouse, *Authentic Witnesses: Approaches to Medieval Texts and Manuscripts* (Notre Dame, 1991).

Rouse, M. A. and R. H. Rouse, 'The Schools and the Waldensians: A New Work by Durand of Huesca', in *Christendom and its Discontents: Exclusion, Persecution and Rebellion, 1000–1500*, ed. S. L. Waugh and P. D. Diehl (Cambridge, 1996).

Salisbury, J. E., 'Human Animals of Medieval Fables', in *Animals in the Middle Ages*, ed. Flores, pp. 49–66.

Scharff, T., 'Schrift zur Kontrolle – Kontrolle der Schrift', *Deutsches Archiv für Erforschung des Mittelalters* 52 (1996), 547–84.

Schmidt, C., *Histoire et doctrine de la secte des Cathares ou Albigeois*, 2 vols. (Paris, 1848–9).

Simons, W., *Cities of Ladies: Beguine Communities in the Medieval Low Countries, 1200–1565* (Philadelphia, PA, 2001)

Smalley, B., *The Study of the Bible in the Middle Ages*, 3rd edn (Oxford, 1983).

Stock, B., *The Implications of Literacy: Written Language and Models of Interpretation in the Eleventh and Twelfth Centuries* (Princeton, NJ, 1983).

Taylor, C., *Heresy in Medieval France: Dualism in Aquitaine and the Agenais, 1000–1249* (London, 2005).

Taylor, C., 'The Letter of Heribert of Périgord as a Source for Dualist Heresy in the Society of Early Eleventh-Century Aquitaine', *Journal of Modern History* 26 (2001), 313–49.

Théry, J., 'L'hérésie des bons hommes. Comment nommer la dissidence religieuse non vaudois ni béguine en Languedoc (XIIe-début du XIVe siècle?)', *Heresis* 36 (2002), 75–117.

Thesaurus Exemplorum Medii Aevi <http://gahom.ehess.fr/thema/>, directed by J. Berlioz, M. A. Polo de Beaulieu and P. Collomb.

Thouzellier, C., 'L'*inquisitio* et saint Dominique', and 'Réponse au R. P. Vicaire', *Annales du Midi* 80 (1968), 121–30, 137–8.

Tremp, K. U., *Von der Häresie zur Hexerei: 'wirkliche' und imaginäre Sekten im Spätmittelalter*, Monumenta Germaniae Historica, Schriften 59 (Hannover, 2008).

Tubach, F. C., *Index Exemplorum: A Handbook of Medieval Religious Tales* (Helsinki, 1981).

Tugwell, S., 'L'évolution des *vitae fratrum*. Résumé des conclusions provisoires', *CF* 36 (2001), 415–18.

Tugwell, S., 'Notes on the Life of St. Dominic', *AFP* 65 (1995), 5–169.

Ullmann, W., 'The Significance of Innocent III's Decretal "Vergentis"', in *Études d'histoire du droit canonique dediées à Gabriel le Bras*, 2 vols. (Paris, 1965), I, 729–41.

Vicaire, M.-H., 'Les Cathares albigeois vus par les polémistes', *CF* 3 (1968), 107–28.

Vicaire, M.-H., 'Note sur la mentalité de saint Dominique', *Annales du Midi* 80 (1968), 131–6.

Wakefield, W. L., *Heresy, Crusade and Inquisition in Southern France 1100–1250* (London, 1974).

Wakefield, W. L., 'Notes on Some Anti-heretical Writings of the Thirteenth Century', *Franciscan Studies* 27 (1967), 285–321.

Wakefield, W. L., 'Some Unorthodox Popular Ideas of the Thirteenth Century', *Medievalia et Humanistica* n.s. 4 (1973), 23–35.

Wakefield, W. L. and A. P. Evans (trans.), *Heresies of the High Middle Ages* (New York, 1969, repr. 1991).

Welter, J. T., *L'exemplum dans la littérature religieuse et didactique du Moyen âge: La tabula exemplorum secundum ordinem alphabeti, recueil d'exempla compilé en France à la fin du XIIIe siècle* (Paris, 1927, repr. Geneva, 1973).

Wessley, S., 'The Composition of Georgius' *Disputatio inter Catholicum et Paterinum hereticum*', *AFP* 48 (1978), 55–61.

Winroth, A., *The Making of Gratian's Decretum* (Cambridge, 2000).

Wolter, H. and H. Holstein, *Lyons I et Lyons II*, Histoire des Conciles Oecuméniques 7 (Paris, 1966).

Zerner, M. (ed.), *Inventer l'hérésie? Discours polémiques et pouvoirs avant l'inquisition* (Nice, 1998).

Ziegler, J., *Medicine and Religion c.1300: The Case of Arnau de Vilanova* (Oxford, 1998).

Index

God's Words, Women's Voices: The Discernment of Spirits in the Writing of Late-Medieval Women Visionaries, Rosalyn Voaden (1999)

Pilgrimage Explored, ed. J. Stopford (1999)

Piety, Fraternity and Power: Religious Gilds in Late Medieval Yorkshire 1389–1547, David J. F. Crouch (2000)

Courts and Regions in Medieval Europe, ed. Sarah Rees Jones, Richard Marks and A. J. Minnis (2000)

Treasure in the Medieval West, ed. Elizabeth M. Tyler (2000)

Nunneries, Learning and Spirituality in Late Medieval English Society: The Dominican Priory of Dartford, Paul Lee (2000)

Prophecy and Public Affairs in Later Medieval England, Lesley A. Coote (2000)

The Problem of Labour in Fourteenth-Century England, ed. James Bothwell, P. J. P. Goldberg and W. M. Ormrod (2000)

New Directions in later Medieval Manuscript Studies: Essays from the 1998 Harvard Conference, ed. Derek Pearsall (2000)

Cistercians, Heresy and Crusadse in Occitania, 1145–1229: Preaching in the Lord's Vineyard, Beverly Mayne Kienzle (2001)

Guilds and the Parish Community in Late Medieval East Anglia, c. 1470–1550, Ken Farnhill (2001)

The Age of Edward III, ed. J. S. Bothwell (2001)

Time in the Medieval World, ed. Chris Humphrey and W. M. Ormrod (2001)

The Cross Goes North: Processes of Conversion in Northern Europe, AD 300–1300, ed. Martin Carver (2002)

Henry IV: The Establishment of the Regime, 1399–1406, ed. Gwilym Dodd and Douglas Biggs (2003)

Youth in the Middle Ages, ed. P. J. P. Goldberg and Felicity Riddy (2004)

The Idea of the Castle in Medieval England, Abigail Wheatley (2004)

Rites of Passage: Cultures of Transition in the Fourteenth Century, ed. Nicola F. McDonald and W. M. Ormrod (2004)

Creating the Monastic Past in Medieval Flanders, Karine Ugé (2005)

St William of York, Christopher Norton (2006)

Medieval Obscenities, ed. Nicola F. McDonald (2006)

The Reign of Edward II: New Perspectives, ed. Gwilym Dodd and Anthony Musson (2006)

Old English Poetics: The Aesthetics of the Familiar in Anglo-Saxon England, Elizabeth M. Tyler (2006)

The Late Medieval Interlude: The Drama of Youth and Aristocratic Masculinity, Fiona S. Dunlop (2007)

The Late Medieval English College and its Context, ed. Clive Burgess and Martin Heale (2008)

The Reign of Henry IV: Rebellion and Survival, 1403–1413, ed. Gwilym Dodd and Douglas Biggs (2008)

Medieval Petitions: Grace and Grievance, ed. W. Mark Ormrod, Gwilym Dodd and Anthony Musson (2009)

St Edmund, King and Martyr: Changing Images of a Medieval Saint, ed. Anthony Bale (2009)

Language and Culture in Medieval Britain: The French of England c.1100–c.1500, ed. Jocelyn Wogan-Browne et al. (2009)

The Royal Pardon: Access to Mercy in Fourteenth-Century England, Helen Lacey (2009)

Texts and Traditions of Medieval Pastoral Care: Essays in Honour of Bella Millett, ed. Cate Gunn and Catherine Innes-Parker (2009)

The Anglo-Norman Language and its Contexts, ed. Richard Ingham (2010)

Parliament and Political Pamphleteering in Fourteenth-Century England, Clementine Oliver (2010)

The Saints' Lives of Jocelin of Furness: Hagiography, Patronage and Ecclesiastical Politics, Helen Birkett (2010)

The York Mystery Plays: Performance in the City, ed. Margaret Rogerson (2011)

Wills and Will-making in Anglo-Saxon England, Linda Tollerton (2011)

The Songs and Travels of a Tudor Minstrel: Richard Sheale of Tamworth, Andrew Taylor (2012)

Sin in Medieval and Early Modern Culture: The Tradition of the Seven Deadly Sins, ed. Richard G. Newhauser and Susan J. Ridyard (2012)

Socialising the Child in Late Medieval England, c. 1400–1600, Merridee L. Bailey (2012)

Barking Abbey and Medieval Literary Culture: Authorship and Authority in a Female Community, ed. Jennifer N. Brown and Donna Alfano Bussell (2012)

Christians and Jews in Angevin England: The York Massacre of 1190, Narratives and Contexts, ed. Sarah Rees Jones and Sethina Watson (2013)

Reimagining History in Anglo-Norman Prose Chronicles, John Spence (2013)

Henry V: New Interpretations, ed. Gwilym Dodd (2013)

Rethinking Chaucer's Legend of Good Women, Carolyn P. Collette (2014)

York Studies in Medieval Theology

I *Medieval Theology and the Natural Body*, ed. Peter Biller and A. J. Minnis (1997)

II *Handling Sin: Confession in the Middle Ages*, ed. Peter Biller and A. J. Minnis (1998)

III *Religion and Medicine in the Middle Ages*, ed. Peter Biller and Joseph Ziegler (2001)

IV *Texts and the Repression of Medieval Heresy*, ed. Caterina Bruschi and Peter Biller (2002)

York Manuscripts Conference

Manuscripts and Readers in Fifteenth-Century England: The Literary Implications of Manuscript Study, ed. Derek Pearsall (1983) [Proceedings of the 1981 York Manuscripts Conference]

Manuscripts and Texts: Editorial Problems in Later Middle English Literature, ed. Derek Pearsall (1987) [Proceedings of the 1985 York Manuscripts Conference]

Latin and Vernacular: Studies in Late-Medieval Texts and Manuscripts, ed. A. J. Minnis (1989) [Proceedings of the 1987 York Manuscripts Conference]

Regionalism in Late-Medieval Manuscripts and Texts: Essays celebrating the publication of 'A Linguistic Atlas of Late Mediaeval English', ed. Felicity Riddy (1991) [Proceedings of the 1989 York Manuscripts Conference]

Late-Medieval Religious Texts and their Transmission: Essays in Honour of A. I. Doyle, ed. A. J. Minnis (1994) [Proceedings of the 1991 York Manuscripts Conference]

Prestige, Authority and Power in Late Medieval Manuscripts and Texts, ed. Felicity Riddy (2000) [Proceedings of the 1994 York Manuscripts Conference]

Middle English Poetry: Texts and Traditions. Essays in Honour of Derek Pearsall, ed. A. J. Minnis (2001) [Proceedings of the 1996 York Manuscripts Conference]

Manuscript Culture in the British Isles

I *Design and Distribution of Late Medieval Manuscripts in England*, ed. Margaret Connolly and Linne R. Mooney (2008)

II *Women and Writing, c.1340–c.1650: The Domestication of Print Culture*, ed. Anne Lawrence-Mathers and Phillipa Hardman (2010)

III *The Wollaton Medieval Manuscripts: Texts, Owners and Readers*, ed. Ralph Hanna and Thorlac Turville-Petre (2010)

IV *Scribes and the City: London Guildhall Clerks and the Dissemination of Middle English Literature, 1375–1425*, Linne R. Mooney and Estelle Stubbs (2013)

V *Robert Thornton and his Books: Essays on the Lincoln and London Thornton Manuscripts*, ed. Susanna Fein and Michael Johnston (2014)

Heresy and Inquisition in the Middle Ages

CPSIA information can be obtained at www.ICGtesting.com
Printed in the USA
BVOW11s0019200116

433539BV00005B/15/P